THEOLOGICAL FOUNDATIONS FOR ENVIRONMENTAL ETHICS

Additional Praise for *Theological Foundations for Environmental Ethics*

"This work will prove to be a major addition to contemporary Catholic theology of nature and environmental ethics in the age of science. In the world of Catholic scholarship I have yet to see such breadth and skill in the retrieval of ecologically relevant patristic and medieval riches as I have in Schaefer's work."

—**John F. Haught**, senior fellow, Woodstock Theological Center, Georgetown University

"An excellent philosophical-theological resource for Catholics seeking links among traditional Catholic doctrine, contemporary Christian environmental theology and ethics, current scientific theories, and pressing ecological issues."

—**John Hart**, professor of Christian ethics, Boston University, and author of *Sacramental Commons: Christian Ecological Ethics*

"Jame Schaefer displays a comprehensive grasp of both historical and contemporary environmental theology. The book is impressively organized and written with exceptional clarity, and the rich and abundant material is readily accessible to the reader."

—**James Huchingson**, Florida International University

"A superb work that will be widely consulted. Schaefer's sustained treatment of the views of patristic and medieval writers is impressive as is her command of the main issues in contemporary ecological ethics. This book breaks new ground and will be read in many graduate seminars where instructors are trying to highlight the breadth of pre-modern creation-centered Christian thinking."

—**William French**, Loyola University of Chicago

"A really well-researched and written book. The author knows the relevant scientific and philosophical background literature well and explains it very clearly, always showing how it is relevant to the topic at hand."

—**Daniel Spencer**, University of Montana

THEOLOGICAL FOUNDATIONS FOR ENVIRONMENTAL ETHICS

Reconstructing Patristic and Medieval Concepts

JAME SCHAEFER

GEORGETOWN UNIVERSITY PRESS
WASHINGTON, D.C.

Georgetown University Press, Washington, D.C. www.press.georgetown.edu

Library of Congress Cataloging-in-Publication Data

Schaefer, Jame.
   Theological foundations for environmental ethics : reconstructing patristic and medieval concepts / Jame Schaefer.
      p. cm.
   Includes bibliographical references (p.) and index.
   ISBN 978-1-58901-268-4 (pbk. : alk. paper)
   1. Human ecology—Religious aspects—Catholic Church. 2. Environmental ethics. 3. Christian ethics—Catholic authors. 4. Fathers of the church.
5. Thomas, Aquinas, Saint, 1225?–1274. I. Title.
   BX1795.H82S32 2008
   261.8′8—dc22

                                                                        2008046567

♾ This book is printed on acid-free, 100% recycled paper meeting the requirements of the American National Standard for Permanence in Paper for Printed Library Materials.

15 14 13 12 11 10 09   9 8 7 6 5 4 3 2
First printing

Printed in the United States of America

For Alek, Nicole, Nathan,
Nadia, Arianell, and Nicholas

CONTENTS

Contents

ACKNOWLEDGMENTS

I am grateful to my students, who have tested these concepts over the past five years and applied them to a plethora of ecological problems that they researched from the scientific, governmental, and advocacy literature. Their efforts aptly demonstrate how helpful and meaningful patristic and medieval concepts can be—some timeless for their significance and others reconstructed to reflect the current scientific understanding of the world.

I am also grateful to my colleagues at Marquette University, who recommended released time from teaching to enable me to work on parts of this project. The College of Arts and Sciences honored me with a summer research grant, and the dean gave me a special development grant that helped considerably. The reference librarians Rose Trupiano and Rosemary Del Toro were especially resourceful in locating the information I needed. Finally, I received perceptive comments from the scholars who reviewed my manuscript for Georgetown University Press, and I was buoyed by the enthusiasm and guidance of Richard Brown throughout the publishing process.

INTRODUCTION:
READING THE CATHOLIC THEOLOGICAL TRADITION THROUGH AN ECOLOGICAL LENS

Earth is imperiled. Human activities are adversely affecting the land, water, air, and myriad forms of biological life that constitute the ecological systems (hereafter, ecosystems) of our planet. Wetlands, forests, grasslands, and aquatic ecosystems are degraded or destroyed daily, endangering or driving into extinction the animal and plant species dependent on these habitats for their survival. Indicators of global warming and holes in the ozone layer inhibit functions vital to the biosphere. Pollutants and toxicants emitted into the air, flushed into waterways, and spread on the land persist in the environment, advance through the food chain, and threaten the survival of myriad types of living entities. The diversity of biological life is declining. Experimental and inadequately safeguarded technologies decimate, injure, and genetically alter living entities and render areas uninhabitable for decades. Highly radioactive and other hazardous wastes accumulate without acceptable long-term solutions for disposition, and even relatively benign wastes are increasingly problematic by their sheer volume prompted by the throwaway mentality that prevails, especially in industrially developed countries. Urban sprawl accompanied by increased automobile use causes a plethora of problems. In one way or another, human damage to the planet becomes damaging to human health and well-being now and in the future, and too often this damage affects people who are least able to protect themselves.

Where does religion fit into this dire picture? Religious communities can play pivotal roles by reminding their members about traditions that can guide their attitudes, thoughts, and actions during this age of widespread ecological degradation. Scholars of religions can help by examining teachings that appear promising, while leaders can instruct their followers on their traditions' ways of thinking about and acting toward other species and systems that constitute Earth. Scholars can also examine traditions that may appear less efficacious, clarify and correct them where necessary, and alert the leaders of their respective communities to problematic dimensions that should be deemphasized.

1

Call and Response to Examine the Tradition

Some prominent leaders of the world's religions have encouraged scholars to examine promising teachings from their traditions. When delivering his 1990 Message on the World Day of Peace, Pope John Paul II underscored the need to
recognize the ecological crisis as a moral responsibility.[1] Many Catholic bishops
from around the world responded,[2] including the United States Conference of
Catholic Bishops, which specifically called upon biblical experts, theologians,
and ethicists "to help explore, deepen, and advance the insights of our Catholic
tradition and its relation to the environment" and especially "to explore the relationship between this tradition's emphasis upon the dignity of the human person and our responsibility to care for all of God's creation."[3] Several other
Christian denominations have issued statements indicating their faith-based positions on caring for God's creation.[4]

Spurred by theologians and other religionists, a series of scholarly conferences
was held at Harvard University's Center for the Study of Religion at which research
findings on the world's religions were shared and from which nine volumes were
generated, each focusing on promising and problematic notions in the teachings of
a religious tradition.[5] Representatives of the Jewish tradition, the Catholic Church,
and other Christian denominations initiated the National Religious Partnership for
the Environment dedicated to integrating care for all of God's creation throughout
religious life—theological reflection, worship, social teaching, education, congre-
gational life, and public policy initiative.[6] Biblical scholars, historians of religion,
systematic theologians, and ethicists have examined their traditions, pointed to notions that are inadequate for responding to ecological concerns, corrected misin-
terpretations of biblical or other texts from which inappropriate conclusions have
been drawn,[7] and endeavored to develop meaningful ways of addressing ecological degradation from their faith perspectives. A historian of environmental ethics
recently characterized these efforts as the "greening of religion."[8]

As a Roman Catholic systematics-ethics theologian who specializes in the
constructive relationship between theology and the natural sciences, I am aware
of the need for more "greening" of the Catholic faith. The ongoing degradation
of Earth requires the fullest possible examination of our tradition in the quest
for expressions of faith that are *relevant* to the condition of Earth, *coherent* with
current knowledge about the world, and *helpful* for addressing the ecological
concerns that plague our planet. Examining the tradition for expressions of faith
that are not helpful is also vital, especially when beliefs or reflections on them
are stilted or taken out of the contexts in which they were written.

Promising Patristic and Medieval Concepts

My examination of the Catholic tradition has revealed some promising concepts,
most of which appear in texts written by patristic and medieval theologians. My

introduction to these texts occurred while I was studying for a doctoral degree after having served in various capacities as a leader of environment advocacy groups, a government official at local, state, and national levels, and a consultant to governments on involving the public in resolving environmental problems.

During my studies I approached every text in the tradition through an ecological lens, seeking to discover ways of thinking and acting that might be helpful toward addressing ecological concerns. The patristic and medieval texts gave me hope. The fact that many were written by eminent theologians revered by the Church as "privileged witnesses" to the Catholic tradition warranted the retrieval of their teachings.[9] Their attribution of goodness, beauty, sacramentality, and integrity to the physical world stimulated my thinking and desire to apply these concepts to ecological problems today. Their reflections on the praise that creatures give to God in their unique "voices" stirred my imagination. The chief moral virtues surfaced as practical guides for human functioning in ecosystems, especially when motivated by the theological virtue of love. These theologians' prescriptions for using the goods of Earth with restraint and gratitude to God loomed as an urgent message that counters the often unconstrained, wasteful, and thankless consumer society that persists, especially in the materially developed societies of the world. Some hagiography about a sense of kinship with other species that some saints conveyed through their words and actions became particularly meaningful in light of evolutionary and molecular biological findings.

However, when probed systematically, some patristic and medieval notions about God's activity, human and other species, and the natural environment appeared incoherent in light of our current scientific understanding of the world. Patristic and medieval theologians reflected from the faith perspective that God created the universe from nothing, determined the exact characteristics of all species, designed their relationships with one another, and ensured their harmonious functioning through laws established by God. Dimensions of their thinking about God in relation to the world were influenced by an eclectic form of Platonism that prevailed in the third to sixth centuries and surfaced especially when theologians commented on the Genesis 1 story of creation,[10] reflected on God as creator of the cosmos from whom all natural entities emanate,[11] and depicted the human quest for union with God through Jesus Christ.

Neoplatonic thinking continued to influence theologians into the medieval period, as Fabro and others have argued convincingly,[12] though the availability of and interest in the translations of Aristotle's corpus from the Greek into Latin led to a Christianized Aristotelian view of the world that dominated the intellectual landscape of the Scholastics, as epitomized in the works of Albertus Magnus and his exemplary student, Thomas Aquinas.[13] They thought about the cosmos as a divinely designed, geocentric, and hierarchically structured organism consisting of fixed species for which God has purposes within the scheme of creation. Humans were at the top of this chain, while God was outside the created order yet actively present to and manifested by it. Descriptions of the natural world were primarily qualitative rather than quantitative, and among the qualities were its goodness, its beauty, and, above all, its sacramentality.[14] Their efforts to reflect on God's relation to the world were earnest attempts at discourse about God in light of their understanding of the world in the contexts of their times, times that were often prompted by discordant or heretical thinking.

Our current worldview contrasts dramatically with the views held by patristic and medieval theologians. When informed by contemporary scientific findings, we depart from their thinking about the world as geocentric and as having been determined by God down to the exact characteristics of any species, ecological system, planet, or galaxy. We have known since the sixteenth century that planets revolve around the sun to constitute a solar system, and our understanding of the totality of the universe is beyond heliocentrism to billions of galaxies in an expanding universe that may not have a center. Its constituents have emerged over cosmological-biological time and space for approximately 14 billion years. An interplay of law and chance seems to be operative, with an openness to a future that cannot be predicted with accuracy. All animate and inanimate entities of Earth are related to and interdependent upon one another. Though humans have capacities beyond any other species in the known universe, our bodies are also products of biological evolution and, thus, radically related to and interconnected with everything living and nonliving in the universe, and especially on our planet. Our species is also radically dependent upon other species and the air, land, and water for our health and well-being.

Following the tradition of preceding theologians who reflected from their faith in God as the purposeful creator and sustainer of the universe informed by their knowledge about the world, some theologians are striving today to construct a discourse about God that is consistent with current scientific findings about the world.[15] The way the world functions helps theologians imagine God's activity in relation to the world while accepting the limitation pressed by Christianized Neoplatonism that humans are incapable of fully comprehending or adequately expressing God or God's activity in and on the world.[16] To achieve the desired goal of theological discourse that coheres with well-established knowledge about the world, theologians accept, at least tentatively, basic scientific findings that are readily available through the various media or "drink deeply of the well of scientific knowledge," as urged by the physicist and minister Robert John Russell.[17] Faith in God precedes their discourse as they humbly work out coherent ways of expressing religious faith in an age of science, technological advancement, and environmental crises.

Whether informed by basic or more in-depth scientific findings, theological discourse can become *coherent*. God, the creator and sustainer of the universe, can at least be understood as having initiated the cosmological-biological evolutionary process, as empowering its functioning, and as continuously sustaining its dynamic existence. God can be understood as having given freedom to the universe to grow and self-organize into diverse kinds of entities through the interplay of law and chance,[18] as persuading forth the self-organization of the vast cosmos, our galaxy, our planet, its ecosystems, and all species, and as calling all to function optimally according to their natures in relation to one another and the totality to its fullest completion. Among these emergents are intelligent beings who have the ability to receive and choose to respond to God's call, to reflect on their place in the developing universe that God actively sustains in dynamic existence, to seek scientific and other information that facilitates their discerning how to act toward the diverse constituents of Earth, and to choose to act in ways that are compatible with the well-being of species, ecosystems, and the biosphere that constitute the community of Earth as the universe advances to completion.[19]

This quest for coherent discourse about God, divine activity, and humans in relation to other creatures leads to questions about the *relevance* of patristic-medieval expressions of the goodness, beauty, sacramentality, and unity of creation, the kinship of creatures and creation's praise for God, the grateful and restrained use of creation, living virtuously, and loving creation in an ecologically endangered world. More specifically, how relevant are attributions of goodness to the more-than-human world? Beauty? Sacramentality? Integrity? The kinship of creatures? Creation's praise for God? Using creation? Living virtuously? Loving creation? If relevant in part, to what extent do these concepts need to be reconstructed so they will reflect our contemporary understanding of the world and can address ecological concerns?

To consider finding answers to these questions means turning to the third major inquiry about the patristic-medieval concepts: To what extent are they *helpful* in guiding the faithful to relate positively to other species, ecosystems, and the biosphere? How the faithful should act on the basis of what they profess to believe remains a looming challenge to Roman Catholics, as does orthopraxis for other Christian denominations and religions professed throughout the world.[20]

A Modest Method for Retrieval, Reconstruction, and Application

In an attempt to answer these questions, five methodological steps are followed in the chapters ahead. The first step is to explore a particular concept that surfaces in patristic and medieval texts, with the aim of ascertaining the extent to which the concept may appear promising for addressing ecological concerns. Each of the nine subsequent chapters explores a particular concept, in this order: The goodness, beauty, and sacramentality of creation; creation's praise for God; the unity and integrity of creation; the kinship of creatures; the restrained and grateful use of creation; living virtuously; and loving Earth. Representative quotations and paraphrasings from patristic and medieval theologians and, in the case of the kinship concept, from hagiographers are grouped according to the key dimensions for each concept.

After these data have been assembled, the next step leads to recognizing the various theologians' views of the world and their philosophical underpinnings in order to grasp the meanings the theologians intended to convey from the contexts of their times and prescientific understanding of the world. Where essential, the circumstances that prompted their writing are identified to facilitate understanding their thinking as fully as possible.

A check for *coherence* constitutes the third step of the methodology employed. Because, as noted above, patristic and medieval theologians wrote from vastly different understandings of the world based on the knowledge available to them, the coherence of their concepts for our time must be determined by their ability to appeal intellectually to the faithful today. Losing touch with reality as it is known through scientific findings and other ways of obtaining knowledge tends to remove theological discourse from the logical reasoning that is essential to human understanding and application, as many theologians and philosophers have argued convincingly.[21] When a patristic-medieval concept is not consistent with basic scientific findings about the world today, my focus turns subsequently to determining how a concept can be expressed more cogently and to reconstructing it accordingly. Most of the concepts explored in the following chapters require reconstruction, whereas others are extended to enhance their responsiveness to ecological concerns.

Relevance to ecological concerns constitutes the fourth methodological step applied to the patristic-medieval concepts in these chapters. This step is generally and briefly employed in this volume, and readers are invited to apply the reconstructed and extended concepts to ecological problems, especially the ones that are most disconcerting for them. There is no shortage of these problems. As originally envisioned, this monograph was intended to include a case study for each concept; however, the text became too cumbersome and overly long.

Finally, the type of behavior a concept suggests is identified for its *helpfulness* in addressing ecological concerns. As a systematics-ethics exercise, each concept culminates in identifying how the faithful will tend to act on the basis of their beliefs that the sensible world is good and beautiful, that it has a sacramental character, that its constituents function as an integral unity, that all creatures are related intimately to more distantly, that species and systems are lovable, that humans are intended by God to use the goods of Earth with restraint and gratitude, and that humans are offered God's grace to live virtuously in relation to the other humans, species, and systems that constitute the community of Earth. This step leads to the identification of a *basic behavior pattern* that a reconstructed patristic-medieval concept suggests (e.g., valuing Earth and its constituents intrinsically and instrumentally from the goodness concept, and cooperating with other constituents to achieve their internal sustainability from the integrity concept).

Throughout this process, the "is-ought" problem of appropriating behavior norms from empirical facts is avoided, because the beginning point is always religious faith in God as the creator-initiator and continuous sustainer of the cosmological-biological process who calls the totality with its diverse interacting constituents to its fullest completion and whose call to human constituents encompasses their moral obligation to choose ways of relating to other constituents that are compatible with God's inclusive call. The various conceptual behavior trajectories (e.g., valuing, appreciating, and cooperating from the goodness, beauty, and integrity concepts) suggested in reflections by some of the most eminent patristic and medieval theologians provide the framework for systematically discerning basic actions that accord with God's call to completion. Scientific findings that point to real and projected effects of human actions contribute to this discernment process.

Altogether, these five steps constitute a *critical-creative* approach to patristic and medieval texts aimed at identifying from the Catholic, Christian tradition some promising ways of thinking about and acting toward other species, ecosystems, and the biosphere. This methodological approach is *critical* in examining patristic and medieval thematic concepts in the contexts of the theologians' times and understandings of the world and recognizing their variances from our contemporary worldview. The method is *creative* in reconstructing the concepts so they are consistent with current scientific findings and coaxing from these reconstructed concepts some basic trajectories of behavior that result from a believer's embracing the concept and desiring to act accordingly. Honing this modest methodology is an ongoing project.

Aside from the basic faith perspective that undergirds all the concepts explored, each stands on its own as a way of thinking about God in relation to the world and humans in relation to the more-than-humans that constitute Earth because of their mutual relation to God as their purposeful creator and sustainer in existence who calls the universe to completion. Each concept suggests a *trajectory* for guiding the behavior of the faithful who embrace the particular quality that patristic and medieval theologians described. Thereby, each posits a model of the human as discussed in the last chapter within the overall model of the human as a responder to God's call to participate in the processional completion of the universe.

Operating under this encompassing model of the human as an informed responder to God's call, each concept has its own appeal when systematically examined, appropriated, and reconstructed or extended. Each is different. And each concept is relatively sufficient to the task of thinking and acting systematically. That this diversity surfaces in patristic and medieval texts demonstrates the richness of the Catholic tradition that theologians embraced and extended in response to the exigencies of their times from their understanding of the world. Theologians today have an opportunity to do no less during this time of widespread ecological degradation and destruction.

Although each concept can stand on its own, the concepts collectively can be viewed as a Catholic system of environmental ethics in response to God's calling. Catholics are called to value the goodness of God's creation both intrinsically and instrumentally. Catholics are called to aesthetically appreciate the beauty of God's creation. Catholics are called to give reverence to the sacramental Earth and universe because they manifest God's presence and character. Catholics are called to respect the various ways in which the diverse constituents of Earth praise God according to their natures. Catholics are called to cooperate with other species and systems to sustain the integrity of our planet. Catholics are called to be companions with other species within the dynamic web of life. Catholics are called to use other constituents of Earth with restraint and gratitude to God. Catholics are called to live morally virtuous lives in relation to one another and to other species and systems now and in the future. Catholics are called to love God's creation, especially Earth. Furthermore, Catholics are called to see themselves within an all-inclusive context of other species, ecosystems, Earth, and the entirety of the universe as called forth to completion by God. Valuing, appreciating, revering, respecting, cooperating, acting companionably, using with constraint and gratitude to God, living virtuously, and loving creation are characteristics that Catholics can develop in themselves and nurture in others. That these characteristics are exemplified in the Catholic theological tradition warrants their serious consideration and celebration.

The Ecclesiastic Stature of Theologians

Each chapter in this book explores concepts expressed by theologians whose stature in the Church varies. One concept—kinship—is built around hagiography. Though some theologians cited are not saints, most chapters are by or about saints who have been honored by the Church for their witness to the Catholic, Christian faith. They demonstrate how some of the most faithful of the faithful think and act. They are, as Yves Congar underscores about the patristic Fathers,[22] witnesses to the tradition that they embraced and extended to reflect the circumstances of their times and understanding of the world. In many cases, as the paucity of these concepts in the current scholarly literature attests, the tradition about the natural world that they embellished is covered with a thick layer of dust.

Nevertheless, the authority of the theologians appropriated for this project varies as witnesses to and teachers of the tradition. Aside from hagiographies, which are probed primarily for certain saints' basic attitudes toward the animals with which they lived and the environments in which they functioned, theologians whose compatible ideas are appropriated and who are not saints are included with those who are revered illuminators of the tradition. Together their reflections suggest basic behavior patterns—valuing, appreciating, reverencing, respecting, cooperating, acting companionably, restraining use, living virtuously, and loving.

Emphasis on the Positive

The following chapters focus on *positive* concepts retrieved from patristic and medieval texts. None deal with concepts that are not helpful or can be construed as harmful. Are there any in the Christian tradition? Permeating these texts is an anthropocentric bias that has prevailed from biblical times to the present, wherein the human is posited as the creature for whom God created all others for human use. As the theologians Paul Santmire and William French and others have shown, this frequent refrain can be found in works by Thomas Aquinas, other great theologians of the patristic-medieval period, and some current theologians.[23] An anthropocentric bias can be construed as noncontributory or harmful to theological discourse in our age of ecological degradation.

However, the anthropocentric perspectives in the works of patristic and medieval theologians that are criticized by present-day theologians and philosophers have not been explored sufficiently from several perspectives, including the contexts of the times in which they lived when compared with our times of ecological degradation and the theologians' worldviews, which predate by many centuries the current knowledge of the approximately 14-billion-year history of the universe. Nor do these criticisms take into consideration the constraints that patristic and medieval theologians imposed on the human use of Earth's constituents and their teachings about the faithful's responsibility to their neighbors and to God for how they regard and use other creatures. If theological discourse is to be cogent, relevant, and helpful for dealing with the ecological crisis, the appearance of *Homo sapiens* within the evolutionary process and the place of humanity in relation to Earth must be acknowledged with deep humility. Theological reflections must acknowledge the human place in a universe where all bodies had their material beginnings in the furnaces of stars billions of years ago, where the human species evolved from other hominid species over a span of approximately 5 million years, and where humans are radically dependent on other species, the air, land, water, ecosystems, the biosphere of Earth, and cosmic bodies, especially the sun, for their health and well-being.[24]

Reconstructed renderings of the human person to reflect reality do not demean members of our species. We are distinct from other creatures. We are knowers of the past and present who should use our intellectual capabilities to discern how to act toward others. We are actors who can choose to function compatibly with other species for our mutual well-being in our shared home. And we are creatures who are responsible to God for how we respond to God's call. How we think about ourselves in relation to others on Earth is key to helping determine how we should act. Toward this end, each concept explored in the following chapters suggests a specific way of thinking about humans in relation to other living and nonliving creatures that constitute Earth because of our mutual relationship with God, the purposeful Creator and empowering sustainer of the universe who calls it with its diverse constituents to authentic existence and completion. These models of the human together fall under the overarching model of the human as a hearer and informed responder to God's call.

Overview of This Book

The chapters of this book explore nine concepts appropriated from the works of patristic and medieval theologians. In chapter 1, the goodness of creation concept provides a behavioral trajectory for valuing Earth and Earth's natural goods, both intrinsically and instrumentally. The beauty of creation suggests behavior that demonstrates an aesthetic appreciation for Earth at various stages of encounter and reflection, as explained in chapter 2. The sacramentality of creation that is explored in chapter 3 sets a course for reverencing Earth because it manifests God's presence and character, albeit dimly. In chapter 4, creation's praise for God leads to respecting each entity's "voice" and the chorus their voices constitute. The functional unity of creation as discussed in chapter 5, points to the need for human cooperation with other species and systems to ensure their internal unity and sustainability. In chapter 6, the reconstructed kinship concept directs the faithful toward a posture of companionship, especially with other species. Consistent teachings throughout the tradition about using God's creation with restraint and gratitude to God are examined in chapter 7. In chapter 8, the chief moral virtues are explored as ways of living in relation to other-than-humans of Earth motivated by love for God and neighbor, whereas chapter 9 focuses on loving God's creation, especially Earth. Chapter 10 recognizes the various models of the human person that surface from the behavior trajectories suggested by the reworked concepts and concentrates on one—the human as a virtuous cooperator, a reconstructed theological anthropology retrieved primarily from the teachings of Thomas Aquinas.

This modest project is open-ended. It is a beginning that needs fine-tuning in order to be responsive to environmental concerns. Some refinements can be made when applying these concepts with their behavior trajectories to the plethora of environmental problems that loom throughout the world and threaten the survival of species including *Homo sapiens,* the functioning of ecosystems, and the integrity of Earth's biosphere.

Taking this experimental approach with my undergraduate and graduate students at Marquette University has been gratifying. Through their research, careful application of the reconstructed concepts to specific environmental problems, and discernment of behavior that can be helpful, my students have proceeded to stimulate thinking and action among their friends, family members, and faith-filled people in their respective religious congregations. Others have moved into the public square and collaborated with members of various religions and with nongovernmental organizations in seeking resolutions to problems that otherwise seemed intractable. Some are teaching and thereby making others aware of the promising patristic-medieval concepts to which they were introduced in my undergraduate and graduate courses. Other students have applied their preferred models to their professional, social, economic, and recreational endeavors.

Using This Book

This book may be useful in several settings. Professors may find it helpful with upper-division undergraduate students who have taken at least an introductory theology course and with graduate students at the master's level so they can become familiar with the various concepts conveyed by patristic and medieval theologians, the reconstruction of their concepts informed by contemporary scientific findings, and some of the behavior trajectories that the reconstructed concepts suggest. To facilitate the application of these concepts to ecological problems, I have included in notes at the beginning of each chapter's section on the behavioral trajectory suggested by the concept, some basic principles that students can apply to ecological problems researched from the scholarly, government, and advocacy literature. Leaving open the opportunity for students to identify additional principles should stimulate their thinking imaginatively and systematically, especially as they apply them to intriguing ecological problems. Requiring them to use the language of each concept consistently is important, however redundant that may appear, so they grasp its significance for reflection and action.

Doctoral-level students may also benefit from this book as an entry into the primary sources, particularly for more detailed exploration of the philosophical underpinnings of those texts. The analysis of how secondary sources view the primary texts should also be fruitful. Students at this level may be prompted to research other theologians during the patristic-medieval and other periods for their views on the God–human–Earth relationship and, of course, to analyze them comparatively.

This book may also be helpful in seminaries for directing those who are preparing for the priesthood, for the diaconate, and for directing religious education programs at the parish level. Through this and other texts, seminary students will be exposed to the positive views that some eminent patristic and medieval theologians had toward the world. This knowledge could aid informed composition of homilies appropriate for Earth Day (April 22), Biological Diversity Day (May 22), and the feast days of Saint Francis of Assisi (October 4) and his predecessors among the saintly desert fathers, Celtic wanderers, and English hermits. The uses to which creative directors of religious education can put the knowledge contained in this book are limited only by their imaginations.

I hope that others may also find this book useful. Scholars of the world religions who are striving to find fruitful concepts and practices in various traditions with which to respond to ecological degradation might find helpful the critical-creative methodology applied to centuries-old discourse in the Catholic theological tradition. Scientists who are interested in knowing what the Catholic tradition offers for responding to the loss of biological diversity may be surprised to find a view that corrects the often-heard criticism that Judeo-Christianity is the cause of the environmental crisis by encouraging the "domination" of the natural world.[25] Environmentalists who are seeking to rally support for projects that address the ongoing degradation of Earth will find rationales for convincing believers to support advocacy efforts.

Finally, lay Catholics who are concerned about the human assaults on our planet should be pleased to find in their theological tradition some promising ways in which they can address local to global issues. For some Catholics who have not yet embraced ecological concerns, recognition of teachings by some of the most revered theologians in the Catholic tradition might be sufficiently persuasive to transform their thinking and direct their actions.

Notes

1. Pope John Paul II, "The Ecological Crisis: A Common Responsibility," Vatican City, January 1, 1990. The pope underscored the moral responsibility that Catholics have for living in harmony with God's creation. His successor, Pope Benedict XVI, speaking at the Church's first "ecofriendly" youth rally, urged world leaders to "save the planet before it's too late." Philip Pullella, "Pope Leads Eco-Friendly Youth Rally," Reuters, September 2, 2007, www.reuters.com/news/video?videoId=65392. Speaking from a stage in Loreto, Italy, and dressed in a green vestment, the pope underscored the responsibility that humans have toward the natural environment: "New generations will be entrusted with the future of the planet," he said, "which bears clear signs of a type of development that has not always protected nature's delicate equilibrium." He continued: "A decisive 'yes' is needed in decisions to safeguard creation as well as a strong commitment to reverse tendencies that risk leading to irreversible situations of degradation." He urged "a strong alliance between man and earth." During the pontificates of both popes, Vatican City has become progressively "green" through conservation efforts including recycling, use of photovoltaic cells on buildings to produce electricity, and hosting a scientific conference to discuss global warming.

2. A composite of statements by the Catholic bishops developed by Heather R. Whittington, one of my honors program students, is accessible from www.marquette.edu/theology/interfacing.

3. United States Conference of Catholic Bishops, *Renewing the Earth: An Invitation to Reflection and Action on Environment in Light of Catholic Social Teaching"* (Washington, DC: USCCB Publications, 1991), 13; also at www.usccb.org/sdwp/ejp/bishopsstatement.shtml. This document is rich in thinking about the human relationship to the natural environment; the bishops call upon biblical scholars, theologians, and ethicists "to help explore, deepen, and advance the insights of our Catholic tradition and its relation to the environment" and especially "to explore the relationship between this tradition's emphasis upon the dignity of the human person and our responsibility to care for all of God's creation."

4. These statements by Christian denominations that participate in the Web of Creation effort with the aim of transforming faith-based communities for a sustainable world can be found at www.webofcreation.org/education/policystatements/index.

5. See, e.g., the series of conferences sponsored by and publications issued from Harvard University's Center for the Study of World Religions, www.environment.harvard.edu/religion/publications/books/book_series/cswr/index.html. Volumes on ecology and Buddhism, Christianity, Confucianism, Daoism, Hinduism, Indigenous Religions, Islam, Jainism, and Judaism were published by the end of 2004, and one is also available from the Shinto perspective.

6. The Coalition on the Environment and Jewish Life (www.coejl.org), the Evangelical Environmental Network (www.creationcare.org), the National Council of Churches of Christ (www.webofcreation.org/ncc/), and the United States Confer-

ence of Catholic Bishops (www.nccbuscc.org/sdwp/ejp/index.htm) constitute the National Religious Partnership for the Environment (www.nrpe.org).

7. Among the theologians who have pointed to inadequacies and ambiguities in the Christian tradition are H. Paul Santmire, *The Travail of Nature: The Ambiguous Ecological Promise of Christian Theology* (Philadelphia: Fortress Press, 1985); Sallie McFague, *The Body of God: An Ecological Theology* (Minneapolis: Fortress Press, 1993); and John F. Haught, *The Promise of Nature: Ecology and Cosmic Purpose* (New York: Paulist Press, 1993). A critique of the Judeo-Christian tradition that precipitated its defense and at least initially some of the more or less constructive "greening" is the historian of medieval technology Lynn White Jr.; see his "The Historical Roots of Our Ecologic Crisis," *Science* 155 (March 10, 1967): 1203–7. A perceptive historical overview of the corrective responses to White's thesis is provided by Elspeth Whitney, "Lynn White, Ecotheology, and History," *Environmental Ethics* 15 (Summer 1993): 151–69.

8. Roderick Frazier Nash, *The Rights of Nature: A History of Environmental Ethics* (Madison: University of Wisconsin Press, 1989), 87. See also Mary Evelyn Tucker and John Grim, "The Greening of the World's Religions," *The Chronicle of Higher Education*, February 9, 2007, B9, available at http://chronicle.com.

9. Yves M.-J. Congar, OP, *Tradition and Traditions: An Historical and a Theological Essay* (London: Burns & Oates, 1966). As Congar explains from his monumental study, the early Fathers of the Church were "'inspired,' raised up, enlightened, guided and strengthened by the Holy Spirit" to contribute significantly to the "permanent form" of the Church's faith by continuing the traditions of the Scriptures. They wielded "a decisive influence on the life of the people of God" at crucial times of the formation of the Church and are, therefore, "Fathers *par excellence*" who hold "special value and historical importance" for the Church (pp. 439–40). As Congar recognizes, the Fathers were conditioned by the culture of their times, including the Neoplatonic influences that provided a framework for thinking about God in relation to the world and the nature of the human person, and they struggled to respond to the heresies of their times while remaining "absolutely theocentric in outlook and reasoning" (p. 450). Retrieval of their teachings for purposes of this project seems especially fitting.

10. Edward Booth, "St. Augustine's '*Notitia Sui*' Related to Aristotle and the Early Neoplatonists," *Augustiniana* 27 (1977):70–132, at 102; Dominic J. O'Meara, "Introduction," *Neoplatonism and Christian Thought*, ed. Dominic J. O'Meara (Norfolk: International Society for Neoplatonic Studies, 1982), ix; and the various essays in *Neoplatonism and Early Christian Thought: Essays in Honour of A. H. Armstrong*, ed. H. J. Blumenthal and R. A. Markus (London: Variorum Publications, 1981).

11. O'Meara, "Introduction," 39. In *De Genesi ad Litteram*, Augustine argued against theological discourse that countered well-established Neoplatonic conclusions about the cosmos. David C. Lindberg provides an overview of Basil's and Augustine's use of natural philosophy in "Science and the Early Church," in *God and Nature: Historical Essays on the Encounter between Christianity and Science*, ed. David C. Lindberg and Ronald L. Numbers (Berkeley: University of California Press, 1986), 19–48. M.-D. Chenu, OP, discusses training in natural philosophy that preceded the advanced study of theology at the university level in *Toward Understanding Saint Thomas*, trans. A.-M. Landry and D. Hughes, OP (Chicago: Henry Regnery, 1964), 20–21.

12. Cornelio Fabro, "The Overcoming of the Neoplatonic Triad of Being, Life, and Intellect by Saint Thomas Aquinas," in *Neoplatonism and Christian Thought*, ed. O'Meara, 97–108.

13. See, e.g., R. T. Wallis, "Divine Omniscience in Plotinus, Proclus, and Aquinas," in *Neoplatonism and Early Christian Thought,* ed. Blumenthal and Markus, 223–35. The importance of understanding the worldviews of theologians is stressed by N. Max Wildiers, *The Theologian and His Universe: Theology and Cosmology from the Middle Ages to the Present* (New York: Seabury Press, 1982).

14. For patristic and medieval theologians, as evident in chapter 3, on the sacramentality of creation, the cosmos mediates God's presence and manifests God's attributes. Ian G. Barbour compares the medieval understanding of the world with our contemporary understanding in *Religion and Science: Historical and Contemporary Issues* (San Francisco: HarperSanFrancisco, 1997), 281–84.

15. Of course, theologians should recognize that scientific knowledge is open to revision as new data are collected, theories revised, and conclusions drawn, so theological discourse informed by scientific knowledge is also open to revision while the basic faith remains intact. Theologians and scientists have pondered this phenomenon of revisionism as various forms of "critical realism," an astute overview of which is provided by the systematic theologian Nels Gregersen, "Critical Realism and Other Realisms," in *Fifty Years in Science and Religion: Ian G. Barbour and His Legacy,* ed. Robert John Russell (Burlington, VT: Ashgate, 2004), 77–93.

16. H. Hilary Armstrong points to the limitations of language in adequately capturing God in "Negative Theology, Myth, and Incarnation," in *Neoplatonism and Christian Thought,* ed. O'Meara, 213–22. Theologians and scientists should share a sense of humility about the limitations of their respective endeavors, whether they operate independently or collaboratively when addressing issues at the boundaries of their disciplines.

17. Robert John Russell, "Introduction," in *Evolutionary and Molecular Biology: Scientific Perspectives on Divine Action,* ed. Robert John Russell, William R. Stoeger, SJ, and Francisco J. Ayala (Vatican City: Vatican Observatory, 1998), ii.

18. Ian Barbour provides a succinct overview of some basic ways of talking about God informed by the biological sciences in "Five Models of God and Evolution," in *Evolutionary and Molecular Biology,* ed. Russell, Stoeger, and Ayala, 419–42.

19. A major effort to explore theological discourse that coheres with more in-depth scientific findings is the series of conferences initiated in 1987 by the Vatican Observatory and organized subsequently with the Center for Theology and the Natural Sciences. In addition to *Evolutionary and Molecular Biology,* ed. Russell, Stoeger, and Ayala, cited above, see *Physics, Philosophy, and Theology: A Common Quest for Understanding,* ed. Robert John Russell, William Stoeger, SJ, and George V. Coyne (Vatican City: Vatican Observatory, 1988); and subsequent volumes, all subtitled *Scientific Perspectives on Divine Action,* including *Chaos and Complexity,* ed. Robert John Russell, Nancey Murphy and Arthur R. Peacocke (Vatican City: Vatican Observatory, 1995); *Quantum Cosmology and the Laws of Nature,* ed. Robert John Russell, Nancey Murphy, and C. J. Isham (Vatican City: Vatican Observatory, 1996); and *Neuroscience and the Person,* ed. Robert John Russell, Nancey Murphy, Theo C. Meyering, and Michael A. Arbib (Vatican City: Vatican Observatory, 1999).

20. Conferences and volumes produced through the efforts of the Center for the Study of World Religions at Harvard University aptly demonstrate the need for examining religious traditions for promising ways for thinking about and acting toward other species, systems, and the biosphere. The results can be viewed from the Harvard

Divinity School website, www.environment.harvard.edu/religion/publications/books/index.html.

21. For examples of this criterion for theological discourse, see Thomas P. Rausch, SJ, "Theology and Its Methods," in *The College Student's Introduction to Theology,* ed. Thomas P. Rausch (Collegeville, MN: Liturgical Press, 1993), 11–23, at 20. Rausch identifies consistency with scientific and other knowledge about the world as one of five tests for theological discourse. Also see Ian G. Barbour, *Religion and Science: Historical and Contemporary Issues* (San Francisco: HarperSanFrancisco, 1997), 113. Arguments and demonstrations for the consistency of theological discourse with scientific knowledge when addressing issues at the boundaries of religion and science can be found in a plethora of articles and books, including several essays by Karl Rahner; see, e.g., his "Natural Science and Reasonable Faith," in *Theological Investigations: Science and Christian Faith,* vol. 21, trans. Hugh M. Riley (New York: Crossroad, 1988), 16–55. Many examples of works aimed at theological discourse that coheres with scientific knowledge of the world appear in the book series focusing on divine action that, as noted above, was organized and published jointly by the Vatican Observatory and the Center for Theology and the Natural Sciences.

22. Congar, *Tradition and Traditions,* 449.

23. Santmire, *Travail of Nature.* See also William C. French, "Subject-Centered and Creation-Centered Paradigms in Recent Catholic Thought," *Journal of Religion* 70 (1990): 48–72. French identifies astutely the human-centered view of the world as an overarching organizing principle in Catholic theology. McFague, *Body of God,* chap. 4, systematically and poignantly explores several problems that occur when taking an unrealistic anthropocentric view of the world.

24. McFague phrases the failure in theological discourse to acknowledge the human place in and of the world as "telling a lie"; McFague, *Body of God,* 112–29. Living an ego-centered life wherein the individual is self-seeking is especially devastating for humans as well as other-than-humans according to W. J. Christie, W. J., M. Becker, J. W. Cowden, and J. R. Vallentyne, "Managing the Great Lakes as a Home," *Journal of Great Lakes Research* 12 (1986): 2–17; Garrett Hardin, "The Tragedy of the Commons," *Science* 162 (December 13, 1968): 1243–48; and National Research Council, *Global Environmental Change: Understanding the Human Dimensions,* ed. Paul C. Stern, Oran R. Young, and Daniel Druckman (Washington, DC: National Academies Press, 1992).

25. See White, "Historical Roots of Our Ecological Crisis," and the review by Whitney, "Lynn White, Ecotheology, and History," regarding the many times this essay has been included in anthologies and referenced to criticize Judeo-Christianity for its role in degrading and destroying the natural environment. White was indeed selective and prone to biblical literalism when addressing his colleagues at the American Association for the Advancement of Science meeting in 1967.

1

VALUING THE GOODNESS OF CREATION

Since the inception of environmental philosophy as an academic field, scholars have struggled to construct an adequate theory of valuing other species, ecosystems, and the greater biosphere. J. Baird Callicott, a leading contributor to this effort, has identified value theory as the "central and most recalcitrant problem" for environmental ethics.[1] Among the important questions with which philosophers have grappled are: (1) Should other-than-humans be valued instrumentally as means to human ends, as Bryan Norton insists,[2] or intrinsically as ends in themselves, as Callicott, Holmes Rolston, Arne Naess, and others argue?[3] (2) If other-than-human entities are valued intrinsically, does their value originate and persist in them to be discovered by humans, as Rolston argues,[4] or is value something that humans create and attribute to other-than-humans, as Callicott proffers?[5] (3) Is one ethic or set of ethics capable of adjudicating conflicts between valued beings, or is a plurality of diverse ethical systems required?[6] As Clare Palmer explains, each of these questions raises others while scholars work toward cogent ways of thinking about valuing other species, ecosystems, and the larger biosphere.[7]

Theologians can benefit from philosophers' identification and refinement of issues regarding the value of the other-than-human beings that constitute Earth. Their work can be particularly helpful to scholars of the world's religions who are striving to develop systematic ways of addressing ecological issues from the data of their various traditions.

A particularly fruitful concept to explore in the Christian tradition is the goodness of creation. As demonstrated in this chapter, thinking about the physical world's goodness is deeply embedded in patristic and medieval texts by some of Christianity's most eminent theologians, including Augustine of Hippo, John Chrysostom, and Thomas Aquinas. They suggest a theologically based theory of valuing from which broad behavioral norms can be discerned and subsequently reworked to reflect current scientific findings. From this process emerges a religiously motivated rationale for intrinsic-instrumental valuing of the physical world's constituents for themselves, their relationships with one another, and their common good. This valuation is realistic, relevant, and meaningful for Christians because of their relationship with the ultimate bestower of value who is God.

This opening chapter begins by exploring various teachings about the goodness of creation in representative texts by Augustine, Chrysostom, and Aquinas. The major dimensions of their teachings center on the goodness of natural beings, gradations of goodness among creatures, the greater goodness of the totality of creation, the common good of creation, God's valuation, and human valuing. Subsequently explained is the need to reconstruct this concept to reflect the current scientific understanding of the world. The goodness concept is reconstructed and compared positively with parallel thinking among secular philosophers who have been struggling with unresolved dilemmas pertaining to intrinsic and instrumental valuing. Ending the chapter is the identification of behavior patterns that are suggested when beginning from a basic faith in God and embracing the reconstructed goodness of creation concept.

Patristic and Medieval Texts

Throughout the patristic and medieval periods, Christian theologians taught that God created the universe of many diverse animate and inanimate beings, they are all good, altogether they constitute a superlative goodness, and they are valued by God. The context of their teachings and the nuances of their reflections varied as some theologians responded to the heresies of their times, others commented on the first but more recent of the two stories of creation that appear in the Book of Genesis,[8] and a few wove their understanding of the goodness of creation into systematic treatments of God's relationship with the world. All shared a faith perspective that is profoundly monotheistic: God is the creator of all the natural beings that constitute the universe, each animate and inanimate being has a God-given purpose, and the entire universe is utterly dependent upon God for its existence.

The Goodness of Natural Beings

For Augustine of Hippo (354–430) nothing exists that does not derive its existence from God, the "supremely good Creator"[9] who created ex nihilo the universe of "good things, both great and small, celestial and terrestrial, spiritual, and corporeal."[10] Some people do not understand that every natural being is good, he wrote against his former companions, the Manicheans, but "Catholic Christians" recognize that there are "generic good things to be found in all that God has created, whether spirit or body."[11] Comparing the body of a human with the body of an ape, he concluded that each has its own characteristics according to its nature and both are good accordingly.[12] The expansiveness of his valuation is exemplified in his great work, *De Trinitate,* where he declared:

> The earth is good by the height of its mountains, the moderate elevation of its hills, and the evenness of its fields; and good is the farm that is pleasant and fertile; and good is the house that is arranged throughout in symmetrical proportions

and is spacious and bright; and good are the animals, animate bodies; and good is the mild and salubrious air; and good is the food that is pleasant and conducive to health; and good is health without pains and weariness; and good is the countenance of man with regular features, a cheerful expression, and a glowing color; and good is the soul of a friend with the sweetness of concord and the fidelity of love; and good is the just man; and good are riches because they readily assist us; and good is the heaven with its own sun, moon, and stars.[13]

Even if a body is diminished and loses its beauty, Augustine insisted, it is good as long as it exists.[14]

Reflecting on Genesis 1, Chrysostom (347–407) dwelled on the text's depiction of God's valuing each type of creature as "good." When God declared that creatures are good, the gifted preacher argued, "who would dare, even if bursting with arrogant folly, to open his mouth and gainsay the words uttered by God?" He identified creatures that are both beneficial and harmful to humans:

Among the growth springing up from the earth it was not only plants that are useful but also those that are harmful, and not only trees that bear fruit but also those that bear none; and not only tame animals but also wild and unruly ones. Among the creatures emerging from the waters it was not only fish but also sea monsters and other fierce creatures. It was not only inhabited land but also the unpeopled; not only level plains but also mountains and woods. Among birds it was not only tame ones and those suitable for our food but also wild and unclean ones, hawks and vultures and many others of that kind. Among the creatures produced from the earth it was not only tame animals but also snakes, vipers, serpents, lions and leopards. In the sky it was not only showers and kindly breezes but also hail and snow.[15]

For Chrysostom, anyone who found fault with these creatures or inquired in any disparaging way about their purpose or use would be showing ingratitude to their Creator.[16]

Aquinas (1224/25–1274) consistently stressed the goodness of the physical world, as Josef Pieper and others have observed.[17] Like Augustine, Aquinas pointed to the first story of creation in the Book of Genesis to affirm the goodness of each type of creature,[18] and he reasoned to their goodness from their existence, which he attributed to God. All natural creatures are good at least by the fact that they exist, Aquinas taught.[19] Moving beyond Augustine's interchange of goodness and existence, Aquinas depicted each entity as perfect in some innate way that was implanted in them by their Creator. Each is endowed with an innate way of existing and, if animate, a way of acting according to its nature. To criticize a creature's nature or its natural inclination is, he insisted, an insult to the Creator of nature.[20]

According to Aquinas, another dimension of goodness is its likeness to God's goodness through its innate way of existing as God intends.[21] Humans are distinct among creatures, however, because each human also bears an image of God through an ability to comprehend.[22] Only the intellectual aspects of the human bear God's image, whereas the nonintellectual aspects, those making up the physical body, retain only a likeness of God's goodness through their existence.[23]

Augustine, Chrysostom, and Aquinas ascribed to the intrinsic valuing of all types of creatures as distinct entities that are essential to the world. As Kavanaugh notes, in Aquinas's thinking, this intrinsic goodness and value persists, regardless of its role as a function of human happiness.[24] Creatures are not islands in the scheme of the world's functioning, however. Inherent in the teachings of these three representative theologians is an understanding that all creatures are related to one another, to the universe as a totality, and to God.

Grades of Goodness

Although patristic and medieval theologians taught that all creatures are good, are valued by God, and should be valued by humans, all creatures nevertheless vary in the extent of their goodness. This variability depends upon their innate makeup and ways of existing. Augustine exclaimed that God did not make "all things equal,"[25] because the level of the goodness of creatures depends upon their "measure, form and order." Some creatures are superior to others according to these innate characteristics. Rational creatures are God's most excellent creatures, he explained, because God gave them the power to be incorruptible if they avoid willing their corruption by remaining obedient to God.[26]

Aquinas reasoned to degrees of goodness among creatures. Arguing against some philosophers' explanations for the differences among creatures, he insisted that their characteristics are attributable only to God, who created them differently and thereby communicated various "grades of goodness" to them.[27] Building upon Aristotle's observations, the great medieval theologian envisioned a simplistic hierarchical arrangement of diverse entities, of which some have greater degrees of goodness than others according to their innate capabilities and complexities: Mixed elements that are more perfect than the primary elements (air, water, fire, and earth), plants than minerals, animals than plants, and humans than other animals.[28]

Aquinas occasionally referred to this arrangement as an "order of conservation," in which the higher relied upon the lower for sustenance. Thus, mixed bodies rely upon the elements, plants upon mixed bodies, animals upon plants, and humans upon animals and plants to sustain their physical needs.[29] Although the higher type of creature is considered more valuable than the lower, primarily because of the higher's innate capabilities, each is essential for the functioning of the universe and is, therefore, valuable. The lower and less capable exists for the sake of the next higher type of being in the hierarchy, he reasoned from his medieval understanding of the world, and all are needed to internally maintain the universe.[30] The universe would not be perfect without all these grades of goodness.[31]

Addressing the role of humans in this hierarchy of beings, Aquinas explained that humans have the highest degree of goodness among physical creatures because humans can embrace and transcend the corporeal world through their ability to reflect on what is stored in their memory,[32] choose to act according to the dictates of reason,[33] and cooperate with God's grace in seeking eternal happiness with God.[34] Humans use other creatures in two ways during their temporal lives: (1) As instruments or means through which human life can be sustained, and (2) as instruments or means through which knowledge of God can be obtained.[35] Humans are supposed to exercise their rational and volitional abilities when using other creatures that are intended to be used to meet human needs.[36] Their needs consist of things that support their bodies, such as food, clothing, transportation,[37] and those things without which they cannot carry on their lives in appropriate ways as they seek eternal happiness with God.[38] He proscribed the exorbitant use of God's other creatures, describing it as inordinate and wasteful,[39] immoderate,[40] disordered, and vicious.[41] The excessive use of other entities was judged sinful in the scheme of the human quest for eternity with God.[42]

Aquinas's teachings that humans can use other creatures to know God reflect his sacramental perception of the physical world as a means through which God's goodness, wisdom, power, and other attributes can be contemplated.[43] The physical world can lead humans to God, Aquinas contended—referring occasionally to Romans 1:20 and Wisdom 13:1–9—especially if they begin from their faith perspective that the world is God's creation and approach it deliberately as a means of knowing and loving God.[44] Through their ability to make and execute informed decisions, an ability that distinguishes them from other material creatures, humans should know that their eternal end is God and should act rightly to achieve this end.[45]

Aquinas extended his understanding of the instrumental use of creatures to humans who use other humans and to God who uses all natural beings for God's purposes. Other humans are the most important creatures a human uses, he reasoned, because they need one another to secure the necessities of life.[46] Moreover, all creatures are like God's instruments created to serve God's purposes,[47] because whoever makes something for a purpose may use it to achieve that purpose.[48]

Clearly, the instrumental value of all creatures looms large in patristic and medieval theological reflections. Creatures are valued instrumentally for what they contribute to the sustenance of the other in the hierarchical chain. In this chain of beings, humans value other creatures instrumentally for their use to sustain human life, not to satisfy superfluous desires.

The Greater Goodness of the Totality

Though patristic and medieval theologians valued each type of creature intrinsically according to their natures and also instrumentally as means through which to sustain themselves in the hierarchy of beings, they valued most highly the entirety of the physical world. They convey an intrinsic valuation of the orderly functioning of the universe. According to their teachings, God wisely created the universe, generously endowed it with the capability to maintain itself internally, and sustains in existence its capacity to maintain itself internally.[49]

Some theologians affirmed the superlative goodness of the physical world when reflecting on Genesis 1:31. For example, Augustine wrote that the ensemble of all entities constitute a "wonderful order and beauty."[50] A "tranquility of order" exists in the arrangement of "equal and unequal" entities in their proper positions" that brings about "the peace of the universe."[51] Indeed, "God has made all things very good."[52]

Aquinas expounded systematically on the goodness of the universe, which is brought about by the orderly functioning of its constituents in relation to one another. From his understanding of the value of each type of creature, he described glowingly the unity brought about by their orderly interactivity as the greatest created good,[53] the highest perfection of the created world,[54] and its most beautiful attribute.[55] The order of things in relation to one another is the nearest thing to God's goodness, he insisted, because every particular good is ordered in relation to the good of the whole.[56] That some things exist for the sake of others and also for the sake of the perfection of the universe is not contradictory, he taught, because some are needed by others to maintain the internal integrity of the universe and all things are needed to contribute to its perfection.[57] When all parts function in relation to one another in innately appropriate ways as intended by God, the universe is indeed perfect, reflects God's goodness, and manifests God's glory.[58]

Although the intrinsic value of the orderly universe appears conclusive in the reflections of these three theologians, Aquinas explicitly addressed the instrumental use of the orderly universe by God. God uses the universe as its principal cause to produce its principal effect,[59] which is a unity of diverse beings that function internally according to the natural law established by God.[60] A universe that functions as intended by God most superbly manifests God's goodness.[61] Thus, the order of instrumentality begins with God and extends hierarchically downward through natural entities. Although all types of beings are intrinsically valuable as essential components of the universe, they are also instrumentally valuable to one another for their sustenance and, as a totality, to God through which God achieves God's purposes.[62]

The Common Good

Closely aligned with the greater goodness of the totality of creation is Aquinas's teaching that God created living and nonliving entities in an orderly relationship with one another to achieve their common good.[63] Paralleling his treatment of the common good of the universe with the common good of citizens of a particular society, he identified the common good as a basic principle of the way God governs the universe and of the way a king rules a kingdom. Both seek the good of many over the good of one.[64]

To achieve the common good, God instilled in each creature a natural inclination toward the good of the whole,[65] so each is inclined intellectually, sensitively, or naturally to the common good.[66] Stones and other entities are inclined naturally to the good of the whole because they do not have the capacity to sense or know.[67] Each is more strongly inclined to the common good than to itself, Aquinas contended, and this inclination is demonstrated by its operation.[68] For example, sometimes a creature suffers damages to itself for the sake of the common good.[69] At the root of this appetite for the common good is each creature's natural inclination for God, who is the absolute common good of all creatures.[70]

Although all parts of creation are inclined toward the common good of the whole, Aquinas explained, entities that have a higher grade of goodness have a greater appetite for the common good and are inclined to seek to do good for others far removed from themselves.[71] The human aptitude for the whole requires a person to will a particular good for the common good; if the person does not, that act of the will is not right.[72]

Because humans often act incorrectly by not directing their wills toward the common good and ultimately toward the individual's lasting relationship with God, God cares providentially for individual humans by offering them grace to help them exercise their wills appropriately.[73] As discussed in more depth in chapter 5 of this volume, on the integrity of creation, God's grace both operates on and cooperates with humans toward their ultimate goal,[74] without interfering in the human exercise of freely making and carrying out decisions.[75] God's grace operates lovingly on the human spirit, so the individual thinks about and acts in ways that are conducive to achieving eternal life.[76] God's grace cooperates with the individual by actively sustaining the innate human capacity to make informed decisions and to choose to act accordingly. God's grace also operates on and cooperates with humans to develop the moral virtues that will aid them in exercising their wills appropriately to achieve the common good in this life because they are motivated to achieve eternal life with God.[77]

Nevertheless, all entities that constitute the universe benefit from being moved toward the common good of the whole, Aquinas taught.[78] Using a parallel example of the leader of an army, he maintained that the leader is ordering all parts to the good of the whole when intending the parts' mutual good.[79] All the parts thus benefit from their ordering in relation to one another, which enables them to function appropriately to bring about the good of the whole.[80]

Aquinas maintained that God intends all entities to cooperate for the good of the whole. In the operations of unintelligible beings, harmony and usefulness in things almost always prevail because they are directed toward their ends by God.[81] God also intends harmony and cooperation to prevail among all the diverse constituents of the universe, including creatures gifted with the ability to think and will the common good.[82] As Legrand observed in Aquinas's teachings, no part of creation or type of creature is excluded from God's intention that all cooperate, combine, or harmonize within the order of the universe that God established to maintain its internal functioning, through which it achieves the good that is common to all.[83]

When Aquinas contended that creatures cooperate in securing the common good, he was not only thinking about creatures cooperating among themselves within the hierarchical scale of beings that ensures their sustainability. He also considered the intercooperation of creatures as cooperating with God. He insisted that the higher creatures on the scale of beings are meant to cooperate with God in acquiring the good of the whole universe. A higher creature receives more abundant goodness from God, as demonstrated by the creature's nature and way of acting. Unless the higher creature cooperates in procuring the good of lower creatures, the abundance of goodness given to the higher creature would be confined to one individual or few.[84] The good of many is better than the good of an individual, he continued, and the good of the universe as a whole is best because it is more representative of the divine goodness.

Furthermore, according to Aquinas, goodness becomes common to many by the fact that the more richly endowed creature cooperates in procuring the good of many.[85] Higher creatures are expected to cooperate in seeking the good of others, and it is with this expectation that God rules lower creatures through higher creatures.

Creatures cooperate with one another for the good of the whole, Aquinas taught, because they are related to God as their Creator. God ordered them to one another with the intention that they achieve their internal common good of sustaining themselves as an integral whole and thereby manifest God's goodness. In one of his most succinct treatments of this subject, he explained that the entire universe of interconnected parts achieves its purpose through the functioning of all the parts in relation to one another in ways that are appropriate to each one's innate characteristics.[86] Functioning in these relational ways as an entirety of interconnected parts as God intended best manifests God's goodness and gives glory to God.[87] Thus, the *created* common good is the good of the whole order of beings functioning in appropriate, relational ways to sustain themselves as intended by God while aiming toward God, who is the *uncreated* common good of the entire universe.

French contends astutely that Aquinas's concept of the common good provides a "cosmological-ecological principle" for his ethical system.[88] From the perspective of ecological degradation today, the good sought in common would be the good of ecosystems, of which humans are integral actors relying on other interacting *biota* (i.e., the fauna and flora of an area) and *abiota* (i.e., the air, land, and water with which and in which the biota interact) for their health and well-being. This ethical framework of the common good for addressing environmental issues also appeals to Longwood, who recognizes the need to remain cognizant of human existence in the "complex and subtly balanced system of the web of life in which all parts function to maintain the quality of the integrated whole."[89]

God's Valuation

Christian theologians embraced the traditional belief in the Genesis 1 story of creation that God values the physical world with its many diverse constituents. Augustine counted the number of times in Genesis 1 that God is depicted as having created a being, looked at it, and proclaimed it good.[90] That God evaluates creatures and finds them good was significant from his faith perspective.[91] For

Augustine, God is the ultimate authority, and, as Ledoux concludes, what God sees, humans would also see as wondrously good when moving beyond their greed and valuing the integrity of natural entities for themselves.[92]

In a celebrated homily on the Book of Genesis, Chrysostom stressed the authority of God's valuation. He warned his flock against the "arrogant folly" of deviating from God's valuing of the physical world. He first told them to "shun . . . like a lunatic" anyone who did not acquiesce to God's judgment about the world's goodness, and subsequently instructed them to inform the ignorant about God's valuation in order to "check" the ignorant person's "unruly tongue."[93] God created everything by his loving and thoughtful kindness; nothing was created idly or without purpose.[94]

Aquinas also ascribed ultimate authority to God for valuing the physical world. Within the *exitus et reditus* schematic of God's creating and governing the orderly universe and ordering its return, Aquinas found compatibility between the Genesis 1 account of God's superlative evaluation of the entirety of creation and Aristotle's reasoning about the order of the universe as the greatest created good.[95] Furthermore, Aquinas insisted that God cares most for the order of the universe. He reasoned that the nearest thing to God's goodness among created things is the good of the order of the universe, because every particular good is ordered to an end—just as the less perfect is ordered to the more perfect, culminating in the human, and each part, including the human, is for the sake of the whole.[96]

From these teachings emerges an understanding of God's intrinsic-instrumental valuing of the entire universe of diverse living and nonliving entities. God values the entire universe most as a functioning whole of intrinsically valuable beings that achieve their purposes for existing by acting or being acted upon according to their natures. Concurrently, God values all types of entities as instruments of others progressively up the hierarchical chain by which the universe maintains itself.[97] For Aquinas, the universe is God's instrument for achieving God's purposes for it.[98]

Human Valuation

Augustine connected human valuing of the physical world to human limitations and self-centered tendencies. Humans are gifted with intellectual abilities, he explained, but their entrenchment in a part of the universe and their condition as mortal beings prevents them from comprehending the universe in its entirety. Only God has this comprehensive ability.

Nevertheless, humans should overcome their narrow-mindedness and self-centeredness as manifested by judging negatively some natural beings and forces that cause personal discomfort. Humans should consider the natures of things in themselves without regard to their convenience or inconvenience, their pleasantness or unpleasantness, their comfort or discomfort. Humans should praise God for all aspects of the physical world and never "in the rashness of human folly" allow themselves to find fault in any way with the work of the "great Artificer." According to Augustine, humans must have confidence in God's overall design, God's continuing care, and God's purpose for all things that constitute the universe.[99]

In addition to addressing the intrinsic value of the physical world, Augustine focused on the human use of other creatures. God created all things in supreme wisdom and ordered them in a perfect relationship that to one another to ensure that they could obtain whatever is needed to sustain them in temporal life. To humans God has given good things suitable to this life, including light to see, air to breathe, water to drink, and food to eat. Every human who uses these goods correctly "shall receive goods greater in degree and superior in kind, namely the peace of immortality" within which God can be enjoyed eternally. The person who uses these goods incorrectly "shall lose them, and shall not receive the blessings of eternal life."[100]

Chrysostom characterized Earth as "mother and nurse," created by God to nourish humans.[101] They are destined by God to enjoy Earth as their "homeland," for which they should be grateful to God.[102]

Aquinas reflected on the human valuation of the physical world from both intrinsic and instrumental perspectives. As Kavanaugh notes, when describing the human as a creature with the cognitive capacity to recognize the goodness of the physical world and the volitional capacity to choose to value it, Aquinas presented humans as intrinsic valuers.[103] His teaching about the human capacity to discover the rational plan by which God directed one creature to the other[104] also opens to recognizing the human as an instrumental valuer. Upon discovering the instrumental relationships of entities to one another that bring about the sustainability of species, ecosystems, and the biosphere of Earth, humans should value them and their instrumental interactions for their mutual sustainability.

That humans should value the physical world with its diverse constituents is also supported by Aquinas's teaching that God gives humans "natural dominion" over God's creation while God maintains "absolute dominion."[105] The natural dominion exercised by humans is based on their ability to know and to will good ends, and humans are always subservient to God's dominion when exercising their dominion, which—contra French—is never "absolute."[106] Thus, human dominion is aimed at cooperating with God in carrying out God's plan and not hindering it in any way.[107]

Another dimension of valuing the physical world intrinsically and instrumentally is Aquinas's teaching that humans can also love the entire world of diverse beings with the highest kind of love—*maxime et caritate*.[108] As discussed in detail in chapter 9 of this volume, on loving God's creation, Aquinas specified two ways of loving most highly: (1) As good entities that should be conserved for God's honor and glory,[109] and (2) as goods needed by other humans as they seek eternal happiness with God.[110] The intrinsic and instrumental valuations surface explicitly from these two ways of loving the world of many varied beings *ex caritate* to the maximum possible extent.

Finally, Aquinas's praise for the orderly interaction of natural beings that maintains the integrity of the physical world provides an exemplar for also valuing its integrity through which the temporal common good—the world's sustainability—is realized. His teaching that humans should seek the common good when willing a particular good provides an entry for thinking more expansively about valuing the world's functioning.[111] The sustainable functioning of ecosystems and the greater biosphere is indeed a good that humans have in common with the other biota and abiota constituting these systems. When humans will this common good, they are conforming their wills to God's valuation of the physical world and God's willing the common good of all the world's constituents.[112]

Reconstructing Patristic and Medieval Concepts for the Twenty-First Century

However promising the patristic and medieval concepts of the goodness of God's creation and its intrinsic-instrumental value appear to be, their reconstruction is essential to reflect our contemporary understanding of the world so the system of ethics developed can be as plausible, relevant, and helpful as possible. Augustine, Chrysostom, Aquinas, and their contemporaries attributed the goodness of the world with its diverse constituents to God's having created them as they are, in their "fixed" specificity, with purposes that fit into God's overall plan for the universe. Only rational beings are endowed with the freedom to make decisions that could run counter to God's intentions.

How can concepts about the "goodness" of creation be reconstructed today when informed by at least basic scientific findings? Because God provides the foundation for all that exists and nothing would exist without God's having initiated and continuing to sustain the existence and capacity of the world to develop itself, goodness must be attributed to the cosmological-biological process out of which all natural entities have emerged over a period of 14 billion years. Goodness must also be attributed to these entities' many diverse natures, their relationships with one another, and their interactions for their common good incrementally as communities, ecosystems, the biosphere, and extraterrestrial systems. The entirety of the physical world can be acknowledged as God's valuable possession, as a manifestation of God's extravagant goodness, and as a readily available subject for discovery. Faithful humans can be understood as discoverers of the physical world's value, as beholders of its value, and as responders to its goodness out of a desire to share in God's valuation of the world.[113]

Reconstructing patristic and medieval concepts about the goodness of creation yields significant implications for behavior that can be responsive to ecological degradation. All species, the air, the earth, and the waters are intrinsically valuable as components of Earth, and they are also valuable instrumentally as needed by other components to sustain themselves within the web of existence. Ecosystems are valuable intrinsically as a composite of intrinsically-instrumentally valuable biota and abiota functioning interdependently to sustain their shared existence, and they are also valuable instrumentally for their contributions to the sustainability of the larger biosphere. The biosphere of Earth is valuable intrinsically as the composite of all systems with biotic and abiotic constituents, along with adjoining marginal areas, that together constitute Earth, and the biosphere is also valuable instrumentally as a home used by humans, other species, and extended ecosystems.[114] The entirety of the physical world with its many diverse constituents is valuable to God, their purposeful creator and sustainer in existence, who endowed humans with the intellectual capacity to discern the intrinsic and instrumental values inherent in the physical world and to determine how to demonstrate these values socially, economically, and politically.

Parallels with Secular Philosophy

Some of these implications for ethics broadly parallel the proposals proffered over the past twenty-five years by secular theorists of intrinsic and instrumental value. A particularly prominent parallel with patristic and medieval thinking is Rolston's position that value is a property of the physical world that preexists humans and is available for discovery by them. This thinking coincides with theologians' teachings that God bestows and upholds the physical world's value, that God's valuing preexists humans, and that faithful Christians who desire eternal happiness with God have a profound incentive for using their intellectual capabilities to discover and value the natural entities that constitute the world. Of course, patristic and medieval theologians grounded their teachings in God as the ultimate source and bestower of value, whereas Rolston limits his philosophical approach to the inherent value of the natural world without reference to God.

Another important parallel between the aforementioned theologians and contemporary environmental ethicists is the good of the whole as the basis for adjudicating conflicts between humans and other species. Callicott promotes adjudicating this common good in principle through Aldo Leopold's "land ethic," Longwood through the Aristotelian concept of "the common good," and French and Kavanaugh through Aquinas's Christianization of Aristotle's understanding of the common good. Maintaining the sustainability of natural entities individually and collectively is their created common good intended by God, as explained in its fullest sense by Aquinas. Thus, all claims would have to be adjudicated on the basis of the extent to which the claim is essential to the sustainability of an entity according to its nature, its purpose within the ecosystem, and the overall sustainability of this system.

Although human claims for using individuals of other species, the air, the land, and the waters would have to meet this common good criterion, human claims could advance beyond bodily existence to also encompass spiritual needs. A primary spiritual need for present and future generations is the opportunity to experience God's presence and goodness through the physical world.[115] Honoring spiritual claims place additional constraints on human use to ensure that other humans now and in the future are not prevented from encountering God through the world. Among these constraints are avoiding actions that would precipitate the extinction of a species, the loss of biological diversity in an ecosystem, the pollution of air, waterways, and land, the widening of the rupture in the ozone layer of Earth, and the littering of outer space.

Requiring humans to constrain their use of other creatures to the necessities of life corresponds with the philosophy of "deep ecology" developed by Arne Naess, Bill Devall, and George Sessions. Deep ecologists recognize the legitimacy of the human use of other species and abiota, though they insist that their use must be balanced by valuing them intrinsically to minimize the impact on the physical environment.[116] Patristic and medieval theologians taught Christians to value God's creation both intrinsically and instrumentally and to consume only what is needed to sustain their temporal lives while preparing for their eternal destiny with God.

A Behavior Pattern for Valuing?

If Christianity is understood generally as an organized way of knowing and orienting oneself to God, and if one way of orienting oneself to God is by valuing God's creation as good both intrinsically and instrumentally, as patristic and medieval theologians taught, how would the faithful think about and act toward other species and ecosystems?[117] Would the faithful acknowledge and value the evolutionary process from which all natural entities have emerged out of a sense of responsibility to God, who initiated and sustains the process in existence? Would they discover and value their intrinsic goodness as entities valuable in themselves and not simply for humans to use? Would they discover and value their instrumental goodness for their value to one another? Would they discover and value the contribution each entity makes to the common good of an ecosystem? Would they discover and value the ecosystems that emerge from the interaction of biota and abiota? Would they discover and value the entire biosphere? These questions prompt a thought experiment to discern answers.

Valuing the Evolutionary Process Intrinsically and Instrumentally

Empowered by God into existence with the internal capacities to develop itself, the physical world has unfolded through an interplay of the basic laws of physics and chance into a vast array of galaxies with billions of stars, other cosmic phenomena, and planets, including at least one with a diversity of biological life, including reflective beings with the capacity to discover value and demonstrate their valuations.[118] Having emerged from and with other entities through this cosmological-biological evolutionary process, the faithful who embrace the belief that the physical world is good will value the evolutionary process by functioning constructively within it so it can continue to evolve with the promise of more good and valuable entities emerging.[119]

The faithful will also value the evolutionary process instrumentally as the conduit through which the necessities of life have emerged to make possible the survival and flourishing of the human species as part of the Earth community. Because there are functional, historical, and evolutionary limits to the physical world, the faithful will strive to know these limits, live within them, and generate changes that are compatible with them.[120] When functioning cooperatively with other species, abiota, ecosystems, and the biosphere, the faithful will be cooperating with God's gratuitous empowerment of this creative process and, thereby, valuing what God values.

Valuing the Intrinsic Goodness of Natural Entities

With Augustine, Chrysostom, and Aquinas, people who profess faith in God will endeavor to discover the intrinsic value of each species, the air, the land, and the water and should demonstrate their valuation accordingly. In addition to *Homo sapiens,* all other species will be valued in themselves as entities that have emerged over time and space with humans. Integral to discovering their value is the need to discern their interests in surviving and their survival needs. Human interference with meeting these needs will be avoided in local to global arenas. Species' habitats will be protected, and lists of threatened and endangered species will diminish. Efforts will be expended to curtail pollutants and persistent toxicants from the air, water, and land to demonstrate the value of the abiotic environment.

Discovering and Valuing Their Instrumental Goodness

Although intrinsically valuable, the instrumental value of species, air, land, and water to one another will also be discerned and valued by people who believe in God as the creator, sustainer, and ultimate valuer of the physical world. Land species use air, water, land, and other species to maintain themselves; marine species use water and select species of food to maintain themselves; and airborne species rely on both water, land, and other species to sustain themselves. Humans use individuals of other species for food and other goods needed for their lives and well-being, though too many humans, especially those who live in economically developed nations, use other biota, abiota, and whole ecosystems to try to satisfy their insatiable desires. Instead of thinking about other species, air, land, and water exclusively from the perspective of their usefulness to humans, however, the faithful will recognize and value the use that other species have for one another and the air, land, and water for their sustenance in the complex web of life.

Valuing the Contributions Each Entity Makes to an Ecosystem

Following Augustine, Chrysostom, Aquinas, and other eminent theologians, people who profess faith in God will discover and acknowledge the contributions that species and abiota make to their shared ecosystems. They will value God's creation as it is valued by God for their contributions to the integrity of ecosystems. Actions that inhibit their contributions will be prevented. Proposed projects will be scrutinized to ensure that each constituent can continue to contribute. Species that are nonnative to ecological systems will not be introduced to them, and efforts will be expended to remove invasive species from ecosystems to which they have been introduced.

Valuing Ecosystems and the Biosphere for Their Common Good

In addition to valuing the contributions that constituents make to their shared ecosystems, the overall functioning of these systems will be valued both intrinsically and instrumentally. The combination of the complex interactions of biota and abiota that create and recreate an ecosystem will be discovered and sufficiently valued intrinsically by avoiding human actions that disrupt a system's natural functioning and, thereby, deter it from achieving its common good.[121] So, too, will those who embrace Aquinas's teachings about the common good value the integral functioning of Earth as the best manifestation of God's goodness.

Because humans rely upon the land, air, waters, and species of ecosystems for their health and well-being, people who profess faith in God will instrumentally value the systems in which they function by taking from them only what is needed to sustain their lives in ways that avoid endangering the system's sustainability. With Aldo Leopold, faithful people will think of themselves as citizens of ecosystems rather than conquerors of them.[122] They will be open to inspiration by Augustine, Aquinas, and the other theologians who have conveyed a sacramental understanding of the physical world and will value the functioning of ecosystems and the biosphere to achieve their common good as the best manifestation of God's goodness.

The sustainability of Earth—the common good of all the plant's constituents—will become the chief organizing principle through which moral decisions are made. As Longwood urges, the common good is the best framework for dealing with the ongoing degradation of Earth.[123] This framework for decision making is conducive to the "cosmological-ecological principle" that French identifies in Aquinas's works[124] and to the "fertile ground" that should satisfy Kavanaugh for ensuring that the valuing of other-than-humans is not merely for human benefit.[125] With Tanner, people who believe in God as the purposeful creator and sustainer of the world will "repudiate any such alternative between concerns for environmental well-being, on the one hand, and sensitivity to issues of human justice, on the other."[126] All actions will be adjudicated on the basis of the shared common good of the constituents of ecosystems and the biosphere to sustain themselves. All conflicts will be settled on the basis of the extent to which the claim seeks to satisfy the needs that sustain the claimant's existence so that the claimant can continue to contribute to the functioning of its shared ecosystem and the greater biosphere. Needs will take precedence over wants in moral decision making,[127] and a vision of the future informed by the present will be essential to making decisions at all levels of human society.[128]

Conclusion

The ethics of intrinsic-instrumental valuing based on reconstructed patristic and medieval concepts of the goodness of creation can provide a cogent, relevant, and potentially effective system of environmental ethics for application today by people who profess faith in God as the creator and sustainer of the world and who believe that humans are responsible to God for how they act in this world. From this perspective of religious faith, people can address the difficult issues with which secular philosophers have been grappling. Other constituents of Earth are valuable intrinsically as well as instrumentally as they seek to sustain their shared existence with humans. The intrinsic value of Earth's constituents originates with God, who empowers the evolutionary process from which all entities emerge. Their intrinsic-instrumental value persists in this ongoing process, and their value is discoverable by humans who have the ability to discern and demonstrate their valuations. Finally, a system of ethics based on the common good—the sustainability of all constituents in their shared ecosystems and the greater biosphere—serves to adjudicate conflicts among valued beings.

A pattern of behavior emerges from reconstructing patristic and medieval concepts of the goodness of the natural world. People who profess faith in God will value the evolutionary process from which all entities have emerged over cosmological and biological time and space. They will also discover and value the innate goodness of the various species and other natural entities, their interests in and needs for surviving, their instrumental relationships with one another, their unique contributions to their shared ecosystems, and the functioning of these ecosystems within the biosphere to achieve their common good—their sustainability—now and in the future. This pattern of thinking and acting is readily available for embracing by the faithful and thus for application to ecological concerns. By valuing Earth with its varied constituents both intrinsically and instrumentally, the faithful are valuing what God values and calls to completion.

Notes

Parts of this chapter have been selected and revised from Jame Schaefer, "Intrinsic-Instrumental Valuing of Earth: A Theological Framework for Environmental Ethics," *Theological Studies* 66 (December 2005): 783–814.

1. J. Baird Callicott, "Intrinsic Value, Quantum Theory, and Environmental Ethics," *Environmental Ethics* 7, no. 3 (1985): 257–75, at 257. Fifteen years later, he repeated this lament in "Introduction" to *Beyond the Land Ethic: More Essays in Environmental Philosophy* (Albany: State University of New York Press, 1999), 15: "The intrinsic-value-in-nature question has been, and remains, the central and most persistent cluster of problems in theoretical environmental philosophy."
2. Bryan G. Norton, "Environmental Ethics and Weak Anthropocentrism," *Environmental Ethics* 6 (1984): 131–48, argues at 141 that "an adequate environmental ethic *need not* be nonanthropocentric and that an adequate environmental ethics *must not* be

limited to considerations of individual interests." Also see Norton's "Why I Am Not a Nonanthropocentrist: Callicott and the Failure of Monistic Inherentism," *Environmental Ethics* 17 (1995): 341–58, in which he argues against Callicott's ecologically centered approach, which Norton thinks is "especially damaging to the cause of a practical environmental philosophy—one that could contribute to real world policy discussions and environmental problem solving" and argues for abandoning the concept of intrinsic value altogether. Ben A. Minteer,"Intrinsic Value for Pragmatists," *Environmental Ethics* 22 (Spring 2001): 57–75, staunchly defends Norton's pragmatism, whereas Laura Westra explains "Why Norton's Approach Is Insufficient for Environmental Ethics," *Environmental Ethics* 19 (1997): 279–97.

3. E.g., see J. Baird Callicott, "On the Intrinsic Value of Nonhuman Species," in *The Preservation of Species,* ed. Bryan G. Norton (Princeton, NJ: Princeton University Press, 1986), 138–72; and J. Baird Callicott, "Intrinsic Value in Nature: A Metaethical Analysis," *Electronic Journal of Analytical Philosophy* 3 (Spring 1995), www.phil.indiana.edu/ejap/1995.spring/callicott.abs.html, reprinted in *Beyond the Land Ethic: More Essays in Environmental Philosophy,* ed. J. Baird Callicott (Albany: State University of New York Press, 1999), 236–61; Arne Naess, "A Defense of the Deep Ecology Movement," *Environmental Ethics* 6 (1984) 265–70; Robert Elliot, "Intrinsic Value, Environmental Obligation and Naturalism," *The Monist* 75 (1992): 138–60; and Eugene C. Hargrove, "Weak Anthropocentric Intrinsic Value," *The Monist* 75 (1992): 183–212.

4. Rolston proffers this position: "To say that something is valuable means that it is able to be valued, if and when (human) valuers come along, but it has this property whether or not humans (or other valuers) ever arrive"; Holmes Rolston III, *Environmental Ethics: Duties to and Values in Nature* (Philadelphia: Temple University Press, 1988), 114. Also see Holmes Rolston III, "Value in Nature and the Value of Nature," in *Environmental Ethics: An Anthology* (Malden, MA: Blackwell, 2003), 143–53, where he argues that value in the natural world preexists humans; is located in individuals, species, ecosystems, and evolutionary processes; and would exist if humans were to become extinct. See, further, Holmes Rolston III, "Are Values in Nature Subjective or Objective?" in his collection of essays cleverly titled *Philosophy Gone Wild* (Buffalo: Prometheus Press, 1989). Also see John O'Neill, "The Varieties of Intrinsic Value," *The Monist* 75 (1992): 119–37, in which O'Neill explores three interchangeable ways of using "intrinsic value."

5. According to J. Baird Callicott, *In Defense of the Land Ethic: Essays in Environmental Philosophy* (Albany: State University of New York Press, 1989), 133–34, values depend upon human judgment and, therefore, are subjective. See also his "On the Intrinsic Value of Nonhuman Species," where he argues that the "source of all value is human consciousness . . . since no value can in principle . . . be altogether independent of a valuing consciousness" (142–43). Value is "projected onto natural objects or events by the subjective feelings of observers. If all consciousness were annihilated at a stroke, there would be no good and evil, no beauty and ugliness, no right and wrong; only impassive phenomena would remain." Hargrove counters this classification of valuing in "Weak Anthropocentric Intrinsic Value," judging Callicott's position "overly subjective" partly because some values are the product of cultural evolution that serve as foundations for individuals.

6. See J. Baird Callicott, "Moral Monism in Environmental Ethics Defended," *Journal of Philosophical Research* 90 (1994): 51–60; and J. Baird Callicott, "The Case against Moral Pluralism," *Environmental Ethics* 12 (1990): 99–124. The use of several systems

of ethics to address a range of moral problems is championed by Christopher Stone, *Earth and Other Ethics: The Case for Moral Pluralism* (New York: Harper & Row, 1987); and Christopher Stone, "Moral Pluralism and the Course of Environmental Ethics," *Environmental Ethics* 10 (1988): 139–54.

7. Clare Palmer summarizes these questions with references to pertinent environmental philosophers; see Clare Palmer, "An Overview of Environmental Ethics," in *Environmental Ethics: An Anthology,* ed. Andrew Light and Holmes Rolston III (Malden, MA: Blackwell, 2003), 15–37. A cursory search of the scholarly literature yields a plethora of articles, anthologies, and monographs on the subject, including an entire issue of *The Monist* 75 (1992).

8. Bernard W. Anderson, *From Creation to New Creation: Old Testament Perspectives* (Minneapolis: Fortress Press, 1994).

9. Saint Augustine, *The Enchiridion: On Faith, Hope, and Love,* trans. J. F. Shaw and ed. Henry Paolucci (Chicago: Regnery Gateway, 1961), 10:10. See also Augustine, *The Nature of the Good against the Manichees* (De natura boni), in *Augustine: Earlier Writings,* trans. and ed. J. H. S. Burleigh, Library of Christian Classics (Philadelphia: Westminster Press, 1953), 1:326. He continues in *Enchiridion* 10:10–11: "By the trinity, thus supremely and equally and unchangeably good, all things were created; and these are not supremely and equally and unchangeably good, but yet they are good, even taken separately."

10. Augustine, *Nature of the Good,* 3:326.

11. Ibid., 327. As the philosopher Arthur O. Ledoux notes, Augustine's view of nature had shifted from negative when he was enmeshed in Manicheanism and subsequently Neoplatonism to positive after he had converted to Christianity whose doctrines affirmed valuing natural entities; Arthur O. Ledoux, "A Green Augustine: On Learning to Love Nature Well," *Theology and Science* 3 (November 2005): 331–44, 333.

12. Augustine, *Nature of the Good,* 14:330, 17:330–31.

13. Augustine, *The Trinity,* trans. Stephen McKenna, CSSR (Washington, DC: Catholic University of America Press, 1963), 8.3.4, 247.

14. Augustine used the concepts of goodness and existence interchangeably as indicated, for example, in *Nature of the Good,* 4:327, 15:330, 17:330. In *Nature of the Good,* 6:328, he insisted that any nature that is corruptible has some dimension of good, because corruption constitutes diminishing the good; see also Augustine, *The Confessions of St. Augustine,* trans. John K. Ryan (Garden City, NY: Image Books, 1960), 7.12.18, 172, where he underscored his thinking that entities deprived of all good cease to exist.

15. John Chrysostom, *Homilies on Genesis 1–17,* trans. Robert C. Hill, vol. 74 of Fathers of the Church (Washington, DC: Catholic University of America Press, 1986), 10.12, 135–37.

16. Ibid.

17. Joseph Pieper, "Of the Goodness of the World," *Orate Fratres* 25 (September 1951): 433–37. According to Piper, Aquinas's summation *omne ens est bonum* (every being is good) is "the deepest, profoundest meaning and root of all those sentences is that every being as being is intended and even loved by the Creator, that every creature at the same time receives its being–real and its being-loved" (433–44). On the initial ethical implications of Aquinas's thinking about the goodness of creatures in relation to the physical environment, see Jean Porter, *The Recovery of Virtue: The Relevance of Aquinas for Christian Ethics* (Louisville: Westminster/John Knox Press, 1990),

178, who contends astutely that the legitimacy of humanity's use of "the subhuman creation" for its own well-being would have to be acknowledged if the
Thomistic framework of thinking were brought to bear on the ecological crisis. She
cautions, however, that the right to use other created things does not mean that humans may treat the rest of corporeal creation in any way they desire, and she offers two parameters from Aquinas's thinking within which the human use of
creation would fall: (1) Any use of the rest of the created world would have to be
directed to the good of *all* humanity, and (2) all created things possess "an intrinsic
goodness apart from their potential usefulness to anything else" that requires "some
form of respect." Also see James F. Keenan, "Goodness and Rightness in Aquinas's
Summa Theologiae," *The Thomist* 58 (1994): 342–48.

18. Thomas Aquinas, *Summa theologiae,* 1.47.2.

19. E.g., see Aquinas, *Summa contra Gentiles,* 3.7; Aquinas, *De veritate,* 20.4, 21.3; and
    Aquinas, *Summa theologiae,* 1.60.1 ad 3.

20. Aquinas, *Summa theologiae,* 1.60.1 ad 3; see, further, 2|2.23.8; 47.1 ad 1, 1.103.7 ad
    1. Also see Aquinas, *De caritate,* 3; Aquinas, *Summa contra Gentiles,* 3.12; Aquinas, *De
    veritate,* 16.2; and Aquinas, *De malo,* 2.12.

21. Aquinas, *Summa contra Gentiles,* 2.46. That a created being achieves a participated
    likeness of the divine also surfaces in his *Compendium theologiae,* 103, where he ex-
    plains that the divine goodness is not only the end of the creature but is also the
    end of every operation of any creature, insofar as each has some participated like-
    ness to the divine goodness. See further Aquinas, *Summa theologiae,* 1.44.4.

22. Aquinas, *Compendium theologiae,* 75. Also see Aquinas, *Summa theologiae,* 1.93.2; and
    Aquinas, *Summa contra Gentiles,* 2.46.

23. Aquinas, *Summa theologiae,* 1.93.6. Also see his *Summa contra Gentiles,* 3.111–12.
    Aquinas considered creatures' likeness to God within a trinitarian framework. Fol-
    lowing Augustine, *The Trinity,* 6.10, Aquinas found a likeness of the Trinity by way
    of a trace in all creatures, insofar as they are caused by the divine persons. He ex-
    plained in *Summa theologiae,* 1.45.7, that the creature represents the person of the
    Father as its cause, the person of the Word as the form conceived, and the person
    of the Holy Spirit as loved and willed to be.

24. John F. Kavanaugh, SJ, "Intrinsic Value, Persons and Stewardship," in *The Challenge
    of Global Stewardship: Roman Catholic Responses,* ed. Maura A. Ryan and Todd David
    Whitmore (Notre Dame, IN: University of Notre Dame Press, 1997), 67–81.

25. Augustine, *Confessions,* 7.12.18, 172. Augustine discussed his theocentric theory
    about the need for inequality in the universe in *Concerning the City of God against the
    Pagans,* trans. Henry Bettenson and intro. John O'Meara (London: Penguin Books,
    1984), 11.22, 453.

26. Augustine, *Confessions,* 13.32.47, 367.

27. Aquinas, *Summa theologiae,* 1.48.2. See also Aquinas, *Summa contra Gentiles,* 3.20.
    Among the many other references to God's having created many grades of good
    entities and ordering them to one another for the perfection of the universe
    are Aquinas, *Summa theologiae,* 1.65.3; Aquinas, *Summa contra Gentiles,* 2.44, 3.71; and
    Aquinas, *Compendium theologiae,* 73.

28. Aquinas, *Summa theologiae,*1.47.2, is one of many examples of his teachings about
    the instrumental order of all beings that constitute the universe. That everything
    God created has a purpose to fulfill in the integral whole and all are related to one
    another in a hierarchical order to achieve their purposes as well as the purpose of

the whole cosmos was a constant in Aquinas's writings. Also see Aquinas, *Summa contra Gentiles*, 3.20, 45, 71.

29. Aquinas, *Summa contra Gentiles*, 3.22. See also Aquinas, *Summa theologiae*, 2 | 2.66.2.

30. Aquinas, *Summa theologiae*, 1.65.2. According to Aquinas, each creature exists for its own proper act and perfection, the lower on the hierarchical scale exists for the higher, but every creature exists for the perfection of the universe, which is ordained toward God inasmuch as it imitates and shows forth the divine goodness to the glory of God.

31. Aquinas, *Summa theologiae*, 1.47.2. When describing this hierarchical configuration, he alluded to Aristotle, *Metaphysics*, 8.10. The concept of a hierarchy of beings has its basis in Greek philosophy, flourished in the patristic and medieval periods, and is the subject of a lecture given by Arthur Q. Lovejoy in 1933 that was published subsequently as *The Great Chain of Being: A Study of the History of an Idea* (Cambridge, MA: Harvard University Press, 1957). Aquinas conveyed an organic understanding of the hierarchical chain.

32. Aquinas, *Summa theologiae*, 1.76.1.

33. Aquinas, *Compendium theologiae*, 18; Aquinas, *Summa contra Gentiles*, 2.46, 2.86, 4.11; Aquinas, *Summa theologiae*, 1.76.1, 1.78.1, 2 | 2.179.1. For Aquinas, humans are the only corporeal creatures capable of transcending the conditions of matter (*Summa theologiae*, 1.76.1) because the human intellectual power is independent of matter (*Summa contra Gentiles*, 2.86) as it elevates the human soul beyond what is corruptible (*Compendium theologiae*, 84). Because the human creature is endowed with intellectual capability, humans have the greatest likeness to God (*Compendium theologiae*, 75; *Summa theologiae*, 1.93.2; and *Summa contra Gentiles*, 2.46).

34. Aquinas, *De veritate*, 24.11, 27.5. For Aquinas, God offers grace to humans to help them seek the temporal good in this life while aiming for eternal happiness. How humans can cooperate is explored in chapters 5 and 10.

35. Aquinas, *Summa contra Gentiles*, 3.78.

36. Aquinas stressed repeatedly that humans should restrict their actions on other creatures to acquiring the necessities of life and knowing God as they seek their eternal goal; e.g., see Aquinas, *Summa theologiae*, Supp. 91.1, 1 | 2.4.6–7, 1 | 2.114.10, 2 | 2.76.2, 2 | 2.83.6, 2 | 2.118.1; Aquinas, *Summa contra Gentiles*, 3.22; and Aquinas, *Compendium theologiae*, 173. Aquinas considered the human use of other creatures for the necessities of life and knowing God as an exercise of natural dominion; e.g., see Aquinas, *Summa theologiae*, 2 | 2.66.1–2; Aquinas, *Compendium theologiae*, 74, 127, 148; and Aquinas, *Summa contra Gentiles* 3.78, 3.111–112. He insisted that God retains absolute dominion over both users and used in *Summa theologiae*, 2 | 2.66.1.

37. Aquinas, *Summa theologiae*, 2 | 2.141.6; see also Supp. 91.1, 2 | 2.64.1, 83.6. Also see Aquinas, *Summa contra Gentiles*, 3.22, 121, 129, 131. Resounding throughout his works is the prescription that humans are intended to use only what is *needed* to sustain human life and not what is *desired* beyond the necessities of life.

38. Aquinas, *Summa theologiae* 1 | 2.4.7; also see 2 | 2.83.6, 118.1, 141.6.

39. Ibid., 2 | 2.83.6.

40. Ibid., 2 | 2.169.1. For his understanding of the "appropriate" use of things by humans, see Aquinas, *Summa contra Gentiles*, 3.129, where he teaches that some uses for the necessities of life are naturally fitting, whereas immoderate uses are naturally unfitting in the scheme of the integrity of the universe and, ultimately, in the human quest for eternal happiness with God.

41. Aquinas, *Summa contra Gentiles,* 4.83.

42. Aquinas, *Summa theologiae,* 2 | 2.118.1; also see 2 | 2.83.6. See, further, Aquinas, *Summa contra Gentiles,* 4.83.

43. Aquinas, *Summa contra Gentiles,* 2.2; see, further, 3.47, 4.1. Also see Aquinas, *Summa theologiae,* 1.65.1, 2 | 2.180.4. This teaching reflects his optimism that humans have been gifted by God with the capacity to rise gradually from the world to limited knowledge of God, though he expressed his sacramental view of the world in ways less emotive than found in works by Augustine, Hugh of Saint Victor, Bonaventure, and Francis of Assisi.

44. Aquinas, *Summa theologiae,* 1.65.1; see, further, 2 | 2.180.4, Supp. 91.1.

45. See, e.g., Aquinas, *Summa contra Gentiles,* 1.92.

46. Aquinas, *Summa contra Gentiles,* 3.128. Also see Aquinas, *Summa theologiae,* 1.96.4, 2 | 2.47.10.

47. Aquinas, *Summa contra Gentiles,* 3.100.

48. Ibid., 3.64.

49. Tarsicius Van Bavel, OSA, rightly points to patristic theologians' ascription to the internal sustainability of the cosmos that God created and sustains in existence; Tarsicius Van Bavel, "The Creator and the Integrity of Creation in the Fathers of the Church, Especially in Saint Augustine," *Augustinian Studies* 21 (1990): 1–33. See also Howard J. Van Till, "Basil, Augustine, and the Doctrine of Creation's Functional Integrity," *Science and Christian Belief* 8 (1996): 21–38.

50. Augustine, *Enchiridion,* 10:11.

51. Augustine, *Concerning the City of God,* 19.13, 870.

52. Augustine, *Confessions,* 7.12.18, 172. Also see Augustine, *Concerning the City of God,* 11.22, for his theocentric theory about the need for "inequality" among creatures in the universe.

53. Aquinas, *Summa contra Gentiles,* 2.39; see, further, 2.44, 2.45, 3.69, 3.144. Also see Aquinas, *Summa theologiae,* 1.15.2, 1.22.1–2.

54. Aquinas, *Summa contra Gentiles,* 2.45; see, further, 2.44.

55. Aquinas, *Summa contra Gentiles,* 3.71. The universe cannot be any better than it is, he wrote in *Summa theologiae,* 1.25.6 ad 3, because of the most beautiful order given to things by God. As John H. Wright concludes from Aquinas's works, the universe is "God's masterpiece" with its excellence found in the ordered harmony of its parts; John H. Wright, *The Order of the Universe in the Theology of St. Thomas Aquinas* (Rome: Apud Aedes Universitatis Gregorianae, 1957), 87.

56. Aquinas, *Summa contra Gentiles,* 3.64, 112. See also Aquinas, *Summa theologiae,* 1.47.2. The integrity of all created beings is described in *Summa contra Gentiles,* 2.45, as the ultimate and noblest perfection in things which in turn are ordered to the ultimate uncreated good who is God.

57. Aquinas, *Summa contra Gentiles,* 3.112.

58. Aquinas, *Summa theologiae,* 1.65.2. The interactive order of all things created by God is the greatest perfection and the most beautiful attribute of creation because it reflects the goodness and wisdom of God, Aquinas wrote in *Compendium theologiae,* 102. Also see Aquinas, *Summa contra Gentiles,* 2.42; and Aquinas, *Summa theologiae,* 1.2.3, 1.4.2, 1.13.2.

59. Aquinas, *De potentia Dei,* 3.7. James A. Weisheipl underscores this point; see James A. Weisheipl, *Friar Thomas D'Aquino: His Life, Thought, and Work* (Garden City, NY: Doubleday Publishing, 1974), 205.

60. Aquinas, *Summa theologiae*, 1 | 2.93.5. For Aquinas, natural law is the result of God's imposition of eternal law upon the universe at its creation to govern all things internally to their ends and ultimately to God; e.g., see *Summa theologiae*, 1 | 2.91.1, 1 | 2.93.1; and Aquinas, *De veritate*, 5.1.6.

61. Aquinas, *Summa theologiae*, 1.65.2; Aquinas, *Compendium theologiae*, 102. See also Aquinas, *Summa contra Gentiles*, 2.39, 44–46, 68; 3.64, 69, 71, 144; and Aquinas, *Summa theologiae*, 1.15.2, 22.1–2; 25.6 ad 3, 47.2.

62. Oliva Blanchette observes in Aquinas's works an order of instrumentality among corporeal things; Oliva Blanchette, *The Perfection of the Universe According to Aquinas: A Teleological Cosmology* (University Park: Pennsylvania State University Press, 1991), 256. However, the order of instrumentality goes beyond human-corporeal parameters to encompasses the totality of existence with God as the ultimate mover of an instrumental order. This more comprehensive instrumental order should be considered by contemporary critics who are troubled by Aquinas's view that other corporeal creatures are instruments for the human; e.g., see H. Paul Santmire, *The Travail of Nature: The Ambiguous Ecological Promise of Christian Theology* (Philadelphia: Fortress Press, 1985), 90–91; William C. French, "Catholicism and the Common Good of the Biosphere," in *An Ecology of the Spirit: Religious Reflection and Environmental Consciousness,* ed. Michael H. Barnes (Lanham, MD: University Press of America, 1994), 177–94, at 193.

63. Aquinas, *Summa theologiae*, 1 | 2.19.10. Aquinas taught that the common good of the universe is its integrity, which results from the order and composition of all its parts. See, e.g., Aquinas, *Summa contra Gentiles*, 3.94; Aquinas, *De potentia Dei*, 1.6.1; and Aquinas, *Summa theologiae*, 1.115.3. Each part has an essential role to play in the whole; whereas some are better than others in their ways of being and acting due to their innate capabilities, all creatures are requisite for the functioning of the whole—contingent and noncontingent, corporeal and incorporeal, corruptible and incorruptible. See his discussion in *Summa contra Gentiles*, 1.85; *De potentia Dei*, 1.6.1; and *Summa theologiae*, 1.103.7.

64. Aquinas, *De veritate*, 5.3.

65. E.g., Aquinas, *Summa theologiae*, 1 | 2.109.3, 2 | 2.26.3.

66. Aquinas, *Summa theologiae*, 2 | 2.26.3.

67. Ibid.; see, further, 1 | 2.26.1.

68. Ibid., 1.60.5; see, further, 2 | 2.26.3 ad 2.

69. Ibid., 2 | 2.26.3; he pointed specifically to citizens who suffer losses to their own property and themselves personally for the sake of the common good of their community.

70. Ibid., 1.60.5 ad 3–5; see, further, 2 | 2.26.3.

71. Aquinas, *Summa contra Gentiles*, 3.24. Also see Aquinas, *Summa theologiae*, 1.57.2.

72. Aquinas, *Summa theologiae*, 1 | 2.19.10; his understanding of what is right is based ultimately on an action's being directed toward finality in God.

73. Ibid., 1.22.2. Also see Aquinas, *Summa contra Gentiles*, 3.112–13; and Aquinas, *De veritate*, 1.5.6–7. According to Aquinas, God's special care is needed for individual humans who have the capacity to think about how to act and choose to act, capacities that humans often misuse. This special divine care for individual humans contrasts with God's general care for other species through natural laws embedded in the physical world because other-than-humans do not have intellectual capabilities or free will with which to deviate from God's intentions. God's care for individual humans and other species should be considered in relation to Aquinas's teaching in *Summa*

contra Gentiles, 3.64, that among God's creation God cares most for the order of all things that constitute the universe.

74. Aquinas, *De veritate,* 24.11; see, further, 27.5.
75. This follows Aquinas's rationale that God governs all things to their end through God's eternal law, which God imposed on the universe in the form of natural law; e.g., see Aquinas, *Summa theologiae,* 1|2.91.1, 93.1–5; and Aquinas, *De veritate,* 5.1.6. On his thinking about rational creatures who are ruled by eternal law and are rulers of themselves to whom God gives grace to seek their ultimate end, see *Summa theologiae,* 1|2.109.1, and *Summa contra Gentiles,* 3.1.
76. Aquinas, *Summa theologiae,* 1|2.110.1.
77. E.g., Aquinas, *Summa theologiae,* 1.111.2; and Aquinas, *De veritate,* 27.5. As Maritain explained when commenting on *Summa theologiae,* 2|2.3.2 ad 2, before humans are "related to the immanent common good of the universe, they are related to an infinitely greater good—the separated common Good, the divine transcendent Whole"; Jacques Maritain, *The Person and the Common Good,* trans. John J. Fitzgerald (New York: Charles Scribner's Sons, 1947), 7–10.
78. Aquinas, *Summa theologiae,* 1.11.3; see, further, 1|2.19.10 on how the common good benefits all constituents of the universe. Also see Aquinas, *Summa contra Gentiles,* 1.70, 2.41, 3.69.
79. Aquinas, *Summa theologiae,* 1|2.9.1.
80. E.g., Aquinas, *De potentia Dei,* 4.2 ad 29.
81. Aquinas, *De veritate,* 5.2.
82. Aquinas, *Summa theologiae,* 1.11.3.
83. Joseph Legrand, *L'univers et l'homme dans la philosophie de Saint Thomas,* 2 vols. (Brussels: L'Édition Universelle, 1946) vol. 1, 40.
84. Aquinas, *Compendium theologiae,* 124.
85. Ibid.
86. Aquinas, *Summa theologiae,* 1.65.2.
87. Ibid.
88. French, "Catholicism and the Common Good of the Biosphere," 192. Though French sees this organizing principle as a promising response to our contemporary ecological morass, he finds it often "overwhelmed" by another organizing principle, which he describes as "the absolute superiority of rational human life over all lesser creatures," a premise for which he sees little room in theological ethics today. However, he does not factor into his evaluation the severe restrictions Aquinas places on how humans function in relation to other creatures because of their mutual relationship to God. See also Robert P. George, "Natural Law, the Common Good, and American Politics," in *The Battle for the Catholic Mind : Catholic Faith and Catholic Intellect in the Work of the Fellowship of Catholic Scholars, 1978–95,* ed. and intro. William E. May also Kenneth D. Whitehead (South Bend, IN: St. Augustine Press, 2001), 308–21; and Brian J. Benestad, "How the Catholic Church Serves the Common Good," in *Battle for the Catholic Mind,* 443–65.
89. Merle Longwood, "The Common Good: An Ethical Framework for Evaluating Environmental Issues," *Theological Studies* 34 (1973): 468–80, at 479–80. I concur with Longwood's astute conclusion that "we have to be cognizant of the way in which we exist in the web of life, which is a complex and subtly balanced system in which all parts function to maintain the quality of the integrated whole, [thus] the concept of the common good seems particularly appropriate. Our conception of the

common good must obviously include the whole biotic community, since the quality and health of human life is integrally tied to the quality and health of the lives of all the other members of the biosphere. There is, after all, only one ecology, not a human ecology on the one hand and a subhuman ecology on the other."

90. Augustine, *Confessions*, 13.29.44, 364.
91. Ibid., 13.31.46, 365: "No less rightly is it said to those who see in the Spirit of God, 'It is not you who see,' so that whatsoever in the Spirit of God they see to be good, it is not they but God who sees that it is good."
92. Ledoux, "Green Augustine," 334.
93. John Chrysostom, *Homilies On Genesis*, 10.13, 137.
94. Ibid.
95. Aquinas, *Summa contra Gentiles*, 3.64.
96. Ibid.
97. Aquinas, *Summa contra Gentiles*, 3.100; following Aristotle's commentary on *De anima*, 2.6, Aquinas noted that animals use plants and inanimate things while plants use inanimate things by taking nourishment and support from them. It is not contrary to the nature of any created thing when it is moved in any way by God, because all things were made the way they are in order to serve God, he taught in *Summa contra Gentiles*, 3.100, and *De potentia Dei*, 5.9; the entirety of creation is like an instrument that produces its principal effect when being used by its principal cause. Weisheipl confirms this view; Weisheipl, *Friar Thomas D'Aquino*, 206.
98. Aquinas, *Summa contra Gentiles*, 3.100; and Aquinas, *De potentia Dei*, 3.7 ad 3, 5.9. See also Weisheipl, *Friar Thomas D'Aquino*, 206. In *Summa contra Gentiles*, 3.100, Aquinas explained that instruments are made for the purpose of subserving the action of the principal agent while being moved by that agent, so it is not contrary to the nature of any created thing when it is moved in any way by God because all things were made the way they are in order to serve God. In *De potentia Dei*, 3.7 ad 3, he taught that the entirety of creation is *like* an instrument that produces its principal effect by being used by its principal cause.
99. Augustine, *Concerning the City of God*, 12.4, 475–76.
100. Ibid., 19.13, 870–72.
101. John Chrysostom, *Homilies on Genesis*, 9.3, 119. He also described earth as the human "tomb" to which the human body would return.
102. Ibid., 10.12, 135–37.
103. Kavanaugh, "Intrinsic Value, Persons and Stewardship," 71. As Kavanaugh notes, the "intrinsic value" approach " stresses that there are certain actions which, no matter what the external factors or the internal motives, are somehow profoundly evil in themselves, independent of their usefulness or our intentions."
104. Aquinas, *Summa contra Gentiles*, 3.78.
105. Aquinas, *Summa theologiae*, 1.96.1.
106. French, "Catholicism and the Common Good of the Biosphere," 192.
107. Aquinas, *Summa contra Gentiles*, 3.78–79.
108. Aquinas, *De caritate*, 7 ad 5.
109. Aquinas, *Summa theologiae*, 2 | 2.25.3.
110. E.g., Aquinas, *De caritate*, 3; and Aquinas, *Summa theologiae*, 2 | 2.23.8, 47.1 ad 1.
111. Aquinas, *Summa theologiae*, 1 | 2.19.10; his understanding of what is right is based ultimately on an action's being directed toward God.
112. Ibid., 1 | 2.19.10.

113. Rolston uses this model for humans to be "beholders of value" in *Environmental Ethics: Duties to and Values in Nature,* 112–17. See also the affirming discussion by Keekok Lee, "The Source and Locus of Intrinsic Value: A Reexamination," *Environmental Ethics* 18 (1996): 297–309.

114. The moral theologian John Hart also recognizes the integral relationship between intrinsic and instrumental valuing of biota and abiota. As he explains in his impressive *Sacramental Commons: Christian Ecological Ethics* (Lanham, MD: Rowman & Littlefield, 2006), 123: "Intrinsic value and instrumental value coexist, cohere, and inhere in a being. To some extent, all aspects and entities of creation have instrumental value, based on such divergent roles as their contributions to an ecosystem or their integrality in cosmic dynamics." See Hart's full discussion of intrinsic-instrumental valuation at 122–25.

115. Teachings on the sacramentality of creation are covered in chapter 3.

116. Arne Naess, "The Deep Ecological Movement: Some Philosophical Aspects," *Philosophical Inquiry* 8 (1986): 10–31; Bill Devall and George Sessions, *Deep Ecology: Living as If Nature Mattered* (Salt Lake City: Gibbs Smith, 1985). Deep ecologists also insist that the human use of other species must be balanced with their intrinsic value, so the impact on the environment is minimal.

117. Among the basic principles that are helpful when addressing ecological problems from the reconstructed concept of the goodness of creation are: (1) Value the evolutionary process out of which all living entities have emerged under God's sustaining power, including *Homo sapiens,* who are related to some extent with other species from whom and with whom they came into existence; (2) recognize and value the intrinsic goodness of the subject, its interests, and its needs to survive in the world and assure that the subject's efforts to sustain itself are not inhibited by human actions; (3) discover and value the instrumental goodness of the subject in relation to others, recognizing their dependence on one another to sustain themselves internally, and assure that their reliance upon one another is not hindered by human actions; (4) value the contributions that the subject makes to the common good of the ecosystem of which it is a constituent and prevent human thwarting of this contribution; and (5) value the ecosystem and/or biosphere and prevent human actions from disrupting its natural functioning for the common good of all its constituents.

118. Ronald Dworkin makes an intriguing observation when reflecting on the creativity of the evolutionary process and the parallel valuing of species by those who believe in God and can view the evolution of species as part of God's authorship of the physical world and by those who ascribe to a purely secular view of species as "achievements of adaptation" over long and complex periods of time. From both perspectives, to cause a species extinction is a "frustration" of "investments" of species that are "worthy of respect." Ronald Dworkin, *Life's Dominion: An Argument about Abortion, Euthanasia, and Individual Freedom* (New York: Alfred A. Knopf, 1993), 76.

119. As Rolston explains, "There is a kind of 'promise' in nature not only in the sense of potential that is promising but in the reliability in the earthen set-up that is right for life. Perhaps the planetary set-up is an accident, but the ongoing after the set-up seems to be loaded with fertility. . . . It seems a shame now for humans to break that 'promise'"; Holmes Rolston III, "Disvalues in Nature," *The Monist* 75 (1992): 250–80, at 268: See, further, John F. Haught, *The Promise of Nature: Ecology and Cosmic Purpose* (New York: Paulist Press, 1993). Callicott insists astutely, when exploring the continuity of self and nature, that "if the self is intrinsically valuable, then nature is intrinsically

valuable. If it is rational for me to act in my own best interests, and I and nature are one, then it is rational for me to act in the best interests of nature"; Callicott, "Intrinsic Value, Quantum Theory, and Environmental Ethics," 275.

120. Steward Pickett, Tom Parker, and Peggy Fiedler point to the shifting mosaic of the physical world, a world that is in continuous flux. They reflect ethically that "human-generated changes must be constrained because nature has functional, historical, and evolutionary limits." Steward Pickett, Tom Parker, and Peggy Fiedler, "The New Paradigm in Ecology: Implications for Conservation Biology above the Species Level," in *Conservation Biology: The Theory and Practice of Nature Conservation, Preservation, and Management,* ed. Peggy L. Fiedler and Subodh K. Jain (New York: Chapman & Hall, 1992), 66–88, at 82.

121. See David Lodge, "From the Balance to the Flux of Nature: The Power of Metaphor in Cross-Discipline Conversations," *Worldviews: Environment, Culture, Religion* 7 (2003): 1–4.

122. Aldo Leopold, *Sand County Almanac: With Essays on Conservation from Round River* (New York: Ballantine, 1966), 203–4.

123. Longwood, "Common Good," 479–80. See note 89 above.

124. French, "Catholicism and the Common Good of the Biosphere," 192.

125. Kavanaugh, "Intrinsic Value, Persons and Stewardship." Kavanaugh explains that Aquinas's "metaphysics and anthropology provide ground fertile enough for raising stewardship as an ethical issue," and he offers an astute account of Aquinas's "intrinsic value" theory as a foundation upon which stewardship can be based. This approach "recognizes an intrinsic goodness and value to every existing being, regardless of its role as a function of our happiness or motives, and finds certain actions as "profoundly evil" in themselves, regardless of external factors and internal motives and independent of their usefulness or human intentions. Kavanaugh makes a good point with which I agree, though the natural instrumental value of species and abiota to one another must also be acknowledged. Ibid., 67.

126. Katherine Tanner, "Creation, Environmental Crisis, and Ecological Justice," in *Reconstructing Christian Theology,* ed. Rebecca S. Chopp and Mark Lewis Taylor (Minneapolis: Fortress Press, 1994), 99–123, at 120: "Putting human and nonhuman beings together in this way within a single community of moral concern helps resolve certain issues for human decision making." Tanner encourages people who believe in God as Creator "to explore ways in which human action might alter circumstances of competition and bring the earth closer to a vision of a truly universal, world-inclusive, equal justice."

127. Callicott argues convincingly that the holistic land ethic is not a case of ecofascism but, instead, tends to supplement, not replace, the more venerable community-based social ethics: "When holistic environment-oriented duties are in conflict with individualistic human-oriented duties, and the holistic environmental interests at issue are significantly stronger than the individualistic human interests at issue, the former take priority"; Callicott, *Beyond the Land Ethic,* 76. For a full explanation, see J. Baird Callicott, "Holistic Environmental Ethics and the Problem of Ecofascism," in *Environmental Philosophy: From Animal Rights to Radical Ecology,* 3rd edition, ed. J. Baird Callicott, Michael E. Zimmerman, George Sessions, Karen J. Warren, and John Clark (Upper Saddle River, NJ: Prentice Hall, 2001), 111–25.

128. A more detailed discussion of prudent environmental decision making can be found in chapter 9.

2

APPRECIATING THE BEAUTY OF CREATION

Aesthetic appreciation for the beauty of the natural environment has been acknowledged widely in the secular literature as foundational for ecological ethics. Among the philosophers who have advanced this status is Eugene Hargrove, the founder and editor of the journal *Environmental Ethics,* who points to the emergence of thinking in Western culture that natural beauty is intrinsically valuable and should be protected.[1] Focusing on the nature of aesthetic appreciation, Noël Carroll stresses the authenticity of appreciation that occurs when the individual is moved emotionally by natural phenomena.[2] Conversely, Allen Carlson dwells on the cognitive dimension of aesthetic appreciation and finds it most appropriate when brought about by scientific knowledge and its "commonsense predecessors."[3] Holmes Rolston fosters aesthetic appreciation for "wild" biological systems and emphasizes the deeper appreciation that occurs when personal experience with natural places (the emotional-subjective dimension) combines with information about it (the cognitive dimension).[4] Stan Godlovitch argues that the only fitting aesthetic regard is appreciation that comes from the mysteriousness or the incomprehensibility of the natural environment.[5]

Although there are many nuances in the works of these and other philosophers who explore the various aspects of aesthetic appreciation for the natural environment, dissecting their subtleties is not the focus of this chapter. What is significant for my purposes is the framing of their discussions about the affective, cognitive, affective-cognitive, and mysterious dimensions of aesthetic appreciation that I find helpful in advancing theological discourse on a parallel concept in the works of some eminent patristic and medieval theologians in the Christian tradition—the beauty of creation. They expressed feelings and thoughts about the beauty of the physical world in ways that resemble contemporary philosophical thinking. Their expressions of appreciation suggest promising foundations for ecological ethics from a theological perspective, especially when their concepts are understood from the worldviews and contexts of the times in which they were written, reconstructed to reflect our scientifically in-formed understanding of the world today, and worked creatively to identify norms for human behavior.

This *critical-creative* approach to appropriating and extending centuries-old concepts about the beauty of creation is demonstrated in this chapter to discern their fruitfulness for addressing ecological degradation today. I begin by explor-ing a sampling of reflections by patristic and medieval theologians who convey their appreciation for the beauty of the world in five discernible ways. The world-views from which these theologians wrote are distinguished subsequently from our current understanding of the world, and the concept of the beauty of cre-ation is reconstructed to reflect broad scientific findings. From this reconstructed concept can be gleaned some patterns of behavior that have potential for address-ing ecological concerns.

The Beauty of Creation in Patristic and Medieval Texts

Among the patristic and medieval theologians who describe the natural world as beautiful are Athanasius of Alexandria, Basil of Caesarea, Augustine of Hippo, Hugh of Saint Victor, an unnamed Cistercian, Bonaventure, Albertus Magnus, and Thomas Aquinas. Their exclamations about the beauty of the physical world span tiny insects to mountain valley vistas to celestial bodies to the entire order of the cosmos, and they always relate this beauty in one way or another to God. Their appreciation for the beauty God created is expressed in four prominent ways that parallel those identified by the aforementioned contemporary philoso-phers: (1) Affective appreciation aroused by the beauty of creatures; (2) affective-cognitive appreciation stimulated by the beauty that is discovered through in-depth study; (3) cognitive appreciation brought about when contemplating the harmonious functioning of creatures; and (4) appreciation precipitated by incom-prehension of the beautiful but complex creation.[6] Because this exploration of their reflections is geared toward its usefulness in developing a response to eco-logical degradation, the details of their rich and complex thinking on other mat-ters are not addressed. Nor are all the possible examples that appear in patristic and medieval texts retrieved for consideration.

Affective Appreciation for Creatures

Exclamations of delight in the beauty of species and vistas appear especially in the works of Basil of Caesarea (ca. 329–79). He depicted natural beauty variously throughout his commentary on the Genesis 1 story of creation.[7] In his second homily, he described the world as august, magnificent, wondrous, marvelous, daz-zling, pleasant, attractive, enjoyable, and excellent. Our senses witness the abun-dance of beauty observable in animals, plants, landscapes and the sky, he insisted. He lauded "cornfields waving in the hollows, meadows verdant and abounding with varied flowers, woodland vales in bloom, and mountain peaks shaded over with forest trees."[8]

In a letter to his friend Gregory of Nazianzus, Basil expressed his visceral appreciation for a place to live that perfectly suites his tastes.[9] Attributing his having found the spot to God's providence, Basil was delighted with the high mountains covered with variously colorful trees, the cool and transparent streams, the evenly sloping plain at the mountain's base, the two deep ravines, the river gliding gently between them, and the whirlpool occurring when the river encountered rocks. He proclaimed the site "most pleasant" and exclaimed that even Homer's beloved Calypso Island was insignificant by comparison. The "exhalations from the land" and "the breezes from the river" elicited his praise, for they added to the overall tranquillity that he experienced at the site.

Although an entire treatise by Augustine of Hippo (354–430) on the beauty of creation is no longer extant,[10] exclamations of awe, astonishment, delight, and wonder about the world permeate his more mature works.[11] In *City of God* he extolled:

> the manifold diversity of beauty in sky and earth and sea; the abundance of light, and its miraculous loveliness, in sun and moon and stars; the dark shades of woods, the colour and fragrance of flowers; the multitudinous varieties of birds, with their songs and their bright plumage; the countless different species of living creatures of all shapes and sizes, amongst whom it is the smallest in bulk that moves our greatest wonder—for we are more astonished at the activities of the tiny ants and bees than at the immense bulk of whales. Then there is the mighty spectacle of the sea itself, putting on its changing colours like different garments, now green, with all the many varied shades, now purple, now blue. Moreover, what a delightful sight it is when stormy, giving added pleasure to the spectator because of the agreeable thought that he is not a sailor tossed and heaved about on it![12]

In *Confessions* he found ferocious animals, elements of the weather, mountains, trees, cattle, and birds all wondrously beautiful, and he urged people in all stations of life to praise God for them: "That you must be praised all these show forth: from the earth, dragons, and all the deeps, fire, hail, snow, ice, stormy winds, which fulfill your word, mountains and all hills, fruitful trees and all cedars, beasts and all cattle, serpents and feathered fowls; kings of the earth and all people, princes and all judges of the earth, young men and maidens, the old with the younger; let them praise your name."[13]

Appreciation for the beauty of creation was conveyed engagingly in the "Description of the Position and Site of the Abbey of Clairvaux" by an unidentified author, most likely a Cistercian monk, in the twelfth century.[14] Throughout this description, the author acclaimed the beauty of the site—"the sturdy oak which salutes the heavens with its lofty top" and the "graceful lime-tree which spreads its arms," the "harmonious concerts of birds of varied plumage," the "clear air" which enables everything to shine, the "delights of colors, of songs, and of odors," the "verdant bank of a pool filled with pure and running water," the "vast plain of meadows" that has "much charm," the "smiling countenance of the earth" that is "painted with varying colors," the "sweet scent" and "bright colors" of the flowers, the "high palisade" of "flexible osiers"[15] on the banks of the lake, the "fragrant air," and, above all, the "sweet fountain" whose waters have so often quenched his thirst. Altogether, the author was "charmed" by "the sweet influence of the beauty of the country."

The affective dimension of aesthetic appreciation seemed operative in these expressions of delight over sites that were observed directly. These expressions fall into Carroll's category of authentic appreciation that occurs when the individual opens to the stimulus of natural phenomena. However, patristic and medieval theologians departed from his model insofar as their expressions of appreciation are always related to God, to whom they give thanks and praise.

Affective-Cognitive Appreciation

Delight for the surficial beauty of the natural environment combined with the delight that is experienced when patristic and medieval theologians observed God's creation in greater detail. For example, in his reflections on the six days of creation as recounted in Genesis 1, Basil marveled at the sense perception of sheep and goats that enables them to avoid harmful plants, starlings whose physical makeup allows them to consume hemlock, the meadows deep with abundant grass, the fertile earth that produces a plethora of goods, the dense woods with their many types of trees, the thick and leafy bushes so distinctly different from one another, and the grapevines heavy with ripening fruit.[16] He observed the similarities and differences of land, winged, and aquatic animals, and he expressed delight in what he found. He studied the activities of bees in constructing honeycombs, the discipline of cranes in flight, the relationship between storks and crows, the monogynous turtledove, and many other creatures.[17] His astute observations seemed to intensify his appreciation for them. He urged his listeners to pay attention to all the creatures, to never cease admiring them, and to give glory to God for them.[18]

Augustine admired the agility of a mosquito and the works of the smallest ants.[19] He urged the serious consideration of all natural beings and forces, from the more excellent and valuable human to the "tiniest fly," for even the smallest of creatures would evoke praise to God, their Creator.[20] He lamented not having adequate time to describe in detail all the beauty he observed around him.[21]

Observing the abbey at Clairvaux and its surrounding environment, the Cistercian's praise for the Aube River was profuse as he reflected perceptively on its labors. In a unique move among patristic and medieval theologians, he personified the river, writing lovingly about its intentional meanderings to seek ways of serving the monks in their tasks. The river was also depicted intentionally as seeking ways to nourish the fish, water the crops and trees, penetrate the earth to facilitate new growth in the spring, and feed the lake. The Cistercian endeavored to list all the services provided by this "friendly," "faithful," and "kindly stream," with the aim of rendering any and all "thanks due to it."[22]

Even beyond this praise for the Aube River, however, was the author's deep appreciation for the natural fountain that so often quenched his thirst. He reproached himself for his ingratitude to the fountain when mentioning it at the end of his description of the site.

In "The Three Days of Invisible Light," Hugh of Saint Victor (1096–1144) admired the characteristics of creatures that enable them to function in ways peculiar to their natures.[23] He acclaimed the crocodile's ability to chew without moving its lower jaw, the ability of the salamander to remain in fire without being harmed, the hedgehog who spikes apples when rolling in them and who "squeaks like a wagon" when it moves, the ant who foresees the upcoming winter and fills its stores with grain, and the spider who weaves a web to capture prey. He was pleased by the consistency of the shape, ribs, and teeth of the leaves of a particular tree and the arrangement of the seeds of mulberries and strawberries.

Hugh expressed delight with the ability of the human senses to discern "very sweet and pleasant" aspects of the natural world. He urged frequent training of the human senses to facilitate investigation of creatures' characteristics according to their various dimensions—arrangement (the composition and ordering of parts to one another), motion (local, natural, animal, and rational activities), appearance (color, shape, and other aspects discernible to the human eye), and quality (perceivable through the other senses, such as a melody heard, sweetness tasted, fragrance smelled, and softness touched).[24]

Exploration of these characteristics from "educated" senses led Hugh to praise God for having designed creatures to act in ways peculiar to their natures: "We cry out in awe and amazement with the psalmist: 'How great are your works, O Lord! You have made them all in wisdom.'" Hugh was joyful that he was not among the foolish or stupid persons who failed to attribute the beauty of creation to God's wisdom: "You have given me delight in what you have made, and I shall exult over the works of your hands. How great are your works, O Lord! Your thoughts are exceeding deep. A foolish person will not know them, and a stupid person will not understand them."[25]

Continuing his predecessors' appreciation for the beauty of God's creation, albeit in less affective tones, Aquinas (1224/25–74) described the many diverse animals, plants, and minerals as good and beautiful. They can give great delight to the observant person, he explained, and their delightfulness should incite humans to love God for having created all the different types of beings that constitute the universe.[26] In unusually poetical tones, Aquinas described natural decay and defective forces in the world analogously as silent pauses contributing to a hymn.[27]

The appreciation for God's creation that is prompted by knowledge of the world was also conveyed in other works of the medieval period, especially those by Aquinas's renowned teacher, Albertus Magnus (ca. 1200–80). He stressed the importance of observation and experimentation in field and laboratory studies of animals, plants, metals, and inorganic elements,[28] and his scholarly efforts legitimized the study of the natural world as a science within the Christian tradition.[29]

He perceived his scientific endeavors as exercises of his God-given human intellectual power to investigate the "natural" causes of things created by God. His efforts served as a way of praising God, "who is the source of wisdom, the creator, establisher, and ruler of nature."[30]

In their works, these patristic and medieval theologians conveyed their appreciation for the bodily characteristics and activities of creatures they observed in detail. Visceral and cognitive dimensions seem to interplay, demonstrating a version of the aesthetic appreciation that Rolston finds meaningful for environmental ethics. Studying God's creation was portrayed by these theologians as a rational way in which humans give glory to God, a way demonstrated especially by Albertus Magnus in his field studies as well as by some of the most renowned scientists who prompted the seventeenth-century scientific revolution.[31] Their faith and confidence in God fueled their quests for information about the beautiful world God created and actively sustains in existence.[32]

Cognitive Appreciation

Some patristic and medieval theologians also demonstrated a deep appreciation for the harmonious functioning of all creatures that seemed to have been prompted primarily by their thinking abstractly about it. Although each natural being has beauty in itself, each was also understood as essential to the greater beauty of the whole universe. For these theologians, God designed all the inanimate and animate beings in the universe to function in specific ways, and their appreciation for the relationship of all beings resounded throughout their works.

The harmony of the diverse entities that constitute the universe prompted Basil's deep regard. From his understanding of the world influenced by Neoplatonic constructs, he taught that God intentionally designed the universe so that all creatures constitute "an unbroken bond of attraction into one fellowship and harmony."[33] The world was, according to Basil, a "mighty" and "elaborate system" brought to "perfection" through powers established by God at the beginning of creation.[34] From his perspective, God empowered all things with innate capabilities to function in relation to one another in orderly ways to the end of time.[35]

Augustine described the world as "a work of such wonder and grandeur as to astound the mind that seriously considers it."[36] Though he deemed the human as the most valuable of all creatures, he insisted that each type of creature has a position in the "splendor" of the "providential order" of creation. Each has a special beauty that contributes to "the whole material scheme" established from the beginning of time and whose continuing existence is sustained by God.[37] Even the decay and death of irrational creatures play vital roles in bringing the beauty of the universe "to perfection" through the succession of new life and the passage of seasons. All beings—rational and irrational, animate and inanimate, decayable and immortal—"fit together to make a scheme of ordered beauty" that Augustine attributed to God.[38] James Alfred Martin describes Augustine's exclamations about the beauty of the orderly universe as "a 'moment' of aesthetic judgment" that occasions a distinctive type of pleasure,[39] a pleasure that comes from thinking deeply about the harmony of all things that make up the universe.

The appreciation that occurs when studying the interrelationship of creatures was demonstrated graphically by the Cistercian when describing the abbey site at Clairvaux.[40] The cooperative interactivity of the monks, the streams of the Aube River, the fertile land, the trees, and the other natural aspects of the site were applauded exuberantly. However, the greatest praise was given for the river proper because it unified all activities.[41]

Aquinas saved his superlatives for the harmonious functioning of all creatures in relation to one another, which yielded the greatest created beauty. Having been endowed by God with innate capabilities to act or be acted upon, they form a hierarchical sustenance chain, with one type of creature providing sustenance to the next.[42] Their interactivity according to their natures unites them.[43] When functioning as intended by God, they constitute a marvelous connection of things,[44] the most beautiful order,[45] the highest beauty,[46] the greatest perfection, and the most beautiful characteristic of the world.[47] As John Wright observes from Aquinas's works, the universe in its entirety is "God's masterpiece."[48]

Thus, patristic and medieval appreciation reached its height when theologians thought about the harmonious relationship of creatures. Though they attributed this harmony to God's detailed design of the static world with its myriad fixed species, they shared Carlson's subsequent emphasis on appreciation that comes from knowing and thinking about the functioning of the world. Patristic and medieval theologians also opened a way to thinking theologically about humans as contributors to the harmonious functioning of the world that is explored in the section below on the basic behavior pattern that flows from thinking about and demonstrating aesthetic appreciation for the beautiful world.[49]

The Incomprehensible Universe

Augustine stressed his deep appreciation for the beautiful universe that, from his perspective, eludes human comprehension. Humans may be gifted by God with great intellectual abilities, he explained in *City of God*,[50] but we cannot fully comprehend the totality of all things that constitute the universe. Our entrenchment in a part of it and our condition as mortal beings prevents us from intellectually grasping the universe in its entirety. God alone, who transcends the universe and time, has this ability.

Furthermore, the narrow-mindedness of humans leads them to judge some natural beings and forces negatively, Augustine lamented. We are "often displeased" by the natural state or behavior of things when we experience discomfort from them. We think only about how we are affected by them personally. Instead of succumbing to our narrow-mindedness and self-centeredness, Augustine cautioned, we should consider the natures of things in themselves "without regard to our convenience or inconvenience" and give God praise for all creatures. However inconvenienced or unpleasant or uncomfortable or adversely affected we are by them, we must never "in the rashness of human folly allow ourselves to find fault" in any way with the work of the "great Artificer." We must have confidence in God's overall design, God's continuing care, and God's purpose for all entities that make up the beautiful universe.[51]

Human words of praise for God seemed inadequate from Augustine's perspective when he contemplated the beautiful world. In allusions to Psalm 148, he called upon the heavens, the angels, the sun, the moon, the stars, and the waters above the heavens to praise God's name.[52] In his commentary on Psalm 103, the beauty of creation became indescribable and his praise for its Creator inexpressible:

> What then are we to say? Our words are wanting, but not our feeling. Let us remember the Psalm lately treated of: we cannot express our feeling; let us shout for joy. . . . *Jubilate unto the God of our salvation. Jubilate unto God, every land. What meaneth, Jubilate?* Utter the ineffable accents of your joy, and let your joy, and let your delight burst forth before Him.[53]

Carol Harrison interprets well Augustine's exclamation as a "voice of love" rather than "a rational consideration of the beauty of creation."[54]

The aesthetic dimensions of Augustine's thinking about the incomprehensible universe were fully displayed when he reflected on the world God created, explained human limitations in understanding it, called upon the various "voices" to praise God according to their natures, and collapsed in shouts of jubilation in the absence of any other way to express his feelings. This theocentric response seems to come close to paralleling the sense of the incomprehensibility or mysteriousness of the world that Godlovitch, from a secular perspective, concludes is the most authentic kind of aesthetic appreciation.

Reconstructing the Concept

Basil, Augustine, Hugh of Saint Victor, Albert, Aquinas, and Bonaventure wrote from the faith perspective that God designed the beautiful universe, determined the exact characteristics of all species, and ensured the sustainable functioning of all creatures through their God-given capabilities to achieve their God-designated purposes. Influenced by Neoplatonic constructs and structures for Christianizing their thinking in the patristic period and by Aristotelian natural philosophy that was accessible through translations from the original Greek to Latin in the medieval period, these theologians systematically extended the traditions they inherited.[55]

As noted above, the patristic-medieval understanding of the world differs vastly from the current worldview in light of scientific findings. Today we depart from their thinking about the world as having been determined by God down to the exact characteristics of any species, ecosystem, planet, or galaxy. The world is beyond heliocentrism to billions of galaxies in an expanding universe that has no center. Its functioning is understood as evolutionary, dynamic, historically emergent, relational, ecological, interdependent, and holistic. An interplay of chance and law seems to be operative, with an openness to a future that cannot be predicted with accuracy. Though humans have capacities not yet found elsewhere, we are products of evolution, radically related to and interconnected with everything living and nonliving in the universe, and especially on our planet. Our species is also radically dependent upon other species and on the air, land, and water for our health and well-being.

Theologians who want their discourse to be responsive to the ecological crisis are becoming informed by at least broad scientific findings so they can reflect more meaningfully on God's relationship with the world, human relations with the more-than-human-others that constitute our planet, and human responsibility to God for functioning in ways that are compatible with the health and well-being of the Earth community.[56] Particularly crucial to cogent theological discourse are scientific findings about the human connectedness with other beings cosmologically, biologically, and ecologically. Also crucial for working out a system of ethics from a religious faith perspective is awareness of the plethora of ecological problems, local to global, and the adverse effects they inflict on human beings, other species, and biological systems.[57]

When focusing on the beauty of creation informed by contemporary scientific findings, theological discourse yields an understanding of God who provides the possibility for the emergence of all the beauty that exists, who endows matter with the capability to create itself, who gives freedom for all beauty to become through random occurrences constrained by the physical laws that God enables and upholds,[58] who continuously empowers the self-organization of the beautiful cosmos, galaxies, planets, diverse species, and ecosystems of Earth, and who underscores the anticipation of the future unfolding of beauty that should not be thwarted by humans.[59] Focusing on the beauty of creation also yields an understanding of the emergence of aesthetically sensitive and intelligent creatures who are capable of appreciating the beauty of the many other entities that have also emerged over vast periods of time, their dynamic harmony amid the decay and waste that has led to more beauty, and the harmonious beauty of Earth when all entities are functioning appropriately. What general patterns of behavior would flow from believing and thinking this way?

Appreciating the Beautiful World

Reconstructing concepts of the beauty of creation suggests a behavioral trajectory in which the faithful are open to the beauty of the natural environment, attentive to the details of natural beauty and alarmed by the ugliness of its degradation, striving to understand and protect the harmonious functioning of the biota and abiota that constitute ecosystems, and committed to acting humbly before the mysteriousness of the world in scientific, technological, and theological endeavors.[60] Each provides a dimension of the total perspective that is essential when addressing the ongoing degradation of the natural environment.

Opening to Earth's Beauty

To be aroused emotionally by natural beauty, believers will show appreciation by being open and receptive to the beauty that God empowered into existence. Carroll claims that opportunities to experience and respond appreciatively to natural phenomena are "quite frequent and even sought out."[61] However, human self-centeredness as individuals or as a species that is superior to or apart from others may impede the human capacity to be open to and appreciative of their beauty.[62] As William C. French contends, the dominance of person-centered theology to the exclusion of the human relatedness to other species and natural systems facilitated this myopic thinking.[63] The overwhelming evidence provided by cosmologists, evolutionary biologists, molecular biologists, and ecologists should correct species-centeredness and enable humans to recognize how radically interrelated and interdependent they are with everything living and nonliving on Earth.[64] To do otherwise would mean "living a lie," as characterized poignantly by Sallie McFague in her exemplary efforts to work out a meaningful and relevant theological anthropology for Christians today.[65]

Patristic and medieval theologians may have perceived humans as the crown of all creatures, but they also demonstrated their openness to and appreciation for the beauty of all the diverse creatures that constitute the cosmos. Moreover, they urged their listeners and readers to be open to and appreciative of the beautiful world God created. Their messages speak across the centuries to convey meaning for monotheists today.

Caressing the Details of Natural Beauty

Appreciation will be shown by the faithful for the beauty of species and vistas by attending to their details. Attention to the details of biota and abiota is synonymous with being a natural scientist today, as it was for Albertus Magnus during the medieval period. Rolston explains that contemporary science cultivates the habit of looking closely and for long periods of time.[66] As Bruce Stutz editorialized in *Natural History,* appreciation for the subjects of observation is enhanced by the detailed knowledge discovered about them.[67] The novelist and lepidopterist Vladimir Nabokov encouraged his students to "caress the details" with a sense of appreciative wonderment about them that could lead to important scientific discoveries.[68] Exclamations by astronauts who observe Earth from the Moon or elsewhere in "space" express their deep appreciation for our planet in comparison with the other phenomena they study. Feminist theologians celebrate the appreciation that comes when the "loving eye" attends to the differences of individuals and species.[69]

When studying the details of species, the faithful will recognize their "interests" in flourishing and their needs in order to flourish. They will also recognize the kind of human behavior that will most likely avoid interfering with species' meeting their needs and act accordingly out of appreciation for them.[70]

Attentiveness to the details will also alert the faithful to the ongoing suffering, decay, and death of individuals in species and between species in the dramatic web of life.[71] That humans share the struggle to survive and flourish with other species during our shared journey of biological emergence will become obvious. Because suffering is inherent in the freedom God has given for all species to emerge, the beauty experienced will become a realistic beauty that is devoid of mere romanticism that provides little toward a workable ethic of aesthetic appreciation.

So, too, will in-depth findings make the faithful aware of the ugliness of genetic damage caused to species by toxic substances emitted into the air, spread on the land, and flushed into waterways. The faithful will lament the ugliness of a double-beaked cormorant, a defoliated stand of maple trees, a yellow stream of sulfur emissions across the horizon, and the absence of another species in a tropical rainforest. The faithful will denounce the insensitive, thoughtless, and ill-informed human activities that have caused this unnatural ugliness. Informed by the causes of defaced beauty and repulsed by the ugliness they encounter, the faithful will be spurred to take ameliorative action and prevent recurrence. Precautionary measures will be taken when an activity threatens human health and the environment, as endorsed by the United Nations, even if conclusive scientific evidence has not definitively established the cause and effect relationship.[72]

Where does attending to the details have relevance for ecological ethics from a theocentric perspective? For people who believe in God as the ultimate source and sustaining ground for the emergence of beauty in the universe, striving to know about the naturally beautiful, appreciating it, and interacting constructively with it constitutes a way of giving glory to God. The faithful will use the intellectual abilities that have been made possible through the evolutionary process to learn about other biota and abiota and to identify how each adds to the beauty of ecosystems and the greater biosphere. When appreciating them, the faithful will use the sensitive faculties made possible by God's generosity to be open to natural beauty and recognize the beautiful other in their midst. When acting constructively toward the diverse beauties of Earth, the faithful will respond to God's generosity by planning to engage in activities that do not interfere with other species' innate quests to survive, flourish, and add their own beauty to ecosystems and the biosphere.

Appreciation that is precipitated by the interplay of knowledge about the natural world and emotional arousal to its beauty could be transforming for Catholics who attribute natural beauty ultimately to God. Paying attention to the details is essential to bringing about this transformation.

Protecting the Harmony of Ecosystems

Grounded in the belief that God's creation is beautiful, people of faith will appreciate the harmony of ecosystems by studying, reflecting upon, and protecting the interactions of the biota, air, land, and water that constitute these systems. The ecologist Eugene Odum demonstrated how ecosystems should be studied when producing the first text organized around the "ecosystem" concept.[73] The eminent naturalist, conservationist, and philosopher Aldo Leopold showed how significant appreciation can come from understanding ecosystem functioning, and he urged acting on that understanding as responsible members and citizens of the land community.[74] Each question about land use should be examined in terms of what is "ethically and aesthetically right," he wrote when proffering his celebrated "land ethic": "A thing is right when it tends to preserve the integrity, stability and beauty of the biotic community. It is wrong when it tends otherwise."[75]

Odum's launching the academic study of ecosystems and Leopold's profound thinking about the integrity, stability, and beauty of the land community resonate somewhat with patristic and medieval theocentric thinking about the harmonious design of all creatures in relation to one another. Especially helpful are the Cistercian monk's descriptions of the harmonious interactions of biotic and abiotic counterparts at Clairvaux and Aquinas's thinking about all natural causes as hierarchically ordered by God to bring about their harmony. Though they and other theologians of their times did not anticipate that humans could disrupt the physical order created and sustained by God, they cautioned against human behavior that fails to conform to God's plan for God's beautiful creation.

Today, scientific as well as economic evidence point to human activities that have disrupted the harmony of terrestrial and aquatic ecosystems. Some have been entirely destroyed. The integrity of the biosphere is in jeopardy, as indicated by the holes observed in the ozone layer of the stratosphere. Humans have not harmonized their activities with members of other species as they strive to work harmoniously within their habitats and the ecosystems of which they are integral parts.

How can the faithful show their appreciation for other species and systems out of a desire to participate in God's plan for the further unfolding of the beautiful world? They will study the needs of ecosystems within which species and abiota strive to harmonize, especially the energy flow, nutrient cycling, and the state of flux between biota and abiota. They will pay attention to the status of the food chain, its primary producers, its primary and secondary consumers, and its decomposers that facilitate the decay of organic matter for biotic use. They will recognize and delight in the dynamic harmony of biotic and abiotic interactions within ecosystems, and they will be inspired to identify and prevent human activities that would interfere with this ongoing harmony. They will deliberately and joyfully avoid activities that threaten the integrity, stability, and beauty of ecosystems. By living harmoniously with other components of these systems, they will demonstrate that humans can be responsible members of the "biotic team," as Leopold described,[76] the Cistercian monk implied, and Aquinas made explicit.

Acting Humbly before the Incomprehensible Universe

Before the admittedly incomprehensible universe, the faithful will act humbly ultimately out of profound humility before God, who grounds and empowers its development and who calls it to completion. The unknown and the incomprehensible dimensions of the universe will prompt deep humility in scientists who profess faith in God and in theologians who reflect on God's relationship to the world. This humility will be played out in two distinct but related ways: Humility in perceiving one's discipline vis-à-vis another, and humility in approaching one's endeavors with caution about the unknown and unpredictable that might adversely affect human and other planetary beings.

Humility in perceiving the natural sciences in relation to theology will be demonstrated by scientists who strive to discover as much as possible about the natural world and whose answers lead to more questions in that quest to know. Cognizant of the physicist Werner Heisenberg's uncertainty principle—which points to the limitations of objective knowledge and on predicting outcomes, due to the inseparable connection between the observer and the observed[77]—scientists will strive for microcosmic to macrocosmic knowledge about the world without the hubristic anticipation that everything there is to know about reality can or will be measured with precision through scientific methods.[78] Scientists will be perceptive to the unknown that transcends scientific discovery. They will avoid falling into the mindset of scientific "materialism,"[79] which moves the scientist from the bona fide realm of a scientific discipline into metaphysics through a claim that science will provide all possible knowledge about reality. They will aim to understand the limitations of their own specialties, value other disciplines for their data and methods of knowing, and seek opportunities for constructive dialogue that can lead to a more comprehensive understanding of the beautiful, harmonious world.

Theologians will also demonstrate humility in their efforts to talk about the relationship between God and the world. Recognizing that patristic and medieval theologians wrote from worldviews vastly different from our current scientific understanding, theologians will engage in discourse informed at least by broad scientific findings. They will discover more relevant and meaningful models of God's relationship with the more-than-human world. They will be especially alert to recognizing the interrelationships of humans and other species, the radical dependence that humans have on the air, land, water, and other biota, and the cognitive-affective giftedness of the human species to know about our intricate biological relationships with other-than-humans, to appreciate these relationships, and to act on them in our mutual interests.

Theologians and scientists who are theists will perceive themselves as providing complementary insights about the world. Neither will expect to provide a definitive account that will remain unchanged, because striving to understand and to articulate that understanding will be considered tentative. All quests for knowledge about the world will proceed in the spirit of humility before God, anticipating that a greater participation in God's knowledge about the world may be experienced as more is learned about the world.

Humility that is fueled by appreciation for the unknown and unpredictable will benefit environmental protection by dictating caution whenever research projects are being planned or technologies are being implemented. Through cautious decision making, adverse effects on human and other beings will be avoided. Caution is requisite for a number of practical reasons, including the human inability to fully understand the interrelationships of species and their interactions with the abiota of ecosystems, the ongoing struggle to model the effects of technologies, and the elusiveness of the synergistic effects of chemicals that are so wantonly emitted into the air, spread on the land, and flushed into waterways. Whether or not scientists will be able to discover all the information essential to facilitate sound decision making remains questionable as the search for answers continues.

Thus, stimulated by appreciation for the unknown, research will be planned to avoid or mitigate the degradation of species, their habitats, ecosystems, and the biosphere. The precautionary principle will be followed, so projects that threaten to endanger public health or the environment will be avoided, even when causal relationships are not certain. Moral theologians will proffer behavioral norms for cautious interactions among humans, both near and far and now and in the future, among humans in relation to other species, and among humans in relation to the air, land, and water that constitute ecosystems. The moral virtues of prudence, justice, temperance, and fortitude will be configured to pave the way for human interactions with other-than-humans.[80] All involved will show appreciation to God for the extent to which they can advance their rational capabilities in their quests for knowledge of the world and for their affective capabilities to respond to its beauty, however limited their capabilities may be to fully comprehend the world's harmonious beauty.

In the absence of solid predictability and with cognizance of ongoing efforts to fill gaps in scientific knowledge, the appropriate response for someone who aesthetically appreciates the beauty of God's more-than-human-world will be to make decisions that are most protective of species and ecosystems rather than risk their degradation or destruction. The faithful will not argue against instituting restrictions or bans on the emission of toxicants into the air that, in laboratory tests, are known to genetically alter or cause anomalies. The search for information that may lead to greater predictability will be understood as striving to participate in a limited way in God's all-encompassing knowledge of the evolving world.

Conclusion

Patristic and medieval theologians expressed their aesthetic appreciation for the beauty of God's creation in at least four ways: An affective appreciation precipitated by their initial encounter with natural beauty; a combined affective-cognitive appreciation from studying the details of natural beings; a cognitive appreciation for the harmonious functioning of the world; and an appreciation that comes with a humble sense of inability to fully comprehend the complex universe. Their expressions of appreciation suggest promising theological foundations for ecological ethics when understood from the worldviews and contexts of the times when they wrote, reconstructed to reflect the current understanding of the world informed by broad scientific findings, and probed creatively to identify basic patterns of behavior when beginning with the reconstructed concept. Among these behavior patterns are striving to be open to the beauty of the natural environment, paying close attention to the details of natural phenomena, endeavoring to understand and protect the harmonious functioning of biota and abiota that comprise ecosystems, and acting humbly before God's incomprehensible universe in scientific and theological endeavors.

The ongoing degradation and destruction of species and ecosystems require responses from theologians that are meaningful and helpful. This examination of reflections on the beauty of creation by some of the most revered theologians in the Christian tradition and the subsequent reconstruction of this concept provide one way that is ripe for tapping.

Notes

This chapter has been revised from Jame Schaefer, "Appreciating the Beauty of Earth," *Theological Studies* 62 (March 2001): 23–52.

1. Eugene C. Hargrove, *Foundations of Environmental Ethics* (Englewood Cliffs, NJ: Prentice Hall, 1989), 179–92.
2. Standing near or under a thundering waterfall and being moved by its grandeur is the example given by Noël Carroll, "On Being Moved by Nature: Between Religion and Natural History," in *Landscape, Natural Beauty and the Arts,* ed. S. Kemal and I. Gaskell (Cambridge: Cambridge University Press, 1993), 244–66. Carroll characterizes this reaction as the "arousal model" in which experiencing nature is more visceral, less intellectual, and apart from any religious inferences.
3. Allen Carlson, "Nature, Aesthetic Appreciation, and Knowledge," *Journal of Aesthetics and Art Criticism* 53 (Fall 1995): 393–400. As an example, he points to the grandeur of a blue whale that moves the informed individual to appreciate its size, force, and the amount of water it displaces; in his model, emotional arousal collapses into cognitive appreciation.
4. Holmes Rolston III's most recent efforts on aesthetics in relation to environmental ethics include "Aesthetic Experience in Forests," *Journal of Aesthetics and Art Criticism* 56 (1998): 157–66. For his instructive perspective on deeper appreciation for the natural environment stimulated by a combination of subjective participation (the eye of the beholder) and objective knowledge (provided by the physical and biological sciences), see Holmes Rolston III, "Does Aesthetic Appreciation of Landscapes Need to be Science-Based?" *British Journal of Aesthetics* 33 (October 1995): 374–86.
5. Stan Godlovitch, "Icebreakers: Environmentalism and Natural Aesthetics," *Journal of Applied Philosophy* 11 (1994): 15–30, at 26. In this model, Godlovitch explains a sense of being outside of or removed from the subject that engenders appreciation; thus, the natural environment is "the aloof, the distant, the unknowable, the Other," leaving mystery without any cognitive-scientific solution.

6. A fifth expression of appreciation for the beauty of creation that has no parallel in philosophical musings is explored in chapter 3, which focuses on the sacramentality of creation.

7. Saint Basil, *On the Hexaemeron,* trans. Sister Agnes Clare Way, *Exegetic Homilies,* 3–150 (Washington, DC: Catholic University of America Press, 1963).

8. Ibid., 2.6–7, 31–32. Reflecting on Gen 1:3, Basil admired the light that God created as having sent out "dazzling rays" that made the air "more pleasant," the "waters brighter," and "all things in general" even more "beautiful." He wonders how humans could ever "conceive anything more delightfully enjoyable."

9. Saint Basil, Letter 14 "To Gregory, His Companion," in *The Letters,* vol. 1, trans. Roy J. Deferrari (New York: Putnam Press, 1926), 46–48.

10. Augustine indicated that he wrote two or three books on the beautiful and fitting; unfortunately, not one is extant. *The Confessions of St. Augustine,* trans. John K. Ryan (New York: Doubleday, 1960), 4.13.20, 106.

11. Carol Harrison's examination of Augustine's thinking about the beauty of creation yields illuminating results in *Beauty and Revelation in the Thought of Saint Augustine* (Oxford: Clarendon Press, 1992).

12. Saint Augustine, *Concerning the City of God against the Pagans,* trans. Henry Battenson (London: Penguin Books, 1972; reprint Penguin Classics, 1984), 22.24, 1075.

13. Augustine, *Confessions,* 7.13.19, 173.

14. "Description of the Position and Site of the Abbey of Clairvaux," in *Life and Works of Saint Bernard,* ed. Dom John Mabillon, trans. Samuel J. Eales, vol. 2 (London: Burns & Oates, 1889), 460–67 (PL 185, 569d-574b), hereafter cited as *Descriptio.* Mabillon attributes this work to Bernard without explanation. However, Pauline Matarasso, translator and editor of *The Cistercian World: Monastic Writings of the Twelfth Century* (New York: Penguin Books 1993), includes *Descriptio* as unattributed. She argues convincingly that the completed irrigation sluices, buildings, and productive activities of the monks described in this piece suggest that it was written by one of the Cistercians sometime after 1135, when the elders urged relocating the abbey down the mountainside and closer to the Aube River where the monks could better provide for their temporal needs.

15. These "osiers" were probably willows or dogwood, whose pliable branches are used to make baskets.

16. Basil, *On the Hexaemeron,* 5.3–8, 70–80.

17. Ibid., 8.1–6, 118–28.

18. Ibid., 5.9, 81. Howard J. Van Till concludes that Basil's description of God's creation has "the style of materials spoken to inspire praise of the Creator"; Howard J. Van Till, "Basil, Augustine, and the Doctrine of Creation's Functional Integrity," *Science & Christian Belief* 8, no. 1 (1996): 21–38, at 26.

19. Augustine, *The Literal Meaning of Genesis,* trans. John Hammond Taylor (New York: Newman Press, 1982), 3.14.22, 89–90.

20. Augustine, *Concerning the City of God,* 22.24, 1071–72. See, further, Augustine, *Confessions,* 7.13.19, 173; also see Saint Augustine, *The Trinity,* trans. Stephen McKenna (Washington, DC: Catholic University of America Press, 1963), 8.3–4, 247–52.

21. Augustine explains his amazement over and gratitude to God for the great variety of beings in the world: "If I decided to take them singly, to unwrap each one, as it were, and examine it, with all the detailed blessings contained within it, what a time

it would take!" Augustine, *Concerning the City of God*, 22.24, 1075. Thereafter, he compares these wondrous blessings in temporal life with the greater blessings anticipated in eternal life with God.

22. Eales, *Descriptio*, 461–63.

23. Hugh of Saint Victor, "The Three Days of Invisible Light" (De tribus diebus invisibilis lucis), book 7, *Eruditionis didascalicae libri septum*, trans. Roland J. Teske, 1996 (PL 176, 811c-838d); hereafter cited as "The Three Days." Wanda Zemler-Cizewski provides an enlightening commentary on this text in "Reading the World as Scripture: Hugh of St Victor's *De tribus diebus*," *Florilegium* 9 (1987): 65–88.

24. Hugh, "The Three Days," 1.

25. Ibid., 4. From Hugh's theocentric view of the world, human gifts should always be used with an eye to one's relationship with God—the ultimate focus of human endeavor.

26. Aquinas, *Summa contra Gentiles*, 2.2, 30–31.

27. Ibid., 3.71, 240.

28. As an example of his insistence on consistent observations, see Albertus Magnus's research on golden eagles that required his being lowered down a cliff in a wicker basket to observe nesting activities over a six-year period. Albertus Magnus, *On Animals: A Medieval Summa Zoologica*, trans. Kenneth F. Kitchell Jr. and Irven Michael Resnick (Baltimore: Johns Hopkins University Press, 1996), 6.6.50, 547. Contemporary assessments of his efforts as a scientist are found in *Albertus Magnus and the Sciences: Commemorative Essays,* ed. James A. Weisheipl (Toronto: Pontifical Institute of Mediaeval Studies, 1980).

29. In 1941, Pope Pius XII declared Albertus Magnus the patron saint of all who cultivate the natural sciences.

30. Albertus Magnus, *Physica*, ed. Paul Hossfeld (Münster: Aschenforff, 1987) 1:1. See further *On Animals*, 21.9.52, 1439, where he indicated that his scientific studies were perfected with God's help.

31. E.g., see Francis Bacon's *Novum Organum* that is dedicated to the glory of God, Johannes Kepler's dedication of the first edition of *Mysterium Cosmographicum,* in which he perceives his work as a way of giving glory to God, Galileo's *Siderius Nuncius,* in which he indicates he was inspired by God, and his "Letter to the Grand Duchess Christina," in which his ability to investigate and reason about the cosmos is described as a gift from God to be used.

32. John F. Haught develops this way of relating theology and the natural sciences under the rubric of a "confirmation" model in *Science and Religion: From Conflict to Conversation* (New York: Paulist Press, 1995), 21–25.

33. Basil, *On the Hexaemeron*, 2.2, 22–24. All diverse animate and inanimate beings created by God have an affinity, a sympathy, for one another that unites them. Tarsicius van Bavel explores this concept with precision in "The Creator and the Integrity of Creation in the Fathers of the Church, especially in Saint Augustine," *Augustinian Studies* 21 (1990): 1–33.

34. Basil, *On the Hexaemeron*, 5.6, 69.

35. That Basil followed a well-established Hellenistic-Jewish-Christian tradition that the created world had a "relative autonomy" is explained by Christopher B. Kaiser, *Creational Theology and the History of Physical Science: The Creationist Tradition from Basil to Bohr* (New York: Brill Academic Publishers, 1997), 32–33. Howard J. Van Till examines Basil's thinking about the functional integrity of creation that precludes

any need for God to perform additional acts of special creation in the natural world now or into the future; see Van Till, "Basil, Augustine, and the Doctrine of Creation's Functional Integrity," 21–38, at 29. Thomas F. Torrance concludes from Basil's commentary on God's majestic fiat in Genesis 1, "Let there be," that "the voice of God in creation gave rise to laws of nature . . . [that] are to be regarded as dependent on the word of God as their source and ground"; Thomas F. Torrance, *The Christian Frame of Mind* (Colorado Springs: Helmers & Howard, 1989), 4.

36. Augustine, *Concerning the City of God,* 22.24, 1072. See, further, Augustine, *Confessions,* 7.13.19, 172–73.

37. Augustine, *Concerning the City of God,* 11.22, 453–54.

38. Ibid., 12.4, 475–76.

39. James Alfred Martin, *Beauty and Holiness: The Dialogue between Aesthetics and Religion* (Princeton, NJ: Princeton University Press, 1990), 20. Martin reached the conclusion that Augustine affirms a distinctive kind of pleasure occasioned by an experience of harmony that entails detachment from practical ends.

40. Eales, *Descriptio,* 460–67.

41. Ibid., 461–63. Clarence L. Glacken considers this work one of the few writings in the medieval period known to him that combines "a strong religious view of nature with an appreciation of natural beauty and with a frank, exultant admiration for the way the monks, through their skill, their techniques, their water mills, can complete what nature has given them." Clarence L. Glacken, *Traces on the Rhodian Shore: Nature and Culture in Western Thought from Ancient Times to the End of the Eighteenth Century* (Berkeley: University of California Press, 1967), 213–14.

42. On the hierarchical order of conservation that has the effect of linking all corporeal creatures to assure their sustenance, see, e.g., Aquinas, *Summa contra Gentiles,* 3.22. See, further, his thinking about the order and composition of parts to constitute the whole universe in ibid., 3.94; on the need for all types to make up a functionable whole, ibid., 1.85; and on creatures as cooperators with God (*Dei cooperatorem*) by functioning in the universe as God intends, ibid., 3.21. See, further, Aquinas, *Summa theologiae,* 1.47.2, 103.7.

43. Aquinas, *Summa contra Gentiles,* 3.69. See, further, Aquinas, *De potentia Dei,* 3.7; also see Aquinas, *Summa theologiae,* 148.1 ad 5. Umberto Eco appropriately characterizes Aquinas's understanding as a sense of the cosmos' "organic wholeness"; Umberto Eco, *The Aesthetics of Thomas Aquinas,* trans. Hugh Bredin (Cambridge, MA: Harvard University Press, 1988), 87.

44. Aquinas, *Summa contra Gentiles,* 2.68.

45. Aquinas, *Summa theologiae,* 1.25.6 ad 3.

46. Aquinas, *Summa contra Gentiles,* 3.71.

47. Aquinas, *Compendium theologiae,* 102.

48. For Aquinas, the functioning of the whole is better than the functioning of any part as explained, e.g., in *Summa contra Gentiles,* 2.43–44. This concept is explored by John H. Wright, *The Order of the Universe in the Theology of St. Thomas Aquinas* (Rome: Apud Aedes Universitatis Gregorianae, 1957), 87.

49. Patristic and medieval theologians demonstrate a version of the classical "design" argument articulated centuries later in various ways by scientists at the threshold of the scientific revolution and even through the present day. For primary sources on the argument to God from design perceived in the universe, see *Science and Religious Belief 1600–1900,* ed. David C. Goodman (Dorchester, U.K.: Open University,

1973). Ian Barbour provides an overview of "design" and "natural theology" in *Religion and Science: Historical and Contemporary Issues* (San Francisco: HarperSanFrancisco, 1997), 19–23, 98–100. An illuminating exploration of contemporary natural theology is provided by W. Norris Clarke, SJ, "Is a Natural Theology Still Possible Today?" in *Physics, Philosophy, Theology: A Common Quest for Understanding,* ed. Robert John Russell, William R. Stoeger, SJ, and George V. Coyne, SJ (Vatican City: Vatican Observatory, 1997), 103–23.

50. Augustine, *Concerning the City of God,* 12.4, 475–76.

51. Ibid.

52. Ibid. Also see Augustine, *Confessions,* 13.33.48, 367, where he sums up his praise to God for the entire creation.

53. Augustine, *Expositions on the Book of Psalms* (Oxford: John Henry Parker, 1853), vol. 5, 44–45.

54. Harrison, *Beauty and Revelation,* 133.

55. An overview of Basil and Augustine's use of natural philosophy is provided by David C. Lindberg, "Science and the Early Church," in *God and Nature: Historical Essays on the Encounter between Christianity and Science,* ed. David C. Lindberg and Ronald L. Numbers (Berkeley: University of California Press, 1986), 19–48. Training in natural philosophy that preceded the advanced study of theology at the university level is discussed by M.-D. Chenu, OP, *Toward Understanding Saint Thomas,* trans. A.-M. Landry and D. Hughes, OP (Chicago: Henry Regnery, 1964), 20–21. N. Max Wildiers stresses the importance of understanding the medieval to contemporary worldviews of theologians in *The Theologian and His Universe: Theology and Cosmology from the Middle Ages to the Present* (New York: Seabury Press, 1982).

56. A major effort to explore cogent theological discourse informed by more in-depth scientific findings is the series of conferences and initiated in 1987 by the Vatican Observatory and organized subsequently with the Center for Theology and the Natural Sciences. See *Physics, Philosophy, and Theology; Chaos and Complexity,* ed. Robert John Russell, Nancey Murphy, and Arthur R. Peacocke (Vatican City: Vatican Observatory, 1995); *Quantum Cosmology and the Laws of Nature,* ed. Robert John Russell, Nancey Murphy, and C. J. Isham (Vatican City: Vatican Observatory, 1996); *Evolutionary and Molecular Biology,* ed. Robert John Russell, William R. Stoeger, SJ, and Francisco J. Ayala (Vatican City: Vatican Observatory, 1998); and *Neuroscience and the Person,* ed. Robert John Russell, Nancey Murphy, Theo C. Meyering, and Michael A. Arbib (Vatican City: Vatican Observatory, 1999).

57. The United Nations Environment Program launched and supported the Environmental Sabbath movement in the 1980s, which facilitated the availability of materials useful for worship services focusing on the ecological crisis during the first weekend in June. A more recent and extensive endeavor to engage the world's religions in addressing ecological concerns was a series of twelve Religions of the World and Ecology conferences hosted by the Harvard University Center for the Study of World Religions from the spring of 1996 to the fall of 1998. Information about the forthcoming series of publications can be found at www.yale.edu/religionandecology.

58. Ian Barbour provides a succinct overview on ways of talking about God informed by contemporary scientific findings in "Five Models of God and Evolution," in *Evolutionary and Molecular Biology,* ed. Russell, Stoeger, Ayala, 419–42.

59. In *Theology of Creation in an Evolutionary World* (Cleveland: Pilgrim Press, 1997), Karl Schmitz-Moormann in collaboration with James Salmon proffers *creatio appellata* as an appropriate way of thinking about God's calling forth the unfolding of the universe.

60. Some principles that work well with the concept of appreciating the beautiful world when applying it to ecological concerns are: (1) Be open to the beauty of the subject (pointing to its specific aspects); (2) be attentive to the details of the natural beauty of the subject and be alarmed at the ugliness of its degradation; (3) strive to understand and protect the harmonious functioning of the subject (identify pertinent related biota and abiota) that constitutes the ecological system and/or habitat of the subject species or system; and (4) be humble before the mysteriousness of the subject in scientific and theological endeavors.

61. Carroll, "On Being Moved by Nature," 245.

62. On "egocentric" thinking to the exclusion of other biota and abiota, see, e.g., W. J. Christie, M. Becker, J. W. Cowden, and J. R. Vallentyne, "Managing the Great Lakes as a Home," *Journal of Great Lakes Research* 12 (1986): 2–17.

63. William C. French, "Subject-Centered and Creation-Centered Paradigms in Recent Catholic Thought," *Journal of Religion* 70 (1990): 48–72.

64. Jeffrey G. Sobosan demonstrates a way to stimulate one's transcendence of myopic self-concerns in *Romancing the Universe: Theology, Science and Cosmology* (Grand Rapids: William B. Eerdmans, 1999).

65. Sallie McFague writes movingly about our "living a lie" in relation to other humans, to other animals, and to Earth in *The Body of God: An Ecological Theology* (Minneapolis: Fortress Press, 1993), 107, 116–17, 118–24, 124–29.

66. Rolston, "Does Aesthetic Appreciation of Landscapes Need to be Science-Based?" 376–77.

67. Bruce Stutz, "Divine Details," *Natural History* 108 (July–August 1999): 6.

68. John Updike included this recollection of one of Nabokov's students in his introduction to Vladimir Nabokov, *Lectures on Literature,* ed. Fredson Bowers (New York: Harcourt Brace Jovanovich, 1980). Also see Brian Boyd and Kurt Johnson, "Nabokov, Scientist," *Natural History* 108 (July–August 1999): 46–50.

69. Marilyn Frye, "In and Out of Harm's Way: Arrogance and Love," in *The Politics of Reality* (Trumansburg: Crossing Press, 1983), 66–72. Annie Dillard demonstrates close attention to embodied differences in *Pilgrim at Tinker Creek* (New York: Harper's Magazine Press, 1974). Sallie McFague explores the "attention epistemology" of feminist theologians in *Body of God,* 49–55.

70. The philosopher Lawrence E. Johnson makes the "interests" of other-than-human-beings the basis for moral significance in *A Morally Deep World: An Essay on Moral Significance and Environmental Ethics* (New York: Cambridge University Press, 1991).

71. Drawing on the theology of Hans Urs von Balthasar, Neil Vaney finds the beauty of creation that mirrors God's beauty as a basis for moral obligation to preserve all other living species; Neil Vaney, "Biodiversity and Beauty," *Pacifica* 8 (1995): 335–45.

72. The "precautionary principle," established in Agenda 21 of the Rio Declaration at the 1992 United Nations Conference on Environment and Development, is binding on the United States, though little work has been done to implement the principle in our country. See the essays in *Protecting Public Health and the Environment: Implementing the Precautionary Principle,* ed. Carolyn Raffensperger and Joel Tickner (Washington, DC: Island Press, 1999).

73. Arthur G. Tansley coined the term "ecosystem" in 1935 to signal a growing understanding among early ecologists that all biota and abiota of an area function as a working unit; Arthur G. Tansley, "The Use and Abuse of Vegetational Concepts and Terms," *Ecology* 16 (1935): 284–307, 299. However, Eugene C. Odum wrote the first textbook organized around the ecosystem concept that transformed "ecosystem" into an idea with vast theoretical and applied significance; Eugene C. Odum, *Fundamentals of Ecology* (Philadelphia: Saunders, 1953). Also see Eugene C. Odum, "Historical Review of the Concepts of Energy Flow in Ecosystems," *American Zoology* 8 (1968): 11–18; Eugene C. Odum, "The Strategy of Ecosystem Development," *Science* 164 (April 18, 1969): 262–70; and Eugene C. Odum, *Systems Ecology: An Introduction* (New York: John Wiley & Sons, 1983). An overview of the ecosystem concept's rise to prominence is provided by Frank B. Golley, *A History of the Ecosystem Concept in Ecology* (Princeton, NJ: Princeton University Press, 1994).

74. Aldo Leopold, *A Sand County Almanac: With Essays on Conservation from Round River* (New York: Ballantine Books, 1966), 240.

75. Ibid., 262.

76. Ibid., 241.

77. Werner Heisenberg, *The Physicist's Conception of Nature,* trans. Arnold J. Pomerans (New York: Harcourt Brace, 1958). Also see Louis de Broglie, *Heisenberg's Uncertainties and the Probabilistic Interpretation of Wave Mechanics,* trans. Alwyn vander Merwe (Boston: Kluwer Academic Publishers, 1990).

78. I have not encountered a text in the patristic or medieval period in which the author claimed that humans would ever know the mind of God! Whether in jest or intended to be serious, this is the theoretical physicist Stephen Hawking's conclusion of his otherwise brilliant and charming *A Brief History of Time: From the Big Bang to Black Holes* (New York: Bantam Books, 1988).

79. Among those who describe scientific materialism succinctly are Haught, *Science and Religion,* 9–17; and Barbour, *Religion and Science,* 78–82.

80. A more detailed discussion of the chief moral virtues appears in chapter 8.

3

REVERENCING THE SACRAMENTAL UNIVERSE

Reflections on the sacramental quality of the world surfaced in the works of theologians throughout the patristic and medieval periods.[1] This particularly powerful and pervasive concept conveys the belief that the visible world mediates God's invisible presence and attributes. Some theologians described the world as a "book" through which God is self-revealing. Whereas few people during their time were able to read the book of scriptures, the "book of nature" was considered readily available for all people to read.

This chapter begins with an overview of the diverse ways in which patristic and medieval theologians reflected on the sacramentality of God's creation.[2] The differences between the worldviews from which they wrote and the current understanding of the world are recognized, and the sacramentality concept is reconstructed to reflect broad scientific findings about the world today. The kind of behavior that is prompted when viewing the world through a sacramental lens is explored subsequently, followed by a regime of training that is needed to awaken the sacramental sensibilities of the faithful. Closing the chapter is a digression on the need to ritualize these reverential actions and the availability of God's grace to facilitate acting reverently toward Earth and its diverse constituents.

The Sacramentality of the Physical World in Patristic and Medieval Texts

Catholics understand sacraments generally as visible signs of invisible grace imparted to persons who are engaged in approved rituals. The materials used, words spoken, and actions taken mediate God. A connection between the visible and the invisible occurs as God gratuitously self-communicates to the participants. Their reception of God's self as grace constitutes a heightened moment of encountering God, and the grace imparted enables individuals to orient their lives to God.[3]

As Martos explains in his historical exploration of the sacraments of the Roman Catholic Church, the term *sacramentum* had been defined more broadly by Augustine as a sign of a sacred reality. All natural entities that constitute the world can be acknowledged as having a sacramental character because they signify God and convey something about God.[4] More specifically, they signify God's presence and aspects of God's character.

Patristic and medieval theologians based their perceptions of the world's sacramental quality on passages from the Old and New testaments.[5] They found readily adaptable to Christianity the Neoplatonic understanding that humans have a capacity for knowing about God by studying God's creation. Thereby, they participate in God's knowledge and wisdom about the world and how it functions.

During the first few centuries of Christianity, theologians underscored the sacramental quality of the world. Often citing Romans 1:20 and occasionally Wisdom 13:1–9, patristic theologians reflected on the world as the first stage toward knowing God, as a means through which God's presence can be experienced, and as the vehicle through which God's attributes are discernible, however dimly and incompletely. They also taught that the sacramental quality of the world should elicit a response of gratitude to God. To this array Augustine of Hippo added an intriguing Trinitarian perspective, whereby characteristics of the three persons in the Blessed Trinity can be discerned when studying the world.

Medievalists elaborated upon approaches introduced by earlier theologians, especially Augustine. They underscored thinking that the entire physical world in its diversity and unity best manifests God, that its sacramental quality requires a response of gratitude to God for self-communicating through the world, and that its contemplation should prompt transformations in human behavior. Also surfacing during this period were reflections on the importance of bodies and the human senses, the need to train the senses to be sacramentally sensitive, and the instructive role the sacramental world plays in deepening a person's faith in God. Mystics conveyed a heightened sense of God's presence that they experienced through the world. The richness of these reflections makes the concept of the sacramentality of creation appealing for exploration today when attempting to respond to the realities of Earth's degradation by humans.

Saint Clement of Alexandria and God's Discernible Power

Clement (ca. 150–216) taught in *Stromateis* that the contemplation of the universe leads eventually to recognizing the powerful rule of God. Though God transcends the created world and is "hard to catch" and "hard to hunt down," God draws near and is "close" by the exercise of "power that has enfolded all things in its embrace."[6] For this Christian apologist and missionary to the Greek cultural world, the power of God is "always present" and "touching us" in ways that are "observant, beneficent, and educative."[7]

Saint Athanasius on God's Activity

In *Contra Gentes,* Athanasius (295–373) distinguished between God's invisibility and the visible constituents of God's creation, though he found them related symbolically. The visible creation points to the invisible Creator, he insisted from his faith perspective.[8] Commenting on Romans 1:20, he taught that God intended humans to use their rational abilities to detect God's invisible attributes from the things God created.[9]

For Athanasius, the revered defender of Christian orthodoxy against the Arian heresy, the sublime order of the universe should stimulate our thinking about God's creative and governing power:

> Seeing the circling of heaven and the course of sun and moon, the positions and revolutions of the other stars, which are opposed and different but in their difference all keep a common order, who would not think that they do not order themselves but that there is another who orders them and who made them? And who, seeing the sun rise by day and the moon shining by night, waning and waxing unchangingly according to an exactly equal number of days, and some stars crossing and variously changing their paths while others keep a fixed movement, who then would not consider that there must be a creator who governs them?[10]

The harmonious functioning of all things tells about God's activity in relation to the physical world, Athanasius reasoned. Contemplating the world leads to forming "an idea of the master who unites and binds the elements together, bringing them into harmony." Even if God is invisible to human eyes, an idea of God as "leader, governor, and king" can be gleaned from the functioning of the many diverse entities that constitute the universe.[11]

Saint Ephrem and the Symbolic Creation

According to the Syrian theologian Ephrem (303–73), symbols of the hidden reality of God are observable throughout the natural world. They can be observed only by the faithful, however, for whom they become more meaningful through the clearer, interior eye of faith.[12]

Reflecting in part to counter the heresies of his day,[13] Ephrem conveyed his understanding of the sacramental creation primarily through poetry and hymns. He expressed therein a sense of wonder and gratitude for the sensible world, because it is full of mysteries that point to the hidden attributes of God.[14] From his faith perspective that all things were created through Jesus Christ, a reflection of his understanding of the prologue to the Gospel of John, Ephrem exclaimed:

> Remaining are all those things the Gracious One made in His mercy.
> Let us see those things that He does for us every day!
> How many tastes for the mouth! How many beauties for the eye!
> How many melodies for the ear! How many scents for the nostrils!
> Who is sufficient in comparison with the goodness of these little things?[15]

The natural world is the "book of creation" that attests to God's presence and to God's character as a craftsman and an artist.[16]

God is essentially incomprehensible from Ephrem's perspective,[17] though God is self-revealing through both scripture and nature.[18] Both are symbolic of God, bear witness to God, and guide the Christian way of life toward God:[19]

> Nature, through man's use of it,
> Scripture, through his reading of it.
> These are the witnesses which reach everywhere
> they are to be found at all times,
> present at every hour.[20]

Symbols of God in both the natural world and scripture are available for all to see, Ephrem instructed:

> In every place, if you look, His symbol is there,
> and when you read, you will find His types.
> For by Him were created all creatures,
> and He engraved His symbols upon His possessions.
> When He created the world,
> He gazed at it and adorned it with His images.[21]

In one poignant hymn, Ephrem depicted God the Creator as painting a self-portrait through the scriptures and nature.[22]

As Murray indicates, Ephrem wanted his readers and listeners to adore God from contemplating symbols of God in nature and scripture.[23] Humans are equipped for this task, Ephrem explained, through the authority over the rest of creation with which God gifted them and the free will with which to exercise this authority. God intended them to use their abilities to contemplate the symbols that they encounter in the world. In response, they are expected to adore God and express gratitude to God.[24] From his impressive studies of Ephrem's poetry, Brock concludes convincingly that the Syrian assumed humans have a responsibility to God for how they exercise their delegated authority over God's creation. This responsibility comes with the freedom and capacity to contemplate the symbols of God that are readily available to them.[25]

Saint Basil of Caesarea and the World's Sacramental Beauty

Basil (329–79) reflected on the significance of the physical world for the faithful: "The world is a work of art, set before all for contemplation, so that through it the wisdom of Him who created it should be known."[26] As a creative act of God, the world manifests God's "artistic processes of thought" and prompts our admiration for God's work.[27] Basil closed his first homily on the six days of creation with this prayer:

> Let us glorify the Master Craftsman for all that has been done wisely and skillfully; and from the beauty of the visible things let us form an idea of Him who is more than beautiful; and from the greatness of these perceptible and circumscribed bod-

ies let us conceive of Him who is infinite and immense and who surpasses all understanding in the plentitude of His power. For, even if we are ignorant of things made, yet, at least, that which in general comes under our observation is so wonderful that even the most acute mind is shown to be at a loss as regards the least of the things in the world, either in the ability to explain it worthily or to render due praise to the Creator, to whom be all glory, honor, and power forever. Amen.[28]

At the end of his sixth homily, Basil stressed God's gift of intelligence to humans, a gift that is intended to be used to study God's creation:

> May he who has granted us intelligence to learn of the great wisdom of the artificer from the most insignificant objects of creation permit us to receive loftier concepts of the Creator from the mighty objects of creation. . . . Truly, it is not possible to attain a worthy view of the God of the universe from these things, but to be led on by them, as also by each of the tiniest of plants and animals to some slight and faint impression of Him.[29]

Perceiving God through the world seems predicated on an unhesitating recognition that the world is truly wondrous: "I want the marvel of creation to gain such complete acceptance from you that, wherever you may be found and whatever kind of plants you may chance upon, you may receive a clear reminder of the Creator."[30] The bishop of Caesarea wanted his flock to have "complete acceptance" of the sacramental character of the microcosmic to macrocosmic phenomena they encountered.

Nevertheless, Basil remained cautious about both the human ability to know God from contemplating God's creation and the capacity of the world to convey God's character. He stressed the need for humans to be open to and appreciate natural phenomena for their innate characteristics as well as for their sacramental qualities. By existing and functioning according to their natures, they manifest God.

Basil is among those Christian theologians of the patristic and medieval periods who also sought moral meaning from God's creation. Reasoning from his faith perspective that God governs the world while maintaining its integrity to function internally from its beginning,[31] Basil taught that God's governance is imbedded in the laws of nature telling us how we ought to act. He provided many examples of moral lessons to be learned from observing animals.[32] He also urged his listeners to obey the laws of nature in their relationships with one another, as do crawling creatures, fish, sea urchins, oysters, sea monsters, and other marine animals.[33]

Saint Augustine of Hippo's Trinitarian Perspective

Augustine (354–430) encouraged his followers to adopt a sacramental attitude toward the physical world because it gives testimony to the "the ineffably and invisibly great, the ineffably and invisibly beautiful" God.[34] He came to this conclusion only after having shed the "vanity" of philosophers[35] who do not approach the created world from a faith perspective and could not, therefore, find

God through God's creation: "I was no longer in that vanity! I had passed beyond it, and by the testimony of the whole creation I had found you, our creator, and your Word, who is God with you, and who is one God with you, through whom you created all things."[36] In his commentary on Psalm 26, he wrote:

> Let your mind roam through the whole creation; everywhere the created world will cry out to you: "God made me." Whatever pleases you in a work of art brings to your mind the artist who wrought it; much more, when you survey the universe, does the consideration of it evoke praise for its Maker. You look on the heavens; they are God's great work. You behold the earth; God made its numbers of seeds, its varieties of plants, its multitude of animals. Go round the heavens again and back to the earth, leave out nothing; on all sides everything cries out to you of its Author; nay the very forms of created things are as it were the voices with which they praise their Creator.[37]

After dismissing Manicheanism and Neoplatonism and converting to Christianity, he concluded that the beauty of the physical world reflects God's wisdom. In *Confessions* and *City of God,* he scoffed at philosophers who do not seek and find this ultimate truth about the universe. Only through faith in God, the architect of the world, can its harmonious beauty and the wisdom it manifests be understood.[38]

Augustine was confident that God self-communicates through the world and that humans have been endowed with a limited capability to know God through the world's diverse constituents. Paraphrasing Romans 1:20, he wrote: "Since the creation of the world, the invisible attributes of God, his everlasting power also and divinity, are seen, being understood through the things that are made."[39] The ability of the human person to see and understand God through the world is assured by the presence of the image of God in the human soul.[40]

To this thinking, Augustine added his belief that the Trinity is self-revealing through the physical world. God produced "sensible and visible effects" in the heavens, on the land, in the seas, and in the air: "To signify His presence, and to reveal Himself in them, as He Himself knows it to be fitting, but without appearing in that substance itself by which He is, and which is wholly unchangeable and more inwardly and more mysteriously sublime than all the spirits which He created."[41]

Reflecting on the refrain in Genesis 1, "and God saw that it was good," he provided a Trinitarian perspective on the sacramentality of creation: "The assertion of the goodness of the created work follows the act of creation in order to emphasize that the work corresponded with the goodness that was the reason for its creation. Now if this goodness is rightly interpreted as the Holy Spirit, then the whole united Trinity is revealed to us in its works."[42] He continued: "The visible and tangible signs . . . signify the invisible and intelligible God, not only the Father, but also the Son and the Holy Spirit, from whom are all things, through whom are all things, and in whom are all things."[43]

For Augustine, all created works "manifest a certain unity, form, and order in themselves." Each is "some one thing, as are the natures of bodies," each is "shaped according to a determined form, as are the figures and qualities of bodies," and each "either seeks for or maintains a certain order, as are the weights and arrangements of bodies." When we "perceive the Creator through the things which have been made, we ought to recognize Him as the Trinity of which a trace appears, as is fitting, in the creature."[44] He insisted that the highest origin of all things, their most perfect beauty, and their most blessed delight is the Trinity.[45] As Harrison explains when examining Augustine's teachings, the world is "a sacrament which veils, and yet, for he who rightly uses and accepts it, reveals its source and reality."[46]

Integral to Augustine's thinking about the sacramentality of the world is God's active but "hidden" governance. God works providentially through the created world, he taught, by having established the innate functioning of all terrestrial and celestial entities and by acting through voluntary beings to enable them to recognize God's hidden providence in and through created works.[47] In the human soul and body, a double providence is operable: (1) *Natural* providence as life in the soul and birth and growth in the body, and (2) *voluntary* providence as the human being learns and exercises free will and provides food and clothing for the body.[48]

How do human creatures reflect the Trinity, according to Augustine? "We resemble the divine Trinity in that we exist," he explained. "We know that we exist, and we are glad of this existence and knowledge."[49] Rejoicing, he prayed and gave thanks to God:

> Let him who sees this, either in part, or through a mirror, or in an obscure manner,[50] rejoice that he knows God, and let him honor Him as God and give thanks. But let him who does not see, strive to see through His piety, and not raise captious objections through his blindness. For God is one, yet a trinity. Nor are the words: 'From whom all things, through whom all things, and unto whom all things,' to be taken in a confused sense, nor as meaning many gods, but 'to him be the glory forever. Amen.'[51]

John Scotus Eriugena on Theophanies

During the so-called Dark Ages in the western part of Europe, another voice entered the chorus regarding the mediating role of the visible creation. John Scotus Eriugena (810–ca. 877), the theologian from Ireland who taught in the palace school of Emperor Charles the Bald and translated the works of Pseudo-Dionysius, stressed the human inability to know God directly, a position commonly taken by Christian Neoplatonists. In his brilliant *Periphysion,* Eriugena shared two major insights. One is that God is ineffable to human understanding—a conclusion that precludes saying anything about God without the aid of metaphor or analogy.[52] The other insight is that God is present in creatures by a process of *theosis,* whereby God descends to all things in the hierarchical scheme of creation and becomes so closely related to them that God self-manifests through them. For Eriugena, theophanies are the means through which humans know God.[53]

The Sacramental Christology of Saint John of Damascus

The sacramentality of the physical world becomes profound when viewed from the perspective of the Incarnation of God in Christ. For John of Damascus (ca. 675–749), the monk and doctor of the Greek and Latin churches whose treatises on the veneration of sacred images placed him in the forefront of the eighth-century iconoclastic controversy, matter is elevated to high regard through the nature and life of Christ. God "became matter for my sake, . . . willed to take His abode in matter, [and] . . . worked out my salvation through matter." Because of the Incarnation, John saluted "all remaining matter with reverence, because God has filled it with His grace and power." The wood of the cross, the mountain of Calvary, the rock-hewn tomb, the ink in the Gospel, and the various metals from which crucifixes are constructed are matter to be honored and venerated for their sacramental quality.[54]

Saint Bernard of Clairvaux and the Importance of the Bodily Senses

Reflecting on Romans 1:20, Bernard of Clairvaux (1090–1153) stressed the indispensable role that the human body and its senses play in the human quest for eternal life with God. "Only through the body does the way, the ascent to the life of blessedness, lie open to us," taught the Cistercian monk, mystic, and founder of the abbey at Clairvaux. Because the "bodily and visible things" God created come to our knowledge only through the bodily senses," bodies are essential to the spiritual lives of humans. Humans cannot achieve knowledge about God that "the blessed" have without our bodily senses, because they provide the initial input about God's creation that enables the ascent to understanding God.[55]

Although Bernard did not explore the sacramentality of creation in any depth, the importance he attributed to bodies should not be overlooked. The bodies of humans and of other creatures encountered by the human senses play key roles in developing a sacramental perception of the world. That both are instrumental to the human spirit's achieving knowledge about and a lasting relationship with God is not problematic when anticipating the need for a constructive response to ecological degradation today. The fact that bodies are crucial as God's mediators is significant, because actions following from this understanding would be geared toward allowing bodies to serve their sacramental functions by being themselves.

Saint Hildegard of Bingen's Heightened Sense of God's Presence

In *Book of Divine Works*, Hildegard (1098–1179) envisioned the enlivening but "hidden" presence of God in all creatures:

> I, the highest and fiery power, have kindled every spark of life. . . . I, the fiery life of divine essence, am aflame beyond the beauty of the meadows, I gleam in the waters, and I burn in the sun, moon, and stars. With every breeze, as with invisible life that contains everything, I awaken everything to life. The air lives by turning green and being in bloom. The waters flow as if they were alive. The sun lives

in its light, and the moon is enkindled, after its disappearance, once again by the light of the sun so that the moon is again revived. The stars, too, give a clear light with their beaming. I have established pillars that bear the entire globe as well as the power of the winds which, once again, have subordinate wings—so to speak, weaker winds—which through their gentle power resist the mighty winds so that they do not become dangerous. . . . And thus I remain hidden in every kind of reality as a fiery power. Everything burns because of me in such a way as our breath constantly moves us, like the wind-tossed flame in a fire. All of this lives in its essence, and there is no death in it. For I am life. I am also Reason, which bears within itself the breath of the resounding Word, through which the whole of creation is made. I breathe life into everything so that nothing is mortal in respect to its species. For I am life.[56]

In *Symphonia,* the German nun, mystic, prophet, and political moralist broke into a song of praise to God, the Creator of the world:

> You, all accomplishing Word of the Father,
> are the light of primordial daybreak over the spheres.
> You, the foreknowing mind of divinity, foresaw all your works as you willed them,
> your prescience hidden in the heart of your power,
> your power like a wheel around the world,
> whose circling never began and never slides to an end.[57]

For Hildegard, humans who approach the world from a Christian faith perspective can see God in every creature.[58] She urged people to "recognize all the divine wonders and symbols" that can be found in the world as signs of God: "All living creatures are, so to speak, sparks from the radiation of God's brilliance, and these sparks emerge from God like the rays of the sun."[59] Her sense of God's immanence in the world was deeply profound.

Hugh of Saint Victor's Meticulous Sacramental Sensibility

Reflection on the sacramentality of creation achieved intricate heights in the works of Hugh of Saint Victor (1096–1141), an Augustinian monk who professed his vows and taught at the Abbey School of Saint Victor in Paris, eventually becoming its master. There he began the tradition of mysticism that made Saint Victor famous throughout the twelfth century. His efforts show the strong influence of Augustine's practical teachings on the contemplative life to which Hugh blended the theoretical teachings of Pseudo-Dionysius.

For Hugh, knowledge about the world serves as an introduction to contemplating God, and he provided in *De tribus diebus* detailed examples of how various attributes of God can be perceived when studying God's many creatures.[60] He began his meditation with Romans 1:20: "From the creation of the world the invisible things of God are seen, having been understood through those things which were made. The invisible things of God are three: his power, wisdom, and goodness. From these three all things proceed; upon these three all things rest, and by these three all things are ruled. For power creates, wisdom governs, goodness preserves."[61]

God's invisible power, wisdom, and goodness are manifested respectively through the immensity of creatures, their beauty, and their usefulness. The immensity of creatures consists in their multitude and greatness, Hugh explained. By multitude he meant many diverse kinds of creatures, and by greatness the creature's weight as well as the amount of space the creature consumes. He proceeded to dissect the various aspects of creatures that point to God's power, exclaiming throughout his amazement at the incredible strength required to produce any one type of being out of nothing. Yet he considered his exclamations inadequate, given "the size of the mountains, the lengths of rivers, the spaces of fields, the height of heaven, [and] the depth of the sea."[62]

Hugh elaborated extensively on the beauty of creatures through which God's wisdom can be perceived. Their beauty can be found in their "arrangement, motion, appearance, and quality":

> Their arrangement is seen in their composition and order; their order is found in place and time and propriety. Motion is fourfold: local, natural, animal, and rational. Local motion is forward and backward, to the right and to the left, up, down, and around. Natural motion is found in increase and decrease. Animal motion is seen in the senses and appetites. Rational motion is found in actions and plans. Appearance is the visible form which is discerned by the eye, such as the colors and shapes of bodies. Quality is an interior property which is perceived by the other senses, such as a melody in sound by the hearing of the ears, sweetness in savor by the taste of the mouth, fragrance in scent by the smelling of the nose, or softness in a body by the touch of the hands.[63]

He insisted that the beautiful world attests to God's wisdom: "Anyone able to investigate these could find in them the marvelous light of the wisdom of God. Would that I could as subtly see them and as competently tell of them as I am able ardently to love them. For I am delighted, because it is very sweet and pleasant frequently to deal with these topics in which the senses are educated by reason and love is roused by emulation."[64]

Education of the human senses should enable the delighted observer to "cry out in awe and amazement" with the psalmist: "How great are your works, O Lord! You have made them all in wisdom.[65] You have given me delight in what you have made, and I shall exult over the works of your hands. How great are your works, O Lord! Your thoughts are exceeding deep."[66]

For Hugh, foolish persons will not know God from the physical creation, and stupid people will not understand their sacramental quality. Only spiritually inclined people are able to perceive the wisdom of God from the beauty of creation:

> This whole sensible world is like a book written by the finger of God, that is, created by the divine power, and individual creatures are like certain characters invented not by human judgment, but by divine choice to manifest and to signify in

some way the invisible wisdom of God. But just as when unlettered people see an open book, they see the characters, but do not know the letters, so foolish people and natural human beings, who do not perceive the things of God, see the external appearance in these visible creatures, but do not understand their inner meaning. But those who are spiritual persons can judge all things insofar as they consider the beauty of the work externally, but grasp within them how much the wisdom of the creator is to be admired.[67]

When referring to spiritually inclined people, Hugh appears to have meant those who approach the world rationally from a monotheistic faith perspective, as Augustine taught.

Hugh urged contemplating the physical world to find "the marvelous rationality and wisdom with which all things have been composed."[68] The rationality and wisdom of God are demonstrated by the harmony of diverse beings that constitute the cosmos, by riverbeds that "glue the earth together," and by the neural structure of the human body.[69] He marveled at God's wisdom, which can be perceived in the endowments of fruit vines, vegetation, wild animals, and metals in different regions, which make them unique,[70] in the sequence of day and night to enable toil and rest, in the four seasons for refreshing life,[71] and in the position of the sense organs on the human face.[72] He delighted in God's wisdom, which is apparent in the motion of streams, sprouting plants, the sensual appetites of irrational animals, and the ability of humans to act rationally.[73]

The comparative appearances of things underscore their wondrous qualities—a whale among fishes, a griffin among birds, an elephant among quadrupeds, and a dragon among snakes. All should be admired, regardless of their size, Hugh taught, because they demonstrate the wisdom of God. Even more marvelous are rare things that are not readily accessible to human beings, having been "hidden away in remote locations" by God.[74] The "monstrous" and "ridiculous" features of creatures prompt questions that go beyond what is initially observable: "Why does the crocodile not move the lower jaw when it chews? And how does a salamander remain in fire without being harmed? Who gave the hedgehog spikes and taught it to roll in apples knocked down by the wind so that loaded down with them it squeaks like a wagon when it moves? And who taught the ant which, foreseeing the coming winter, fills its stores with grain? And the spider which weaves its webs from its innards to capture prey?"[75] Their intriguing characteristics and activities are, Hugh concluded, witnesses to the wisdom of God who, when creating the world, intended creatures to be the way they are and to serve specific purposes in the scheme of creation.

The colors of the sun, moon, stars, precious gems, and sprouting plants that please the eye are also attributed to God's wisdom.[76] So, too are fragrances, sounds, sweets, and textures.[77] All senses have significance from Hugh's sacramental perspective, and he urged their training to assure that they are applied appropriately toward experiencing God's presence and discerning God's character.[78]

Moving to another attribute of God, Hugh perceived God's goodness as manifested in the usefulness of things. He discussed their utility for humans according to four dimensions—the necessary, the advantageous, the fitting, and the pleasant:

> The necessary for each thing is that without which it cannot readily exist, such as bread and water in human nourishment, wool or hide in clothing, or any such garment. The advantageous is that which, though at times it produces more delight, life can still be lived without it, such as in human nourishment a cup of wine and the eating of meat; in clothing linen and silk and any other softer clothing. The fitting or suitable is that which, though it does not benefit its users, is appropriate to use, such as the dyes of various colors, precious stones, and other things of this sort. The pleasant is that which is not useful and yet is delightful to look at, such as certain kinds of plants and animals as well as birds and fishes, and the like.[79]

Hugh provided two explanations for why God created things that are not necessary for humans: One is to serve humans in useful ways guided by the virtue of temperance. The other reason is moral—to enable humans to recognize in creatures "the sort of invisible good that they ought to seek" in the "superabundant riches of [God's] goodness."[80]

In *De sacramentis Christianae fidei,* Hugh considered the entirety of creation as a sacrament through which God teaches rational creatures that they must strive toward intellectual and moral perfection.[81] He stressed in *Didascalicon* the necessity of pursuing knowledge about the world in order to be restored to the blessings that come from knowing and loving God, blessings that had been lost in "the fall" of the human being as described in Genesis 3. By contemplating the orderly world that God has created, humans can recognize how they ought to act as part of the process of being restored to intellectual and moral perfection.

From Hugh's perspective, nothing in the universe that God created lacks fecundity.[82] All nature speaks of God. All nature teaches the human how to function theocentrically.

Alan of Lille and the Fecund Sacramental World

For Alan of Lille (1128–1202), the Cistercian monk, theologian, and poet, the natural world reflects God.[83] In *De planctu naturae,* Alan personified the physical world as "Nature" and depicts it as representative of an inexhaustible divine fecundity, from which springs a multiplicity of beings, their laws, their order in relation to one another, and their beauty. Nature is God's deputy whose pen is guided by God's hand. Nature is active, efficacious, and aware of the reasonableness and holiness of her God-given laws.[84]

Alan lamented the violation of natural laws by humans. When they refuse to follow nature's laws, they violate the principle of love that God instilled in the world, thereby separating the human being from nature. Whereas the land, stars, winds, land, sea, fish, and rain all function according to their innate capabilities and in harmony with one another as God intends, humans choose to act against God's intentions. Disharmony results, and nature's ability to reflect God's intentions for the world is defaced.[85]

Saint Bonaventure's Trinitarian Sensibility: The First Step to Contemplating God

The sacramentality of creation was a significant topic for Bonaventure (1217–74) in *Itinerarium mentis in Deum*,[86] in which he contemplated the physical world as the first step by which the human ascends to God.[87] His reflections were grounded in Augustine's thinking, with references to the speculative tradition of Christian theology found in Pseudo-Dionysius and Anselm of Canterbury. They also converge with Francis of Assisi's sense of religious awe that is awakened by God's wondrous creation.

In this masterpiece, the Seraphic Doctor meditated on the vastness of the physical world God created and saw reflections of God's power, wisdom, and goodness. All creatures were identified as vestiges (literally, footprints) of the Holy Trinity, and the faithful were urged to use their five senses as entry-level tools to contemplating God.[88] Repeating a theme familiar by the end of the twelfth century, he insisted that those who do not use their senses for this purpose are "foolish" indeed.

For Bonaventure, the natural world is "a ladder" by which the faithful ascend to God.[89] He stressed the need to approach it from a position of faith in God and to seek God's help in making the ascent.[90] "We cannot rise above ourselves," he asserted, "unless a higher power lifts us up."[91] Nothing will come of the human being's efforts "unless accompanied by divine aid." God's help is readily available "to those who seek it from their hearts, humbly and devoutly," by means of a dependent "sigh," and by fervent prayer.[92] Franciscan humility and a profound sense of dependence on God permeates this engaging reflection.

Using a triadic structure, Bonaventure described the specific aspects of the physical world through which God's supreme power, wisdom, and benevolence shine forth. The bodily senses convey these perceptions to the interior senses, he reasoned, thereby enabling the human intellect to investigate the created world rationally, to believe fully, and to contemplate it theocentrically.[93]

He dissected three characteristics that distinguish creatures—their weight, number, and measure: "Weight, by which they tend to their position; number, by which they are distinguished; and measure, by which they are limited. Thus we see in them mode, species and order as well as substance, power and operation. From these, as from a vestige, we can rise to knowledge of the immense power, wisdom and goodness of the Creator."[94] When reasoning about the nature of each type of creature, the human being may understand God's power, wisdom, and goodness as living, intelligent, purely spiritual, incorruptible, and unchangeable.[95]

Extending his reflection to the properties of creatures that testify to God's power, wisdom, and goodness, Bonaventure considered the origin, magnitude, multitude, beauty, fullness, activity, and order of all things relative to one another. The origin of things in their distinction and embellishment proclaims "the divine power that produces all things from nothing, the divine wisdom that clearly distinguishes all things, and the divine goodness that lavishly adorns all things."

The magnitude of things can be seen in their length, width, depth, and efficiency of operations. Their multitude is observable from the many diverse creatures that constitute the universe, their beauty from the variety of light, shape, color, and the diversity of beings, their fullness through their potential to emerge from matter, and their order in relation to one another from the harmonious functioning of the universe.[96]

The ability to recognize God's attributes from the works that God has created requires openness to their sacramental quality, appropriate use of the human senses, and a deeply felt honoring of God in response to God's self-revelation through the physical world. Bonaventure warned those who do not comply:

> Whoever, therefore, is not enlightened by such splendor of created things is blind;
> whoever is not awakened by such outcries is deaf; whoever does not praise God
> because of all these effects is dumb; whoever does not discover the First Principle
> from such clear signs is a fool. Therefore, open your eyes, alert the ears of your
> spirit, open your lips and *apply your heart* so that in all creatures you may see, hear,
> praise, love and worship, glorify and honor your God lest the whole world rise
> against you.[97]

Through these warnings, Bonaventure underscored the physical world's sacramental significance and, as urged by Hugh of Saint Victor, the need to train the human senses toward this end. Although Bonaventure moved beyond sensible beings to higher levels of ascent to God, this beginning rung of the ladder to God must be cherished as an indispensable first step toward knowing God, albeit incompletely, during temporal life.

Aquinas on the Entire Universe as Most Revelatory of God

That the universe is revelatory of God is also integral to the systematic theology of Thomas Aquinas (1224/25–74), though in much less emotive ways when compared with Hugh of Saint Victor's and Bonaventure's reflections. Aquinas taught that each creature manifests God in some way, but the best manifestation of God's goodness and wisdom is the beautifully ordered universe of all creatures functioning in relation to one another as God intended when creating the world.[98] God created distinct creatures and ordered them in relation to one another to achieve the good of the whole universe, Aquinas reasoned.[99] This mutual ordering of distinct parts to achieve its overall good most nearly reflects God's goodness.[100]

For Aquinas, the relationship among creatures is a hierarchical chain of diverse beings, with each type of creature finding its purpose in the other progressively up the chain by providing something the creature needs to sustain itself. Although some creatures exist for the sake of others, all creatures exist for the sake of the universe by contributing something essential to its perfection.[101] The order of all things in relation to one another is described as the ultimate and noblest perfection to be found in creatures.[102] That some things have instrumental value by existing for the sake of others while also having intrinsic value for the sake of the universe's perfection is not contradictory from Aquinas's theocentric valuing of all natural things as God's orderly creation.

Aquinas's thinking that corporeal creatures serve as stepping stones to knowledge about God was driven by Romans 1:20 and Augustine's *De vera religione.*[103] Creatures take on the characteristics of sacramental signs of something holy,[104] especially divine wisdom and goodness, Aquinas taught.[105] They are sacramental signs in a sense similar to the scriptures that convey spiritual matters under the guise of written words.[106]

Elaborating on Augustine's thinking in *De Trinitate,* that a trace of the Trinity may be found in all creatures,[107] Aquinas held that the creature represents the person of the Father as its cause, the person of the Word as the form conceived, and the person of the Holy Spirit as loved and willed to be.[108] Although only a trace of the Trinity may be found in the human body, an image of the Trinity exists in the human mind, enabling the human being to transcend matter and encompass the physical world intellectually.[109]

Meditating on God's works of creation plays a pivotal role for the faithful, Aquinas stressed. They can advance their admiration for God's wisdom in having created all the wondrous works that constitute the universe. They can grow in reverence for God's sublime power, a power much greater than the power of all the works God has created. They can be incited to love God's goodness for having provided a plethora of good, beautiful, and delightful creatures. They can attain a greater likeness to God, who contemplates all things in their entirety. Contemplation of the universe can also destroy errors concerning God, including the divinity of stars and forces of nature, Aquinas insisted from his faith perspective and medieval understanding of the world.[110]

Saint Gregory Palamas and Indirect Knowledge of God

For Gregory (1296–1359), the Eastern Orthodox theologian and archbishop of Thessalonica, the world serves as a mirror that reflects knowledge about its Creator, as taught earlier by Augustine and his followers.[111] Humans recognize "the power, wisdom and providence of God" when studying the world, but this knowledge is incomplete and limited.[112] Gregory also contrasted indirect knowledge of God with direct knowledge of God, which he believed was given to humans from the beginning of creation, obscured by human sin, and reestablished by Christ.[113] Whereas this direct knowledge of God constitutes a "supernatural union with the more than resplendent light" that is "the sole source of sure theology,"[114] the ability to gain knowledge of God by studying the world is a natural gift given by God to all humans. However, effort must be expended to acquire this knowledge. The fact that no one attains indirect knowledge of God without effort and practice distinguishes this natural gift from the supernatural gift of grace through which direct knowledge of God is given gratuitously to humans.[115]

When contemplating that "great work of God, I mean the whole visible" creation, Gregory exclaimed, the faithful are "filled with praise and wonder." Their praise and wonder are considered ways of giving "glory to the Creator."[116]

Summation

The sacramentality of creation was a prominent concept among theologians during the patristic through medieval periods. Reflecting either explicitly or implicitly on Romans 1:20, with allusions to Wisdom 13:1–9, they taught that God's invisible presence can be experienced through the physical world and, when studying the world, characteristics of God can be discerned—especially God's power, wisdom, and goodness. At least one theologian taught emphatically that the functioning of all creatures in relation to one another as intended by God manifests God's character more fully than any one or several types of creatures. Those who proceeded from a Trinitarian perspective reflected on the presence and character of the three persons in one God in and through the physical world. For these theologians, the universe is translucent, and the human senses should be trained to seek and find God through the world God has created.

These theologians also taught that contemplating the physical world prompts transformations in ways of thinking and acting. When considered as a means for instructing people in their faith, studying the world through a sacramental lens stimulates a greater reverence for God and prompts expressions of gratitude to God. Furthermore, the activities of other creatures according to the natural laws instituted by God provide instruction on how to act morally.

The question that must be answered at this point is whether or not the concept of the sacramentality of creation as constructed by the patristic and medieval theologians from biblical renderings coheres with current scientific knowledge about the world. Of primary importance is determining what studying the world today can tell us about God's presence and character, especially God's goodness, wisdom, and power. To answer these questions, the worldviews of the patristic and medieval theologians must be compared with the current scientific understanding of the world.

Reconstructing the Sacramentality Concept

As noted in the introductory chapter, the sacramental quality of the world about which patristic and medieval theologians wrote was a divinely designed, static, and geocentric organism with fixed species, all of which have God-given purposes for existing and acting. Their teleological view of the world was structured hierarchically, with humans at the top of the chain of material beings and God outside the created order yet actively present to it. Descriptions of the natural world were primarily qualitative rather than quantitative, and, as shown above, a sacramental view of the world reigned, so all natural beings were believed to manifest God's presence and character.[117]

With the shift to a mechanistic worldview prompted by the onset of modern science, the qualitative descriptions of the world gave way to quantitative descriptions. The laws of physics determined the way the world functioned, and the future was considered predictable if sufficient knowledge about the past and present was available. A series of mechanical causes replaced teleological purposes, and an increasingly reductionistic approach to studying the world became the norm. For some people holding influential positions in society,[118] the world was like a clock that God had created, wound up, and left to unwind on its own without any interference, interaction, or adjustment. Thus, God was understood as distant from the world while remaining interiorly present to humans, and the "book of nature" had been closed to theological and quasi-theological reflection.

Subsequent discoveries by quantum physicists, cosmologists, evolutionary and molecular biologists, and ecologists stimulated the reopening of the book of nature. Through their scientific lens, the natural world appears historically emergent, evolutionary, dynamic, holistic, and open to a future that cannot be predicted with accuracy. The biota and abiota that constitute Earth are relational, ecologically interdependent, and mutually affected by random occurrences constrained by the basic laws of physics. Humans are products of evolution, and each is radically related to everything living and nonliving in the universe, and especially to our planet. Humans are also radically dependent upon other species, the air, land, and water for their health and well-being socially and economically.

These findings prompt new ways of thinking about God, the world, and humans as its constituents. Particularly significant are opportunities to think about God as having initiated the cosmological-biological evolutionary process approximately 14 billion years ago, as continuously sustaining the universe as it organizes and develops itself through an interplay of law and chance and produces myriad forces and bodies, and as calling all emerging entities and the entirety of the universe to completion.[119] Among these entities are intelligent creatures who can reflect on their place in the universe and can choose to act in ways that are conducive to its fullest possible completion.[120]

The attributes of God's power, wisdom, and goodness favored by patristic and medieval theologians take on new meaning when informed by contemporary scientific findings. God's power can be recognized as voluntarily self-limiting through the freedom given to the universe to evolve at its own pace in expanding place and extending time.[121] God's goodness can be recognized through the seemingly endless potentialities with which God has endowed matter to develop creatively.[122] God's wisdom can be recognized through the physical laws within which chance occurrences are operative as God directs the universe to become itself in increasing diversity and complexity,[123] with the promise of fulfillment in the future.[124]

When theological discourse is informed by the contemporary sciences, some new and renewed attributes of God surface: Empowering. Freedom giving. Generous. Caring. Patient. Humble. Encouraging. Through the dynamic unfolding of the universe, God can be perceived as *empowering* the universe forward to complete itself while serving as its invigorating spiritual ground. God can be perceived as *freedom giving* through the ability of the universe to self-organize and produce entities out of many possibilities without dictation or oppressive coercion. God can be perceived as *generous* through the many diverse beings and forces that can be observed and measured by providing the possibility for their emergence over

eons of time in expanding space. God can be acknowledged as *caring* by continuously sustaining the evolution of an internally self-sufficient universe of diverse
beings that function harmoniously. God can be perceived as *humble* by allowing
the universe with its diverse beings to emerge without interference and to play
itself out in surprising ways amid considerable suffering, decay, waste, and death.
God can be perceived as *patient* through the billions of years of the universe's
expansion from a very small entity to billions of galaxies out of which at least
one planet evolving around a medium-sized, middle-aged star has produced a
magnificent array of ecosystems with their varied biota, including intelligent beings who have the ability to receive and respond to God's self-communication
through the universe. God can be perceived as *encouraging* the universe with its
many diverse entities to become fully themselves, to function according to their
natures in relation to others, and to complete itself at the end of time.

How can God's presence be understood when theological discourse on the
sacramentality of creation is scientifically informed? God's presence is continuously available for experiencing at every moment of the universe's unfolding by
those who are open to its mediating quality. God's presence is accessible through
flora, fauna, air, land, water, vistas, and other natural phenomena as the empowering ground of their emergent existence. Every natural being that is seen, heard,
touched, smelled, or tasted stimulates a sense of God's presence in relation to
all natural entities. Awe, wonder, amazement, fascination, astonishment, curiosity, and surprise are among the feelings precipitated initially in the person as an
entry to thinking about God in relation to the subject that is encountered.

As persons move beyond the sensual to contemplate the connections of natural phenomena in rainforests, coral reefs, prairies, and other ecosystems, God's
presence is experienced as they strive to know about the ecological relationships
among the constituents of ecosystems, to determine how they ought to relate
to the more-than-human others that are encountered, and to choose to relate to
them in ways that respect their distinctiveness as parts in the sustainable whole.
God's presence is experienced as persons act responsibly toward other entities
and systems on all social, political, and economic levels. God's presence is experienced as humans identify and overcome obstacles to sacramentally envision-
ing the physical world. In these moves beyond the immediate act of sacramental
sensing, God remains actively present to all, relating to them according to their
natures, and energizing them to function, to develop, and to respond according
to their natures. The response of humans who believe in God as the source and
energizing force of the universe is to think and act in ways that show reverence
to God who is present in and through the physical world.

Reverencing the Sacramental World

If the physical world is embraced as a medium through which God's presence is
experienced and a glimpse of God's character is manifested, reverence for the nat-

ural world and its constituents seems warranted as a way of responding to God.[125] Of course, reverential behavior by believers does not constitute reverence for the natural world in itself. From the perspective of this concept in particular and Christianity in general, the world with its diverse biota and abiota is not sacred. God alone is sacred, in the strict sense of the term. Reverential behavior is aimed toward God, whose presence and character are mediated by the sensible world. By studying and knowing about the world, faith-filled people can know about God, reflect on God in ways that are compatible with scientific knowledge about the world, and revere God through worship in words and action.

When viewed from a sacramental perspective, individuals of species, communities of biota, ecosystems with their interconnected components, the entire biosphere, and the totality of the universe will be revered because they mediate God's presence and God's attributes. Reverential behavior will aim to ensure that species, ecosystems, and the larger biosphere are not prevented from being and acting according to their natures so they can continue to mediate God's presence and character.

Those who embrace the concept that the world and its diverse living and abiotic constituents have sacramental qualities will encounter biota and abiota cautiously to avoid degrading their capacities to mediate God. They will want to know as much as possible about the subjects of their encounter because, by knowing as fully as possible about them, they can better discern God's presence and character through them. They will preserve species and ecosystems so they can continue to mediate God's presence and character in the future. They will react cautiously when other biota threaten their health, domiciles, and well-being. They will identify and implement rationales for relating to ecosystems and the larger biosphere. They will limit their use of other ecosystem components in ways that assure their mutual sustenance. And they will engage in ongoing efforts to identify and combat forces that thwart opportunities to discern the sacramental quality of the world. A closer look at these behavior trajectories is warranted.

Encountering Biota and Abiota with an Anticipatory Pause

People who believe that God's presence and character are manifested through the sensible world will encounter biota and abiota cautiously with an openness to their sacramental quality and will avoid any immediate actions that impede their ability to mediate God's presence and character. All individuals of species, areas of land, bodies of water, and air regimes will be approached with the anticipation that God is self-communicating through them. No component will be seen, touched, smelled, heard, or tasted without reference to God, whose generosity is manifested in the plethora of diverse entities that have emerged through the evolutionary process. No natural entity will be dismissed immediately or acted on negatively at the beginning of an encounter, unless the beholder's life and necessities are immediately and irrevocably jeopardized. Sacramental beholders will pause with the anticipation of revering natural entities when initially encountering them because they mediate God.

Learning about the Subjects of Sacramental Encounters

To be able to experience God's presence and discern some aspects of God's character, the faithful will want to know as much as possible about the subjects of their encounters. By knowing their natures, how they relate to others, how they function within ecosystems, and their significance in the greater biosphere, the faithful can better discern God's attributes and experience God's presence. Knowing about them will enable the faithful to reflect on God's giving species the freedom to evolve and develop, sustaining their development through their interactions with others, being patient and humble while they develop without physical interference, and encouraging their development by calling them to be fully themselves as themselves and in their relation to others.

Preserving Other Species and Systems for Their Sacramental Quality

The faithful will preserve other species and ecosystems so they can continue to mediate God's presence and character now and into the future. Although natural historians have discovered that species extinction occurs naturally, the reverential behavior that flows from believing that God is manifested by the world will prompt the faithful to halt human activities that accelerate the rate of extinction of species and initiate efforts to protect them locally to globally. Laws requiring the identification and listing of endangered species will be supported and implemented vigorously at the requisite levels of government. Wilderness areas will be preserved, and marginal areas will be monitored to mitigate adverse human effects on wild places, so some relatively pristine areas can progress through the evolutionary process. Appropriate actions will be taken at local levels of government to prevent species from endangerment, to restore habitats, and to prohibit their being destroyed for superfluous development projects. The significance of particular species, their habitats, and greater ecosystems will be conveyed through educational programs readily available to the public, especially in regions where species and systems are at risk. The biological, social, and economic losses that occur when species are driven to extinction will be lamented.

Reacting Cautiously to Threatening Encounters

When threatened by members of other species and natural phenomena, the faithful will react cautiously to avoid the unnecessary destruction of means through which God's character can be discerned. Human life, homes, and well-being may be threatened occasionally by other species, but efforts will be made to minimize these threats by living and functioning in ways that do not lure wild and pest species into human habitats. Sacramental believers will identify methods that cause the least amount of residual damage to threatened species. To deal with animals whose habitats have been appropriated for human use, the faithful will transplant them to natural reserves and take steps to avoid attracting them back into the human-occupied areas. Natural reserves will be advocated as compensation to species whose habitats have been taken over by humans.

Relating within the Structure of the Sacramental World

To avoid impairing the internal functioning of ecosystems, the faithful will identify ways of relating within the structure of ecosystems and the biosphere. Species and systems can more accurately reflect God's empowering them to function and God's providential care when unimpaired by human interference. Encouragement and support will be given to identifying ways in which humans can contribute to the health and well-being of ecosystems, and responsibility will be assumed, from the most local ecological level (e.g., a river tributary) upward to more encompassing levels (e.g., the basin of a composite group of lakes) to assure their integrity.[126] Because natural systems affect one another across political boundaries, national and international efforts will be expended to assure the integrity of ecosystems. so they can continue to manifest God in some way.

Limiting the Use of Earth's Sacramental Goods

Sacramental believers will limit their use of Earth's "goods" to whatever is essential to sustain themselves, other species, and ecosystems when striving to resolve conflicting claims among humans. Consideration will be given to current and future generations to ensure the availability of goods that will sustain life. Because, as Aquinas taught, God's attributes are best conveyed by the physical world's internal functioning as a dynamic self-sustaining whole, with entities taking from one another whatever is needed to sustain themselves as parts of the whole, sacramental beholders will function in relation to other species, the air, land, and water with a view to Earth's sustainability.

Human use of Earth's goods will proceed from a recognition of the interrelationships among humans, other species, and abiota in maintaining the internal functioning of our mutual home while striving for eternal happiness with God. Toward this end, the faithful will consume only those goods of Earth that are needed for their temporal lives instead of aiming to satisfy their excessive wants,[127] avoid using up nonrenewable goods because their depletion would eliminate their roles in the physical world's functioning and deny future generations access to them in meeting their needs in life,[128] and develop renewable goods in ways that are compatible with the functional integrity of the planet.[129] Humans who are meeting their needs in life will help those who are not, beginning at the individual level and proceeding incrementally to additional levels are necessary, as warranted by the principle of subsidiarity.

Seeking Opportunities to Directly Encounter the Sacramental World

The faithful will seek opportunities to encounter other species and their habitats directly, with the aim of knowing about their natures and their interrelationships as a basis for reflecting more deeply on their sacramental qualities. Direct encounters are especially important at a time when the forces of consumerism are reducing exposure to highly commercialized and digitalized images.[130] The perils of human estrangement from "the natural scale and rhythms of life on earth" were highlighted by the Catholic bishops of the United States in a 1991 statement addressing the ecological crisis from the perspective of Catholic social teaching. As "heirs and victims of the industrial revolution, students of science and beneficiaries of technology, urban-dwellers and jet-commuters," the bishops teach, Americans of this century do not readily perceive the sacramental quality of the physical world.[131] Those who do will seek access to other species, their natural habitats, and larger ecosystems directly and cautiously. They will also facilitate access by others, especially through church communities wherein they can disseminate information and facilitate reverential encounters with other-than-human constituents of Earth.

Implicit in the practice of reverential behavior is the expectation that the faithful will use their intellectual capabilities both individually and collectively to determine the probable effects of various courses of action on other species and natural systems that are encountered. Also implicit is the opportunity to choose the course of action that avoids inhibiting the sacramental quality of the physical world and to execute that action.

Training Sacramental Sensibilities

Because the reconstruction of patristic and medieval teachings on the sacramentality of creation has significance for ecological concerns, developing a sacramental sensibility is paramount. It will require training and practice. This task may seem formidable in light of the dualism that has prevailed since the Enlightenment period and the onset of modern science, when reflection on the sacramental character of the physical world waned and the world was reduced to an object for human investigation and exploitation.[132]

Nevertheless, as the theologian June O'Connor explains, some contemporary strains of theological discourse express "unity, continuity, and connection" more than "disunity, discontinuity, and separation," especially in the works of feminist and process theologians.[133] She also detects a sacramental sensibility of wholeness that remains "a rich and meaningful category for many people today, not only for those who find that traditional formulations satisfy their spiritual and theological needs, but also, for those who, dissatisfied by past formulas and formulations, seek to give new expression to the richness of sacramentality."[134]

Attempting to provide a renewed expression of the sacramentality of creation is the task at hand. Fortunately, this effort has been invigorated by biologists who underscore human unity, continuity, and connection with other biota as well as abiota. Their studies of microscopic detail prompt some scientists to express awe, wonder, and a sense of the sacred, expressions that can be probed for sacramental meaning among people who believe in God is the source and sustainer of the world through which God self-communicates.[135]

Hugh of Saint Victor and Bonaventure are particularly helpful for the task of renewing the sacramental sensibilities of the faithful. They explicitly encouraged training the human senses to be open to the sacramental quality of the physical world. Given the widespread ecological degradation apparent in areas of the world where Christianity is the dominant religious faith professed, training is undoubtedly needed to sense the sacramental quality of the biota, abiota, and ecosystems that humans encounter in their daily lives.

What does sacramental sensibility training encompass? At the outset, it presupposes belief in God as the ultimate source of the beginning and the continuing existence of the universe, a belief that is basic to Christianity, Judaism, and Islam. Sacramental sensibility training also assumes a biblical tradition of perceiving the physical world as a means through which God self-communicates, and the texts explored above attest to a deeply imbedded sacramental vision in the Christian theological tradition. To attempt to train the sensibilities of anyone who does not adhere to these faith perspectives may be futile.[136]

Beginning from these two presuppositions, the senses can be trained in five steps. The first is to be open to the sacramental quality of all natural entities that are encountered. Not one is seen, touched, smelled, heard, or tasted without reference to God's active presence or the anticipation of revealing some aspect of God's character. Reactions of wonder, awe, astonishment, surprise, fascination, and curiosity over other species, vistas, and systems need to be related to God. Sacramental sensing should be practiced so biota and abiota are encountered consistently from a sacramental perspective. Throughout, stress is placed on striving to be open to the sacramental quality of natural systems and on practicing sacramental sensing skills. This training aims to condition the individual to anticipate God at every encounter with natural entities and to express gratitude for this entry level into experiencing the sacred.

Sacramental sensibility training moves subsequently to an awareness of oneself in relation to the subject sensed. In this second step of training the senses, initial sensations from the sacramental encounter are geared toward wondering about the individual in relation to the sensible other, wondering about the greater reality within which the individual and the sensible other exist in time and place, and wondering about God, who continuously upholds and empowers the dynamic existence of all beings. Feeling small and humble within the greater reality before God is encouraged. Demonizing natural beings is avoided. Pausing before taking action becomes routine.

Wondering about oneself in relation to others leads to the quest for information about this relationship and a mutual relationship with God. Among the findings pursued in this third training step are basic scientific facts about the sensed, including its needs to sustain itself; its interests in flourishing, its surroundings, its functioning in relation to the sensing self and others in its shared space, and its contributions to meeting the actual needs of others, including oneself, family, and community. More expansive findings to be sought include the relationship of the entity sensed with the larger ecological setting that manifests God's

presence and character more fully and the evolutionary history of their relationships that conveys God's empowerment of beings to emerge and function. Also
sought are the real or possible effects of alternative actions on the sensed, its
surroundings, the larger ecological system, and other human sensors now and
into the future that could impede experiencing God's presence and discerning
God's character. The need to know these relationships to the greatest possible
extent is drilled, so inquiry prefaces every response to an encounter with the individual of a species, a habitat, or a vista to ensure that they can continue to manifest God's presence.

The ongoing degradation of the natural environment requires a fourth step
in training the senses—developing the skill to recognize impediments to sensing God's presence and discerning evidence of God's goodness, wisdom, freedom giving, empowerment, generosity, caring, humility, patience, and
encouragement to fullness and completion. The manifestation of God's empowering matter and energy forward to diversify, to become more complex, to
live, to behold, and to respond to God's self-revelation is impeded by human
actions that deter diversification, complexification, and thriving. The manifestation of God's generosity is thwarted by human actions that degrade natural
systems and extinguish species at rapid rates. The manifestation of God's freedom giving is stunted by human interference with the self-organization of
ecosystems and the biosphere to develop and function. The manifestation of
God's providential caring is disrupted when components of ecosystems—the
air, land, water, and biota—are destroyed and their harmonious functioning for
the good of the whole is prevented. The manifestation of God's humility in
allowing diverse beings to emerge with respect and without interference is
defaced by self-serving and speciesistic manipulation. The manifestation of
God's patience is obliterated by human impatience propelled for short-term self-
gratification. The manifestation of God's encouragement is overcome by human coercion, oppression of others, and myopic aggression driven by individual self-interest.

If training in sacramental sensibility is to be as thorough as possible, readi-
ness to react negatively to ecological abuse is an indispensable fifth step. Among
the negative reactions to ecological abuse that are to be solicited and encouraged
during this stage of training are:

- *Disgust* for a blemished habitat;
- *Abhorrence* of sulfur emissions across an otherwise blue sky, oil washed up
  on beaches and weighing down the wings of wildlife, silos of high-level radioactive spent fuel along a lakeshore, cattle grazing in an area that had
  been a lush rainforest, or a highway through prime agricultural land;
- *Alarm* when yet another species is endangered;
- *Lament* for the extinction of yet another species; and
- *Intolerance* for the racial injustice and damage to human health precipitated by ecological abuse.

All five steps toward sacramental sensitivity training are essential. They are complementary. Together they constitute a process that should prompt the discernment of action to be taken at the most appropriate levels of human endeavor.

Ritual and Grace

The sacramentality of creation provides an entry into exploring a role for ritual in the development of reverential behavior toward the world because it mediates God's presence and manifests God's character. The doctrine of grace also has significance for understanding efficacy of appropriating and applying this concept in an age of ecological degradation.

Ritualizing Reverential Behavior

Rituals are understood generally as social, symbolic processes that have the potential to communicate meaning. As a social process, a ritual is the product of society's creation to reenact cherished traditions. As a symbolic process, a ritual employs objects, words, activities, gestures, spatial arrangements, and relationships to convey meaning. Some symbols used in rituals are core to the beliefs and values that give identity to a religious tradition, though core symbols can gain or lose meaning as the social process unfolds. The shared beliefs and values of a religious tradition are strengthened through rituals, and they serve as occasions for engaging in critical reflection on beliefs and values. They also can play significant roles in resolving crises and making transitions within a society.[137]

Catholic and other monotheistic traditions with sacramental practices should consider using rituals to address the ecological crisis.[138] Ripe for tapping are liturgies and other symbol-filled activities that could be directed toward worshiping God by revering the natural environment because it mediates God. Some religious denominations have celebrated commemorative liturgies around Earth Day, the feast day of Francis of Assisi, and the Environmental Sabbath weekend promoted by the United Nations Environment Program during the 1980s. Songs, activities, and nature settings have been used for liturgical celebrations to emphasize the significant role religious faith can play in bringing about a transformation in the ways in which people think about and act in the more-than-human world. Some organized religions have used these occasions to facilitate critical thinking about their scholastic heritage, the extent to which their concepts can be responsive to the ecological crisis, and the need for new, more effective ways of thinking. Strong ties among religions have been formed with a shared commitment to protecting the natural environment, and shared rituals have been enacted at gatherings like the Earth Summit held in Rio de Janeiro in 1992 to express mutual concerns.[139]

Efforts should also be made to explore how to incorporate the sacramentality of creation into rituals cherished by religions traditions. Especially ripe for this purpose are the Catholic sacraments of reconciliation and confirmation. A communal ritual for receiving the sacrament of reconciliation could be geared toward confessing sins of ecological degradation,[140] seeking forgiveness for them at all levels of existence—as individuals, families, neighborhoods, communities, participants in biological regions, and dwellers on Earth—and resolving to avoid committing ecological sins again. The sacrament of confirmation could provide an opportunity for recipients to make their commitments in a ceremony set in the wilderness and geared toward awakening their senses to God's presence and character and toward facilitating reflection on how the gifts of the Holy Spirit can be applied to environmental issues. Through these and other established rituals, participants may be aided in experiencing the joy of being open to God's self-communication through the physical world and responding reverently.

The notion of ritual could also be extended beyond established sacramental practices by structuring formats through which reverence can be shown for the world's sacramentality. For example, a stepwise approach to sacramental sensing could be initiated, beginning with a prayer of intention to be open to experiencing God's presence and character through a particular natural place, moving through a process of sensing the place in increasing detail with attention to relationships between it and the encountering persons, thinking through constructive ways of relating to the place, and ending with a prayer of gratitude to God for it. Other rituals that could be developed include patterned ways of using the goods of a particular ecosystem to meet human needs while avoiding their being used up, minimizing waste, recycling, and assuring the ecosystem's sustainability so its capacity to manifest God is not marred. The enactment of these practices would acknowledge the traditional Christian belief in God as self-revealing through the world and would give contemporary meaning to this belief in response to the ecological crisis.

Because many theistic traditions use symbols in the rituals that express their core beliefs and values, enacting practices that ritualize the exercise of moral virtues to respond to the ecological crisis seems most appropriate when proceeding from a sacramental understanding of the physical world. The moral virtues of prudence, justice, temperance, and fortitude have been evoked throughout the Christian tradition to appeal for right behavior among humans. Rituals that build on the moral virtues from a sacramental worldview could invigorate constructive ways in which humans would behave toward other creatures and ecosystems.

If elevated to the level of ritual, individual and communal practices that build on the sacramental quality of the physical world could become patterned ways of acting with reverence for God, who empowers humans forward and gives us freedom to function cooperatively as integral but unique participants in God's creation. This reverence for God would be conveyed by practices that are compatible with the preservation of species and the dynamics of their habitats, greater ecosystems, and the biosphere so they are not inhibited from being themselves and, thus, mediating God. Because so many mediators have been blemished or destroyed forever through accelerated species extinction, habitat destruction, and damage to the biosphere, developing rituals of preservation and conservation activities could prompt attitudes and practices that are essential today.[141]

Empowering Grace

The doctrine of grace has been explored and refined over the centuries by Christian theologians and the teaching authority of the Catholic Church.[142] This effort to reconstruct the concept of sacramentality through a contemporary lens provides an opportunity to consider grace in the context of ecological degradation.

At its most fundamental meaning, grace is understood as God's gratuitous gift of self that is offered lovingly to persons who can choose to respond. This gift of God is categorically supernatural.[143] It is given above and beyond the innate makeup of the individual. The graced individual is one who freely receives God's gift of self and thereby becomes empowered to orient his or her life toward eternal happiness with God.

As noted above in the discussion of the nature of sacraments, one occasion for receiving God's gift of self as grace occurs when persons are engaged in rituals sanctioned by the Church. The materials used, words spoken, and actions taken mediate God. A connection between the visible and the invisible occurs as God's saving grace is communicated to the participants. Their reception constitutes a heightened moment of encountering God, though the grace imparted continues in the daily life of the participant who is empowered by the supernatural virtues of faith, hope, and love to express the moral virtues and to exercise the gifts of the Holy Spirit. According to the teachings of the Second Vatican Council, God's gift of self should provoke gratitude for a gift intended to be appreciated and used to bring forth the fruits of God's grace by actions toward others that are oriented ultimately toward God.[144]

What significance does grace have when the sacramentality of creation is considered in an ecological context? If accepted as a medium through which God self-communicates the divine presence and character, the physical world can be recognized as God's gift given freely so God's presence can be sensed and some dimensions of God's character can be recognized and contemplated. God offers the divine self through the world in a way that parallels the materials used, words spoken, and actions taken in sacramental rituals and ceremonies. God's gift of self through the natural world is offered to persons who can choose to receive grace humbly with gratitude and allow grace to facilitate the orientation of their lives toward God. Empowered by the infused virtues of faith, hope, and love, the individual demonstrates the reception of grace by functioning in morally virtuous ways in relation to the world. All the actions that follow express gratitude to God for God's self-communication through the world.[145]

Demonstrating grace that has been received, the individual approaches other species, habitats, and vistas fortified to act morally toward them out of faith in God who communicates through the world, out of hope for its serving relatively unblemished as the vehicle for God's self-communication, and out of love for God who intends to convey the divine presence and character through the world.

Grace received empowers the individual to demonstrate the virtue of prudence by identifying appropriate actions that minimize the degradation of biota and natural systems and avoid their destruction now and in the future. Grace received fortifies the individual to demonstrate the virtue of justice by ensuring that the activities in which the individual is engaged alone or with other humans are not preventing other species from meeting their survival needs. Grace received empowers the individual to avoid consuming more of Earth's constituents than is essential for temporal sustenance as eternal life with God is advanced. And grace received energizes the individual to act courageously when defending the natural world through which God's presence is experienced and God's character is contemplated.[146]

The availability of grace as God's freely given gift of self demonstrates God's continuous presence and generous self-communication through the world. The acceptance of grace to avoid blemishing a means through which God self-communicates demonstrates the individual's openness to the world's sacramental quality and commitment to its unimpeded access.

Finally, grace received strengthens the sacramental sensibilities of the individual who is fortified to more keenly look, touch, listen, taste, and smell the mediums through which God self-communicates. Their diversity is relished.[147] Their characteristics are cherished. Their place in the scheme of the complex world is respected. Their abilities to manifest God's presence and character are protected. From these graced sensibilities, the individual is able to more deeply contemplate God through the world and to react in responsible ways to God's self-communication.

Especially poignant for this discussion is Bonaventure's thinking about the need to seek and rely on God's help when approaching the physical world in the quest for God. With Bonaventure, faithful persons can recognize the need for God's gift of self as grace that enables them to experience and know God. With Bonaventure, the faithful can chant: "We cannot rise above ourselves unless a higher power lifts us up." The faithful will recognize that nothing will come of human efforts "unless accompanied by divine aid," aid that is readily available "to those who seek it from their hearts, humbly and devoutly." The faithful can do so by means of a dependent "sigh," a fervent prayer, and a grateful openness to God through the world.[148]

Conclusion

The exploration of theological reflections on the sacramentality of creation in patristic through medieval texts yields a faith-based understanding that the physical world mediates God's presence and conveys some aspects of God's character, especially God's power, wisdom, and goodness. When reconstructed to reflect the current scientific understanding of the world, this concept suggests a promising way of thinking that should prompt people who believe in God to revere the diverse species, ecosystems, and biosphere that constitute Earth. They are means through which God can be experienced and known when they are existing and functioning according to their natures.

Among the attributes of God that can be discerned when studying the world today are freedom giving, empowering, generous, caring, humble, patient, and encouraging. A trajectory of behavior surfaces from this reconstructed concept suggesting that the faithful will encounter other species, lands, waters, and levels of air with an openness to their sacramental quality, learn about the subjects of sacramental encounters in order to reflect more accurately on God's attributes, preserve species and ecosystems in their integrity so they can continue to manifest God, react cautiously toward other species when human life and well-being are jeopardized, identify and implement structural ways of relating to ecosystems and the biosphere that avoid impairing their functioning now and in the future, and combat forces that thwart the discernment of the world's sacramental quality. A reverential posture before the world can lead to formulating ritualized ways of acting out of reverence for God. Grace takes on profound meaning as the gift of God that enables the faithful to grow in their sacramental sensitivities and to be steadfast in acting reverently toward the world because it mediates God.

As a prevalent concept in the Christian tradition, the sacramentality of the world is ripe for appropriating today. Its reconstruction produces a cogent, relevant, and helpful approach to addressing the plight of Earth. For people who believe in God as the purposeful creator and continuous sustainer of the world, this concept can be highly meaningful.

Notes

Sections of this chapter were selected and revised from Jame Schaefer, "Acting Reverently in God's Sacramental World," in *Ethical Dilemmas in the New Millennium II,* ed. Francis A. Eigo (Villanova, PA: Villanova University Press, 2001), 37–90. Copyright permission was granted by Darlene Weaver, director, Theology Institute, Villanova University, on November 4, 2006.

1. E. P. Meijering underscored the popularity of sacramental thinking in *Athanasius: Contra Gentes* (Leiden: Brill Academic Publishers, 1984), 115–17.
2. This exploration does not attempt to exhaust the rich Christian tradition but merely to provide examples. Much more is available for appropriation and application.
3. Bernard Cooke stresses the transformative power of Christian sacramental practices for humans in *Sacraments and Sacramentality* (Mystic, CT: Twenty-Third Publications, 1989).
4. Joseph Martos, *Doors to the Sacred: A Historical Introduction to Sacraments in the Catholic Church* (Tarrytown, NY: Triumph Books, 1991), 4. An informative overview of the narrowing of this definition to seven sacraments of the Church and the ongoing development of sacramental theology can be found in "Sacrament," by Kevin W. Irvin, in *The New Dictionary of Theology,* ed. Joseph A. Komonchak, Mary Collins, and Dermot A. Lane (Collegeville, MN: Liturgical Press, 1987), 910–22. The need

for more giving more attention to the sacramental quality of God's creation is advanced by the following exploration of the physical world as a sign of God's constant self-communication and self-revelation.

5. Schaefer, "Acting Reverently in God's Sacramental World," 39–40. Among the biblical referents to this concept are passages in the Hebrew Bible that recount the Israelites' belief that God was present in natural phenomena that marked their history (e.g., plagues, rainbows, thunderbolts, earthquakes, and creative word); see Wisdom 13:1–9, in which the beauty and rational study of the universe was thought to convey God's attributes by analogy and anyone who did not was characterized as "foolish." In the New Testament, see Saint Paul's letter to the Romans 1.19–20, 22–25, Colossians 1, and Acts 14:15–17, 24–29.

6. Saint Clement of Alexandria, *Stromateis,* trans. John Ferguson (Washington, DC: Catholic University of America Press, 1991), 2.2.5.1–5, 160.

7. Ibid.

8. Saint Athanasius, *Contra gentes,* ed. and trans. Robert W. Thomson (Oxford: Clarendon Press, 1971), 35, 95–97.

9. Meijering, *Athanasius,* 118.

10. Athanasius, *Contra gentes,* 35, 95–97.

11. Ibid., 38, 103–5. Athanasius reflected from his understanding of the cosmology of his time that all species and entities comprising the cosmos were fixed and determined by God as observed by humans.

12. Sebastian P. Brock, *The Luminous Eye: The Spiritual World Vision of Saint Ephrem* (Kalamazoo: Cistercian Publications, 1992), 56, 162.

13. These were primarily the heresies of Bardasian, Mani, and Marcion. See, e.g., Kathleen E. McVey's discussion of Ephrem's polemics against their teachings in her collection of his *Selected Prose Works,* trans. Edward G. Matthews Jr. and Joseph P. Amar (Washington, DC: Catholic University of America Press, 1994), 40, 64. An impressive overview of the literature on Ephrem's polemics against heresies is provided by Mathai Kadavil, *The World as Sacrament: Sacramentality of Creation from the Perspectives of Leonardo Boff, Alexander Schmemann, and Saint Ephrem* (Louvain: Peeters, 2005), 247–51.

14. Saint Syrus Ephrem, *Hymns on Virginity and the Symbols of the Lord,* in *Ephrem the Syrian: Hymns,* trans. Kathleen E. McVey (New York: Paulist Press, 1989), 5.16, 286; 20.12, 348; 31.16–17, 401–2. See also Ephrem's *Hymns on Paradise,* trans. Sebastian Brock (Crestwood, NY: St. Vladimir's Seminary Press, 1998), IX.25–26, 145; XV.2–4, 82–83. See also Syrus Ephrem *Hymnen de fide,* trans. Edmund Beck (Louvain: L. Durbecq, 1955), 41.7, 111; 84.2, 219. In *Hymnen de Ecclesia,* trans. Edmund Beck (Louvain: Secrétariat du Corpus SCO, 1960), hymn 24.3, 53, Ephrem indicated that faith enables a person to see hidden things. That faith needs to be accompanied by love and prayer was exclaimed in *Hymnen de Fide* 4:11, 11–12.

15. Ephrem, *Hymns on Virginity,* 31.16–17, 401–2. See also hymn 11, 307–9.

16. Ephrem, *Hymns on Paradise,* VI.1, 108–9.

17. Kathleen McVey, "General Introduction," in *Selected Prose Works* by Saint Ephrem the Syrian, trans. Edward G. Mathews Jr. and Joseph P. Amar and ed. Kathleen McVey (Washington, DC: Catholic University of America Press, 1994), 49–52.

18. In *Hymns on Virginity,* hymns 27–30, pp. 382–83, Ephrem characterized the natural world, the Old Testament, and the New Testament as three harps on which God plays for humans to hear. This fundamental joint economy of nature and scripture

is substantiated well by Robert Murray, "The Theory of Symbolism in St. Ephrem's Theology," *Parole de l'Orient* 6–7 (1975–76): 1–20, at 5; Ephrem, *Ephrem the Syrian: Hymns,* 48; Kadavil, *World as Sacrament,* 234–35; and, Brock, *Luminous Eye,* 41. In *Evidence of Greek Philosophical Concepts in the Writings of Ephrem the Syrian* (Louvain: Peeters, 1999), 60–61, Ute Possekel explores three meanings of *kyânâ* in Ephrem's works—all created entities and their order, the inner nature of God's creation, and the primary elements including fire, air, water, and earth.

19. Ephrem, *Hymns on Virginity,* 1.3, 262.

20. Ephrem, *Hymns on Paradise,* VI.2, 102–3.

21. Ibid., 20.12, 348–49. As McVey notes, Ephrem is referring to the ancient custom of marking one's belongings.

22. Ephrem, *Hymn on Virginity,* 28.2, 386.

23. Robert Murray, SJ, *Symbols of Church and Kingdom: A Study in Early Syriac Tradition* (Cambridge: Cambridge University Press, 1975), 89.

24. Ibid.; David D. Bundy, "Language and Knowledge of God in Ephrem Syrus," *Patristic and Byzantine Review* 5 (1986): 91–103, at 103.

25. Brock, *Luminous Eye,* 164–65; Brock argues from his studies of Ephrem's poetry that human responsibility arises from the awareness of the hidden power inherent in nature itself. See also Sebastian Brock, "Humanity and the Natural World in the Syriac Tradition," *Sobornost* 12, no. 2 (1990): 131–42, esp. 138–39. See also Kadavil, *World as Sacrament,* 178. In Ephrem's *Commentary on Genesis* II, 9:3, in McVey's edition of Ephrem, *Selected Prose Works,* the Syrian interpreted the human relationship to God's creation through the story of Adam's naming the animals. Therein, a harmony reigned in the God–human, human–creation, and animal–animal relationships. The subsequent story of the misuse of free will by Adam and Eve destroyed this harmony, according to Ephrem, and it will only be recovered fully at the end of time.

26. Basil of Caesarea, *On the Hexaemeron,* in *Exegetic Homilies,* trans. Sister Agnes Clare Way, Fathers of the Church 46 (Washington, DC: Catholic University of America Press, 1963), 3–150, esp. homily 1.7, 112.

27. Ibid., 1.1–3, 3–54.

28. Ibid., 1.11, 19.

29. Ibid., 6.11, 102–3. Even "the abyss" to which Psalm 148 refers contributes to the glory that the whole universe gives to God, Basil wrote in homily 3.9, 52–53.

30. Ibid., 5.2, 69.

31. See, e.g., Tarsicius van Bavel, "The Creator and the Integrity of Creation in the Fathers of the Church, Especially in Saint Augustine," *Augustinian Studies* 21 (1900): 1–33; and Howard J. Van Till, "Basil, Augustine, and the Doctrine of Creation's Functional Integrity," *Science & Christian Belief* 8 (April 1996): 21–38.

32. Especially see Saint Basil, *On the Hexaemeron,* 7–8, pp. 105–34. Among the lessons humans can learn from the actions of bees constructing their honeycombs is how to work without injuring one another or their product. He doesn't seem as kind to wives, whom he urges to take lessons from the viper who embraces the sea lamprey fiercely, so they may come to tolerate their rough, fierce, brawling and drunken husbands to whom they are "united by Nature"!

33. Ibid., 7.4, 112.

34. Saint Augustine, *Concerning the City of God against the Pagans,* trans. John O'Meara (London: Penguin Books, 1972), 11.4, 432. See also Saint Augustine, *The Confessions of St. Augustine,* trans. John K. Ryan (Garden City, NY: Image Books, 1960), 7.17.23,

175–76; 9.10–23–25, 221–22; and Saint Augustine, *The Trinity,* trans. Stephen McKenna (Washington, DC: Catholic University of America Press, 1963), 2.25, 81–82.

35. These were most likely Manicheans and Neoplatonists, with whom he had been engaged sequentially before converting to Christianity.

36. Augustine, *Confessions,* 8.2, 182.

37. Augustine, *On the Psalms,* Ancient Christian Writers 29 (New York: Newman Press, 1960), 272.

38. Augustine, *Confessions,* 5.3.5, 116; Augustine, *Concerning the City of God* 11.4, 432. He distinguishes between the purviews of faith and the rational observation of the world. Carol Harrison points to Augustine's stress on the need for the faithful to actively search for God through the world and to avoid dependence on God's creation to lead them passively to God; Carol Harrison, *Beauty and Revelation in the Thought of Saint Augustine* (Oxford: Clarendon Press, 1992), 114.

39. Augustine, *The Trinity,* 2.15.25, 81–82.

40. Ibid., 11.5.8, 326–28. The image of God is thought to be in the human being by virtue of the rational soul, which Augustine teaches is nearer to God in its capacity to respond to God's call, to turn to God, to be formed/made beautiful by God, and, thus, to know God. Also see books 8–10, where he works out a way of defining the human being as having been created in the image of God, and books 11–15, where he explains how self-knowledge as image can be turned towards God. He proceeds through various triads until he reaches memory, understanding, and will as the final definition of human image. On his thinking about signs of divinely bestowed favors, see letter 138 in *Letters,* by Augustine, vol. 3, trans. Sister Wilfrid Parsons, SND (New York: Fathers of the Church, 1953), 36–53.

41. Augustine, *The Trinity,* 3.4.10, 105.

42. Augustine, *Concerning the City of God,* 11.24, 457.

43. Ibid. This is evidently an allusion to Rom 11:36.

44. Augustine, *The Trinity,* 6.10.12, 214.

45. Ibid.

46. Harrison, *Beauty and Revelation in the Thought of Saint Augustine,* 266. According to Augustine, Harrison concludes, the entirety of God's creation is the human mirror through which its Creator can be seen.

47. Along with other theologians before and after his time until Alfred Russel Wallace and Charles Darwin shared their findings about the evolution of species, Augustine adhered to the doctrine of fixed species—all types of creatures derive their basic characteristics from God at the beginning of creation.

48. Augustine, *The Literal Meaning of Genesis,* vol. 2, trans. John Hammond Taylor, SJ (New York: Newman Press, 1982), 8.9.12, 45–46. Thus, Augustine works with two types of divine providence—natural and voluntary providence. Natural providence is God's hidden governance at work in the world via natural law established by God. Augustine explains this divine activity through his theory of causal or seminal reasons that contain the potential and inevitable life, growth, decay, and the end of all things. See the discussion by Jules M. Brady, "Augustine's Theory of Seminal Reasons," *New Scholasticism* 38 (1964): 141–58.

49. Augustine, *Concerning the City of God,* 11.26, 459–60.

50. Cor 13:12.

51. Augustine, *The Trinity,* 6.10.12, 214–15, citing Rom 11:36. A unity comprised of a distinction of persons is assumed.

52. John Scotus Eriugena, *Periphyseon* (The Division of Nature), trans. I. P. Sheldon-Williams; rev. John J. O'Meara (Washington, DC: Dumbarton Oaks, 1987). Eriugena insisted on the ineffability of God, as exemplified by apophatic theology—nothing can be said properly about God because God transcends human understanding. However, metaphorical and analogical affirmations can be made by observing God's creation. Eriugena holds these notions in tension throughout *Periphyseon,* his most celebrated work.

53. E.g., see Eriugena, *Periphyseon* 3, 249–51, 305–6; 5, 577, 592–93, 645, 667–68, 685.

54. Saint John of Damascus, *On the Divine Images: Three Apologies against Those Who Attack the Divine Images,* trans. David Anderson (Crestwood, NY: St. Vladimir's Seminary Press, 1980), 1st apology, 16–17:23–26. In the vein of the great Christian mystics, including Pseudo-Dionysius, John Scotus Eriugena, Meister Eckhart, John of the Cross, and John Chrysostom, John of Damascus contends that God is best known through an apophatic theology, which makes no positive statements about God. William Temple (1881–1944), the archbishop of Canterbury and leader of the ecumenical movement during the first half of the twentieth century, stressed the sacramentality of creation from a Christ-centered perspective; see William Temple, *Readings in St John's Gospel* (London: Macmillan, 1939), xx–xxi. Also see Arthur R. Peacocke, "A Sacramental View of Nature," in *Man and Nature,* ed. Hugh Montefiore (London: Collins, 1975), 132–42, esp. 134, 141–42.

55. Bernard of Clairvaux, *Selected Writings,* trans. G. R. Evans (New York: Paulist Press, 1987), sermon 5, 227–31.

56. Hildegard of Bingen, *Book of Divine Works,* ed. Matthew Fox and trans. Robert Cunningham (Santa Fe: Bear & Co., 1987), vision 1.2.8, 10–11.

57. Hildegard of Bingen, *Symphonia: A Critical Edition of the Symphonia armonie celestium revelationum,* 2nd edition, ed. and trans. Barbara Newman (Ithaca, NY: Cornell University Press, 1998), 259. See also Hildegard of Bingen, "Song to the Redeemer," in *Symphonia,* 263.

58. Hildegard, *Book of Divine Works* 2.15, 36.

59. Ibid., 4.11, 86–87.

60. In "Reading the World as Scripture: Hugh of St Victor's *De Tribus Diebus,*" *Florilegium* 9 (1987): 65–88, Wanda Cizewski suggests that this text might best be read as the contemplative end to Hugh's *Didascalicon.* In that work, Hugh sets forth a program for studying a whole complex of the traditional arts. He prescribes a particular order that all humankind should follow as a means of relieving the physical weaknesses of earthly life and of restoring that union with the divine Wisdom for which the human being was made. He teaches that the human being's immortal mind is capable of pursuing systematic study of all things, beginning with the visible.

61. Hugh of Saint Victor, "The Three Days of Invisible Light," trans. Roland J. Teske, SJ, Marquette University, June 1996. The quotations here are used with Fr. Teske's permission, given October 30, 2006.

62. Ibid., 3.

63. Ibid., 1.

64. Ibid., 4.

65. Ps 103:24.

66. Ps 91:5–7.

67. Hugh, "Three Days," 4.

68. Ibid., 5.

69. Ibid.
70. Ibid.
71. Ibid., 6.
72. Ibid., 7.
73. Ibid., 8.
74. Ibid., 9.
75. Ibid., 12.
76. Ibid.
77. Ibid., 13.
78. Ibid., 4, 12.
79. Ibid., 14.
80. Ibid.
81. See Jerome Taylor, "Introduction," in *Didascalicon: A Medieval Guide to the Arts,* by Hugh of Saint Victor, trans. Jerome Taylor (New York: Columbia University Press, 1961), especially his summation at 29–30.
82. Hugh of Saint Victor, *Didascalicon* 6.5, 145.
83. Alan shared in the mystic reaction of the second half of the twelfth century against the prevailing Scholastic philosophy, adopting an eclectic Scholasticism that combined rationalism and mysticism.
84. Alan of Lille, *The Plaint of Nature,* trans. James J. Sheridan (Toronto: Pontifical Institute of Mediaeval Studies, 1980).
85. Ibid., 8.4, 131–38. See also Clarence L. Glacken, *Traces on the Rhodian Shore: Nature and Culture in Western Thought from Ancient Times to the End of the Eighteenth Century* (Berkeley: University of California Press, 1967), 217.
86. Saint Bonaventure, *The Soul's Journey into God* (Itinerarium mentis in Deum), Classics of Western Spirituality, trans. Ewert Cousins (New York: Paulist Press, 1978), 59–68.
87. Bonaventure used the Latin term *speculatio* (whose root *speculum* means "mirror") to convey reflection, speculation, contemplation, and consideration. As customary in his use of certain key words, he often intends all these meanings in a given instance.
88. Though the meditation on creation in *The Soul's Journey* correlates with Francis of Assisi's "Canticle of Brother Sun" in the sense of wonderment about creation and its signification of God, Bonaventure seems to be more captivated by the intelligible structure of creation and meditates extensively on it in conceptual terms rather than citing specific creatures.
89. Like Augustine and others centuries before, Bonaventure characterizes the universe sometimes as a mirror through which we pass over to God. Although he begins here with the material world as a ladder to God, he climbs up the ladder, leaving the sensible world behind to reach the intellectual state and finally to contemplating God. Some contemporary theologians find this approach problematic because it posits the physical world as valuable only instrumentally as a beginning step to God. E.g., see Larry L. Rasmussen, *Earth Community, Earth Ethics* (Maryknoll, NY: Orbis Books, 1996), 273, and H. Paul. Santmire, *The Travail of Nature: The Ambiguous Ecological Promise of Christian Theology* (Philadelphia: Fortress Press, 1985), 98–102. What these scholars fail to recognize is that theologians during the patristic and medieval periods valued natural entities as capable of mediating God's presence and character by the very fact of their natures and functioning as intended by God. Furthermore, the ladder to God is grounded in the sensible world where the "climb" begins; thus, the world is indispensable to this task.

90. Cousins explains in the introduction to his translation of *The Soul's Journey*, 23, that Bonaventure does not hold in his other works that one must move precisely from sensation to soul to God because knowledge of God is innate in the soul and does not have to be derived from sense data by a reasoning process.

91. Ps 83:6–7.

92. Bonaventure, *The Soul's Journey*, 1.1, 59–60.

93. Ibid., 1.10, 63–64.

94. Ibid., 1.11, 64.

95. Ibid., 1.13, 64.

96. Things have a "fullness" in the sense that matter is full of forms because God placed seminal principles (*rationes seminales*) in matter when creating the universe, out of which specific types of creatures emerge in the future. The equivalent of the contemporary understanding of evolutionary biology is not presumed by Bonaventure or by Augustine, who taught the doctrine of seminal principles.

97. Bonaventure, *The Soul's Journey*, 1.15, 67–68, quoting from and reflecting on Proverbs 22:17.

98. E.g., see Aquinas, *Summa theologiae*, 1.47.1.

99. Aquinas, *Summa contra Gentiles*, 2.39; also 44–45, 3.69, 144.10. See also Aquinas, *Summa theologiae*, 1.15.2, 22.1–2.

100. Aquinas, *Summa contra Gentiles*, 3.64. See also Aquinas, *Summa theologiae*, 1.47.2.

101. Aquinas, *Summa contra Gentiles*, 3.112; also see 3.113 and 145, where he explains that the entirety of the ordered creation of diverse beings is ordered ultimately to the uncreated good who is God. As rational beings endowed with free will, humans are intended by God to will their use of all creatures for knowledge and sustenance of their bodies ultimately to God. See, further, Aquinas, *Summa theologiae*, 1.47.2, 2 | 2.83.6, 118.1 ad 1; and Aquinas, *Compendium theologiae*, 173. In *Summa contra Gentiles* 1.92, he evaluates this limited human use of other creatures as "right use."

102. E.g., see Aquinas, *Summa contra Gentiles*, 2.44–45.

103. Aquinas, *Summa theologiae*, 2 | 2.180.4; also see 3.60, Supp. 91.

104. Ibid., 3.60.4.

105. Ibid., 3.60.2.

106. Ibid., 3.60.4.

107. Ibid., 1.45.7.

108. Ibid.

109. Ibid.

110. Aquinas, *Summa contra Gentiles*, 2.1–3.

111. John Meyendorff, *A Study of Gregory Palamas*, trans. George Lawrence (Crestwood, NY: St. Vladimir's Seminary Press, 1998), 119. Meyendorff considers Palamas "the greatest Greek theologian of the Middle Ages."

112. Palamas, *The Triads*, ed. John Meyendorff; trans. Nicholas Gendle (New York: Paulist Press, 1983), 2.3.15–16, 59–61. Also see Meyendorff, *Study of Gregory Palamas*, 119.

113. See Meyendorff's summation in *Study of Gregory Palamas*, 120.

114. Palamas, *The Triads*, 2.3.15, 59–60. Also see Meyendorff, *Study of Gregory Palamas*, 120.

115. Palamas, *The Triads*, 1.1.22, 29–30. Also see Meyendorff, *Study of Gregory Palamas*, 119. The influence of Neoplatonic thinking is obvious.

116. Palamas, homily 34. Daniel Roglich provides helpful insight in "Homily 34 of Saint Gregory Palamas," *Greek Orthodox Theological Review* 33, no. 2 (1988): 135–66.

117. E.g., see Ian Barbour, *Religion and Science: Historical and Contemporary Issues* (San Francisco: HarperSanFrancisco, 1997), 281–84.

118. This was true especially for the Deists, among whom numbered the founding fathers of the United States of America.

119. Though the theological concept of being "called" by God has been limited traditionally to humans, calling the universe forth to completion is plausible for its inclusiveness and effectiveness in an age of ecological degradation. See Karl Schmitz-Moormann with James F. Salmon, SJ, *Theology of Creation in an Evolutionary World* (Cleveland: Pilgrim Press, 1997), 121–25, for an insightful reflection on this calling, which they refer to as *creatio appellata*.

120. Ian Barbour provides a succinct overview on ways of talking about God informed by contemporary scientific findings; Ian Barbour, "Five Models of God and Evolution," in *Evolutionary and Molecular Biology: Scientific Perspectives on Divine Action* (Vatican City: Vatican Observatory, 1998), 419–42.

121. Arthur Peacocke tries out several analogies to characterize God's relationship to the world informed by contemporary evolutionary and molecular biology, including thinking about God as acting like a choreographer who leaves much of the dance to the dancers. See especially Arthur Peacocke, *Theology for a Scientific Age* (London: SCM Press, 1993).

122. See Paul Davies, *The Cosmic Blueprint* (New York: Simon & Schuster, 1988). See also Paul Davies, *The Mind of God* (New York: Simon & Schuster, 1992).

123. Schmitz-Moormann, *Theology of Creation.*

124. John F. Haught makes this point in *The Promise of Nature: Ecology and Cosmic Purpose* (New York: Paulist Press, 1993).

125. Principles that this reconstructed concept suggests for application to ecological problems include: (1) Encounter the subject reverently to avoid degrading its capacities to be fully itself according to its nature so it can mediate God; (2) preserve the subject so it can continue to be itself and thereby mediate God's presence and character in the future; (3) react cautiously and carefully when the subject threatens the health, domicile, and well-being of humans; (4) identify and implement rationales for relating to the subject so its natural functioning can reflect God's empowering character; (5) limit use of other components of the subject's ecological system in ways that assure their mutual sustenance so altogether they can reflect God's attributes; and (6) engage in ongoing efforts to identify and combat forces that thwart the discernment of the sacramental character of the subject.

126. The principle of subsidiarity should be followed so actions are taken at the most local level and referred to a higher levels when the lower level is inadequate to accomplish the goal. For an explanation of this ethical-political principle, including its first articulation by Pope Pius XI in *Quadragesimo Anno* and the teachings of Aquinas that served as a basis for this principle, see Benjamin S. Llamzon, "Subsidiarity: The Term, Its Metaphysics and Use," *Aquinas* 21 (January–April 1978): 44–62. Also see the many references to the principle of subsidiarity on social issues as discussed by the Pontifical Council for Justice and Peace, *Compendium of the Social Doctrine of the Church* (Washington, DC: United States Conference of Catholic Bishops, 2004).

127. E.g., see Aquinas, *Summa contra Gentiles,* 3.141, wherein he explains the use of material things as means to the ultimate end in God and never as ends. Also see ibid., 3.113; and Aquinas, *Summa theologiae,* 2–2.83.6; 18.1; 1–2.114.10.

128. Even in the thirteenth century, when teaching on the virtue of justice, Aquinas observed in *Summa theologiae*, 2–2.118.1 ad 2, that one individual cannot have an abundance of external riches without other individuals lacking them.

129. Too often in the economically developed areas of the world, consumption prompted by wanting and taking more than is needed to sustain life translates into excessive use by a few for their own self-interests and short-term gain while others go hungry, do not have adequate shelter or clothing, and are subjected to the perils of ecological abuse.

130. The Christian environmental ethicist Ted Nunez alerted me to contemporary high-technology images of the physical world while pressing his advocacy of bona fide experiences of nature.

131. United States Conference of Catholic Bishops, *Renewing the Earth: An Invitation to Reflection and Action on Environment in Light of Catholic Social Teaching* (Washington, DC: USCCB Publications, 1991), III-A.

132. Carolyn Merchant provides a perceptive historical overview of the dualistic and mechanistic world view of early modern science that sanctioned the exploitation of the physical world; Carolyn Merchant, *The Death of Nature: Women, Ecology and the Scientific Revolution* (San Francisco: Harper & Row, 1980).

133. June O'Connor, "Sensuality, Spirituality, Sacramentality," *Union Seminary Quarterly Review* 40 (1985): 59–70, at 61.

134. Ibid.; Rasmussen, *Earth Community*, 247, concludes that "an evolutionary sacramentalist cosmology offers the richest conceptual resources for addressing earth's distress, if infused with a profound earth asceticism and married to prophetic efforts aimed at 'the liberation of life,'" as advocated by Charles Birch and John B. Cobb Jr., *The Liberation of Life: From the Cell to the Community* (Denton, TX: Environmental Ethics Books, 1990).

135. A plethora of examples springs to mind. Among the most recent is by the biochemist Ursula Goodenough, *The Sacred Depths of Nature* (New York: Oxford University Press, 1998). Stephen J. Gould, *Wonderful Life: The Burgess Shale and the Nature of History* (New York: W. W. Norton, 1989), remains a favorite. Bruce Stutz editorialized recently on scientists' aesthetic appreciation for subjects of their study; see his "Divine Details," *Natural History* 108 (July–August 1999): 6.

136. John Hart insists insightfully that people who are open spiritually to the sacramentality of a place are able to see the signs of the divine presence through it; John Hart, *Sacramental Commons: Christian Ecological Ethics* (Lanham, MD: Rowman & Littlefield, 2006), xiii.

137. I draw upon an informative discussion of ritual that appears in "Ritual," by Margaret Mary Kelleher, OSU, in *The New Dictionary of Theology*, ed. Joseph A. Komonchak, Mary Collins, and Dermot A. Lane (Collegeville, MN: Liturgical Press, 1987), 906–7.

138. Douglas G. Adams, "Sacramental Worship for Creation Consciousness," in *Cry of the Environment*, ed. Philip N. Joranson and Ken Butigan (Santa Fe: Bear & Co., 1984), 430–35.

139. Noel J. Brown and Pierre Quiblier, eds., *Ethics & Agenda 21: Moral Implications of a Global Consensus* (New York: United Nations Environmental Program, 1994).

140. The term "sin" was applied explicitly to human degradation of the environment by a major religious leader when His All Holiness Bartholomew, Patriarch of the See of Constantinople, the mother church of Orthodox Christianity, was on a month-long

visit to the United States in 1997. Popularly known as the "green patriarch," Bartholomew told a symposium on religion, science, and the environment at an Orthodox church in Los Angeles: "To commit a crime against the natural world is a sin. . . . For humans to cause species to become extinct and to destroy the biological diversity of God's creation, for humans to degrade the integrity of the Earth by causing changes in its climate, stripping the Earth of its natural forests, or destroying its wetlands; . . . for humans to contaminate the Earth's waters, its land, its air, and its life with poisonous substances—these are sins." Larry B. Stammer, "Harming the Environment Is Sinful, Prelate Says," *Los Angeles Times,* November 2, 1997.

141. Theodore Runyon appeals for a theology of ecology and an ethic of responsibility which joins Christians to Christ's own redemptive work of bringing order out of ecological chaos; Theodore Runyon, "The World as the Original Sacrament," *Worship* 54 (November 1980): 495–511.

142. See, e.g., the overview, "Ritual," by Quentin Quesnell, in *New Dictionary of Theology,* ed. Komonchak, Collins, and Lane, 437–50.

143. According to Karl Rahner and Herbert Vorgrimler, God's self-communication is supernatural so humans do not have claim to it and could, in principle, be denied by God. Karl Rahner and Herbert Vorgrimler, "Grace," in *Dictionary of Theology,* rev. ed. (New York: Crossroad, 1990), 196–200, at 197. A more cogent way of thinking about God's gift of grace that deserves in-depth exploration in a dedicated article is to consider God as gratuitously offering grace continuously, to which the faithful can choose to be open and to receive. Taking that approach to grace avoids any inkling that God may be construed as capricious or preferential.

144. Particularly helpful is Quesnell's interpretation of Vatican II's implicit efforts on grace; Quesnell ,"Ritual," 447–49.

145. That grace is essentially God's freely imparted self-communication to the human being is drawn from a number of Roman Catholic sources, including Rahner and Vorgrimler, "Grace." Especially instructive and meaningful for the topic at hand is Rahner and Vorgrimler's stress on God's self-communication as actual grace permanently offered to humankind and as sustaining the act by which grace is freely accepted.

146. Aquinas's teachings on the moral virtues provide some fruitful avenues to explore for ecological ethics as indicated in the chapter below on living virtuously.

147. Joseph Sittler described grace for an ecological age: "Grace comes in black and white and yellow and red! Grace comes in colors. That is a quite different understanding of grace, for it is bound up with the unthinkable variety of God the Creator who loves all colors, textures, forms, nuances, and modes of life. It is grace as the joyful acknowledgment of the variety that God loves, the variety he has made." Joseph Sittler, "Ecological Commitment as Theological Responsibility," *Zygon* 5 (June 1970): 172–81, at 180–81.

148. Bonaventure, *The Soul's Journey,* 1.1, 59–60.

4

RESPECTING CREATION'S PRAISE FOR GOD

The imaginative concept of creation's praise for God in the Catholic tradition requires the reader to consider living organisms, bodies of water, terrains, air regimes, and cosmic phenomena as having "voices" with which they praise God and together as a chorus that praises God. Although the Bible and texts throughout the Christian tradition are replete with praises for God, reflections that affirm and call upon natural entities to praise God are scant. The few patristic and medieval theologians who thought about living and inanimate creatures as praising God often referred or alluded to the poetic and hymnic literature in the Old Testament, especially Psalm 148 and Daniel 3:57–81.

Today, the "voices" of many animate and inanimate beings cry out in anguish as they become endangered, altered by genetic manipulation, and destroyed by toxicants. The destruction of habitats under the guise of "progress" continues to accelerate the rate of species extinction, resulting in an alarming loss of biological diversity throughout the ecosystems of Earth. Some of these species are crucial to human life and well-being now and into the future, so the voice of *Homo sapiens* is also at risk.

Following the format of prior chapters, I examine the patristic and medieval texts in which theologians contemplate creatures' praise for God. Explained subsequently is how this concept coheres with our current understanding of the contributions that various biota and abiota make to ecosystems and the greater biosphere. In the concluding section, I explore the kind of human behavior that embracing this concept suggests.

Patristic and Medieval Sources

Saints Basil of Caesarea, Augustine of Hippo, Francis of Assisi, and John of the Cross thought about creatures as praising God according to their natures. Basil and John also explicitly reflected on all creatures as constituting a chorus that praises God by relating to one another as God intends. Each of their views is examined sequentially with reference to the biblical texts that inspired their reflections.

Saint Basil of Caesarea, the Languages of Creatures, and the Chorus of Creation

Basil of Caesarea (ca. 329–79) was one of the most prominent theologians who thought about creatures as giving praise to God according to their natures and all creatures together as constituting a chorus of praise for God. Within his third homily on the *Hexaemeron,* Basil examined Psalm 148 in which the hymnist calls upon the sun, moon, shining stars, Earth, sea monsters, fire and hail, snow and mist, storm winds, mountains and hills, orchards and cedars, wild animals and cattle, reptiles and birds, kings, nations, and all people to praise God.[1] Basil underscored the inclusiveness of this call to praise, noting that "even the deep" was not rejected by the psalmist for "even it harmoniously sings a hymn of praise to the Creator through the language assigned to it."[2] Each "language" is known by God who "approves them individually" in light of God's "final aim" for the natural world,[3] whereas their relationships with one another exhibit a "beauty of relationship"[4] in which they harmonize as "the general chorus of creation"[5]

For Basil, God is the creator of the chorus of creatures, each of which has been endowed with a language of its own. All are intended to harmonize with one another through their interrelationships, and all have been empowered by God to do so from the beginning of the world.[6] God is also the director of the chorus, calling it to fulfill its purpose by being itself and thereby giving glory to God.[7]

Saint Augustine's Exuberant Call for Creation to Praise God

In *Confessions,* after praising God profusely for the marvels of the natural world that God created, Augustine (354–430) followed the list of creatures in Ps. 148, asking God to also let them praise their Creator:

> Let me never say, "These things should not be!" If I considered them alone, I might desire better things; but still for them alone I ought to praise you. That you must be praised all these show forth: from the earth, dragons, and all the deeps, fire, hail, snow, ice, stormy winds, which fulfill your word, mountains and all hills, fruitful trees and all cedars, beasts and all cattle, serpents and feathered fowls; kings of the earth and all people, princes and all judges of the earth, young men and maidens, the old with the younger; let them praise your name. And from the heavens also let these praise you, let these praise you, our God, in the high places, all your angels, all your hosts, the sun and the moon, all stars and light, the heavens of heavens, and the waters that are above the heavens, let them praise your name.[8]

As he explained in *On Free Will,* creatures "praise God" by existing or acting according to their natures as God intended when creating them.[9] Further into *Con-*

fessions, Augustine connected his and creation's praise for God as a way of loving God. "Your works praise you, to the end that we may love you, and we love you to the end that your works may praise you."[10]

When commenting on Psalm 26 with its stress on hope in God, he referred to creatures as crying out "God" as their author in their assigned "voices":

> Let your mind roam through the whole creation; everywhere the created world will cry out to you: "God made me." Whatever pleases you in a work of art brings to your mind the artist who wrought it; much more, when you survey the universe, does the consideration of it evoke praise for its Maker. You look on the heavens; they are God's great work. You behold the earth; God made its numbers of seeds, its varieties of plants, its multitude of animals. Go round the heavens again and back to the earth, leave out nothing; on all sides everything cries out to you of its Author; nay the very forms of created things are as it were the voices with which they praise their Creator.[11]

Here Augustine linked the idea of creation's praise for God with creatures' disclosure of God. Only God could have created such marvels, Augustine insisted throughout his works, countering the teachings of Mani that material things are created by an evil principle whereas God creates spiritual things.

Saint Francis of Assisi's Poetic Calls

In "The Canticle of Brother Sun," Francis of Assisi (1181/82–1226) praised God through the moon, stars, water, fire, earth, and other natural entities.[12] He urged them to praise God directly in several other poems, often alluding to various psalms and the creation hymn in Daniel 3. For example, in "The Exhortation to the Praise of God," he urged heaven and earth (Psalm 68:35), rivers (Daniel 3:78), and the birds of the heavens (Daniel 3:80 and Psalm 148:10) to praise God. His most inclusive exhortation appeared in the prayer "Let Every Creature" where he called upon all creatures "in heaven, on earth, in the sea and in the depths" to give "praise, glory, honor, and blessing" to God who "suffered so much for us" and who "has given so many good things, and will do so for the future."[13] In "The Praises To Be Said at All the Hours," Francis conveyed his desire that the Friars Minor express their praise for a loving God and called upon "heaven and earth," and "every creature that is in heaven and on earth and under the earth and in the sea" to "praise and glorify" God "forever." Clearly, Francis of Assisi was striving to include all creatures in rendering praise to God.

Saint John of the Cross and the Symphony of Creation

A renowned mystic and founder of the Discaled Carmelites, John of the Cross (1542–91) contemplated the nature of the diverse voices of creatures and their harmonizing to provide a "symphony of sublime music" that surpasses "all concerts and melodies of the world."[14] Though not a medieval theologian, he poignantly extends Basil of Caesarea's thinking about the chorus of creation, so including John provides a more rich exposition of this concept.

According to John of the Cross, each creature is endowed with "a certain likeness of God" as the kind of entity God intended when creating it. Each "gives voice to what God is in it" through its God-given way to existing and/or functioning.[15] God is "in" the creature as the giver and foundation of its existence, and the creature's exercise of its innate capabilities is its "voice" through which it gives testimony to God. In "its own way, bearing God within itself according to its capacity," the creature conveys its "likeness of God" and thereby "magnifies God."[16]

John lauded the diversity of creatures' voices with which they praise God. "As each one possesses God's gifts differently, each one sings His praises differently."[17] Yet the mystic found great joy in the collective music of all creatures who together voice themselves. "All these voices form one voice of music praising the grandeur, wisdom, and wonderful knowledge of God," he exclaimed.[18] "All of them together form a symphony of love,"[19] one that is "continually" giving praise and testimony to God.[20]

Their collective music is "silent," however, at least to "the natural senses and faculties." It is silent because the chorus of voices constitutes "tranquil and quiet knowledge" of how all creatures voice themselves harmoniously "without . . . sound."[21] Key to understanding their music as "silent" is knowing that their voices harmonize to praise God by giving testimony to God as God's creation that exists and functions as God intends. Their collective voices testifying to God's presence in them constitute spiritual knowledge that the faithful have of God. They are means to knowing God, providing "sounding solitude for the spiritual faculties.[22]

The receiver of this "symphony of spiritual music" that creatures convey collectively "knows and enjoys" it.[23] However, as John of the Cross moved to creatures' spiritual significance, the knowledge of God that is received by the faithful through them is devoid of their natural characteristics: "When these spiritual faculties are alone and empty of all natural forms and apprehensions, they can receive in a most sonorous way the spiritual sound of the excellence of God, in Himself and in His creatures."[24] Knowledge of the collective harmony of creatures is interior. It is deep. It goes beyond the sensible to the spiritual. It is "tranquil wisdom that all creatures, higher and lower ones alike, according to what each in itself has received from God" magnify God together.[25]

Consonance between Patristic-Medieval Thinking and Contemporary Science

Creation's praise for God parallels the concepts of the goodness, beauty, and sacramentality of creation explored in the three preceding chapters. In each concept, every creature is important in itself and in relation to others, whereas the totality of creatures best conveys the underlying concept (e.g., the greatest good, supreme beauty, and best manifestation of God's presence and character).

That the praising concept shares this overall individual-collective approach should not be surprising, because these concepts are different ways in which patristic and medieval theologians expressed their faith about God's relation to the universe.

However, the praising concept tends to be more imaginative in requiring the faithful to think about all types of creatures—living and inanimate—as having "voices" through which they express themselves. Some of these expressions may be through actual vocalizations, but all creatures have ways of existing that are more than sound. One significant way of existing is relating to one another to constitute a grand chorus of all voices that harmonize in their praise of God by functioning according to their natures as God intends. Can this highly imaginative patristic-medieval concept resonate with our current understanding of the world?

Consonance with the Biosphere and the Gaia Theory

Thinking about all biota and abiota as constituting a harmonious chorus has consonance with the scientific understanding of the biosphere of Earth—the life-supporting stratum of Earth's surface that extends from a few kilometers into the atmosphere to the deep sea vents of the ocean where organisms derive energy and nutrients from nonliving components.[26] The biosphere is the area in which life evolved in increasing complexity after the geosphere—the inorganic area of the primitive Earth consisting of rock and soil (lithosphere), water (hydrosphere), and air (atmosphere)—was bombarded with energy by the sun and underwent chemical and physical reactions millions of years ago. This process eventually led to the emergence of the first form of life.

Today this zone of life contains myriad species that have evolved over time from single-celled organisms that interacted with the physical environment. Eventually these relationships lead to the formation of ecosystems[27] (e.g., forests, grasslands, lakes, and wetlands). Within these systems, the various biota interact continuously with abiota (e.g., soil, air, water, and minerals).[28] On the periphery of these ecosystems are ecotones, where a mixture of their components occurs. All these systems, with their plethora of biotic, abiotic, and system components, constitute the biosphere. As a type of biological life, humans are constituents of the biosphere along with members of other species, interact variously with them and the abiota within ecological and peripheral systems, and, by their actions, affect the biosphere—the dynamic zone of life.[29]

Some scientists are dissatisfied with focusing on the biosphere in light of the intricate relationship that biota have had with the geosphere historically and that they currently have in constituting one planet. Studies of the chemical composition of the atmosphere have been particularly compelling to this reality. To underscore the totality of Earth, James E. Lovelock, the British chemist and inventor of the electron capture detector,[30] proffered the hypothesis that living organisms regulate the atmosphere in their own interests to make Earth habitable for themselves.[31] The novelist William Golding suggested "Gaia," a name used in ancient Greece,[32] as Earth's appropriate name, and the "Gaia hypothesis" was introduced to the scientific community. As Lovelock explains in *The Ages of Gaia,* Gaia is Earth in its totality:

> The name of the living planet, Gaia, is not a synonym for the biosphere—that part of the Earth where living things are seen normally to exist. Still less is Gaia the same as the biota, which is simply the collection of all individual living organisms. The biota and the biosphere taken together form a part but not all of Gaia. Just as the shell is part of the snail, so the rocks, the air, and the oceans are part of Gaia. Gaia, as we shall see, has continuity with the past back to the origins of life, and in the future as long as life persists. Gaia, as a total planetary being, has properties that are not necessarily discernable by just knowing individual species or populations of organisms living together.[33]

Thus, Earth is a single living entity from the Gaian perspective.[34] In an interview, Lovelock explained the historical notion of Gaia and its significance for scientific study today:

> Most of us sense that the Earth is more than a sphere of rock with a thin layer of air, ocean and life covering the surface. We feel that we belong here as if this planet were indeed our home. Long ago the Greeks, thinking this way, gave to the Earth the name Gaia or, for short, Ge. In those days, science and theology were one and science, although less precise, had soul. As time passed this warm relationship faded and was replaced by the frigidity of the schoolmen. The life sciences, no longer concerned with life, fell to classifying dead things and even to vivisection. Ge was stolen from theology to become no more the root from which the disciplines of geography and geology were named. Now at last there are signs of a change. Science becomes holistic again and rediscovers soul, and theology, moved by ecumenical forces, begins to realise that Gaia is not to be subdivided for academic convenience.[35]

This new way of looking at Earth generated a storm of controversy among biologists and other scientists,[36] because finding plausible control mechanisms appeared elusive. Lovelock, the microbiologist Lynn Margulis—his primary collaborator[37]—and other scientists sought the missing links.[38] Their cumulative scientific research elevated the hypothesis to provisional theory status, as framed by Lovelock: "Organisms and their material environment evolve as a single coupled system, from which emerges the sustained self-regulation of climate and chemistry at a habitable state for whatever is the current biota."[39]

More specifically, the temperature, oxidation, state, acidity, and certain aspects of the rocks and waters are kept constant, and this homeostasis is maintained by active feedback processes operated automatically and unconsciously by the biota.[40] The Gaia theory postulates the need for a comprehensive description of Earth rather than taking the specialized, fragmented approach that is epitomized by the reductionistic way in which the individual sciences operate. Through this comprehensive perspective, the Gaia theory has been widely credited for having stimulated the development of Earth systems science, which requires a multidisciplinary approach to understanding our planet's biological and geophysical realms and their interactions.[41] One impressive example is the work of the eminent Canadian biochemist George Ronald Williams who has been exploring the molecular biology of Earth.[42] Other prominent investigations have been initiated by Earth systems scientists, who are discovering links between the activity of living entities and the physical environment.[43]

Lovelock's view of Earth also helped raise interest in the environment,[44] though, ironically, his notion of Earth as self-regulating may lead some to conclude that Gaia will fix any problems humans cause to the atmosphere. However, if all animals, plants, and the air, land, and water are considered parts of a single organism, the need to know about, respect, and protect all parts is essential for the organism to operate naturally. Human interference with one or more parts may disrupt or destroy the organism to a point that its self-regulatory capabilities are altered. However, the extent to which Earth's self-regulating capabilities can be altered by adverse human activities is difficult to predict due to the many variables that must be factored into scientific testing. Also worrisome are the effects that artificial and toxic materials humans are emitting into the air, depositing on the land, and flushing into the biosphere. Particularly problematic are two phenomena. One is the occurrence of holes in the ozone layer of the planet caused by emissions of chlorofluorocarbons and other chlorinated compounds into the atmosphere that open Earth to harmful rays from the sun.[45] The other highly problematic phenomenon is global warming, which occurs when carbon dioxide, methane, nitrous oxide, and other greenhouse gases are emitted into the air, trap excessive heat near the surface of Earth, cause glaciers to melt, sea levels to rise, and a plethora of other changes to the climate.[46]

When thinking about these and other problems from the perspective of the praising concept, holes in the ozone layer and excessive greenhouse gases are thwarting the capacity of Earth to praise God. Both the individual voices and the collective voices are adversely affected. To avoid thwarting their praise of God, directives are needed to guide human behavior.

Biospheric Ethics? Gaian Ethics?

Stimulated by scientific findings about the biosphere of Earth and Lovelock's more all-encompassing Gaia theory, some philosophers have attempted to develop a system of ethics that is geared toward Earth's well-being. The philosopher Paul Taylor has been at the forefront urging a system of "biocentric" ethics that focuses on the need to respect all living entities.[47] However, his system does not directly address abiota or the entire planet, though an argument could be made that protecting habitats, ecosystems, or the biosphere could result from actions taken to protect species.

Dorion Sagan and Lynn Margulis have argued for a Gaian ethic that is amorally "natural." According to this "ethic," all living entities exhibit "the urge to grow and reproduce and make the world over in their image."[48] They interact, readjust, and regulate the planet's physiology accordingly.[49] Human behavior becomes part of the "continuity" of life that flounders in "the ethical abyss" until Earth no longer exists in 5,000 million years.[50] There are no good or evil actions in this schematic, only amoral actions that feed into the self-regulation of the planet that is Gaia.

Thus, a Gaian ethic is not an ethic per se with moral norms to guide human behavior. Instead, a Gaian ethic from Sagan and Margulis's shared perspective seems to entail an acceptance of the inevitability that human actions will fit into the modulation of the Gaian environment. Their acceptance is both optimistic about Gaia's capacity to adjust to human actions and pessimistic about the human capacity to anticipate actions that might hinder Gaia's self-regulating capacity and to choose to avoid those actions.

Some environmental philosophers have explored other options for ethics based on thinking about the biosphere and the Gaia theory, but they have been found inadequate for one reason or another. For example, after carefully examining several possibilities, Anthony Weston finds inadequate an emphasis on the self-regulating powers of Earth to maintain a balance of life and prefers to stress human responsibility toward that end. He wisely points to the paradox that the "Gaian perspective" poses to environmental protection.[51] If our planet is considered capable of regulating itself, why impose limits on naturally present compounds like methane, which produces significant quantities of carbon monoxide, along with nitrous oxide and methyl chloride, which are known potent ozone depleters?[52]

Lovelock argues that the concept of atmospheric "pollution" may be "irrelevant in a Gaian context," because Earth has been adjusting to fluxes of atmospheric gases and particulates over time.[53] Though his approach to the addition of increasing amounts of gases and particulates to the atmosphere is not sufficiently cautious,[54] he has warned against degrading and destroying wetlands, rainforests, and other "vital organs" of Gaia.[55] He also has encouraged environmental engineering and the generation of electricity by nuclear fuel, despite the many hazards this technology poses at all levels of the fuel cycle to the disposition of highly radioactive spent fuel.

As Weston concludes astutely, ethics based on the Gaia theory "may undercut rather than reinforce many of the legal safeguards that environmentalists have established." Ethics based on the Gaia theory may also "knock the props out from under the utilitarian sorts of arguments that persuade most policy makers and the general public."[56] Other problems with ethics from a Gaian perspective include the difficulty in according value to individuals of species, to individual natural formations, deep bodies of water, and to ecosystems because of the Gaian focus on valuing Earth as a self-regulating totality. Although valuing the capability of Earth to regulate itself has merit, Weston asserts convincingly, "the Gaia hypothesis cannot ground a *complete* environmental ethic."[57] Nevertheless, though arguments can be made indirectly for respecting all components that contribute something essential in themselves and through their interactions with others to constitute the biosphere.

Other philosophers have explicitly or implicitly advocated treating Earth in a way that is analogous to individual persons who should be valued intrinsically and respected accordingly. From this perspective, Kenneth Goodpaster points to the biosphere's "integrated, self-sustaining unity" and its "successful self-protection," which make Earth enough like a person to warrant its respect.[58] Of course, Earth has other characteristics that parallel the characteristics of human persons and living nonpersons (e.g., amoeba and plants). Like Earth, they also have self-protective and sustaining features, so reasons for respecting Earth and human persons are restricted to the few to which Goodpaster points.[59] Although stretching a case for Earth's personhood, his approach at least expands the circle of respect that is usually reserved for humans. However, he leaves other animals and ecosystems on the periphery to be defended in other-than-person terms.

David Abram approaches the question of Gaian ethics by systematically exploring the implications of reflecting perceptively on Earth. Humans are literally parts of Earth, he insists. Our bodies are parts of the physiology of Earth, and we are constantly in "communion" with Earth through our senses.[60] If we live in the reality of our sensory communion with Earth, Abram explains we can know directly when Earth is stressed. We can be shocked. We can feel Earth's pain. Presumably, we will avoid causing further pain, ameliorate the circumstances that cause the pain, and prevent causing it in the future. Abram's approach to ethics from a Gaian perspective is commendable indeed.

However, as Weston notes, being lifelike enough to sense Earth's distress appears to be the criterion for respect, just as being personlike appeared to be Goodpaster's criterion for respect.[61] Inanimate entities are left out of the ethics picture, at least directly. A system of ethics that is responsive to Earth must encompass all of Earth's constituents—biota and abiota in themselves as individual types, in their interactions, and in their collective totality.

Some theological reflections on the Gaia theory have generated interest in identifying moral norms,[62] though a system of ethics that is responsive to the planet in its entirety has not been forthcoming. One possibility inspired by patristic and medieval teachings about creation's praise for God is the need to respect the voices of Earth's constituents so they can continue to praise God individually according to their natures and collectively as a chorus of many diverse voices that interact to constitute one planet.

Respecting Creation's Praise for God

With Basil, Augustine, Francis, and John of the Cross, we can assume that each creature has a unique "voice" with which it praises God.[63] With Basil and John, we can also assume that the greatest praise for God is raised when the voices of all creatures harmonize like a chorus. What behavior patterns emerge from this thinking? To respect humans and other-than-humans requires regarding them in high esteem and exhibiting behavior that demonstrates this esteem. A theological perspective requires a person who believes in God as the purposeful creator and active sustainer of the universe to respect the praise that creatures give to

God through their unique ways of existing and functioning. What kind of behavior would flow from extending this imaginative, biblically based tradition into the twenty-first century?

Respecting Animate and Inanimate Ways of Praising God

The ways in which other species, lands, waters, and airways praise God according to their natures will be respected. The faithful will "listen" to their voices with an openness to recognizing their distinctive characteristics. They will recognize how species and abiota function according to their natures. They will recognize their need for space within which to praise God. Actions appropriate to their continuing to praise God will be taken, and actions that inhibit their praise will be avoided.

Respecting the Interacting Voices

The faithful will maintain a posture of respect for the interactions of air, land, water, and types of biological life that constitute grasslands, lake basins, coral systems, mountain ranges, river valleys, deserts, wetlands, and other ecosystems. They will be respected for their interacting "voices" through which they praise God. Destructive logging practices in forests, development projects in wetlands, the introduction of invasive species to the land and water, and other inhibitors of the natural praise that constituents of ecosystems give to God will no longer be allowed.[64]

Respecting the Biosphere's Capacity to Praise God

The biosphere will be respected for its collection of ecosystems and ecotones that together praise God as one chorus. The faithful will share the sentiments of the astronauts who expressed their respect for Earth when viewed from outer space. As the U.S. astronaut Loren Acton exclaimed: "Looking outward to the blackness of space, sprinkled with the glory of a universe of lights, I saw majesty—but no welcome. Below was a welcoming planet. There, contained in the thin, moving, incredibly fragile shell of the biosphere is everything that is dear to you, all the human drama and comedy. That's where life is; that's where all the good stuff is."[65] Representing the former USSR, the cosmonaut Aleksei Leonov remarked: "The Earth was small, light blue, and so touchingly alone, our home that must be defended like a holy relic. The Earth was absolutely round. I believe I never knew what the word round meant until I saw Earth from space."[66] They were awed by Earth, the unique blue planet within our solar system, and they were motivated to protect their home.

While these astronauts were exclaiming their awe of Earth, panels of scientists in increasing numbers have been issuing warnings about global warming and other threats to the biosphere.[67] Their findings show that Earth's voice is being squelched by excessive greenhouse gases emitted from clearing the land and burning fossil fuels to run cars, factories, and electricity generation facilities. Carbon dioxide and other greenhouse gases emitted through human activities are accumulating in the atmosphere, where they act like a blanket to keep Earth warm and heat up the surface of the land, oceans, and air. The ramifications of this global warming appear significant for all ecosystems and the biosphere, because ecosystems are "moderately to highly sensitive to changes in climate," with effects likely to include harmful changes to some systems that precipitate beneficial changes to other systems. Enhanced-growth scenarios occur under the least amount of simulated global warming, whereas the severe decline or dieback scenarios occur under the greatest projected global warming.[68]

Human actions that cause Earth's temperature to increase are disrupting its cumulative voice. Instead of blending into a symphony of praise for God, the voices of Earth are disparate. They bleat in a cacophony. They are hoarse and harsh due to the excessive amounts of carbon dioxide and other greenhouse gases that humans are emitting into the atmosphere. Earth groans in travail as it waits for redemption from the degradation that humans are inflicting on its voice. A transformation in human thought and action is essential to allow Earth's praise of God.

Adding the Human Voice to the Chorus of Creation

A conscious effort to add the human voice to all other living and nonliving creatures' praise for God will launch the transformation of human thinking and action that is needed today. Believers who contribute their voices will minimize the disharmony that has distorted and squelched the voices of other species, abiota, and ecosystems. Dissonance in the chorus will be curtailed when the faithful implement appropriate measures in their homes, their modes of travel, and their places of work. Dissonance in the chorus will also be curtailed when the faithful clamor for administrative and legislative efforts at appropriate levels of government to address the accelerated rate of species extinction, ecosystem degradation and destruction, and threats to the biosphere.

From this concept's perspective, human disrespect for individual and cumulative voices of the biosphere constitutes disrespect for God. God is due to be praised by all creatures through their collective voices. When humans do not add their voices to the praise for God given by other biota and abiota according to their natures, the praise that is due to God is incomplete.

Conclusion

Some sources in the Catholic theological tradition celebrate the notion that all creatures praise God according to their natures, while the totality of creatures praise God as one chorus. Basil of Caesarea, Augustine of Hippo, Francis of Assisi, and John of the Cross are major contributors to this creative thinking. Informing their reflections with recent scientific findings suggests a type of behavior that can guide the faithful in living more compatibly with other creatures of Earth. Embracing this behavior will lead to respecting ways in which species, land, atmosphere, and waterways praise God according to their physical makeup, respecting the ways in which they interact to constitute ecosystems, and respecting the biosphere's ability to praise God as a functioning collective of all constituents of Earth. The collective is complete when the human voice is added through actions that harmonize with all living and nonliving beings that constitute Earth.

Unfortunately, Earth's ability to express itself is being thwarted by human activities. By alerting the faithful to thinking about Earth as a "chorus" that unifies all the various voices of our planet in praising God, they may be inspired to blend their voices with the more-than-human others, complete the chorus, and sing joyfully through their attitudes, thoughts, and actions.

Notes

1. Psalm 148, Cosmic Hymn of Praise. An informative and illuminating exegesis of Psalm 148 is provided by Terence E. Fretheim, "Nature's Praise of God in the Psalms," *Ex Auditu* 3 (1987): 16–30, which includes a critical history of various interpretation of the psalm; points to thinking in the rest of the Old Testament that illumines the psalmist's suggestion of God's call–response relationship to the more-than-human world; and concludes with a sanguine, poignant, and ecologically sensitive reflection on the interaction of human and other beings in praising God. Also see Duane Warden, "All Things Praise Him (Psalm 148)," *Restoration Quarterly* 35 (1993): 101–8. See also Ps 65:13–14, where valleys shout for joy; Ps 66:1–4 and Ps 89:6, where the whole earth worships God; and Ps 68:9, where nature, like man, fears God and trembles in God's presence.

2. Saint Basil, *On the Hexaemeron,* in *Exegetic Homilies,* trans. Sister Agnes Clare Way (Washington, DC: Catholic University of America Press, 1963), 3–150, esp. homily 3.9, at 52–53. Basil exclaimed that even the waters above the heavens (waters that yield rain, snow, sleet, and hail) are "sometimes invited to praise the common Master of the universe."

3. Ibid., 3.10, 53.

4. Ibid., 3.9, 53.

5. Ibid., 52–53.

6. Ibid.

7. Ibid., 3.10, 53.

8. Saint Augustine, *The Confessions of St. Augustine,* trans. John K. Ryan (Garden City, NY: Image Books, 1960), 7.13.19, 172–73. Though this truly great work consists primarily of Augustine's confessions of his sins, vices, temptations, and intellectual errors, it also serves as a profession of his profound faith and trust in God. He wrote this text shortly after becoming Bishop of Hippo in 396 CE. Through it, the African Christians who constituted his flock and who tended to idealize their bishops would know him; his struggles, which led him eventually to embrace Christianity; and his understanding of God.

   Regarding the waters above the heavens that are called to praise God, Augustine adopted the ancient psalmist's world view in which the sky was encased in a firmament, holding the rain, hail, and snow until sluices in the firmament released them. He discussed elsewhere the plausibility of the existence of waters above the heavens as depicted in the Hebrew Old Testament and bows to the authority of scripture while finding an allegorical interpretation where there is conflict with the Greek science of the day. See, e.g., *On the Literal Interpretation of Genesis/De Genesi ad litteram*, 2.5, 1.19. See, further, J. L. E. Dryer, "Medieval Cosmology," in *Theories of the Universe: From Babylonian Myth to Modern Science,* ed. Milton K. Munitz (New York: Macmillan Publishers, 1957), 115–38, at 120.

9. Augustine, *On Free Will*, in *Augustine: Earlier Writings,* trans. John H. S. Burleigh (Philadelphia: Westminster Press, 1953), 3.15.42, 196.
10. Augustine, *Confessions,* 13.33.48, 367.
11. Augustine, *On the Psalms,* Ancient Christian Writers, vol. 29 (New York: Newman Press, 1960), 272.
12. Saint Francis of Assisi, "The Canticle of Brother Sun," in *Francis and Clare: The Complete Works,* trans. Regis J. Armstrong, OFM, and Ignatius C. Brady, OFM (New York: Paulist Press, 1982), 37–38.
13. Francis of Assisi, "Let Every Creature," in *Francis and Clare,* 71.
14. Saint John of the Cross, "The Spiritual Canticle," in *The Collected Works of St. John of the Cross,* trans. Kieran Kavanaugh, OCD, and Otilio Rodriguez, OCD (Washington, DC: ICS Publications, 1973), para. 25, 472–73.
15. Ibid., 472.
16. Ibid., 473.
17. Ibid., para. 26, 473.
18. Ibid., para. 27, 473.
19. Ibid., para. 26, 473.
20. Ibid.
21. Ibid., paras. 25–26, 472–73.
22. Ibid., paras. 26, 473.
23. Ibid., paras. 25–26, 472–73.
24. Ibid., para. 26, 473.
25. Ibid., para. 27, 473.
26. Parallels may also be found with well-defined ecosystems that are addressed and demonstrated in chapter 5, on the functional unity of creation concept.
27. When emphasis is placed on the interaction of biotic and abiotic components of an area, the term "ecosystem" is appropriate, whereas "community" places emphasis on the population of species while excluding the abiotic factors.
28. The abiotic, or nonliving, constituent of each ecosystem in the biosphere includes the flow of energy, nutrients, water, and gases and the concentrations of organic and inorganic substances in the environment. The biotic, or living, portion includes three general categories of organisms based on their methods of acquiring energy: the primary producers, largely green plants; the consumers, which include all the animals; and the decomposers, which include the microorganisms that break down the remains of plants and animals into simpler components for recycling in the biosphere.
29. "Biosphere," *Encyclopædia Britannica,* Encyclopædia Britannica Online, http://search.eb.com/eb/article-9117266. See also Mitchell B. Rambler, Lynn Margulis, and René Fester, eds., *Global Ecology: Towards a Science of the Biosphere* (New York: Academic Press, 1989) in which the biosphere and the processes that occur within

it are described and interpreted; Richard J. Huggett, *Climate, Earth Processes, and Earth History* (New York: Springer Press, 1991), on the changing biosphere over time; *Environmental Evolution: Effects of the Origin and Evolution of Life on Planet Earth,* ed. Lynn Margulis, Clifford Matthews, and Aaron Haselton, 2nd ed. (Cambridge, MA: MIT Press, 2000), on the interaction of life and the abiota as life evolved and changes were made to the biosphere; and William K. Purves, David Sadava, Gordon H. Orians, and H. Craig Heller, *Life: The Science of Biology,* 7th ed. (Sunderland, MA: Sinauer Associates and W. H. Freeman, 2003), which deals in part with theories about the origin of life.

30. A device used in gas chromatography that can detect minuscule amounts of chemical compounds in the atmosphere and elsewhere on Earth. This device, which is 1 million times more sensitive than thermal conductivity detectors, made possible the detection of chlorofluorocarbons, other halogenated compounds, and nitrous oxide, which revolutionized our understanding of the atmosphere and pollutants. See the autobiography by James Lovelock, *Homage to Gaia: The Life of an Independent Scientist* (New York: Oxford University Press, 2000), for accounts of his many outstanding contributions to understanding the atmosphere and pollutants, including his establishment of first atmospheric halocarbon monitoring station in Ireland, his detection of trace quantities of polychlorinated biphenyls (PCBs) and organic mercury compounds that facilitated the development of environmental protection policies, methods of analyzing lunar soil, and investigation of the possibility of life on Mars.

31. Lovelock worked on the Gaia hypothesis in the 1960s, formally initiated it in 1972, and explained it at length in 1979 in *Gaia: A New Look at Life on Earth* (New York: Oxford University Press, 1979). Lovelock subsequently collaborated with the American biologist Lynn Margulis in further developing the hypothesis. In addition to Lovelock's *Homage to Gaia,* see James Lovelock, *The Ages of Gaia A Biography of Our Living Earth* (New York: W. W. Norton, 1989); and James Lovelock, *Gaia and the Theory of the Living Planet* (Eastbourne, U.K.: Gardners Books, 2005).

32. James Lovelock, "The Living Earth," *Nature* 426 (December 18–25, 2003): 769–80, at 769.

33. Lovelock, *Ages of Gaia,* 19.

34. Anthony Weston, "Forms of Gaian Ethics," *Environmental Ethics* 9 (Fall 1987): 217–30.

35. James Lovelock, "What Is Gaia?" James Lovelock's website, www.ecolo.org/lovelock/what_is_Gaia.html. See also Anna Primavesi, *Gaia's Gift: Earth, Ourselves, and God after Copernicus* (New York: Routledge Publishing, 2003); and Lawrence E. Joseph, *Gaia: The Growth of an Idea* (New York: St. Martin's Press, 1990).

36. The Gaia hypothesis and its upgrade to theory status have been viewed both favorably and unfavorably in the overviews by Stephen Schneider, "What Gaia Hath Wrought: The Story of a Scientific Controversy," *Technology Review* 92, no.5 (July 1989): 54–61; and Stephen Schneider, "Debating Gaia," *Environment* 32 (May 1990): 4–9, 29–32. Specific examples of criticisms by scientists are found in *Scientists on Gaia,* ed. Stephen H. Schneider and Penelope J. Boston (Cambridge, MA: MIT Press, 1991); and *Scientists Debate Gaia: The Next Century,* ed. Stephen H. Schneider (Cambridge, MA: MIT Press, 2004).

37. Especially see Lynn Margulis, *Symbiotic Planet: A New Look at Evolution* (New York: Basic Books, 1998); also see Lynn Margulis, *Slanted Truths: Essays on Gaia, Symbiosis, and Evolution* (New York: Copernicus Press, 1997). And see the overview by Jane

Bosveld, "Life according to Gaia: Cooperation, Not Competition, May Drive Evolutionary Diversity on Earth," *Omni* 14, no. 1 (October 1991): 66–70.

38. See, e.g., Connie Barlow and Tyler Volk, "Gaia and Evolutionary Biology," *BioScience* 42, no. 9 (October 1992): 686–93; and Richard A. Kerr, "No Longer Willful, Gaia Becomes Respectable," *Science* 240 (April 22, 1988): 393–95.

39. Lovelock, "Living Earth," 769.

40. Lovelock, *Ages of Gaia*.

41. Ronald E. Martin, "Gaia Out of Equilibrium?" *Bioscience* 55, no. 9 (September 2005): 799–81.

42. George Ronald Williams, *The Molecular Biology of Gaia* (New York: Columbia University Press, 1996), www.netlibrary.com.libus.csd.mu.edu/Reader/. As indicated in his prologue, Williams proposes looking for the beginnings of life "among the molecular processes that introduce the simple molecules of the inorganic environment into the complex chemistry of living systems" (p. xii). He admits that finding "a causal path from a change in the interatomic relationships in a particular enzyme to the level of cellular function . . . has never been easy," but "to extend that chain of cause and effect to the ecological level will be that much harder—and even more difficult when we move to the global level." Unless some evidence can be "convincingly displayed" about the role of molecular regulation of ecosystem behavior, "Gaia may remain a fringe idea in a biological counterculture." Williams contributed to the first Gaia Congress held in 1988; see George Ronald Williams, "Gaian and Nongaian Explanations for the Contemporary Level of Atmospheric Oxygen," in *Scientists on Gaia,* ed. Schneider and Boston, 167–73.

43. An earlier overview is Bosveld, "Life according to Gaia," 68–70. In-depth studies are provided by Timothy M Lenton, "Gaia and Natural Selection," *Nature* 394, no. 6692 (July 30, 1998): 439, in which the feedback mechanisms stemming from naturally selected traits of organisms are considered as a source for the planet's self-regulation; Earth's "biogeochemical" processes are explored by Tyler Volk, *Gaia's Body: Toward a Physiology of Earth* (Cambridge, MA: MIT Press, 2003); and Simon A. Levin, "Self-Organization and the Emergence of Complexity in Ecological Systems," *Bioscience* 55, no. 12 (December 2005): 1075–79. Information about the scientific investigations through the Earth Observing System is provided by Patricia D. Lock, "EOS and Terra: Seeing Earth as a System," *Odyssey* 13, no. 2 (February 2004): 14–15.

44. See William Cooper, "Scenes from Science: Who's for Gaia?" *The Spectator,* March 3, 1990, 23; Stephen H. Schneider, "Debating Gaia," *Environment* 32 (May 1990): 4–9, 29–32; Samanta Sen, "Environment: A People's Move to be Heard at Johannesburg Summit," Global Information Network, March 29, 2002, 1; and "Friends of the Earth: African NGOs Tell Ministers to Say No to Terminator Technology," M2 Presswire, February 17, 2006. Fred Pearce notes that Lovelock criticized environmentalists for being too concerned with narrow issues instead of focusing on the planet as a whole; Fred Pearce, "A Hero for the Greens?" *New Scientist,* September 23, 1989, 63. Joseph notes in *Gaia: The Growth of an Idea,* 153–55, that Lovelock discovered the accumulation of chlorofluorocarbons (CFCs) in Earth's atmosphere, but for two decades scorned environmentalists' and scientists' warnings linking CFCs to depletion of the ozone layer. See Lovelock's, *Homage to Gaia,* 191–93, 206–40, regarding his use of the electron capture detector to find how CFCs were accumulating in the atmosphere—a discovery that lead to the Montreal Protocol and the ban on releasing CFCs into the atmosphere.

45. See, e.g., "Earth's Ozone Layer Starting to Heal," Environmental News Service, May 8, 2006, www.ens-newswire.com/ens/may2006/2006-05-08-05.asp. This article reports on a paper by Betsy Weatherhead of the U.S. National and Oceanic and Atmospheric Administration and Signe Bech Andersen of the Danish Meteorological Institute in which the authors document a leveling off of ozone depletion since 1987 when the Montreal Protocol was signed, calling for the phasing out, production, and consumption of chlorofluorocarbons, halons, carbon tetrachloride, and methyl chloroform. The United States is among the 180 nations that have endorsed the protocol since it was initially signed.

46. See the three volumes by the United Nations' Intergovernmental Panel on Climate Change, *Climate Change 2007* (Cambridge: Cambridge University Press, 2007), accessible at www.ipcc.ch/ipccreports/index.htm.

47. Paul Taylor, *Respect for Nature: A Theory of Environmental Ethics* (Princeton, NJ: Princeton University Press, 1986). Also see the perceptive probing of Taylor's biocentric ethics by Joseph Claude Evans, *With Respect for Nature: Living as Part of the Natural World* (Albany: State University of New York Press, 2005), esp. 77–128; Mikael Stenmark, *Environmental Ethics and Policy-Making* (Burlington, VT: Ashgate, 2002), 64–79; Ian Barbour, *Ethics in an Age of Technology* (San Francisco: HarperSanFrancisco, 1993), 61–62; and a practical application by Douglas E. Booth, *Biocentric Environmental Values and Support for the Ecological Restoration of an Urban Watersheds* (Milwaukee: Institute for Urban Environmental Risk Management, Marquette University, 2000).

48. Dorion Sagan and Lynn Margulis, "Gaia and the Ethical Abyss: A Natural Ethic Is a G[o]od Thing," in *The Good in Nature and Humanity: Connecting Science, Religion, and Spirituality with the Natural World,* ed. Stephen R. Kellert and Timothy J. Farnham (Washington, DC: Island Press, 2002), 91–102, at 97.

49. Ibid.

50. Ibid., 100.

51. Weston, "Forms of Gaian Ethics," 220.

52. Especially see Lovelock, *Gaia,* 110, where he laments human ignorance about planetary control systems within which associations of species "co-operate to perform some essential regulatory functions" including the adaptation of species to then-present levels of methyl iodide.

53. Ibid., 110.

54. James Lovelock and Michael Allaby, *The Greening of Mars* (New York: St. Martin's Press, 1984). The authors propose exporting Gaia's planetary-homeostatic mechanisms to reconstitute Mars' atmosphere. Lovelock has also been a foremost advocate of the nuclear generation of electricity as indicated, e.g., in the unsigned newspaper article "James Lovelock: Nuclear Power is the Only Green Solution," *The Independent,* May 24, 2004, www.ecolo.org/media/articles/articles.in.english/love-indep-24-05-04.htm; and James Lovelock, "Nuclear Energy: The Safe Choice for Now," www.ecolo.org/lovelock/nuclear-safe-choice-05.htm.

55. Lovelock, *Gaia,* 118–20.

56. Weston, "Forms of Gaian Ethics," 220.

57. Ibid., 221.

58. Kenneth Goodpaster, "From Egoism to Environmentalism," in *Ethics and Problems of the 21st Century,* ed. K. E. Goodpaster and K. M. Sayre (Notre Dame, IN: Notre Dame University Press, 1979), 21–35; a primary example of Earth's "self-sustaining

unity" is putting solar energy to work "in the service of the planet's "growth and maintenance." See also Kenneth Goodpaster, "On Being Morally Considerable," in *Ethics and the Environment,* ed. Donald Scherer and Thomas Attig (Englewood Cliffs, NJ: Prentice-Hall, 1983), 30–40; and Peter Bunyard, "The Gaia Hypothesis and Man's Responsibility to the Earth," *The Ecologist* 13, no. 5 (1983): 158–59.

59. Other distinguishing characteristics include self-awareness and some capacity for making informed decisions and acting autonomously.

60. David Abram, "The Perceptual Implications of Gaia," *The Ecologist* 15, no. 3 (1985): 96–103, at 98. Abram shares an impressive treatment of the impetus that a deep, sensual experience with Earth can lead to identifying ways of living ethically in *The Spell of the Sensuous: Perception and Language in a More-than-Human World* (New York: Pantheon Books, 1996).

61. Weston, "Forms of Gaian Ethics," 228.

62. Rosemary Radford Ruether, *Gaia & God: An Ecofeminist Theology of Earth Healing* (San Francisco: HarperSanFrancisco, 1992). See also Celia Deane-Drummond, *A Handbook in Theology and Ecology* (London: SCM Press, 1996), 98–114; Celia Deane-Drummond, *Biology and Theology Today: Exploring the Boundaries* (London: SCM Press, 2001), 165–83; Alister E. McGrath, *The Re-enchantment of Nature: Science, Religion and the Human Sense of Wonder* (London: Hodder & Stoughton, 2003), 26–52; and Anne Primavesi, *Sacred Gaia: Holistic Theology and Earth System Science* (New York: Routledge, 2000).

63. Among the principles that stimulate thinking about the concept of creation's praise for God are: (1) Respect the way in which the subject praises God in its unique "voice" according to its nature; (2) respect the praise that the subject and the constituents with which it interacts give praise to God through their interactions and avoid interfering with their praise; (3) respect the biosphere's capacity to praise God and avoid interfering with its cumulative praise; and (4) add the human voice to the chorus of the other "voices" giving praise to God. This imaginative concept should stimulate imaginative principles that can be added to this list.

64. Pacific Northwest Research Station, "Meeting the Challenge: Invasive Plants in Pacific Northwest Ecosystems," www.fs.fed.us/pnw/calendar/invasive-plants/index.shtml.

65. Calvin J. Hamilton, "Earth from Space: Quotes from Astronauts," www.solarviews.com/eng/earthsp.htm#quote. For the U.S. astronaut James Irwin, "the Earth reminded us of a Christmas tree ornament hanging in the blackness of space. As we got farther and farther away it diminished in size. Finally it shrank to the size of a marble, the most beautiful marble you can imagine. That beautiful, warm, living object looked so fragile, so delicate, that if you touched it with a finger it would crumble and fall apart. Seeing this has to change a man, has to make a man appreciate the creation of God and the love of God." Another U.S. astronaut, Edgar Mitchell, shared this reaction: "Suddenly, from behind the rim of the moon, in long, slow-motion moments of immense majesty, there emerges a sparkling blue and white jewel, a light, delicate sky-blue sphere laced with slowly swirling veils of white, rising gradually like a small pearl in a thick sea of black mystery. It takes more than a moment to fully realize this is Earth . . . home." And Ulf Merbold of the Federal Republic of Germany stated: "For the first time in my life I saw the horizon as a curved line. It was accentuated by a thin seam of dark blue light—our atmosphere. Obviously this was not the ocean of air I had been told it was so many times in my

life. I was terrified by its fragile appearance." Finally, Taylor Wong of China and the United States said: "A Chinese tale tells of some men sent to harm a young girl who, upon seeing her beauty, become her protectors rather than her violators. That's how I felt seeing the Earth for the first time. I could not help but love and cherish her."

66. Ibid.

67. E.g., by initiation in 1988 of the United Nations Environment Program and the World Meteorological Organization, the Intergovernmental Panel on Climate Change brought together 2,500 of the world's leading scientists to assess the scientific and technical literature on climate change, the potential impacts of changes in climate, and options for adaptation to and mitigation of these changes. Since its inception, the panel has produced a series of assessment reports, special reports, technical papers, methods of assessment, and other products that have become standard works of reference widely used by policymakers, scientists, and other experts. The various reports are accessible from www.ipcc.ch/ipccreports/index.htm.

68. Intergovernmental Panel on Climate Change, "Summary for Policymakers," in *The Regional Impacts of Climate Change: An Assessment of Vulnerability,* ed. R. T. Watson, M. C. Zinyowera, and R. H. Moss (Cambridge: Cambridge University Press, 1998), www.ipcc.ch/ipccreports/sres/regional/512.htm. Many uncertainties persist in calculating the long-term effects.

5

COOPERATING WITHIN THE INTEGRITY OF CREATION

Patristic and medieval reflections on the integrity of creation build upon the goodness concept by recognizing the instrumental interactions among animate and inanimate creatures that unify them. According to the theologians of these periods, God equipped, empowered, and continuously sustains the universe with the capability of functioning to sustain itself internally. After exploring their teachings about the integrity of creation, I turn to a detailed description of a site in France during the twelfth century that depicts cooperative human interactivity with other entities of the area. Following this exposition is a discussion of the need to adjust patristic-medieval understanding to reflect current knowledge about the functioning of ecosystem constituents when the human species is considered one type of biota that ineracts with other species and abiota (land, air, and water). Acting cooperatively out of a desire to cooperate with God is the human behavioral trajectory suggested by the reconstructed concept.

Patristic and Medieval Theologians

Alluding occasionally to the orderly composition of the world, as indicated in the Genesis 1 story of creation and in Psalm 103, patristic and medieval theologians reflected on how God intends creatures to function in relation to one another in order to constitute an orderly cosmos. Among these theologians are Saint Basil of Caesarea, Saint Augustine, Pseudo-Dionysius, John Scotus Eriugena, and Saint Thomas Aquinas. Each theologian's contribution to this topic is explored for its significance in advancing the integrity of creation concept.

Saint Basil on the Fellowship of Creatures

Reflecting on the Genesis 1 story of creation, Basil of Caesarea (330–79) described God as creating the world by speaking, knowing what the world needed to function in the future, giving directions for how it should function, and empowering it to function accordingly at the beginning of time.[1] Among Basil's examples are

God's empowerment of Earth to bring forth, grow, and sustain vegetation[2] and animals of all types, and Earth's response.[3] When explaining God's foresight in assuring that the world would have sufficient water, which, with fire, is needed for terrestrial life, Basil taught: "He who disposes all things by weight and by measure (for, "easily numbered by Him are even the drops of rain," according to Job)[4] knew how long a time He had appointed to the world for its continuance, and how much had to be set aside from the first for consumption by the fire. This is the explanation for the superabundance of water in creation."[5] God knew what God was doing when creating the world, Basil insisted. God spoke, and the world responded accordingly, fully equipped by God with the capacity to function as God intends.

Basil was enamored with the cooperative interactions of the diverse entities God created. From his patristic view of the world, he insisted that God intentionally designed the universe of many different creatures to relate appropriately to one another. Together, they constitute "an unbroken bond of attraction into one fellowship and harmony."[6] The world is a "mighty" and "elaborate system" that was brought to "perfection" through powers established in the world by God at the beginning of creation.[7] From this bishop's perspective, God empowered all creatures with innate capacities to function in relation to one another in orderly ways through the end of time.

For Basil, creation acts throughout time with its God-given capacities to carry out God's will. Yet God is not distant from the world. The Holy Spirit remains with the world, preparing it to do as the Creator intends. Interpreting the Genesis 1:2 depiction of the Spirit hovering above the waters, Basil explained that the Spirit was "preparing the nature of water for the generation of living beings" like "a bird brooding upon eggs and imparting some vital power to them so they are being warmed."[8] God remained intimately with creation, according to Basil, nurturing the world's productivity through the Holy Spirit without interfering in or disrupting its internal functioning.

As the historian of science Christopher B. Kaiser contends, the relative autonomy of the world to function with the capacities that God gave to it at the beginning of creation had already been "clearly fixed" in the Hellenistic-Jewish-Christian tradition that Basil inherited.[9] Basil continued this tradition, insisting that the world is only relatively autonomous because it depends on God's sustaining it in existence.

Saint Augustine on the Commonwealth of Creatures

Augustine of Hippo (354–430) shared Basil's view of the internal integrity of the universe and its ability to function through its God-given capabilities. Like Basil, Augustine attributed the orderly universe to God's will. He focused on the changeable nature of the universe, "the order of things in the heavens, on the earth, and in the sea," and pointed to the unchangeable wisdom of God as the source.[10] In this order of creatures, "grosser and lower" material bodies are "directed in a certain order by subtler and stronger bodies" (e.g., the irrational by the rational), and the will of God is the commander of the order of all things in relation to one another:

> The will of God is the first and the highest cause of all the forms and movements of the corporeal being. For nothing happens in a visible and sensible manner, throughout the most immense and boundless commonwealth of all creation, that is not commanded or permitted by that inner, invisible, and spiritual court of the supreme ruler, in accordance with the ineffable justice of His rewards and punishments, and of His graces and retributions.[11]

God remains active but "hidden" in governing the commonwealth of diverse creatures, Augustine instructed, by having established within the world the innate functioning of all terrestrial and celestial entities that act involuntarily, and by having empowered creatures who have the ability to act voluntarily to recognize God's hidden providence in and through created works.[12] To help creatures who can will their own actions to recognize God's presence, God produced "sensible and visible effects" in creatures of Heaven and creatures of Earth.[13] Recognizing God's presence through them serves as a reminder to affirm and deepen their faith in God and direct their actions toward God.

If, as Augustine taught, God is the ultimate source of the changes that occur in the world, what vehicle did God use to enable the world to make ordinary changes without God's direct intervention in the world's functioning? Reflecting on the Genesis 1 story of creation,[14] Augustine explained that God instilled rational "seeds" in the world at the time of creation that remained hidden in the corporeal elements of the world. These seed-like principles make possible the generation of specific visible entities when the conditions suitable for their development occur.[15] Whatever becomes visible receives its first beginnings from hidden seeds, takes its own distinctive form, and grows gradually according to rules that have been fixed from the beginning of time when God created the world.[16]

Thus, for Augustine, the orderly world God created has within itself the God-given power to function internally, to generate living beings, and to facilitate their growth. God empowered the world to function in this way and sustains that ability.

Pseudo-Dionysius and Eriugena on God's Unifying Love

The sixth-century mystic Pseudo-Dionysius attributed the cohesive functioning of all creatures to God's unifying love.[17] Due to the existence of "the Good" who is God, all sentient creatures have "soul and life," all plants have "nourishment and life and motion," and all lifeless matter exists.[18] God causes and transcends them as "superabundant Life . . . [and] . . . wisdom,"[19] giving "Light" to the "highest and most perfect forms of being to the very lowest" while remaining above and beyond them. God "gives light to everything capable of receiving it," and "keeps them alive, [and] preserves and perfects them." God is responsible for nourishing living creatures, causing them to grow, "purifying them, and renewing them." God "loves all things in the superabundance of his goodness," by which all things were made, are brought together in perfection, and are held together.[20]

God, as the active cause and end of the universe, "returns all things" to God's self and "gathers together whatever may be scattered," Pseudo-Dionysius reflected. Each creature looks to God as its "divine Source and unifier of the sum total of things," and as "the agent of cohesion" for all creatures.[21] The many different entities that constitute the world relate harmoniously to one another according to their God-given natures. They have an "innate togetherness" in which they all intermingle and persist,[22] as God intends: "Subordinate is returned to superior, equal keeps company with equal, superior turns providentially to subordinate, each bestirs itself and all are stirred to do and to will whatever it is they do and will because of the yearning for the Beautiful and the Good."[23]

Creatures' desire and yearning for God unify them into "an alliance" that constitutes "a particular commingling" in God, Pseudo-Dionysius continued. Their commingling is "a capacity" that "preexists" through God, is dealt out by God, and "binds the things of the same order in a mutually regarding union" that "moves the superior to provide for the subordinate" and "stirs the subordinate in a return toward the superior."[24] They show "friendship" for one another that Pseudo-Dionysius describes as "inherent harmony." All are constituents of nature falling under the "laws of nature" that derive from "the universal system of nature" instituted by God.[25]

John Scotus Eriugena (810–ca. 877) shared Pseudo-Dionysius's thinking about the unifying action that God's love affects on all creation. Eriugena wrote about love as "a bond and chain by which the totality of all things is bound together in ineffable friendship and indissoluble unity." Love is "the end and quiet resting place of the natural motion of all things that are in motion." Love moves the higher entities to provide for the lower, those that are equal to influence one another, and the lower to turn to those above them. God is "the Cause of all love and is diffused through all things and gathers all things together into one and involves them in Himself in an ineffable Return," Eriugena reflected. All natural entities remain in "the pacific embrace of universal love" that "gathers all things together into the indivisible Unity [of God's self] and holds them inseparably together."[26]

Saint Thomas Aquinas on the Unifying Interactivity of Diverse Creatures

Aquinas approached the unity of all creatures from two intertwined perspectives—sacramental and functional. From the sacramental perspective, as discussed in chapter 3, Aquinas taught that God created the many diverse entities that exist in the universe to communicate the divine goodness and, thereby, better represent it than any one (or presumably several) creatures could.[27] From the functional perspective, he recognized the distinctiveness of natural entities from nonliving elements to the living vegetation, sensible/irrational creatures, and rational creatures that God created. Aquinas attributed their differences to God's having communicated various grades of goodness to establish a perfect universe, and he praised God's wisdom in ordering them to act in relation to one another to achieve the universe's common good—its functioning to maintain itself internally while God sustains the existence of the universe.[28] By functioning as God intended when creating the universe, it best reflects God's goodness.

How creatures function in relation to one another did not escape Aquinas's attention. They function through their interactivity. He posited four types of interactivity: (1) The causal activities of creatures when a higher or more capable cause acts on a lower cause or an inanimate entity, with the rational creature considered the highest actor due to the capacity to make and choose to carry out informed decisions; (2) their tendency toward finality, through which they achieve their purposes in a hierarchical relationship with one another (plants draw from the elements that constitute Earth, animals feed on plants, and humans feed on animals and plants); (3) their mutually beneficial activities, wherein lower creatures serve as sustenance for higher creatures and as means through which knowledge about God can be obtained[29] and higher creatures help, move, protect, or provide for lower creatures by enabling them to serve their purposes in the scheme of the universe;[30] and (4) their collaboration for the good of the whole.[31] By either acting or being acted upon, creatures are unified. They become a "community of creatures," as John Wright characterizes them perceptively from Aquinas's teachings.[32] Thomas Gilby portrays Aquinas's the unity of interacting constituents teachings on as "one organism" composed of "essential, integral or functional parts."[33]

Particularly intriguing for purposes of reflection during our age of widespread ecological degradation is the sense of cooperation that emerges among natural entities when the lower look to the higher for help and the higher provide for the lower. Aquinas used various versions of *cooperator*[34] to convey four distinct but related types of cooperation: (1) Creatures cooperate by acting or being acted upon according to their God-given natures for their individual and common good in conformity with the orderly world that God created and sustains;[35] (2) living creatures cooperate with God, their primary cause for existing, by acting as secondary agents on other creatures to carry out God's plan for the universe;[36] (3) God both operates on and cooperates with humans for their temporal and eternal good;[37] and (4) humans cooperate with God's grace by acting on others in ways that achieve good in temporal life as they seek their eternal good—eternal happiness with God.[38] These modes of cooperation are elaborated upon in chapter 10, laying out one example of a way of thinking about humans today in relation to one another, to other species, to ecosystems, and to the biosphere of Earth.

From Aquinas's medieval view of the world, the hierarchical arrangement and interaction of creatures are essential for the perfection of the universe. Each constituent contributes its own innate perfection to the universe by acting or being acted upon according to its nature,[39] the lower rung of the hierarchy serves the one above incrementally through the chain of being that culminates in rational creatures,[40] and their relationships together achieve the internal functioning of the universe that is its common internal good.[41] Although the integrity of the world's orderly functioning is its internal common good, the overall internal ordering is for the ultimate good of ordering all things to God[42] through human knowing and loving.[43] Humans also have the intellectual capacity to know the rational plan by which God directs one creature to the other, and they can participate more fully in God's providential activity by exercising the natural dominion God gave them over other creatures.[44] Aquinas taught that their natural dominion over other creatures is always subservient to God's absolute dominion over all.[45]

Unfortunately, Aquinas lamented, humans do not always use their intellectual abilities as God intends. Humans sometimes put aside their reasoning ability or allow it to be impeded by some passion,[46] seek good for themselves through means of their senses, and cause evil to occur. Failure to use their ability to reason and to seek the common good explains why evil is a majority occurrence in one species,[47] whereas the use of one's reasoning ability should lead the person to seek the created common good of all and, ultimately, the uncreated common Good who is God.[48]

Because Aquinas identified the finality of the universe with the finality of human moral activity, human sin violates in general not only the human's order in relation to God, as Wright explains, but also the order of the whole universe in relation to God.[49] Human sin violates the ordering of the universe in relation to God because the human is intended to function in ways that are conducive to the human position in the hierarchical order of creatures by using their intellectual abilities to know the common good and to will it accordingly.[50]

Like Athanasius,[51] Aquinas taught that humans who stray from the order of creation that is aimed ultimately toward God can be restored to that order through Jesus Christ.[52] As Wright explains: "Just as [human] sin is against the order of the whole universe to God, so the work of redemption affects the whole universe. . . . To restore the order of the universe to God while preserving the created and meritorious character of this activity, it was necessary that a man should be born who was also God."[53] Aquinas taught that Jesus Christ entered the universe to heal the disorder of the human fall from the order of creatures established by God. Through the Incarnation, Jesus became the head of creation and the common good of the universe.[54] He is the Savior through whom humans can be restored to their intended place within the order of the universe.

God provides the grace humans need to follow Christ, to do good works that will lead to happiness, to seek the common good, and to love God over one's self.[55] With the assistance of God's grace, humans can act in ways that are conducive to the common created good and seek their finality in the common uncreated Good. Thereby, the entire internal order of the universe can be restored and reordered in relation to its finality in God.

Summation

Patristic and medieval reflections on the integrity of creation conveyed a metaphysical understanding of how and why the world functions in an orderly fashion from a profound faith perspective in God as the world's purposeful creator and continuous sustainer. God lovingly endowed the world with everything it needs to function internally, and its proper functioning yields the common good of all. However, humans do not always choose to seek the common good, and thereby they disrupt the world's internal functioning. God lovingly offers them grace, through which they can seek the common good so the orderly world God created can function as God intends.

Although these religiously based reflections provide a conceptual understanding of how theologians thought the world functioned and why, a graphic depiction of the cooperative functioning of humans with other species and the natural environment is warranted to advance the purpose of this chapter. A twelfth-century text provides an example that is both informative and inspiring.

Description of Cooperative Activity at the Clairvaux Abbey

Discovered in the literature of the Cistercian Order founded by Saint Bernard of Clairvaux, *Descriptio Positionis Seu Situationis Monasterii Clarae-vallensis* exudes the unnamed[56] author's deep appreciation and gratitude for the cooperative interactivity of humans, other species, the land, water, and air that ensured their mutual sustainability and maintained the site's integrity.[57] This view predates by centuries the efforts of contemporary philosophers to reflect on the human relation to other biota and abiota that constitute ecosystems, to develop ethical principles that can guide human functioning as integral parts of these systems,[58] and to facilitate systematic thinking about "sustainable development" strategies encouraged by the United Nations World Commission on Environment and Development.[59]

Although these secular considerations are demonstrated graphically in *Descriptio,* the text's author proceeded from a deeper meaning rooted in religious faith. Faith in God, who created and sustains the world, is the foundation from which the twelfth-century text was written, and the behavioral norms suggested are theocentrically motivated. Christians who embrace the underlying notions of this medieval text and inform them with broad scientific findings are offered meaningful ways of thinking about how they ought to relate to other animate and inanimate beings for their mutual benefit and the overall sustainability of ecosystems.

For the purposes of this chapter, I refer to the unnamed author of *Descriptio* as "the Cistercian" because the writer is, at the very least, Cistercian in spirit. Among the indicators that justify this designation are the author's familiarity with the site, reference to frequent reliance on the fountain, a profession of deep faith in God as the ultimate source of their well-being and the ultimate end of their existence, and appreciation for the monks' efforts to meet their basic physical needs at the site by cooperating with God's other creatures.[60] Further justification for "the Cistercian" attribution is the author's humility before God's creation, a virtue required by and nurtured within the Benedictine tradition.[61]

The Twelfth-Century Text

The Cistercian begins with the express intention of describing the site so precisely that the reader will be able to envision it clearly.[62] Starting with the overall topography, the author surveys the site and finds an area bounded by two mountains connected by a widening river valley. The bottom half of each mountain is cultivated, one covered with vineyards and the other with corn. On the upper halves of the mountains, the monks collect dry branches and clear the land between the trees for an express purpose: "So that there may be no impediment to the sturdy oak which salutes the heavens with its lofty top, to the graceful lime-tree which spreads its arms, to the ash-tree whose wood is so elastic and easily split, or to the leafy beech, as the one shoots upwards and the other spreads its lateral shade."[63]

Focusing on the abbey proper, the author points to the broad plain that extends from the house. A significant part of the area is enclosed by a wall the brethren constructed.[64] Within this space are many fruit trees of various types whose branches support singing birds. Monks with health problems walk among the trees, find shade from the hot sun, rest their eyes amid the "pleasant green of the trees and of the turf," listen to "the sweet and harmonious concerts of birds of varied plumage," inhale "the air fragrant with the scent of hay," and delight in the abundance of ripening fruit.[65] The overall therapeutic atmosphere of the orchard is attributed to God's generosity: "See how, in order to cure one sickness, the goodness of God multiplies remedies, causes the clear air to shine in serenity, the earth to breathe forth fruitfulness, and the sick man himself to inhale through eyes, and ears, and nostrils the delights of colours, of songs, and of odours."[66]

In the garden beyond the orchard, the sick monks find another "pleasing site" on the bank of a pond where they watch "the sports of little fish in water clear as crystal" as they "swim to and fro in shoals like marching armies."[67] The water in the pond is fed by "a constant current" channeled from the Aube River to a system of square irrigation ditches the monks constructed throughout the garden area.[68]

Attention turns to the movement of the Aube within and around the abbey. Pointing to the channel the monks built to divert water from the river, the Cistercian personifies the stream and interprets its movement as aggressively aimed toward cooperating as fully as possible with the monks: "The river . . . passes nowhere without rendering some service, or leaving some of its water behind. It divides the valley into two by a sinuous bed, which the labour of the brethren, and not Nature, has made, and goes on to throw half of its waters into the abbey, as if to salute the brethren."[69]

The diverted water seeks to aid the monks through an extensive system of ducts and sluices designed to feed and power their workshops.[70] Many tasks are accomplished by the cooperative interactions of the monks and the water as it drives the wheels of the mill where meal is ground, fills a boiler that is heated to prepare an unidentified liquid beverage that the monks will drink when the supply of wine is short,[71] and seeks diligently and ungrudgingly to aid the monks in their endeavors. The stream "does not hesitate nor refuse any who require its aid," the Cistercian exclaims.[72]

Water from the Aube relieves the monks of their heaviest tasks, the Cistercian proclaims gratefully. It even shares the monks' fatigues. Its many services to them are acknowledged as consolations provided by God: "O God, how many consolations Thou givest to Thy poor, so that they may not be entirely weighed down by the extreme stress of their labour! What alleviations of punishment to the penitent, that they may not be altogether absorbed by excessive sorrow! How many horses would this labour tire! Of how many men would it weary the arms! And the kindly stream relieves us from it altogether."[73] Without its help, the Cistercian insists, the monks would have neither food to eat nor cloth to make their garments.[74]

The diverted water asks little from the monks in return for its vital assistance, the author recognizes. The only compensation it requires is to be allowed "to go free upon its way" after diligently completing its many tasks.[75]

The end of the river's cooperation with the monks draws near as it enters the workshop where sandals are being made. Separating into many troughs built by the monks, the water "penetrates all the workshops, and lends itself to everyone's need, everywhere looking for assistance that it may be able to render."[76] The author indicates a desire to be as thorough as possible in acknowledging the Aube's contributions to the site and lauds the water for also seeking to remove all the visible wastes remaining from the monks' labors: "Lastly, in order that I may not omit any thanks due to it, nor leave the catalogue of its services in any way imperfect, the river carries away all dirt and uncleanness, and leaves all things clean behind it."[77] Unfortunately, the Cistercian is not concerned about the fact that the river is being polluted by the wastes it is carrying away.[78]

With this last task completed, the grateful monks cooperate with the diverted water's modest request, and it proceeds rapidly to join the rest of the Aube: "After having accomplished industriously the purpose for which it came, it returns with rapid current to the stream, and renders to it, in the name of Clairvaux, thanks for all the services which it has performed."[79] Its swift departure and reunification with the Aube are interpreted as a "worthy response" to the monks' thanks for all the services it performs for them.[80] With obvious delight, the Cistercian observes the reunion of the stream to the river proper:

> Immediately [the Aube] receives into its bosom the waters that it had lent to us, and the two streams become only one. They are so perfectly mixed that no trace of their union can be found, though the onrush of the diverted water hastens the current that had been delayed, diminished, and rendered less active when part of its waters had been withdrawn.[81]

Recognizing that the water diverted by the monks from the Aube had affected its flow, the Cistercian seems pleased that the monks fulfilled their responsibility to the river by returning the water to its place in the riverbed.[82]

Focus turns to the meadows where water channeled from the river filled the irrigation ditches the monks had built.[83] The streams are depicted as seeking to aid the abiota and the biota that constitute the site. They wander in "careless curves" through the meadows, penetrating and refreshing the earth to enable the sprouting and growth of plants. The streams provide all the moisture needed in the meadows, the Cistercian declares confidently. They have no need for "drops from the clouds" because they are fed sufficiently by the generous river.[84]

Traversing the vast plain of the meadows, the author finds "much charm" for soothing the monks' weary minds and for relieving their anxieties and cares: "The smiling countenance of the earth is painted with varying colours, the blooming verdure of spring satisfies the eyes, and its sweet odour salutes the nostrils."[85] Yet these pleasing surroundings go beyond satisfying the monks' aesthetic senses. They also prompt the monks' theological reflection: "While I am charmed without by the sweet influence of the beauty of the country, I have not less delight within in reflecting on the mysteries which are hidden beneath it."[86] The author assumes the sacramental quality of the visible creation, a common perception during the patristic through medieval eras that the physical world mediates the presence and attributes of God.[87]

Turning to the immediate benefits of the ongoing cooperation in the meadows, the Cistercian catalogs the many services the irrigation waters render to the monks, the plants, and the lake. The streams send moisture to the vegetation that is being cut to make hay, a process requiring twenty days of heavy work by the monks, lay brothers, and hired laborers.[88] The streams also intentionally feed a lake through narrow, irrigation ditches thirty-six feet long that assure sufficient water for the fish to thrive and provide nourishment for the monks. To keep the water at a constant level, the monks maintain overflow pipes that lead back to the Aube. Their impressive technology, the streams from the generous river, and the absorbing meadows maintain the area's integrity.[89]

At the height of delight with this productive interactivity taking place in the meadows, the author suddenly expresses remorse for having overlooked a vital component and failing to be grateful for it: "While I breathlessly mount the steep slopes, or traverse the brightly-coloured surface of the meadow, painted by the hand of Wisdom, or describe the ridges of the mountains clothed with trees, I am accused of ingratitude by that sweet fountain of whose waters I have so often drunk, which has merited so well of me and which I have repaid so ill."[90] The fountain is depicted as chastising its observer: "It reminds me in a tone of reproach that it has often quenched my thirst, that it has given me water to wash my hands and even my feet, and that it has rendered to me many such offices of kindness and benevolence. It says to me that all these good offices I have repaid with ingratitude, that it has been the last mentioned of all the places I have described, and, indeed, that it scarcely found a place at all."[91] For "all the respect I owe to it," the author continues, "it should have been placed first."[92]

Yet the author wonders retrospectively if the fountain intends to be secretive, to be silent and hidden, as its waters pass through subterranean channels and reappear within the monastery enclosure.[93] Here the fountain returns "to life" and offers itself "to charm the sight and supply the wants of the brethren." Perhaps, the author conjectures, the fountain is "not willing to have communication with any others than saints."[94] With this strong sense of affinity between the fountain and the saintly monks, the Cistercian concludes *Descriptio*.

Appreciation and Gratitude for Cooperative Interactivity

Throughout this charming and enthusiastic description of the Abbey site, the Cistercian conveyed deep appreciation of and gratitude for the cooperative interactivity of humans, other species, water, air, and land to achieve their mutual flourishing and the overall sustainability of the monastery site. The author lauded the Aube River for moistening the meadows and providing steady streams to the lake, the lake for providing a setting in which the fish can swim, the trees for preventing the earth from crumbling into the lake,[95] and the tree branches for serving as perches for the singing birds.[96] The author lauded the cooperation of the river when "lending" the monks the water they needed to perform their daily tasks,[97] the cooperation of the fountain when quenching the monks' thirst,[98] the therapeutic services offered to the sick monks by the air, shade trees, birds, and fish,[99] and the meadows that cooperate with the monks by soothing their weary minds and relieving their anxieties.[100] The author lauded the monks' cooperation with the ground by collecting dry branches and brushwood that were considered disfiguring, with the oak trees by digging up roots of other plants that were thought to impede the trees' growth,[101] with the river by constructing a channel through which its diverted water could aid the monks[102] and allowing it to return to the riverbed after rendering its services,[103] and with the lake by installing overflow pipes to ensure that the lake levels remained stable enough for the fish to flourish.[104] From the Cistercian's perspective, this cooperative interactivity ensured that the needs of the monks, trees, birds, meadowlands, lake, river, and air were all met. The end result was the harmoniously functioning site with each of the components appreciated for contributing something essential to one another and, in turn, assuring the integrity of the site.

Underlying this sense of cooperation that the Cistercian conveyed was a faith perspective in God as having created all components of the site and sustaining their interactivity for their overall sustenance. God caused the air to shine, the earth to "breathe forth fruitfulness," and the steady streams from the Aube River that filled the pool of water in which fish swam.[105] God's "wisdom" painted the brightly colored surface of the meadow,[106] the author insisted from his faith perspective. Humans have made nothing that equals God's beautiful creation.[107] The air, meadows, river, trees, fountain, lake, fish, birds, and plants were valued components of the site provided by God and intended to be rendered with care and humility by the monks, which, in the Benedictine tradition, was considered a way of serving God.[108] All constituents of the site were perceived as means through which God's presence was experienced and God's goodness was affirmed.[109]

Furthermore, the Cistercian's praise for the interactivity of all components that constitute the site gave way to explicit expressions of deep gratitude. When cataloging the services rendered by the river, the author endeavored to avoid missing any "thanks" due to it.[110] The author lamented not having sufficiently respected the fountain by mentioning it first instead of last.[111] Utmost gratitude was given to God for creating the site with its diverse components and for enabling them to function harmoniously in relation to one another. Appreciation, respect, and gratitude were Cistercian hallmarks of a fitting reaction to the Clairvaux site that flowed from faith in God.

However profusely the Cistercian conveyed appreciation and gratitude for the natural environment, especially the Aube River and the fountain, one type of practice at the monastery proved to be highly problematic in the future: the flushing of wastes into a waterway. The Cistercian assumed that the river absorbed the wastes from the workshops without any ramifications. As detailed in chapter 7, in too many parts of the world, flushing various kinds of wastes into waterways is ongoing with serious ramifications on the use of creation. Furthermore, the knowledge about pollutants and toxicants obtained during the twentieth-century precludes making an assumption today that a river could carry away all waste products without a "trace," because many toxins and pollutants are invisible to the unaided eye. Thus, this account provides an early example of the pollution of waterways, a practice that continued after the twelfth century and escalated into the twentieth century, when some governments began to place restrictions on effluents into water, emissions into the air, and deposits on the land.

Another practice at Clairvaux that has also escalated around the world is the diversion of surface water and groundwater for multiple purposes. Though diversion of water from the Aube River was aimed at supporting a sustainable lifestyle at the monastery, the diversion of water today for agricultural business has become a serious problem worldwide, as also discussed in chapter 7.

Ecosystem Philosophy

Although the worldviews of patristic-medieval theologians and the Cistercian differed vastly from the current scientific understanding of the world, their reflections on and depiction of the cooperative interactivity of humans, other species, and abiota resonates with current philosophical thinking about the human being as an integral *part of* an ecosystem. The Cartesian duality of the human as *apart from* the physical world is unrealistic today in light of the radical human connectedness with other beings in ecosystems, the inescapable effects of human actions on others now and into the future, and the emergence of humans from and with other species through the evolutionary process.

Ecosystem philosophy reflects on findings that fall within the discipline of ecology, a subspecialty of biology. Tansley coined the term "ecosystem" in 1935 to signal a growing understanding among early ecologists that all the biota and abiota of an area function as a working unit.[112] By the 1950s, the term had become a central organizing idea in ecology,[113] due in large part to Odum, who wrote the first textbook organized around the "ecosystem" concept[114] and transformed it into an idea with vast theoretical and applied significance.[115]

Although the term "ecosystem" is expansive and has been attributed to an area as small as a pond and to one as vast as an ocean basin,[116] ecosystems share major characteristics that have significance when relating to parallel thinking in the Cistercian's text. Among these are the "holistic, whole-system property" or "integrity" that is more than the sum of the ecosystem's parts, the interactivity of its various components that brings about its holistic character, the diversity of each part that brings into play something unique and vital to constituting the whole, and the hierarchical control that some components exert over others. Other ecosystem characteristics that depart from the Cistercian's worldview include the evolutionary nature of ecosystems in which new levels of organization emerge periodically, strive to achieve stability, and bring about changes as species adapt to one another, are modified, or become extinct.[117] These characteristics underscore the interdependence of all components in constituting, developing, maintaining, and changing the identity of an ecosystem over long periods of time.

Though these characteristics were not and should not be expected to have been explored conceptually in any twelfth-century text, the medieval author graphically described the site as a whole system made up of distinctive biota and abiota, each of which actively contributed to and received something essential to the area that made it sustainable. Of course, the site was not planned using the ecosystem concept as embraced by some ecologists today, but a sense of harmony of all parts working together was prominent in the twelfth-century author's view of the abbey and its surroundings. The monks were considered cooperators among cooperators, contributors among contributors, and significant receivers among receivers of the Aube River ecosystem.

When describing the characteristics of ecosystems, some ecologists and philosophers of science have not treated humans as parts of ecosystems but, rather, as forces external to them. However, informed by ecology and eschewing Cartesian dualism, Odum contends that an understanding of the "ecosystem" concept and the realization that the human species is part of the complex biogeo-chemical interactions of an ecosystem is fundamental to ecology and to human affairs.[118] Nothing in this concept inherently excludes humans from consideration as a part of the ecosystem, whereas the concept appears naturally to include humans who, like other living organisms, evolved within the biosphere, have adapted to its structure, functions, and chemical composition, are dependent on the water, air, land, and other biota of their shared ecosystems for survival, and are subject to physical and biological constraints when conducting social, economic, and political affairs.[119]

Among the negative factors that warrant including humans as integral parts of ecosystems are the demands humans make on other ecosystem components, the actions that place at risk the stability, diversity, and functioning of ecosystems, the air pollutants and other mobile toxicants induced in one ecosystem that affect neighboring ecosystems, and the acceleration of ecosystem change and species extinction precipitated by the choices made and technologies employed.[120] If humans are acknowledged as integral parts of the ecosystems in which they function, proponents contend, they can also consider themselves subject to the self-regulating rules and limitations of ecosystems.[121]

Jacobs insists that humans should be considered a natural but highly specialized constituent of ecosystems if the human role in them is to be comprehended and if human activities are to become compatible with ecosystem functioning.[122] Thinking about *Homo sapiens* in this way links humans inextricably to the sustainability of ecosystems and the greater biosphere. The management of ecosystems from this perspective requires perceiving all human actions—biological, technological, economic, and social—within the framework of the ecosystem's carrying capacity and the compatibility of human actions with maintaining the ecosystem's integrity. When managing ecosystems, human needs and the needs of the ecosystem with all its components are understood as complementary, and the human use of other ecosystem components is tempered by the goal of ensuring the system's sustainability.[123]

Among the efforts to adopt and implement the ecosystem concept as a basis for management is the Great Lakes Water Quality Agreement signed by the United States and Canada in 1978. The two nations defined the ecosystem of the Great Lakes as "the interacting components of air, land, water and living organisms, including man" within the lakes' drainage basin (article 1) and committed themselves "to restore and maintain the chemical, physical, and biological integrity" of its waters (article 2). This action provided a conceptual framework for addressing widespread degradation throughout the Great Lakes Basin.

Thinking about the human as part of an ecosystem does not exclude economic concerns. As noted above, humans are highly dependent on the other biota, water, land, and ambient air of an ecosystem for their economic well-being. How humans function within an ecosystem and use its components determine the options for occupations, recreation, and health now and in the future. Recognizing this nexus between economic and environmental well-being, the World Commission on Environment and Development has encouraged the development of the economy in ways that sustain ecosystems and the larger biosphere.[124] Similar sentiments have been expressed by scientists and philosophers, who urge managing the human use of ecosystem components on a sustainable basis for future generations.[125]

Behaving Cooperatively

For moral theologians who have struggled with the dualistic perception of the physical universe as merely the object of human study and exploitation, the human-in-ecosystem approach provides a scientifically informed paradigm for thinking about how humans should consider functioning as integral parts of God's creation.[126] A basic model existed centuries ago in the depiction of the Cistercian monks' cooperation with the other forms of biological life and the abiota that constituted the Clairvaux site[127] and in metaphysical conceptualization by patristic to medieval theologians. Although the Cistercian's description and the theologians' reflections were written centuries before scientists developed the field of ecology, the patristic-medieval faith-based efforts complement current scientific findings. Together they provide inspiration for identifying a behavioral trajectory that could be helpful today—cooperation.[128]

Cooperating with Other-Than-Humans on Behalf of Humans

Faithful persons will be inclined to cooperate with the other living and abiotic components of their shared ecosystems by thinking about the health and welfare of other humans now and in the future within the context of the health and well-being of the ecosystem in which they function. Because humans live, work, play, and otherwise function within ecosystems, their personal welfare and the well-being of their families will not be contemplated outside these physical contexts. This ecological frame of reference is warranted by the human connection with other species over cosmological and biological evolutionary time, humans' radical reliance on other species and abiota for their health and well-being, and the adverse effects of human activities on the ecosystem that, in turn, have adversely affected or threaten to affect other humans near and far, now and into the future. All concerns about human welfare will be weighed with special attention to the poor, the vulnerable, and the disadvantaged, who are least able to sustain themselves within the ecosystem context.[129]

Acknowledging Biotic and Abiotic Contributions to Ecosystems

The contributions that living and nonliving constituents make to their shared ecosystems will be discovered and acknowledged. Efforts will be made to seek at least basic knowledge about the species, air, land, and water that constitute the ecosystem and the contributions they make to its integrity. Knowledge about at-risk species and abiota will also be sought, with the aim of identifying activities that jeopardize their existence and the overall effect on other species and abiota that constitute their shared ecosystem. Knowing these facts will lead to acknowledging and cooperating with the biota and abiota for their mutual flourishing with humans, as exemplified in *Descriptio*. Acknowledging their contributions will lead the faithful to express their gratitude to them, following the Cistercian centuries ago who lauded the Aube, the fountain, the trees, the meadows, the birds, the fish, the air, and the sunshine at Clairvaux. To forget any one constituent will be lamentable, as was the Cistercian, who almost forgot the fountain that met the monks' vital needs.

Avoiding Interference with Ecosystem Interactions

Ways of acting that do not inhibit or interfere with the contributions that species, air, land, and water make to their respective ecosystems will be identified and implemented by those who proceed from believing that God created and sustains the functional integrity of Earth and who know that they are responsible to God for living cooperatively within the ecosystem. The faithful will exercise their innate abilities to identify and act in ways that avoid interfering with other species' quests for nourishment and self-preservation within their shared ecosystem. Efforts will be made to investigate the projected ramifications of their actions and to choose to act at home, at work, and at play with the aim of assuring the viability of the other species and abiota that constitute the ecosystem. At-risk species will be protected, invasive species will be removed, minimum standards for affecting environmental quality will be instituted and followed, the consumption of nonrenewable biota and abiota will be self-restricted, and the renewable goods of God's Earth will be used in sustainable ways.

Assuring the Sustainability of Ecosystems

The faithful will cooperate with the many different creatures that constitute an ecosystem with the aim of ensuring their shared sustainability into the future. Grounded by their belief in God and informed by ecologists' findings, human activities will be geared toward maintaining the relative stability, resilience, and biotic diversity of an ecosystem in ways that do not interrupt its natural evolution.[130] Where the stability of the biological populations becomes unbalanced, efforts will be expended to return to the equilibrium that had existed before human disruptions.[131] Where the ecosystem's resilience has been diminished, efforts will be initiated to reduce stress on the ecosystem so it can become more robust.[132] Where biological diversity has been reduced, efforts will be made to restore it. Human cooperators will follow the "precautionary principle" when ecosystem health and well-being are threatened, opting to err on the side of caution rather than waiting for conclusive scientific evidence of the cause–effect relationship.[133]

Seeking Communitywide Cooperation

Communitywide cooperative actions will be initiated by the faithful to achieve the sustainability of their shared ecosystem. The plethora of ecosystem problems today transcend the capacity of one or several persons to bring about the needed changes in thinking and acting. Although a few faithful individuals may lead an effort, the cooperative action by many is essential, beginning in the home and moving upward to whatever level of social, economic, and political activity is necessary to achieve sustainability. Reaching out to the faithful of other religious traditions in an area will demonstrate cultural cooperation within an ecosystem.

Voluntary efforts will be encouraged, but restrictions and penalties for noncompliance will be instituted where and when necessary. The principle of subsidiarity will guide decision making, so all possible means of cooperation at one level are employed before moving onto the next level.[134] Vigilance will be exercised to enable the faithful to recognize and correct obstacles to cooperation that persist in political and economic systems.

Being Penitent for Noncooperation

For actions that prevent biota and abiota from cooperating with one another and thereby jeopardizing the sustainability of an ecosystem, the faithful will be penitent. Human activities that disrupt the cooperative interactivity of the other species, air, land, and water will be perceived as failures of the human spirit to acknowledge the rightful place of humans as responsible citizens of ecosystems. The faithful will be responsive to the other humans, species, air, land, and water that constitute ecosystems by outwardly admitting their failures to cooperate, professing their intentions to avoid repeating these activities, and performing penance that is aimed at facilitating the reinvigoration of ecosystem species and the restoration of ecosystem sustainability.

To reverse their noncooperative courses of action, believers will embrace Aquinas's teaching that God offers grace to believers to aid them in cooperating with others as a way of cooperating with God. They will accept God's grace to be cooperative with other species, airwaves, land masses, and waterways that constitute ecosystems. They will be open to receiving God's grace in their thinking about how to cooperate with others for their mutual sustainability.

Conclusion

From their faith perspective in God as the purposeful Creator and sustainer of the world, patristic and medieval theologians reflected on God's having provided all that was needed for the universe of many diverse creatures to function cooperatively. Their cooperative interactions ensured the internal self-maintenance of the world, the theologians taught, while God continuously sustained its capability to function. A twelfth-century text graphically depicted the cooperative interactivity among the monks, birds, trees, meadow, mountains, river, lake, spring, and air that constituted the Cistercian abbey site at Clairvaux. The cooperative functioning of humans with the other biota and abiota at Clairvaux parallels contemporary metaphysical reflections, in which humans are considered highly specialized, integral, and responsible components of the ecosystems of the areas where they live, work and play.

When the human-in-ecosystem approach proceeds from faith in God, who continuously empowers the interactivity of all species, air, land, and water, the faithful will be inclined to cooperate with other humans, other species, and the abiota of their shared ecosystem for their mutual sustainability, paying special attention to those who are least able to seek the sustenance they need. The faithful will become knowledgeable about the contributions that other species, air, land, and water make to their shared ecosystem that brings about its sustainability and be grateful for their contributions. The faithful will avoid interfering with interactions of ecosystem components that thwart its sustainability. The faithful will strive to ensure the sustainability of their shared ecosystem in their economic and social endeavors and seek communitywide cooperation for this purpose.

When the faithful do not cooperate with the other components of their shared ecosystem, they will be penitent to one another and to the other components. They will commit themselves to being cooperative in the future, ultimately out of their desire to be cooperative with God, with whom eternal happiness is sought. Finally, they will be open to accepting God's grace to act cooperatively toward that desired end.

Notes

1. The theologian Howard J. Van Till argues convincingly that Saint Basil pictured God as bringing the world into existence ex nihilo and equipping it with all that was needed for the future. Howard J. Van Till, "Basil, Augustine, and the Doctrine of Creation's Functional Integrity," *Science and Christian Belief* 8 (April 1996): 21–38.
2. Saint Basil, *On the Hexaemeron,* in *Exegetic Homilies,* trans. Sister Agnes Clare Way, CDP (Washington, DC: Catholic University of America Press, 1963), homily 5, 67–82. Thomas F. Torrance stresses the importance in Basil's reflections that God empowered the world to function internally without interference; Thomas F. Torrance, *The Christian Frame of Mind* (Colorado Springs: Helmers and Howard, 1989), 4.
3. Basil, *On the Hexaemeron,* 9.2, 136–39.
4. Jb 36:27.
5. Basil, *On the Hexaemeron,* 3.5, 45.
6. Ibid., 2.2, 22–24. All diverse animate and inanimate beings created by God have an affinity, a sympathy, for one another that unites them. Tarsicius van Bavel explores this notion with precision in "The Creator and the Integrity of Creation in the Fathers of the Church, Especially in Saint Augustine," *Augustinian Studies* 21 (1990): 1–33.
7. Basil, *On the Hexaemeron,* 5.6, 69.
8. Ibid., 2, p. 31.
9. Christopher B. Kaiser, *Creational Theology and the History of Physical Science: The Creationist Tradition from Basil to Bohr* (New York: Brill Academic Publishers, 1997), 32–33. At the forefront among scientists who are engaged in constructive dialogue with theologians on religion-science issues, the physicist Howard Van Till finds in Basil's writing a "sufficiently robust" description of God's creation of the world to function in a way that does not require additional acts of special creation in time by God as proffered by current "creation scientists" and intelligent design advocates; see Van Till, "Basil, Augustine, and the Doctrine of Creation's Functional Integrity," 29. Torrance, *Christian Frame of Mind,* 4, points to the significance of God's majes-

tic fiat in Genesis 1: "Let there be" as giving "rise to the laws of nature" through which the world functions. Also see Kaiser, *Creational Theology,* 29.

10. Saint Augustine, *The Trinity,* trans. Stephen McKenna, CSSR, Fathers of the Church 45 (Washington, DC: Catholic University of America Press, 1963), 3.2.7, 100.

11. Ibid., 3.4.9, 104.

12. Along with other theologians before and after his time until Alfred Russel Wallace and Charles Darwin shared their findings about the evolution of species, Augustine adhered to the doctrine of fixed species—all types of creatures derive their basic characteristics provided by God at the beginning of creation.

13. Augustine, *The Trinity,* 3.4.10, 105.

14. Esp. Gn 1:20–25.

15. Augustine, *The Trinity,* 3.8.13, 108. Augustine was not advancing a theory of evolution; he attempted to explain through his "rational seeds" theory that God empowered the world with the secondary causative capacity to generate living beings through the operation of natural laws. See Jules M. Brady, SJ, "St. Augustine's Theory of Seminal Reasons," *New Scholasticism* 38 (1964): 141–58, esp. 149.

16. Augustine, *The Trinity,* 3.8.13, 109. Interestingly, Augustine thought that the good angels know the rational seeds by the "subtlety of their intelligence and body, . . . scatter them secretly through suitable mixtures of the elements, and thus provide the favorable opportunities for the birth of things and accelerate their growth." Not creators per se, the angels and other entities act as secondary causes to God's primary causality that empowers them to create through God's power.

17. Pseudo-Dionysius, *The Divine Names,* in *The Complete Works,* trans. Colm Luibheid; notes and trans. collaboration by Paul Rorem; introduction by Jaroslav Pelikan, Jean LeClerq, and Karlfried Froehlich (New York: Paulist Press, 1987), 4.1–10, 71–80.

18. Ibid., 4.2, 73.

19. Ibid., 4.3, 73.

20. Ibid., 4.10, 79–80.

21. Ibid., 4.4, 74–75.

22. Ibid., 4.7, 77.

23. Ibid. 4.10, p. 79.

24. Ibid., 4.12, 81.

25. Ibid., 4.26, 92.

26. Johannes Scotus Eriugena, *Periphyseon* (The Division of Nature), trans. I. P. Sheldon-Williams and rev. John J. O'Meara (Washington, DC: Dumbarton Oaks, 1987), 117–21.

27. Aquinas, *Summa theologiae,* 1.47.

28. Ibid., 1.47.2; see also 1.47.3, in which Aquinas considered the various degrees of "perfection" in which the constituents of the cosmos exist, with the mixed things more perfect than the elements, plants than minerals, animals than plants, and humans than other animals. In each of these types of constituents, one type is more perfect than others, he contended. The universe would not be perfect if only one grade or degree of goodness existed. See, further, 1.65.2.

29. E.g., see Aquinas, *Compendium theologiae,* 148; Aquinas, *Summa theologiae,* 2 | 2.64.1; and Aquinas, *Summa contra Gentiles,* 3.22, 128. Aquinas taught in *Summa contra Gentiles,* 3.47, that humans progress to knowledge of God from God's effects, and he uses both Rom 1:20 and Saint Augustine's *De vera religione* to support his thinking

that corporeal creatures serve as stepping stones to the knowledge of God, as indicated in *Summa theologiae*, 2|2.180.4, 3.60.4, Supp. 91.1, a notion that is held by many of his peers as indicated in the above chapter on the sacramentality of creation. As explained in *Summa contra Gentiles*, 2.2, among the precise ways in which creatures fill this quest for knowledge about God are (1) as things through which humans can admire and reflect on God's wisdom, a likeness of which God has communicated widely to created things; (2) as entities through which humans can admire God's sublime power and through which human hearts can be inspired to revere God; (3) as creatures of goodness, beauty, and delightfulness that incite human souls to love God's goodness within which all the goodness of various creatures are united as their source; and (4) as things known by humans that render in them a likeness to God's wisdom.

30. That some things help others is a basis for the ordering of things in relation to one another, Aquinas explained in *Summa contra Gentiles*, 1.42, 2.41. That some depend on others is stressed in reference to how some created things are preserved in existence by others in a secondary way, as indicated in *Summa theologiae*, 1.104.2 ad 2. Higher beings also benefit lower by leading them to goodness by being acted upon as God intended (*De veritate*, 5.8), thereby making them more like God's ideas of them when they were created (*Summa contra Gentiles*, 3.24; see also *Compendium theologiae*, 73, 124) on how God rules lower creatures by higher so they can procure the good of many and *Summa theologiae*, 2–2.2.3, where he taught that creatures more capable of acting at a high level can lead lower creatures to perfection as God intended when creating them.

31. John H. Wright, *The Order of the Universe in the Theology of St. Thomas Aquinas* (Rome: Apud Aedes Universitatis Gregorianae, 1957), 107–8.

32. Ibid., 100.

33. Thomas Gilby, "Introduction," in *Summa theologiae*, vol. 8, trans. Blackfriars (New York: McGraw-Hill, 1964), 102 n. f.

34. Ibid., 30–113. The *Index Thomisticus* identifies 286 entries of these usages of *cooperator*: 20 regarding the cooperation of creatures, 106 on their cooperation with God, 45 in which humans cooperate freely with God or God's grace, and 115 on divine grace operating on humans and cooperating with human actions.

35. See, e.g., Aquinas, *Summa theologiae*, 1.61.3, 111.2, 1|2.9.1, 19.10; Aquinas, *De veritate*, 9.2, 27.5; Aquinas, *Compendium theologiae*, 124; and Aquinas, *Summa contra Gentiles*, 1.70, 3.21, 3.69–70.

36. When God works through secondary causal agents, Aquinas taught in *Summa theologiae*, 1.105.5, the innate efficacy of their causal powers is left absolutely intact. God's activity in them does not displace or obviate their actions; it sustains and guides their actions lovingly toward their ultimate end. Aquinas perceived God's employing secondary causes to govern other creatures as a way of communicating the dignity of causality to creatures as indicated, for example, in *Summa theologiae*, 1.23.8, and explained by Etienne Gilson, *The Christian Philosophy of St. Thomas Aquinas*, trans. L. K. Shook (New York: Random House, 1956), 184. In *Summa contra Gentiles*, 3.21, Aquinas cites Pseudo-Dionysius and 1 Cor 3:9 to support his thinking that creatures operating on others according to the innate characteristics given to them by God are *Dei cooperatorem*.

37. E.g., see Aquinas, *De veritate*, 27.5. Also see Aquinas, *Summa theologiae*, 1.105.4–5, for his understanding of God's will acting on rational creatures.

38. According to Aquinas, *De veritate,* 24.11, 27.5, God offers grace to humans to enable their cooperation with God's intention that they seek the temporal good in this life while aiming for eternal happiness.

39. Aquinas, *Summa contra Gentiles,* 3.22, 71. His point is clear: God has given creatures innate capabilities to act or be acted upon according to their natures, God allows them to use their capabilities to bring about the orderly universe. Throughout book 3 of *Summa contra Gentiles,* Aquinas stressed God's providentially working through secondary causes—actions of some on others—without taking away or interfering with their innate capacities; see, for example, 3.75–77.

40. E.g., see Aquinas, *Summa contra Gentiles,* 3.22, wherein he designated elements as existing for the sake (*propter se*) of mixed bodies and they exist for the sake of living bodies, among which plants exist for animals and animals for humans—a sustenance chain. In *Summa theologiae,* 1.96.1, Aquinas describe the use of natural things in terms of grades of perfection with the imperfect for the use of the more perfect (e.g., plants make use of the earth for their nourishment, and animals make use of plants, and humans make use of both plants and animals).

41. Aquinas, *Summa contra Gentiles,* 1.65. See also *De potentia Dei,* 7.9, where Aquinas explained that all creatures are ordered in relation to God both as to their beginning and as to their end because the order of the parts of the universe results from the order of the whole universe to God. In *Summa theologiae,* 1.61.3, Aquinas taught that the mutual relationship of creatures makes up the good of the universe. But no part is perfect if separate from the whole.

42. Aquinas, *De veritate,* 5.1.9. For Aquinas, this twofold ordering is both God's work of art in arranging the constituents of the world hierarchically so they can function internally in relation to one another and God's providence in ordering them to their end to achieve their common good and the good of the universe. God's ordering the constituents of the universe to one another is the cause of the ordering of the parts to each other.

43. E.g., see Aquinas, *Summa theologiae,* 1.65.2, 1│2.6.1; and Aquinas, *Summa contra Gentiles,* 3.25. Contrast his depiction with nonintellectual beings that are moved toward their end by God's determination, as he indicated in *Summa theologiae,* 1│2.23.2, and *Summa contra Gentiles,* 3.85, 111.

44. Aquinas, *Summa contra Gentiles,* 3.78.

45. Aquinas, *Summa theologiae,* 1.96.1. Aquinas distinguished between human rule over other creatures as a natural dominion to use them in restricted ways while God retains absolute dominion over all. Other corporeal creatures are subordinate to the governance of humans, according to Aquinas in *Compendium theologiae,* 74, 127, 148, because they have an intellectual nature and the capacity to control their acts by freely moving their wills, whereas other corporeal creatures have strictly material natures through which they act by instinct in determined patterns. See also Aquinas, *Summa contra Gentiles,* 3.111, 112.

46. See Aquinas, *Summa contra Gentiles,* 3.108.3, 81.6. See also Aquinas, *Summa theologiae,* 1│2.18.8, 2│2.158.2.

47. See Aquinas, *Summa theologiae,* 1.49.3 ad 5. See also Aquinas, *Compendium theologiae,* 186, 192.

48. Aquinas, *Summa theologiae,* 1│2.109.3; also see 77.4.

49. Wright, *Order of the Universe,* 55.

50. Aquinas, *Summa theologiae,* 1│2.19.10.

51. See Saint Athanasius, *On the Incarnation*, trans. and ed. A Religious of CSMV (Crestwood, NY: St. Vladimir's Seminary Press, 1978), 7.43, 78–79, where he explains why God manifested God's self in human form: "Some may then ask, why did He not manifest Himself by means of other and nobler parts of creation, and use some nobler instrument, such as sun or moon or stars or fire or air, instead of mere man? The answer is this. The Lord did not come to make a display. He came to heal and to teach suffering men. For one who wanted to make a display the thing would have been just to appear and dazzle the beholders. But for Him Who came to heal and to teach the way was not merely to dwell here, but to put Himself at the disposal of those who needed Him, and to be manifested according as they could bear it, not vitiating the value of the Divine appearing by exceeding their capacity to receive it. "Moreover, nothing in creation had erred from the path of God's purpose for it, save only man. Sun, moon, heaven, stars, water, air, none of these had swerved from their order, but, knowing the Word as their Maker and their King, remained as they were made. Men alone having rejected what is good, have invented nothings instead of the truth, and have ascribed the honour due to God and the knowledge concerning Him to daemons and men in the form of stones."

52. Aquinas, *Summa theologiae*, 3.3.8.

53. Wright, *Order of the Universe*, 179.

54. Aquinas, *Summa theologiae*, 3.4.5 ad 2. Also see Wright, *Order of the Universe*, 181.

55. Aquinas, *Summa theologiae*, 1 | 2.109.3.

56. *Descriptio Positionis Seu Situationis Monasterii Clarae-vallensis* (cited hereafter as *Descriptio*), which was found in Migne's *Patrologia Latina* 185:569–74 (cited herein as *PL*), is attributed to Bernard by Dom John Mabillon (1623–1707), and included on pp. 460–67 of vol. 2 of his edition of *Life and Works of Saint Bernard*, trans. Samuel J. Eales (London: Burns & Oates, 1889), and quoted throughout this chapter. However, Pauline Matarasso, translator and editor of *The Cistercian World: Monastic Writings of the Twelfth Century* (New York: Penguin Books, 1993), includes the description on pp. 287–92 without definitive attribution in light of the completed irrigation sluices, multiple buildings, and productive activities of the monks that suggest *Descriptio* was written by one of the Cistercians sometime after 1135 when the elders urged relocating the abbey down the mountainside and closer to the Aube River where the monks could better provide for their temporal needs. On Bernard's initial resistance to the move, see Arnald of Bonneval's *Vita Prima*, 2.2.29–31, as cited by Matarasso, *Cistercian World*, 285.

57. This section is revised from Jame Schaefer, "Grateful Cooperation: Cistercian Inspiration for Ecological Ethics," *Cistercian Studies Quarterly* 37, no. 2 (2002): 187–203.

58. E.g., see Aldo Leopold, *A Sand County Almanac: With Essays on Conservation from Round River* (New York: Ballantine Books, 1966); J. Baird Callicott, *In Defense of the Land Ethic: Essays in Environmental Philosophy* (Albany: State University of New York Press, 1989); Laura Westra, *An Environmental Proposal for Ethics: The Principle of Integrity* (Lanham, MD: Rowman & Littlefield, 1994); Bill Devall and George Sessions, "The Development of Nature Resources and the Integrity of Nature," *Environmental Ethics* 6 (1984): 293–322; Lawrence E. Johnson, "Toward the Moral Considerability of Species and Ecosystems," *Environmental Ethics* 14 (1992): 145–57; and Holmes Rolston III, *Environmental Ethics: Duties to and Values in the Natural World* (Philadelphia: Temple University Press, 1988).

59. World Commission on Environment and Development, *Our Common Future* (New York: Oxford University Press, 1987). An astute overview and evaluation of various "sustainability" concepts is provided by Robert U. Ayres, Joroen C. J. M. van den Bergh, and John M. Gowdy, "Strong Versus Weak Sustainability: Economics, Natural Sciences, and 'Consilience,'" *Environmental Ethics* 23 (2001): 155–68. Also see Wilfred Beckerman, "Sustainable Development: Is It a Useful Concept?" *Environmental Values* 3 (1994): 191–209; J. Baird Callicott, "The Wilderness Idea Revisited: The Sustainable Development Alternative," *Environmental Professional* 13 (1991): 235–47; and Bryan Norton, "Sustainability, Human Welfare and Ecosystem Health," *Environmental Values* 1 (1992): 97–111.

60. The goal of achieving a sustainable site follows the Benedictine tradition as legislated in principle by Rule 66.6: "The monastery should be so set up that everything necessary is carried on within the monastery, that is, the water, the mill, the garden, and the various crafts." "Of the Gatekeepers of the Monastery," in *The Rule of Benedict: A Guide to Christian Living,* trans. Monks of Glenstal Abbey (Dublin: Four Courts, 1994), 303.

61. Rule 31 designates all components of a monastery's property as "consecrated vessels of the altar" to be treated with care and rendered with humility by the monks; "Of the Monastery's Cellarer: What Type of Person He Should Be," in *Rule of Benedict*, 174–75. Commenting on rule 31, at pp. 177–79, Abbot Holzherr explains Benedict's intention that the monks reflect the prophetic image of the Servant of God in their work so it is perceived as "priestly activity" aimed ultimately at serving God. Rule 7 prescribes twelve steps of humility that lead the monk to a theocentric way of life in which all actions habitually become virtuous.

62. Eales, *Descriptio*, 460.

63. Ibid.

64. Ibid., 461.

65. Ibid.

66. Ibid.

67. Ibid.

68. Ibid.

69. Ibid., 462. The Cistercian obviously appreciates the irrigation system that the monks have constructed to divert water from the Aube. Of course, this is a technological change that is ongoing today with more advanced means to control natural systems and much less attention to their sustainability and devoid of the gratitude that the Cistercian demonstrates for the river.

70. In the introduction to her translation of *Descriptio* on p. 287, Matarasso, *Cistercian World,* points to Arnald of Bonneval's account in *Vita Prima* 2.2 of the extensive digging to create this irrigation system.

71. Eales, *Descriptio*, 462. Though the identity of the beverage the monks were preparing is not known with certitude from the *filia . . . festucae* verbiage used, it probably was an ale made from the grain of a straw-like weed that grows among barley or barley itself. See, e.g., *A Latin Dictionary: Founded on Andrews' Edition of Freund's Latin Dictionary,* rev., enlarged, and rewritten by Charlton T. Lewis and Charles Short (Oxford: Clarendon Press, 1955), 743; also see *Dictionary of Medieval Latin from British Sources,* prepared by R. E. Latham under direction of the British Academy Committee (London: Oxford University Press, 1975), 933; and Gilbertus Foliot's letter in 1162 (PL 190.1040A-B), where another *festucae filiam* configuration

appears in reference to *turbatioris subere cervisia* that is "hateful to noble folk." In a letter attributed to Bernard (*PL* 182.0512C-513A), *cervasia* was used to toast visitors at Clairvaux. The Trappist Chrysogonus Waddell at the Abbey of Gethsemani reports "numerous references to *cervisia*" in the Cistercians' General Chapter statutes of the twelfth century and is "generally taken to mean beer made out of barley grain" (letter from Waddell, November 4 2001). I am grateful to Fr. Waddell and to Marquette professors Stephen Beall, medieval Latin scholar, and theologian Wanda Zemler-Cizewski, who specializes in twelfth-century texts, for their help in interpreting this terminology.

72. Eales, *Descriptio,* 462.
73. Ibid., 463.
74. Ibid.
75. Ibid. Though accomplished to support the sustainable lifestyle at Clairvaux, the diversion of surface water and groundwater for agricultural businesses has become a major problem today as indicated in the seventh chapter pertaining to the use of creation.
76. Ibid.
77. Ibid.
78. An early example of water pollution resulting from thinking that dilution is the solution to disposing of waste products from human endeavors.
79. Eales, *Descriptio,* 463.
80. Ibid.
81. Ibid.
82. Ibid.
83. Matarasso, *Cistercian World,* 285, reports that Arnold of Bonneval describes at *Vita prima,* 2.2.29–31, the digging of the network of channels, ducts, and sluices that fed and powered the monks' workshops.
84. Eales, *Descriptio,* 464. The Cistercian is obviously impressed with the water-diverting network that the monks built to power their workshops and irrigate their fields in order to maintain a sustainable lifestyle at Clairvaux.
85. Ibid.
86. Ibid.
87. Ibid. The "sacramentality of creation" concept is explored in chapter 4.
88. Eales, *Descriptio,* 465.
89. Ibid., 466.
90. Ibid.
91. Ibid.
92. Ibid.
93. Apparently the monks situated the abbey above a subterranean channel of water to take advantage of the fountain for their daily needs. The point the author makes, however, is that the fountain is an integral component of the site, providing a necessity of life for the monks, who in turn should appreciate and be thankful for its contribution.
94. Eales, *Descriptio,* 467.
95. Ibid., 466.
96. Ibid., 461.
97. Ibid., 463–64.
98. Ibid., 466.

99. Ibid., 460–61.

100. Ibid., 462.

101. Ibid., 460.

102. Ibid., 462.

103. Ibid.

104. Ibid.

105. Ibid., 461.

106. Ibid., 466.

107. Ibid., 464–65. The significance of thinking that God's creation is beautiful is discussed in chapter 2.

108. See, e.g., Benedict's Rule 31, "Of the Monastery's Cellarer," in *Rule of Benedict,* 175. See also in this text the commentary by Abbot Holzherr at p. 179, who provides a basis for and meaning toward the twelfth-century author's viewing the site's biotic and abiotic constituents as "consecrated vessels of the altar."

109. Eales, *Descriptio,* 464.

110. Ibid., 463.

111. Ibid., 466.

112. Arthur G. Tansley, "The Use and Abuse of Vegetational Concepts and Terms," *Ecology* 16 (1935): 284–307, at 299. See also J. L. Chapman and M. J. Reiss, *Ecology: Principles and Applications* (New York: Cambridge University Press, 1992), 185; R. V. O'Neill, D. L. DeAngelis, J. B. Waide, and T. F. H. Allen, *A Hierarchical Concept of Ecosystems* (Princeton, NJ: Princeton University Press, 1986); and Frank B. Golley, *A History of the Ecosystem Concept in Ecology: More Than the Sum of the Parts* (New Haven, CT: Yale University Press, 1994), 8–11.

113. Robert E. Ricklefs, *Ecology,* 3rd ed. (New York: W. H. Freeman, 1990), 179. See also Donald Worster, *Nature's Economy: The Roots of Ecology* (San Francisco: Sierra Club Books, 1977), 378; and Paul R. Ehrlich and Jonathan Roughgarden, *The Science of Ecology* (New York: Macmillan, 1987). The term "ecosystem" is not used by all ecologists. The focus in ecology is progressively on individuals, populations, communities and, according to some, ecosystems. In their work, Michael Begon, John L. Harper and Colin R. Townsend do not distinguish a separate ecosystem level of organization, treat the community as the highest level acting in a given environment, and attribute to the community level all the structure and function; Michael Begon, John L. Harper and Colin R. Townsend, *Ecology: Individuals, Populations, and Communities,* 3rd ed. (Boston: Blackwell Scientific Publications, 1996).

114. Eugene P. Odum, *Fundamentals of Ecology* (Philadelphia: Saunders, 1953).

115. Golley, *History of the Ecosystem Concept,* 1.

116. Tansley, "Use and Abuse of Vegetational Concepts," 299. See also Odum, *Fundamentals of Ecology,* 1–12; and Kenneth E. Boulding, "What Went Wrong, If Anything, since Copernicus?" *Science and Public Affairs* 30 (January 1974): 17–23, esp. 17.

117. See, e.g., Anthony W. King, "Considerations of Scale and Hierarchy," in *Ecological Integrity and the Management of Ecosystems,* ed. Stephen Woodley, James Kay, and George Francis (Delray Beach, FL: St. Lucie Press, 1993), 19–46; Ricklefs, *Ecology,* 174–77; Bernard J. Nebel, *Environmental Science: The Way the World Works,* 3rd ed. (Englewood Cliffs, NJ: Prentice Hall, 1990), 15; O'Neill et al., *Hierarchical Concept of Ecosystems;* and Eugene Odum, "The Strategy of Ecosystem Development," *Science* 164 (April 18, 1969): 262–70.

118. Odum, *Fundamentals of Ecology*, 1–12. See also Golley, *History of the Ecosystem Concept*, 66.

119. Riley E. Dunlap and Kent D. Van Liere provide a detailed analysis of the assumptions that underlie the emergence of the human-in-ecosystem paradigm in "The 'New Environmental Paradigm': A Proposed Measuring Instrument and Preliminary Results," *Journal of Environmental Education* 9 (1978): 10–19. Further analysis is given by William R. Catton Jr. and Riley E. Dunlap, "A New Ecological Paradigm for Post-exuberant Sociology," *American Behavioral Scientist* 24 (September–October 1980): 15–47. See also F. H. Buttell, "Social Science and the Environment: Competing Theories," *Social Science Quarterly* 57 (1976): 307–23; Riley E. Dunlap and Kent D. Van Liere, "Land Ethic or Golden Rule," *Journal of Social Issues* 33 (1977): 200–207; and D. E. Morrison, "Growth, Environment, Equity and Scarcity," *Social Science Quarterly* 57 (1976): 292–306.

120. Jürgen Jacobs, "Diversity, Stability and Maturity in Ecosystems Influenced by Human Activities," in *Unifying Concepts in Ecology: Report of the Plenary Sessions of the First International Congress of Ecology, The Hague, The Netherlands, September 8–14, 1974*, ed. W. H. van Dobben and R. H. Lowe-McConnell (The Hague: Dr. W. Junk BV, 1975), 187–207, esp. 205; and Great Lakes Science Advisory Board, *The Ecosystem Approach: Scope and Implications of an Ecosystem Approach to Transboundary Problems in the Great Lakes Basin* (Windsor: International Joint Commission, 1978), vii. See a similar point made by Jared Diamond, *The Third Chimpanzee: The Evolution and Future of the Human Animal* (New York: HarperPerennial, 1992); and Bernard J. Nebel and Richard T. Wright, *Environmental Science: The Way the World Works*, 4th ed. (Englewood Cliffs, NJ: Prentice Hall, 1993), 102.

121. R. L. Thomas, J. R. Vallentyne, K. Ogilvie, and J. D. Kingham, "The Ecosystems Approach: A Strategy for the Management of Renewable Resources in the Great Lakes Basin," in *Perspectives on Ecosystem Management for the Great Lakes*, ed. Lynton K. Caldwell (Albany: State University of New York Press, 1988), 31–57, esp. 41.

122. Jacobs, "Diversity, Stability and Maturity," 203–4. See also Golley, *History of the Ecosystem Concept*, 66.

123. Golley, *History of the Ecosystem Concept*, 48.

124. World Commission on Environment and Development, *Our Common Future* (Oxford: Oxford University Press, 1987).

125. Thomas et al., "Ecosystem Approach," 32–33, 41–46.

126. Initial principles for the concept of behaving cooperatively that are open to particularization and application to specific ecological problems include: (1) Cooperate with the subject by thinking about the health and welfare of *other humans* now and into the future within the context of the health and well-being of ecosystems; (2) cooperate with the subject by recognizing the contributions it makes to the constitution of the ecosystem; (3) cooperate with the *many different creatures* that constitute an ecosystem with the goal of assuring its sustainability into the future; (4) seek to collaborate with people of other religions to initiate community-wide cooperative actions that aim to achieve the sustainability of their shared ecosystem; (5) be open to receiving God's grace that enables the faithful to act cooperatively with the subject and the ecosystem of which it is a part; and (6) be *penitent for conduct* that prevents biota and abiota from cooperating with one another and jeopardizing the sustainability of an ecosystem or the greater biosphere.

127. Although Clarence J. Glacken, in *Traces on the Rhodian Shore: Nature and Culture in Western Thought from Ancient Times to the End of the Eighteenth Century* (Berkeley: University of California, 1967), 214, finds in *Descriptio* an understanding that the human being serves as "a partner of God, sharing in, changing, and improving creation to his own best uses because these accomplishments are for the greater glory of God," I am impressed by the Cistercian's more humble depiction of the cooperation of monks, other biota, and abiota to assure their mutual sustainability and the integrity of the site, all of which are attributed ultimately to God's sustaining goodness. The deep appreciation of the interactivity of the site's constituents and the gratitude expressed add to this sense of humility that permeates the Cistercian's account and serves as an example for how the faithful should act today.

128. Although the notion of cooperation has unique meaning when addressing human cooperation with other species and physical systems, the concept of cooperation among humans as a moral responsibility has permeated the Catholic tradition for centuries as enumerated by the Pontifical Council for Justice and Peace, *Compendium of the Social Doctrine of the Church* (Washington, DC: United States Conference of Catholic Bishops, 2004). Reconstructing this concept today for reflection and action is indeed promising.

129. This principle acknowledges the "option for the poor" that prevails in Christian theology and has been a cornerstone of Catholic social thought for many decades. Sallie McFague, in *The Body of God* (Minneapolis: Fortress Press, 1993), 200–1, describes "nature" poignantly as "the new poor—the oppressed, victimized, deteriorating, excluded" that "deserves our solidarity in its vulnerability." The point she makes is also compelling for any system of ethics that aims to be responsive to the ecological crisis.

130. An informative review of the various approaches to thinking about the sustainability of ecosystems is provided by Robert U. Ayres, Jeroen C. J. M. van den Berrgh, and John M. Gowdy, "Strong versus Weak Sustainability: Economics, Natural Sciences, and Consilience," *Environmental Ethics* 23 (2001): 155–68. See also Mick Commons and Charles Perrings, "Towards an Ecological Economics of Sustainability," *Ecological Economics* 6 (1992): 7–34.

131. E.g., considerable efforts are under way to identify and make plans to restore the integrity of forty-two "Areas of Concern" around the Great Lakes that the International Joint Commission prioritized in 1987 as highly toxic. Progress is slow, primarily for "institutional and financial rather than technical reasons," according to a special report on successful strategies from the International Joint Commission, *Beacons of Light/Des Lumièères dans la Nuit,* March 1998, www.ijc.org/boards/annex2/beacon/beacon.html.

132. Charles Perrings, in "Resilience in the Dynamics of Economy-Environment Systems," *Environmental and Resource Economics* 11 (1998): 503–20, explains two variants requiring consideration: (1) the time taken for a disturbed system to return to its initial state; and (2) the magnitude of disturbance that a system can absorb before it changes to another state. See also Crawford S. Holling, "Resilience and Stability of Ecological Systems," *Annual Review of Ecological Systems* 4 (1973): 1–24.

133. The "precautionary principle" established in Agenda 21 of the Rio Declaration at the 1992 United Nations Conference on Environment and Development is binding on the United States, though little work has been done to implement the principle in this country. See the essays in *Protecting Public Health and the Environment:*

Implementing the Precautionary Principle, ed. Carolyn Raffensperger and Joel Tickner (Washington, DC: Island Press, 1999).

134. As noted in earlier and subsequent chapters, this ethical-political principle is discussed from historical to current times by Benjamin S. Llamzon, "Subsidiarity: The Term, Its Metaphysics and Use," *Aquinas* 21 (January–April 1978): 44–62. See also examples of various ways in which the principle of subsidiarity has been applied to social issues as recounted briefly in *The Compendium of the Social Doctrine of the Church* by the Pontifical Council for Justice and Peace.

6

ACKNOWLEDGING KINSHIP AND
PRACTICING COMPANIONSHIP

As they contemplated a close and unencumbered relationship with God, the early Christian desert fathers, Celtic wanderers, and English hermits conveyed a variety of positive attitudes toward the animals and natural environment of their temporal homes. Primary among these attitudes was an affinity—a *kinship,* in the broadest sense of the term[1]—for a close and caring relationship with other animals, as conveyed in the hagiographies produced by their contemporaries.[2] Writings by and about Francis of Assisi heightened this attitude as he interacted with the wild animals he encountered and other natural phenomena he experienced.

The human relationship with other species is even more profound today. Cosmological and biological findings underscore the relatedness of humans to other species over vast periods of time—from the initial beginning of the universe and the subsequent death of stars that yielded elements essential to life, through the formation of galaxies with at least one solar system and a planet within which simple forms of life emerged, and through the evolutionary process that yielded increasingly complex species, including *Homo sapiens.* When the sentiments of the Christian saints are informed by the facts and theories of evolutionary, molecular, and ethological biology, the behavior pattern suggested should propel more responsible attitudes and actions toward other species.

This chapter provides examples of the various ways in which the saintly desert fathers, Celtic wanderers, English hermits, and Francis of Assisi expressed their intimate relationships with wild species and natural places.[3] Subsequently explained are current evolutionary and molecular biological findings that underscore the close relationship between humans and other species. The next section explores the significance for Christian ethics that the metaphysical hypothesis of biophilia posits for rethinking the human relationship with other species and the natural environment. In the conclusion, I identify some basic

patterns of behavior that are suggested when the kinship concept, with its ac-
companying notion of companionship, is informed by subdisciplines of biology.

Early Christian and Medieval Hagiography

The various attitudes that the Christian desert fathers, Celtic wanderers, English
hermits, and Francis of Assisi conveyed toward animals and the natural environment were precipitated by several factors. Among these are the reasons why
they moved into remote settings, the topographies of the places in which they
settled, and the types of animals they encountered. One constant factor prevailed among these saints—their shared faith in God as their creator, sustainer
in existence, and redeemer, in whose presence they wished to spend eternal life.

According to the "History of the Monks of Egypt" and other hagiographies,
the desert fathers individually left the trappings of urban life in considerable
numbers during the fourth century and retreated to remote, wild areas where,
in solitude, they purified themselves through prayer and self-denial as they sought
a lasting relationship with God.[4] Among these hagiographies are accounts of their
physical and spiritual battles with a devil who, allegedly driven out of urban areas by Christian prayer, sometimes exerted control over wild animals and was
manifested by them.[5] According to these stories, the devil not only wanted to
deter the fathers from their God-centered goals; it also aimed to deter them from
filling the desert with their holiness.[6] Yet the fathers prevailed, despite the hard-
ships of their lives that they accepted with humility. They adjusted to the desert
environment, learned to live in relative harmony with the many large animals
and few reptiles whose habitats they shared, and attributed to the providence of
God their existence in the desert as the place where they could best lead holy
lives.[7] The diverse literature by and about the desert fathers indicates that they
were influenced by four sources: (1) The Hebrew and Christian scriptures;[8] (2) fa-
bles circulating in the third and fourth centuries about a variety of animals, including those favored by the desert fathers, that were intended to provide
instruction on moral behavior;[9] (3) widespread beliefs that holy men have a special relationship with animals and natural phenomena; and (4) Greco-Roman
mythology and philosophy.[10]

The holy lives of the desert fathers influenced the Celtic monks significantly,
as stories about the former spread to distant lands.[11] However, in contrast with
the desert fathers who usually remained in one place for long periods of time,
the Celtic solitaires were wanderers who spread the message of Christianity during their travels.[12] For this reason, they were referred to as *peregrini* because, as
the historian Deborah Vess explains, they journeyed as if on a God-centered pil-
grimage. The theologian, ecologist, and environmental ethicist Susan Power
Bratton argues persuasively from her research on Celtic Christianity that the
wandering monks combined "the best of their ethnic heritage as nature lovers"

with their adoration of Jesus their Savior to produce a "magnificent wilderness literature" that is too often neglected.[13]

Because they were residents of pasture, woodland, and moor, and they had no cities like Alexandria to abandon as did the desert fathers, there is little discourse in Celtic hagiography about withdrawing to remote and wild places. Nor can many antiurban sentiments be found in accounts of their experiences from the sixth to the twelfth centuries. What can be found are countless stories about how the saints fondly treated not only a wider variety of wild animals than the desert fathers, but also how they related to domestic animals and appreciated natural places,[14] especially forests, lakes, and islands.[15] Their attention to diverse landscapes reflects their travels when spreading Christianity and their eventual gravitation toward a variety of areas in which to establish hermitages and monasteries.[16]

Francis of Assisi (1181 or 1182–1226 CE) brought the prior attitudes of the desert, Celtic, and English saints to new heights,[17] as indicated in his writings and in biographies by his contemporaries. He was interested in all aspects of the natural world, where he encountered and responded with piety[18] to creatures of all kinds, though the legends about his interactions with song birds and rabbits greatly outnumbered narratives about large wild animals. As Bratton notes, the animals that Francis encountered were primarily "creatures of the domesticated countryside" who were seldom threatening and controlled with relative ease.[19]

However, the humility and affection with which Francis interacted with other species and the egalitarianism suggested by some of his words and actions, as recounted below in this chapter, heightened the sense of companionship that had been conveyed by the desert fathers and especially by some of the Celtic solitaires who may have influenced his thinking.[20] His attitudes and actions still serve as a model for the Friars Minor that is being built upon today by members and auxiliaries of his order.[21] In 1979, the late Pope John Paul II proclaimed Francis "the heavenly Patron of those who promote ecology"[22] because "he offers Christians an example of genuine and deep respect for the integrity of creation."[23]

Enumerated in this section are a variety of attitudes the saints expressed toward the animals they encountered and natural places in which they lived while striving to be closer to God. They protected and fed wild animals. They acted with relative compassion, love, affection, kindness, devotion, and steadfastness toward them. They loved, appreciated, and desired to preserve the natural environment. They perceived animals as reciprocating their care and compassion by feeding, serving, and mourning them and other holy people. Some thought about animals as their followers or disciples, and a few used familial language when referring to animals and natural phenomena.

None of the following synopses should be taken literally as having happened exactly the way they are recounted. They are hagiographies—legends about the saints. Nevertheless, these stories convey the saints' overall attitudes toward and affinity for the animals and the places they mutually inhabited. The animals with whom some saints shared their remote settings were often the only other living beings with whom they interacted in their otherwise solitary lives.

Physically Protecting and Giving Nourishment to Animals

The hagiographies of the desert fathers, Celtic solitaires, English hermits, and Francis of Assisi are replete with accounts of their having protected and fed wild animals. In some cases, the animals lingered with the saints, conveying a sense of affinity the animals had for their saviors. A few examples will have to suffice.

The Celtic solitaire Maedoc, the first bishop of Ferns (ca. 558–626), was praying in the woods, saw a stag pursued by hounds, and threw the corner of his plaid[24] over the stag's horns to protect it from the hounds, who subsequently were unable to find a trace of the stag as they approached him.[25] One of the great saints of Ireland, Kevin (ca. 498–618) was described as saving a boar from a huntsman who followed it into the glen where Kevin was praying under a tree while "a crowd of birds perched on his shoulders and his hands" and others were "flitting about him" and "singing" to him. The huntsman was "dumbfounded" by this scene, and, "for the sake of the holy solitary's blessing, let the boar go free."[26] The saintly Patrick (387–461) prevented a fawn from being killed by his companions when they found it lying on the spot where a church was subsequently built.[27]

The English hermit Godric of Finchale (1070–1170) saved a beautiful stag from the huntsmen's hounds when the stag sought refuge in his hermitage and pleaded for help with "plaintive cries." According to the legend, "the old man came out, saw the stag shivering and exhausted at his gate, and moved with pity bade it hush its moans, and opening the door of his hut, let it go in. The creature dropped at the good father's feet." Shutting the door behind him, the holy man sat down in the open while the hounds followed the scent of the stag to the hermitage and encircled it. In response to the baying of their hounds, the huntsmen hacked a path through the surrounding brushwood of thorns and briars, came upon the hermit in his poor rags, questioned him about the stag, looked at "the angelic beauty of his countenance, and in reverence for his holiness," fell before him, and "asked his pardon for their bold intrusion." Godric let the stag go free that evening, but "for years thereafter" the stag went out of its way to visit him and lie at his feet, "to show what gratitude it could for its deliverance."[28] Other hunted animals came to his hermitage as if "by some divine instinct" that they could find refuge with the holy man. After Godric saved them, he would "send them away to their familiar haunts."[29]

Godric also freed birds and other little animals that had been captured by servants:

> If anyone in his service had caught a bird or little beast in a snare or a trap or a noose, as soon as he found it he would snatch it from their hands and let it go free in the fields or the glades of the wood. So that many a time they would hide their captive spoils under a corn measure or a basket or some more secret hiding-place

still: but even so they could never deceive him or keep it hidden. For often without any telling, and indeed with his serving-man disavowing and protesting, he would go straight to the place where the creatures had been hidden: and while the man would stand by crimson with fear and confusion, he would lift them out and set them free.[30]

Many stories were told about Francis of Assisi's saving doves, fish, waterfowl, and rabbits that others had captured. For example, he freed some turtledoves that a boy had caught in a snare, was carrying to market, but, "inspired by God," gave them to the holy man when he asked: "Good boy, please give me those doves so that such innocent birds, which in Holy Scripture are symbols of pure, humble and faithful souls, will not fall into the hands of cruel men who will kill them."[31] Francis also released a rabbit that had been caught in a trap[32] and told it to go wherever it wished.[33]

Several legends focus on solitaires who fed large wild animals. For example, an unnamed hermit who lived about twelve miles from the Nile River was described as having taken his guests to an oasis where they encountered a lion: "The wild beast—you would say it was at the command of God—modestly withdrew a little way and sat down, while the old man plucked the fruit from the lower branches. He held out his hand, full of dates; and up the creature ran and took them as frankly as any tame animal about the house: and when it had finished eating, it went away."[34]

John Moschus (ca. 550–619) included in *Pratum spirituale*[35] a legend about a hermit of "great virtue" who "would welcome the lions into his cave with him, and offer them food in his lap."[36] The church historian Rufinus of Aquilea (ca. 340–410 CE) described the hermit Theon's going into the desert followed by "a great troop of the beasts of the desert"—most likely gazelle, goats, and wild ass—drawing water from his well, and offering cupfuls to the beasts "in return for their kindness in attending him."[37] After curing a blind hyena whelp that its mother brought to him,[38] the desert father Macarius of Alexandria (?–ca. 395 CE) promised to feed her if she could not find wild game to eat: "The hyaena bowed her head to the ground, and dropped on her knees, bending her paws, moving her head up and down, looking at his face as if she were promising him. . . . From time to time she would come to seek the old man; if she had not been able to find food, she would come to him and he would throw her a loaf."[39] Maedoc of Ferns was "seized with pity" when encountering some starving wolves and fed them with eight lambs.[40] He also fed a calf to wolves who came to him while he was in his cell.[41]

The holy men were also depicted as quenching the thirst of animals. In *Life of Hilarion,* Jerome (331–420), one of the most learned of the desert fathers who visited and wrote about many of them, described Antony's allowing wild asses to drink the water on which he relied, though he forbade their from eating the fruit and vegetables of his garden because they did not help sow it.[42] Kevin commended his monastery to the care of trustworthy monks, built a tiny hunt in a narrow strip between the mountain and the lake, and gave water "from his hands" to the wild animals who "would drink . . . like domestic creatures."[43]

Expressions of Piety toward Animals

In its full medieval sense, piety encompassed several key attributes—loving, affectionate, kind, faithful, compassionate, devoted, and, in a sacramental sense, reverential. The fullest expression of piety in word and action can be found in works by and about Francis of Assisi, though these attributes were demonstrated centuries before by some of the desert fathers, Celtic wanderers, and English hermits. Many of these legends are about the holy men and birds, for, as Bratton notes, "an ultimate sign of saintliness is never to have molested a bird."[44]

When Ciaran (?–ca. 530 CE), the first bishop of Ossory, was a "lad," a hawk swept down from the sky upon a small bird brooding on its nest, caught it, and carried it away. Ciaran prayed for the bird, the hawk returned and laid it mangled and half-dead before him. Under his "pitying gaze," the bird was "made whole" and "sat brooding on her nest, happy and unhurt."[45]

Godric's "gentleness" of heart prompted him to watch over "the very reptiles and the creatures of the earth" even in harsh weather:

> In winter, when all about was frozen stiff in the cold, he would go out barefoot, and if he lighted on any animal helpless with misery of the cold, he would set it under his armpit or in his bosom to warm it. Many a time would the kind soul go spying under the thick hedges or tangled patches of briars, and if haply he found a creature that had lost its way, or cowed with the harshness of the weather, or tired, or half dead, he would recover it with all the healing art he had.[46]

The English hermit Bartholomew of Farne (?–1193) was moved to compassion by the birds that inhabited Holy Island off the coast of Northumbria where Cuthbert (ca. 634/35–687) served as bishop of a great Benedictine Abbey. One of the ducklings who was following its mother fell into a cleft of a creviced rock. In distress, the mother went to Bartholomew, tugged at the hem of his cloak with her beak, and led him to where the chick could be seen clinging to the rock. Climbing down, the hermit rescued the duckling and returned it to its mother.[47]

During one Lenten season, Kevin was praying in a little hut "in his accustomed fashion, with his hand outstretched through the window and lifted up to heaven." A blackbird settled on his hand and laid an egg in it. "So moved was the saint that in all patience and gentleness he remained, neither closing nor withdrawing his hand . . . until the young ones were fully hatched." As a sign of remembrance of this incident, images of Kevin throughout Ireland show a blackbird in his hand.[48]

Francis of Assisi "was filled with compassion" not only for people in need, but also for "dumb animals, reptiles, birds and other creatures," according to his first biographer, Thomas of Celano.[49] Bonaventure, a subsequent biographer and minister general of the Order of Friars Minor that Francis founded, devoted a chapter of his *Life of St. Francis* to exploring the saint's affectionate piety toward wild animals and how they were affectionate toward him. "True piety," Bonaventure wrote, "had so filled Francis's heart and penetrated its depths that it seemed to have appropriated the man of God completely into its dominion."[50] For example, Francis made nests for the doves he purchased from the boy who had snared them, telling them: "I want to rescue you from death and make nests for you where you can lay your eggs and fulfill the Creator's commandment to multiply." Bonaventure continued: "And the doves settled in the nests made by St. Francis, and laid their eggs and reared their young right among the friars, and they increased in numbers. They were so tame and familiar with St. Francis and the other friars that they seemed to be like chickens that had always been raised by the friars. And they did not leave until St. Francis gave them permission, with his blessing."[51]

According to Bonaventure, the rabbit that Francis released from a trap was told to go wherever it wished. However, when set free and called back, the rabbit demonstrated a mutual affinity for the holy man:

> "When the kind father called, it ran and jumped into his arms. He fondled it with warm affection and seemed to pity it like a mother. After warning it gently not to let itself be caught again, he let it go free. But as often as he placed it on the ground to run away, it always came back to the father's arms, as if in some secret way it perceived the kind feeling he had for it. Finally, at the father's command, the friars carried it away to a safer place far from the haunts of men."[52]

Bonaventure also described the affinity Francis had with a waterfowl that a fisherman gave to him: "Francis took it gladly and opened his hands to let it go, but it did not want to. He prayed for a long time with his eyes turned to heaven. After more than an hour, he came back to himself as if from another realm and gently told the bird again to go away and praise God. Having received his permission with a blessing, the bird expressed its joy in the movements of its body, and flew away."[53]

When offered a large fish, Francis put it back into the water. However, the fish also showed an attachment to the saint: "The fish played about in the water in front of the man of God; and, as if it were attracted by his love, it would not go away from the ship until it received from him his permission with a blessing."[54]

Bonaventure's *Life of St. Francis* is filled with similar accounts of the saint's greeting lambs, birds, and other animals who responded in extraordinary ways.[55] He also pointed to the joy Francis exuded when encountering birds and how he was charmed by their beauty and variety as well as their attention and familiarity with him for which he gave thanks to their Creator.[56] Thomas of Celano exclaimed the following about Francis's love for creatures: "Toward little worms even he glowed with a very great love, for he had read this saying about the Savior: *I am a worm, not a man.* Therefore he picked them up from the road and placed them in a safe place, lest they be crushed by the feet of the passerby. What shall I say of the lower creatures, when he would see to it that bees would be provided with honey in the winter, or the best wine, lest they should die from the cold."[57]

Loving, Appreciating, and Preserving the Natural Environment

According to Athanasius, Antony fell "in love" with his third and final home "as if it had been offered to him by God."[58] Jerome further described the mountain environment in which Antony lived:

There is a tall and rocky mountain, about a mile in circumference, that produces water at its foot, some of which is absorbed by the sand while some flows down to the lower area, gradually forming a stream. Above this stream grow innumerable palm trees which make the place very pleasant and comfortable. Here you might have seen the old man Hilarion rushing from one place to another with the blessed Antony's disciples. 'Here,' they said, 'he used to sing psalms; here he used to pray. Here he would work and here he would rest when he was tired. He planted these vines and bushes himself.'[59]

Antony gardened for his own subsistence and eventually to feed the visitors who sought spiritual direction from him. Other monks followed his example by providing for their necessities of life within their hermitages. They harvested palm fronds and other natural sources for their needs, and their disruption of the natural environment was minimal. Among the monastic virtues they sought, as indicated in *The Sayings of the Fathers,* are quietness, self-restraint, lacking in material possessions, patience, and contemplation.[60] Though they chose this lifestyle in order to focus on their relationship with God, the virtues they developed also led to their exemplifying environmentally compatible ways of functioning in their hermitages.

Antony expressed another dimension of appreciation for the natural environment. When a philosopher asked him how he contented himself when he did not have "the comfort of books," he replied: "My book, philosopher, is the nature of created things, and as often as I have a mind to read the words of God, it is at my hand."[61] For Antony, the natural world was created by God and is revelatory of God.[62]

Macarius of Alexandris and Kevin of Ireland also expressed love for the natural environment. According to Rufinis of Aquliea, Macarius "was a lover beyond all other men of the desert, and had explored its ultimate and inaccessible wastes."[63] God sent an angel to Kevin to lead him and fifty monks to a place God appointed for them. The angel told him that God would level the four mountains that enclose the valley "into rich and gentle meadow lands." However, Kevin replied that he did not want to sadden the wild creatures who were his "house mates": "I have no wish that the creatures of God should be moved because of me: my God can help that place in some other fashion. And moreover, all the wild creatures on these mountains are my house mates, gentle and familiar with me, and they would be sad of this that thou hast said."[64] The mountains were not leveled as Kevin requested. He and his monks adjusted their lifestyle to the area to which the angel led them.[65]

Some stories tell of the holy men's desire to protect forests. For example, Columba (521–97) was so opposed to the unnecessary felling of trees that he did not place his sanctuary in the traditional position facing east.[66] According to Lady Gregory, Columba composed the following hymn of praise for the oak-covered Doire in Ireland:

It is the reason I love Doire, for its quietness for its purity;
it is quite full of white angels from the one end to the other.

It is the reason I love Doire, for its quietness for its purity;
quite full of white angels in every leaf of the oaks of Doire.
My Doire my little oakwood, my dwelling and my white cell;
O living God in Heaven, it is a pity for him that harms it![67]

Kevin "promised hell and short life" to anyone who would burn the wood, whether dry or green, from a particular forest.[68] Other saints who explicitly expressed their appreciation for wooded areas include Mochuda of Lismore (sixth–seventh centuries CE) who walked through the woods singing psalms,[69] Maedoc who prayed in the "recesses of a wood,"[70] and Francis of Assisi who meditated in the woods.[71] According to Bratton, these saints produced one of the first preservationist ethics on record.[72] Francis also promoted a conservationist ethic when he "forbade the brothers to cut down the whole tree when they cut wood, so that it might have hope of sprouting again."[73]

Additional directives that Francis issued to the Friars Minor demonstrated his appreciation for other natural settings from another perspective—their sacramentality in manifesting the presence of God:

> He commanded the gardener to leave the border around the garden undug, so that in their proper times the greenness of the grass and the beauty of the flowers might announce the beauty of the Father of all things. He commanded that a little place be set aside in the garden for sweet-smelling and flowering plants, so that they would bring those who look upon them to the memory of the eternal Sweetness.[74]

Of course, the desert fathers, Celtic wanderers, English hermits, and Francis of Assisi appreciated natural, solitary settings for prayer and contemplation, as indicated above. Special holy seasons, particularly Lent, propelled them to seek solitude for prayer and penance. For example, Francis sought a quiet place for Lent, crossed over to an island in a lake, went into "a dense thicket in which many thorn bushes and small trees had made a sort of little cabin or den. And he began to pray and contemplate heavenly things in that place. And he stayed there all through Lent without eating and without drinking, except for half of one of those little loaves of bread ."[75] He divided the rest of his time between ministering to the people and withdrawing to the woods and mountains where he could contemplate in "peaceful ecstasy."[76]

Furthermore, according to Thomas of Celano, Francis bore a "very great affection . . . for all things that are God's." This affection stemmed at least in part from his sacramental sensibility—that all natural entities manifested the attributes and presence of God:

> Who would be able to narrate the sweetness he enjoyed while contemplating in creatures the wisdom of their Creator, his power and his goodness? Indeed, he was often filled with a wonderful and ineffable joy from this consideration while he looked upon the sun, while he beheld the moon and while he gazed upon the stars and the firmament. O simple piety and pious simplicity! Toward little worms even he glowed with a very great love, for he had read this saying about the Savior: I

am a worm, not a man. Therefore he picked them up from the road and placed them in a safe place, lest they be crushed by the feet of the passerby. What shall I say of the lower creatures, when he would see to it that bees would be provided with honey in the winter, or the best wine lest they should die from the cold.[77]

Though their impact on the areas in which they settled as hermits was minimal, due to their vows of self-discipline and self-denial, some monks eventually established monasteries for community living in wilderness areas, introduced the moldboard plow for subsistence farming,[78] and thereby encouraged the trend begun by the Romans toward opening the wilderness to land clearing.[79] However, as Bratton concludes convincingly, the monks were more interested in occupying oak forests than in destroying them, and they often left the forests standing at the sites of their sanctuaries and hermitages.[80] Some Celtic monastic settlements were built in lowland areas that had been forested previously, thereby minimizing the monks' disruption to the natural contours of those areas.[81]

Animal Reciprocity by Aiding, Feeding, and Protecting the Solitaires

The abundant stories about the monks having been fed, served, protected, and mourned by wild animals have often been interpreted as God's providence working through animals and the natural environment.[82] Tales were also told about the monks ordering animals to aid them and animals departing when the monks were no longer holy. Some of the animals' services were portrayed as reciprocal to the monks for their services to them.

According to Jerome, a raven that had fed half a loaf of bread to Paul the Hermit for sixty years dropped a whole loaf to him when Antony visited him in his cave.[83] Macarius of Alexandria ran out of water when traveling in arid lands, found a herd of antelope, and took some milk from the udder of one that followed him back to his cell and "continued to nurse him."[84] Journeying in the desert under "the excessive blazing of the sun" and "unbearable heat," Antony "knelt down and stretched out his hands in supplications to the Lord," after which "the tears fell from his eyes" and "there burst forth a bubbling spring in the exact spot where he was praying." Antony and the monk traveling with him "quenched their thirst, cooled their burning limbs, filled their waterskins, and found the camel so it could also drink from the spring."[85] The monk Sabas needed a source of water for a monastery he was establishing and found "an even supply that never fails" when a wild ass was digging for water."[86] An otter brought salmon to some of Kevin's monks but, when one monk decided the otter would look better as a glove, the otter recognized his danger, ceased to come, and left the monks without salmon.[87] Cuthbert received a fish from an eagle,[88] a "portion of hog's lard" from a raven that he used for greasing the shoes of monks who visited him,[89] bread from a horse,[90] and, from the sea, timber for flooring "on the very spot" on which he was planning to build a hut.[91]

Stories varied about animals aiding the monks. The Abba Helle was ferried across the river by a crocodile that had terrorized the neighborhood.[92] Crocodiles also carried Pachome across the river on their backs.[93] Otters warmed Cuthbert's feet with their pantings and tried to dry them with their fur while the saint was praying on the beach.[94] A lion entered the holy hermit Poemen's cave on a cold evening and slept beside him to keep him warm while a visitor remained extremely cold.[95] A stag came daily to Ciaran of Ossory, lay down before the monk, and allowed him to use its antlers as a reading stand.[96] A cow who used to lick Kevin's cloak when put out to pasture became frenzied and stopped producing prodigious amounts of milk when the herdsman berated the monk and called him uncomplimentary names.[97] Kevin accidentally dropped his Psalter into a lake and an otter returned it to him dry and readable.[98] Columba, who founded a monastery on Iona, off the coast of Scotland, forgot his books and a stag returned them to him on his back.[99]

In another highly imaginative legend, a cock, a mouse, and a fly are described as aiding Colman (605–76), the bishop of Lindesfarne. The cock crowed to awaken the saint at night so he would be on time for Lauds. The mouse would not allow him to sleep or lie at peace beyond the fixed hour that he had established for himself according to his vows. The fly rendered an even stranger service to Colman. When he was reading his holy books, the fly would "trot up and down his codex" and, at the saint's command when called to his duties, would sit down upon the line at which he had stopped reading and remain there until the saint returned. Colman was disheartened when "the three little creatures died" and "their kind service and company was lost" to him. The legend's author indicated that Colman attributed the creatures' service as an example of the "amazing kindness of God" by directing the animals to rendering their "good offices" as "a kind of human ministering" according to God's "divine wisdom."[100]

Bonaventure described therapeutic services that a live pheasant and a falcon rendered to Francis when he was ill. A nobleman sent the pheasant to him, and the pheasant "was drawn to him with such affection" that it would not be separated from him. When the pheasant was given to another man, it refused to eat and was finally brought back to Francis, where it "showed signs of joy and ate heartily." The pheasant remained with Francis until he recovered from his illness and the pheasant was dismissed.[101] The falcon became attached to Francis "as a friend" when the saint was staying at La Verna and woke him up by "making noise and singing" when it was time for him to say the divine office and "shook out of him all sluggish laziness." When Francis was ill, "the falcon had pity" on him and did not wake him up for the early vigils.[102]

In some cases, the holy hermits ordered animals to serve them. Mochuda commandeered two deer to pull a poor man's plow.[103] Abban ordered wolves to tend his sheep.[104] And Abba Amoun called upon snakes to guard his cell.[105] Kevin commanded a doe to provide milk for a foster fawn; when a wolf killed the fawn, the holy man ordered the wolf to take the place of the fawn so the doe would continue to provide milk.[106] On another occasion, he made a stag pull a chariot.[107]

Goods and services rendered to the holy solitaires by the sea, seacoasts, islands, forests, and other natural settings are recounted in many legends. The remote natural settings that they sought offered the solitude they needed and wanted so they could repent their sins in quiet and without disruption by other humans.[108] At least implicitly but often explicitly, the solitaires attributed to God's providence the goods and services rendered to them.[109]

Animals' Laments for Dying and Deceased Solitaires

When Cellach of Killala (? ninth century) was dying, all the birds of the forest waited in hushed appreciation.[110] The lion, whose infected paw the Abbott Gerasimus had treated, refused to leave him, grieved upon his death, lay down roaring on his grave, and eventually died there.[111] Lions rushed to mourn the death of Paul the Hermit, as recounted by Jerome from Antony's observations:

> Two lions came running from the inner desert, their manes flowing over their necks. At first Antony was terrified at the sight of them but when he focused his mind on God he was able to stand still without fear as if what he saw was a pair of doves. They came straight towards the corpse of the blessed old man and stopped there; wagging their tails in devotion they lay down at his feet, roaring loudly as if to show that in their own way they were lamenting as best they could. They then began to dig the ground nearby with their paws: vying with each other to remove the sand, they dug out a space large enough for one man. They then went straight up to Antony, their necks bent and their ears laid back, and licked his hands and feet as if demanding a reward for their hard work. He realized that they were asking him for a blessing. Immediately he burst out in praise of Christ because dumb animals, too, were able to understand that there was a God. . . . Making a sign to them with his hand, he ordered them to depart, and they obeyed.[112]

When a puzzled cleric saw a bird lamenting the death of Molua (554–622/23), an angel appeared and told him: "Molua MacOcha has died, and therefore all living creatures bewail him, for never has he killed any animal, little or big; so not more to men bewail him than the other animals, and the little bird thou beholdest."[113]

Animals as Followers, Disciples, and Companions of Holy People

When Ciaran of Ossory became a hermit in Munster, he sat under a tree and encountered "a fierce boar." The boar "fled in sore terror, . . . and then, made tame by God," returned to Ciaran "as though to be his serving-man" and became "Ciaran's first disciple or monk . . . in that place." The storyteller continued:

> That boar, as the man of God watched, began with great vigour tearing down twigs and grass with his teeth to build him a little cell. At that time there was no one with the saint he had left his disciples behind him and escaped alone to that solitude. Later on other animals came from their dens in the wilds to St. Ciaran, a fox, and a badger, and a wolf and a deer: and they stayed with him, tame and gentle. And they obeyed the saint's word in all things, as if they had been his monks.[114]

The animals lived there for the rest of their lives, "tame and familiar," while men from throughout the area sought Ciaran's direction for their lives and a monastery was formed.[115]

Bonaventure indicated in *Life of St. Francis* that the founder of the Friars Minor had a little lamb "out of reverence for the most gentle Lamb of God" and that Francis considered the lamb his "disciple." When Francis left Rome, he left the lamb in the care of a noble woman:

> Now the lamb went with the lady to church, standing reverently by her side as her inseparable companion, as if it had been trained in spiritual matters by the saint. If the lady was late in rising in the morning, the lamb rose and nudged her with its horns and woke her with its bleating, urging her with its nods and gestures to hurry to the church. On account of this, the lamb, which was Francis's disciple and had now become a master of devotion, was held by the lady as an object of wonder and love.[116]

Some stories describe animals as following the monks' instructions, especially those given by Francis. According to Bonaventure, a sheep "carefully observed" Francis's instructions. When the sheep heard the friars chanting in choir: "It would enter the church, genuflect without instructions from anyone, and bleat before the altar of the Virgin, the mother of the Lamb, as if it wished to greet her. Besides, when the most sacred body of Christ was elevated at mass, it would bow down on bended knees as if this reverent animal were reproaching those who were not devout and inviting the devout to reverence the sacrament."[117] Bonaventure indicated that Francis converted the wolf of Gubbio in "the best monastic tradition" as the desert monk Gerasimus with the lion and Ciaran with the wild boar. Following "the example of the Franciscans," the wolf "became a humble, mind-manner beggar."[118]

Other accounts refer to the animals' responsiveness to the monks' preaching. Abba Bes in Egypt preached to both hippos and crocodiles; inspired by his words, they ceased ravaging the countryside.[119] After founding his order of monks, Francis saw on some trees "a great multitude of birds" and told his companions to wait for him while he went to preach to them: "Entering into the field, he began to preach to the birds which were on the ground, and suddenly all those also on the trees came round him, and all listened while St. Francis preached to them, and did not fly away until he had given them his blessing. And Brother Masseo related afterwards to Brother James of Massa how St. Francis went among them and even touched them with his garments, and how none of them moved."

According to Bonaventure, Francis delivered the following sermon to the birds:

> My little bird sisters, you owe much to God your Creator, and you must always and everywhere praise him, because he has given you the freedom to fly anywhere—also he has given you a double and triple covering, and your colorful and pretty clothing, and your food is ready without your working for it, and your singing that was taught to you by the Creator, and your numbers that have been multiplied by the blessing of God—and because He preserved your species in Noah's ark so that your race should not disappear from the earth. And you are also

indebted to Him for the realm of the air that He assigned to you. Moreover, you neither sow or reap, yet God nourishes you, and He gives you the rivers and the springs to drink from. He givess you high mountains and hills, rocks and crags as refuges, and lofty trees in which to make your nests. And although you do not know how to spin or sew, God gives you and your little ones the clothing that you need. So the Creator loves you very much, since He gives you so many good things. Therefore, my little bird sisters, be careful not to be ungrateful, but strive always to praise God.[120]

Francis was "charmed with their beautiful variety" and with "their attention and familiarity, for all which he devoutly gave thanks to the Creator." Having finished his sermon, Francis "made the sign of the cross, and gave them leave to fly away."[121]

Francis also preached to the flowers and invited them to praise God. "So it was with cornfields and vineyards, rocks and woods, and all the beauties of the fields, splashing fountains, lush green gardens, earth and fire, air and wind," Thomas of Celano reported, that Francis would "in complete sincerity, urge to love God and to serve him with gladness."[122]

Anthony of Padua (1195–1231 CE) delivered to fish a sermon similar to Francis's sermon to birds that is quoted above. Anthony called the fish to "listen to the word of God, since the faithless heretics refuse to hear it." He tailored his sermon to the nature and habitats of the fish, exhorting them "to praise and bless the Lord" who has given them "so many more blessings than to other creatures."[123]

The Use of Familial Language

Although Francis of Assisi is known for his use of sibling language when addressing nonhuman animals and natural phenomena, at least one precursor paved the way. The Celtic monk Ciaran of Ossory used the term "brother" during the sixth century—seven centuries before Francis founded his mendicant order—when speaking to the fox, the badger, the wolf, and the boar, who he characterized as his "disciples" who were "like monks."[124]

Francis used the terms "brother" and "sister" frequently, as indicated in his works and those about him. In *Life of St. Francis,* Bonaventure wrote that the founder of his order was "filled with even more abundant piety, calling creatures, no matter how small, by the name of brother or sister, because he knew they had the same source as himself."[125] One celebrated example is "The Canticle of Brother Sun," in which Francis perceived God as being praised through "Sir Brother Sun," "Sister Moon and the stars," "Brother Wind," "Sister Water," "Brother Fire," and "Sister Mother Earth."[126]

As noted above, when describing Francis's sermonizing to birds, he referred to them as "sisters." Bonaventure told about one experience when Francis went to the hermitage of La Verna to observe a forty-day fast in honor of the Archangel Michael: "Birds of different kinds flew around his cell, with melodious singing and joyful movements, as if rejoicing at his arrival, and seemed to be inviting and enticing the devoted father to stay. When he saw this, he said to his companion:

'I see, brother, that it is God's will that we stay here for some time, for our sisters the birds seem so delighted at our presence.'"[127]

Francis occasionally used familial language with a mixture of joy and admonishment, according to Bonaventure. The admonishment may convey some degree of control over other animals. For example, when he was walking with a friar through the marshes of Venice and came upon a large flock of birds singing among the reeds, he said to the friar: "Our sisters the birds are praising their Creator; so we should go in among them and chant the Lord's praises and the canonical hours." They entered and began to pray, but the birds were making so much noise that the friars could not hear one another's prayers. Francis told "Sister birds" to "stop singing" until the friars had finished their "duty of praising God!" At once they were silent and remained so until Francis "gave them permission" to resume their singing.[128]

Francis marveled at the "magnificence" of a cricket that perched on a fig tree beside his cell and sang. According to Bonaventure,

> [Francis] called it one day, and it flew upon his hand as if it had been taught by God. He said to it: "Sing, my sister cricket, praise the Lord Creator with your joyful song!" It obeyed without delay and began to sing; nor did it stop until at his command it flew back to its usual place. There it remained for eight days, coming each day, singing and returning, all at his command. Finally the man of God said to his companions: "Let us give our sister cricket permission to go away now, for she has cheered us enough with her singing and has aroused us to praise God over the space of eight days." With his permission, it departed and never appeared there again, as if it did not dare to disobey his command in the slightest way.[129]

When offered "a large live fish," he addressed it "brother in his usual way and put it back into the water by the boat. The fish played about in the water in front of the man of God; and as if it were attracted by his love, it would not go away from the ship until it received from him his permission with a blessing."[130]

Francis also used familial language when "taming" a fierce animal—the wolf of Gubbio. At a time when he was staying in the town of Gubbio, he learned about "a fearfully large and fierce wolf which was so rabid with hunger that it devoured not only animals but even human beings." Francis "had pity on the people and decided to go out and meet the wolf." He called for "Brother Wolf" to come to him and proceeded to admonish him, using the familial salutation eleven times according to the account in *The Little Flowers of St. Francis*.[131]

Though he used sibling terminology with many different animals and natural phenomena as identified above, he had a favorite. Bonaventure explained: "He embraced more affectionately and sweetly those creatures [lambs] which present a natural reflection of Christ's merciful gentleness and represent him in Scriptural symbolism. He often paid to ransom lambs that were being led to their death, remembering that most gentle Lamb who willed to be led to slaughter [Is 53:7] to pay the ransom of sinners."[132]

When a "ferocious sow" killed a little lamb one night, Francis is alleged to have exclaimed: "Alas, brother lamb, innocent animal, you represent Christ to men."[133] Thus, the lamb had a sacramental quality that made it particularly beloved.

Anthony of Padua referred to the fish to whom he was sermonizing as "brother fish."[134] Like Francis, he seemed to understand and appreciate the nature and habitats of the fish and geared his interaction with them accordingly.

Although Ciaran, Francis, and Anthony used familial language for nonhuman animals, hagiographies that describe their preaching, admonishing, or preferring one over another temper the conclusion that they considered animals and natural phenomena equal to humans. Yet the use of "brother" and "sister" suggest an affinity the monks had for them that should not be overlooked or dismissed as merely romantic. When coupled with other positive attitudes toward animals and natural settings in which the monks lived as they sought a closer relationship with God, familial language may best be understood as strengthening the sense of companionship the holy men had toward the other species in their midst.

Summation

The hagiographies of the desert fathers, Celtic wanderers, English hermits, and Francis of Assisi indicate that these holy men protected and fed wild animals; expressed varying degrees of piety toward them; appreciated, loved, preserved, and conserved natural settings as well as other natural phenomena; perceived animals as aiding, feeding, and protecting them as manifestations of God's providing for them; interpreted animal actions toward the dying and dead monks as lamenting them; considered animals their followers, disciples, and companions; and addressed animals in familial language. Although the hagiographic accounts cannot be taken literally,[135] they can be appropriated for the meaning that the storytellers seem to have been conveying about the attitudes and actions of the saints during their times and from their understanding of the world. Making this attempt is especially warranted in order to ascertain to what extent they can be helpful in providing guidance for those who share their religious faith. Doing so is especially important during our time, when the rate of species extinction is accelerating, a rapid loss of biodiversity is occurring, the ongoing degradation and destruction of ecosystems is well documented, and adverse affects of human actions on the biosphere are identified.

The basic meaning conveyed in the literature by and about the aforementioned saints is that they had a close affinity with the animals and the deserts, forests, glens, and mountains where they dwelled. As they retreated from contacts with other humans, they treated other animals as their companions during their temporal lives. Those who wrote stories about the desert fathers, Celtic wanderers, English hermits, and Francis of Assisi at the very least intended to inform the faithful about the exemplary lives they led as they struggled to overcome impediments to a lasting relationship with God.

Evolutionary, Molecular, and Ethological Biology

Although the saintly desert fathers, Celtic *peregrini*, English hermits, and Francis of Assisi had an affinity for the animals and the environments in which they lived, they did not know how closely related humans are to other species biologically. Nor did the saints know that all species and phenomena have a common beginning approximately 14 billion years ago. When informed by contemporary cosmology and biology, the sense of companionship that the saints had toward animals and natural phenomena becomes even more profound, and the guidance for human behavior that the accounts of their lives suggest becomes more realistic, helpful, and meaningful when understood within the Christian faith context.

In this section, the facts and theories of cosmologists, biophysicists, evolutionary and molecular biologists, and ethologists are examined sequentially for their contributions to understanding the relatedness of *Homo sapiens* to other species and natural systems while also recognizing the distinctiveness of humans when compared with other species. These findings reinforce and deepen the sense of kinship that people of faith should have today, especially toward other species. When grounded in faith in God, the purposeful creator and sustainer of the cosmological-biological continuum, a scientifically informed kinship sensibility should prompt the faithful to live companionably with one another, other species, and their shared habitats.

The Emergence of Life from the Early Universe

Born from an explosive finite singularity, often referred to as the "Big Bang," the infant universe was composed of hydrogen and helium. Some quantities of these two elements were converted eventually in the furnaces of dying stars into carbon, nitrogen, oxygen, sulfur, iron, and other heavy elements that were spewed into interstellar space. Subsequently, they collected, perhaps under the binding power of new galaxies, to form new stars that were enriched with the building blocks of planets and their living and nonliving constituents.[136] As the biophysicist Harold Morowitz explained, "the atoms of every living thing, including each one of us, were at one time in the history of the universe cooked up deep in the core of some unbelievably hot star."[137] The principal investigator of the National Aeronautics Space Administration's Stardust Project, a project that is charged with collecting and examining interstellar materials from comet Wild 2, reflected recently on the significance of the human–stardust relationship: "The relation between humans and stardust, amazingly is that, virtually all the atoms in our bodies were in little grains like the ones we're bringing back from the comet."[138]

Approximately 10 billion years after the universe came into existence, our sun, a third-generation star of average size, began to condense from a complex brew of hydrogen, helium, carbon, nitrogen, oxygen, and other interstellar elements that resulted from supernovae. Planets also condensed from the same mix of material. Earth attained its basic form about 4.5 billion years ago and kept gathering material as comets and asteroids fell into its gravitational center. Whenever there was a large impact, the surface of the planet was heat-sterilized and all the oceans boiled up into the clouds. About 4 billion years ago, Earth cooled down sufficiently to allow life to emerge and persist, though exactly how living organisms came into existence has not been determined conclusively. On the basis of ongoing experiments, Morowitz suspects that molecules could have been formed "with relative ease in deep rift zones on the ocean floor" from which living organisms eventually emerged.[139] The fact that fossils found in Australia are estimated to be 3.56 billion years old indicates that living organisms appeared soon after the physical circumstances were in place to allow their emergence.[140]

For the first 2 billion years of life on Earth, the dominant form of living organisms was probably prokaryotes—simple one-celled organisms with a minimum of internal structure, the most common forms of which are bacteria.[141] They "busily explored the available chemical domains," and one or more of their experiments led to the invention of photosynthesis, "a fundamental development" that produces oxygen from water. As organisms that were capable of photosynthesis multiplied, the amount of oxygen in the atmosphere began to rise very rapidly, providing new ways of obtaining energy that led to radical changes on the surface of the planet. Organisms developed with a more clearly defined nucleus, a nuclear membrane, well-defined chromosomes, and other significant characteristics.[142] Their evolution into the eukaryotic organisms with which we interact today—plants, animals, and other humans—is the subject of evolutionary biology.

The Emergence and Uniqueness of Homo sapiens

With a "healthy dose of chance"[143] constrained by some basic laws of physics and affected by shifting environmental conditions, some eukaryotic organisms eventually organized into a lineage from which *Homo sapiens* evolved. The hominid lineage probably diverged from the chimpanzee lineage about 5 to 7 million years ago on the African continent. According to the evolutionary biologist Francisco Ayala, fossils discovered in Africa date the appearance of the bipedal and small-brained *Australopithecus anamensis* at about 4 million years ago, the prolific toolmaker *Homo habilis* at approximately 2 million years ago,[144] and the continent-wanderer *Homo erectus* at 1.5 million years ago.[145] The transition of *Homo erectus* to *Homo sapiens* may have occurred about four hundred thousand years ago,[146] though whether this transition occurred consonantly in various parts of the world or *Homo sapiens* first arose in Africa or the Middle East sometime prior to one hundred thousand years ago and spread throughout the world is the subject of considerable controversy.[147] The anthropologist Ian Tattersall posits another possible "family tree" leading to *Homo sapiens: Homo habilis* to possibly *Homo ergaster,* which branched to *Homo antecessor* to *Homo heidelbergensis* to *Homo sapiens.*[148]

Biologists and anthropologists point to distinct biological features and behavioral traits of *Homo sapiens* when compared with the primates from which our species evolved. These features include erect posture, a large brain, opposing thumbs, arms and hand changes, a reduction of the jaw and remodeling of the face, changes in skin and glands, a reduction in body hair, cryptic ovulation, slow development, modification of the focal tract and larynx, and a reorganization of the brain.[149] The neurophysiologist Paul MacLean stresses the increase in the size of the brain, its complexity, and additional new structures as especially distinct characteristics of the human species. At the base of human brains are the oldest structures that our species shares with reptiles and birds. These structures control respiration, the cardiovascular system, and instinctive behavior, which is rigidly programmed genetically. The midbrain or limbic system that humans share with animals controls our hormones and emotional life (e.g., pleasure, fear, sex, and hunger). The outer layer or neocortex that is prominent in higher mammals and humans controls perceptual, cognitive, and communicative processes that make possible more complex forms of language, learning, and intelligence.[150] Distinctive human behavioral traits include subtle expressions of emotions, intelligence (abstract thinking, categorizing, and reasoning), the use of symbolic language, awareness of self and death, tool making and technology, the development of the sciences and humanities, the formation of religions and the articulation of moral norms, the organization of social structures, the formation of political institutions, and the development of legal codes.[151]

Although evidence for the evolution and nature of our species was gathered by paleontologists, comparative anatomists, embryologists, and biogeographers during the latter half of the nineteenth and early twentieth centuries, several other disciplines—including genetics, cell biology, physiology, and ecology—yielded new knowledge during the first half of the twentieth century that can only be understood within the framework of the scientific theory of evolution. The birth and blossoming of molecular biology during the second half of the twentieth century provided convincing evidence of biological evolution and the means to reconstruct the evolutionary history of living organisms with detail and precision.[152] Molecular biological findings indicate that African chimpanzees and modern gorillas share more than 99 percent of their DNA with the DNA of humans, but that 1 percent accounts for some striking differences.[153] Steps toward probing these differences and finding biological answers to questions about the makeup of humans have been accelerated by the recent deciphering of the chimpanzee's DNA, the production of a long list of DNA differences between humans and chimpanzees, and some hints about which differences may be crucial.[154]

Comparisons with primates on the basis of research conducted thus far elucidate some distinctive behavioral traits in humans. Primates are socially organized, but their organization is much less complex than human social organization.[155] Chimpanzees can be taught limited forms of symbolic communication, though they are not fully capable of language as are humans because primates lack a larynx necessary for articulated speech.[156] Chimpanzees have a rudimentary self-awareness,[157] but humans have a self-consciousness that seems without parallel in primates. Humans have a greater capacity to remember the past, to anticipate the future, to use abstract symbols that liberate us from our immediate time and place, to imagine possibilities that are distantly related to present experience, and to reflect on goals that go beyond meeting immediate needs. Humans are also aware of their finitude and the inevitability of death, and they ask questions about the meaning of their lives.[158] Whereas primates as well as other animals and many species of insects live in complex social orders with definite roles and patterns of cooperative behavior,[159] humans have many more ways of transmitting information from generation to generation (e.g., writing, the public media, education, and various institutions).[160] Finally, scientific discoveries, technologies, imaginative literature, and the varied expressions of the humanities testify to the intellectual power and creativity of humans. Humans have the capacity to reflect rationally about themselves and make informed decisions. Humans are capable of making moral choices. And humans are agents with at least limited freedom, despite the constraints of both their genes in which their capabilities are rooted and their cultures that guide their decision making.[161]

Barbour poignantly summarizes the uniqueness of humans:

> "In short, humanity is part of nature, but a unique part. We are the product of a long evolutionary history and retain a powerful legacy from the past. But we also have creative abilities and potentialities without parallel among the species of the earth. We are biological organisms, but we are also responsible selves. If research in recent decades has at some points found greater similarities with other life forms than had been previously suspected, these findings should lead us to greater respect for those forms, not to the denial of human dignity."[162]

The human capacity to make moral choices is particularly relevant when investigating the concept of the kinship of creatures as a religious foundation for environmental ethics. Ayala argues that ethical behavior, which he defines as the proclivity to judge human actions as either good or evil, has evolved as a consequence of the natural selection of high intelligence that is characteristic of the human species.[163] Although the capacity to behave ethically is an attribute of human nature that has evolved biologically, moral norms are the products of cultural evolution[164] that have been superimposed on biological nature to produce religious and ethical traditions, language, scientific knowledge, the humanities, technologies, and other creations of the human mind.[165] Cultural communities are wise to establish moral codes that are consistent with the *needs* of the biological nature of humans, or our species will become extinct. Our biological nature may predispose us to accepting certain moral norms, but it does not constrain us to accept them or to behave according to them. The intellectual abilities that make ethical behavior possible also give us the power to accept some moral norms and to reject others, despite natural inclinations in one direction of choice over another.

Studies of Animals' Emotions and Cognitive Abilities

Although the differences between human and nonhuman animals are vast, studies by cognitive ethologists illumine the Darwinian insight of differences in degrees rather than kind. Their findings have significant implications for human attitudes toward and treatment of other animals. Particularly informative are the results of ongoing research conducted by the ethologist Marc Bekoff and his colleagues. Their efforts indicate that animals experience a wide variety of emotions, have mood swings, feel pain, communicate with one another in languages unique to their natures, think, make choices, and relate to others within and outside of their species, with some demonstrating strong familial associations within their species.[166]

These behavioral characteristics that vary among animals require an effort to understand them, a transformation in attitudes toward them, and a formulation of ethical norms to guide human behavior toward them. For Bekoff, humans should be "minding animals," which consists of "caring for other animal beings, respecting them for who they are, appreciating their worldviews, and wondering what and how they are feeling and why"[167] Using the widest sense of the term "kin" to convey the human connectedness with other animals and the need to have empathy for them, Bekoff advocates thinking about humans as "strolling" with animals as their "kin."[168]

As the theologian Donna Yarri argues, Bekoff and his colleagues' efforts affect Christian theology by challenging the heretofore prevalent thinking that humans are absolutely superior to other animals, urging the development of a more comprehensive moral theology regarding our treatment of them, and taking advantage of opportunities to deepen Christian spirituality by exploring the similarities between humans and other animals.[169] The saintly desert fathers, Celtic *peregrini,* English hermits, and Francis of Assisi point us in that direction. Advocates of what is known as the biophilia hypothesis may provide additional direction toward recognizing an affinity that humans have toward other animals.

The Biophilia Hypothesis

As proffered by the eminent evolutionary biologist Edward O. Wilson, the biophilia hypothesis asserts that humans have a biologically based need to affiliate with other living organisms.[170] This need is demonstrated by a complex of "hereditary learning propensities" in humans that began with the origin of hominids, molded feelings along several emotional spectra "from attraction to aversion, from awe to indifference, from peacefulness to fear-driven anxiety,"[171] and spread by natural selection in a cultural context. Wilson identifies this process as "biocultural evolution"[172] through which *Homo sapiens* has survived as a species. Other species are "our kin," he continues, because all higher eukaryotic organisms—from flowering plants to insects, animals, and humans—are thought to have descended from a single ancestral population that lived about 2 billion years ago, whereas single-celled eukaryotes and bacteria are linked by even more remote ancestors. For Wilson, all organisms claim at least a "distant kinship," one that is stamped by "a common genetic code and elementary features of cell structure."[173]

A biological kinship of varying degrees among all organisms must be acknowledged, though their relationship may be traced chemically as far back as the hydrogen and helium that emerged at the beginning of the universe followed by the novae that produced the heavier elements essential for life. For organisms, the biophilia hypothesis suggests that affiliation with life and lifelike processes has conferred distinctive physical, emotional, and intellectual advantages in the human evolutionary struggle to adapt, persist, and thrive as individuals and as a species. As in the past, the human inclination toward affiliating with living entities and processes functions today as "a basis for healthy human maturation and development,"[174] "emotionally, cognitively, aesthetically, and spiritually,"[175] according to the social ecologist Stephen Kellert, that enhances the human potential for attaining satisfying and secure lives.[176] When the human affiliation with other species and natural systems is degraded, the biophilia hypothesis intimates the likelihood of "a deprived and diminished" existence in "a wide variety of affective, cognitive, and evaluative respects."[177] The hypothesis asserts strongly, Kellert contends, that "the human search for a coherent and fulfilling existence is intimately dependent upon our relationship with nature."[178]

Kellert qualifies the notion that humans have an inherent inclination to affiliate with other species and the natural environment. He explains that the various expressions of biophilia are not hard-wired instincts like breathing and eating. The human affinity for nature represents "a collection of relatively *weak* biological tendencies," and all the various strains of biophilia depend on adequate learning and experience; otherwise, they lie "dormant and frustrated."[179] That is why the different aspects of biophilia are best viewed as products of "biocultural evolution," wherein inborn tendencies are shaped by the mediating influence of learning, culture, and experience.[180] These learning propensities can be "fine-tuned variously by an adjustment of sensory thresholds, by a quickening or blockage of learning, and by modification of emotional responses."[181]

Wilson is concerned about replacing biophilic learning propensities. When humans remove themselves from the natural environment, he cautions, "the biophilic learning propensities are not replaced by modern versions that are equally well adapted to artifacts; instead, they persist from generation to generation, atrophied and fitfully manifested in the artificial new environments into which technology has catapulted humanity."[182]

Testing the Hypothesis

What evidence exists for identifying these tendencies that humans have toward affiliating with other living beings and processes? Wilson laments the slowness with which cognitive psychologists have addressed the consequences of humanity's relationship with the natural environment, especially because it is rapidly disappearing.[183] On the basis of his research with colleagues on a wide array of cultures and human perspectives on nature,[184] Kellert points to nine human valuations of nature that adapted over evolutionary time in the human struggle to survive, thrive, and attain fulfillment:

- Utilitarian, for physical sustenance and security;
- Naturalist, for mental and physical development of curiosity and outdoor skills;

- Ecological-scientific, for knowledge, understanding, and observational skills;
- Aesthetic, for inspiration, harmony, peace and security;
- Symbolic, for communication and mental development;
- Humanist, for group bonding, sharing, cooperation, and companionship;
- Moralist, for order and meaning in life, kinship, and affiliational ties;
- Dominionist, for mechanical skills, physical prowess, and ability to subdue; and
- Negativist, for security, protection, and safety.

Together, these nine biologically based values of nature constitute "an expression of the biophilia tendency" that has facilitated the human ability to adapt, persist, and thrive.[185]

How sound is this research for testing the biophilia hypothesis? Kellert admits to "a limited empirical corroboration" of the biophilia hypothesis, and he acknowledges that these studies do not prove the hypothesis.[186] He recognizes that the data offer "restricted support" for his nine value categories as biologically based expressions of human dependence on nature, even though the occurrence of the value types "across cultures, taxa and time" has adaptational significance.[187] Nevertheless, considerable research is needed to advance the hypothesis to a solid theory that can be tested rigorously.[188]

A Basis for Ethics?

Another challenge to the biophilia hypothesis centers on the extent to which, if any, ethical behavior toward nature can be attributed to natural selection over evolutionary time. Wilson bases the ethic of love for all life forms—biophilia—in humans' self-preserving genes. As an award-winning evolutionary biologist, proponent of sociobiology, and advocate for preserving biodiversity, Wilson finds the genetic basis for ethics that aims to preserve the human "more powerful and intellectually convincing" than other bases for environmental ethics.[189] Only "a robust and richly textured anthropocentric ethic . . . based on the hereditary needs of our own species" will suffice in our time when biological diversity is rapidly declining.[190] Kellert follows Wilson in promoting an ethic of human self-interest, though he bases his ethic specifically on the nine aforementioned human tendencies to value nature that adapted in the human struggle to survive, thrive, and attain fulfillment. His notion includes the valuing of opportunities for emotional bonding and companionship, a connection that he describes as "so intense that it sometimes engenders feelings of love."[191]

The environmental philosopher Holmes Rolston argues brilliantly against Wilson's reductionist approach to ethics. While lauding Wilson's intentions to proffer a system of ethics that protects biodiversity, Rolston explains that genes do not have behavior options; nor do the genes choose them. Furthermore, natural selection is directed at individual organisms, not at genes. No gene is "fit" by itself, because it has fitness only with the company it keeps, and the only "self" about which a gene can be selfish is also only in the company it keeps.[192] According to Rolston, Wilson views the organism as "nothing but an aggregation of genes and their outposts," with each gene "individually 'selfish'" for its life and not that of the organism.[193] The organism must attend to the immediate somatic needs of the genes and reproduce itself in the next generation; it has no options other than to do so.[194] Thus, as Rolston explains convincingly, Wilson cannot get the ethic of biophilia out of selfish genes: "This is because a single gene is really, so to speak, only a fragment of biophilia, a bit of life information. A gene is nothing much in and of itself; there is no self there to be selfish about. But these genes collectively, in their wholes, share and spin together the vital drama of life."[195]

Instead of looking to genes for an environmental ethic, Rolston insists, humans must obtain one from outside biology. Furthermore, they must "defeat their biology"[196] to be selfish if biotic communities are to be loved and respected.[197] Rolston appeals to Wilson to opt for a basis of a conservation ethic that is more "joyous" than the selfish gene:

> There is no need for a person with such an admirable love of life to retreat into a killjoy explanation of his love. Why not rise to a joyous explanation? The home planet is prolific with life, exuberantly projected up from the primeval ooze and mud, an emergent vitality expressed in 10 million species. The planet loves life and so do we. This is the evolutionary epic, and we are this love of life become conscious of itself. We do not want to depress life into nothing but selfishness, borrowing inappropriately a depressing category from human moral failure. We want to respect the life that has so marvelously expressed itself over evolutionary history, and reaching that respect will itself be an elevating moral achievement.[198]

Although a genetic predisposition for a biophilia-based environmental ethic has not been scientifically established and considerable research lies ahead for the development and testing of a bona fide theory, the possibility that there might be a partly genetic predisposition to respond positively to nature seems plausible to "many" scientists, as the health systems designer Roger S. Ulrich explains.[199] He points to a cascade of convincing studies showing that biological or genetic factors play a role in alcoholism, mathematical skills, and "numerous other aspects of human behavior and response."[200] Thus, the possibility of a partly genetic predisposition to biophilia cannot be ruled out. If natural selection proves to be a factor, all the influences on the individual after birth/nurture must also be considered.

Religion is one of those influences that should be investigated, especially because it may be the most powerful influence on people who profess a religious faith.[201] Thus, the kinship attitudes of the desert fathers, Celtic wanderers, English hermits, and Francis of Assisi toward the animals they encountered and natural settings in which they lived are ripe for tapping to identify a behavioral trajectory to guide Christians when informed by contemporary scientific findings.

From Kinship to Companionship

Thinking about other species and natural places as companions in the journey of one's life has been proffered by the Lutheran theologian Joseph Sittler and the Catholic theologians Michael J. Himes and Kenneth R. Himes.[202] Both Sittler and the Himeses stress the mutual dependence that all creatures have on God for their existence and their intrinsic value versus strictly instrumental value for humans. They also use familial language when referring to other species, thereby conveying a sense of intimacy, dignity, and equality to them to thrive according to their natures.

As one of the first theologians to address environmental concerns, Sittler criticized the subsuming of the natural environment under humanity to serve merely as a resource for human needs, thereby leaving the environment divested of "her own and proper life" and "devoid of interests in herself." Yet he also dismissed subsuming humanity under the natural environment, which abdicates responsibility for human actions—the "glory of the human spirit." The only viable alternative is to have humans stand alongside nature as "her cherishing brother, for she too is God's creation and bears God's image."[203] For Sittler, reflecting on Psalm 104, humankind, other species, and the natural environment are mutually dependent upon God; all derive their significance from their origination in God, all find fulfillment in praise of God, and all are distinct yet totally related. Sittler characterized the degraded environment as our "violated sister who is heard groaning 'in pain and travail'" because humans are not functioning in relation to the rest of creation as God intends. Instead of treating other creatures "like a cherished brother and sister," humans are abusing them.[204]

The Himeses build upon the "companionship" notion in Genesis 2 that indicates God's intention for humans to live in positive relationships with one another and with the rest of creation. The basis for their companionship ethic is the sacramental vision of creatures' capacity to reveal God's loving and creative power by being thoroughly themselves according to their natures.[205] This expansive sacramentality is identifiable in Francis of Assisi's interweaving of poverty with the brotherhood and sisterhood of all creatures.[206] For Francis, poverty is the realization that all creatures are fundamentally contingent upon God for their existence—they would not exist if God had not lovingly willed their existence. They share this "iffiness" that is "true poverty, the poverty of the spirit," that unites them and renders them equal insofar as they have intrinsic value. Thus, the Himeses insist, humans have no more claim to intrinsic value than a plant or an animal, a star or a stone.[207] When relating to other species and natural places, humans should value them for themselves instead of valuing them strictly for their usefulness to humans.[208] Furthermore, to denigrate any creature implicitly denigrates every creature,[209] because all are revelatory of God's loving gift to be themselves.

Although the saintly desert fathers, Irish *peregrini,* English hermits, and Francis of Assisi wrote from vastly different understandings of the world than

Sittler and the Himeses, they share utter faith in God as the creator of the world whose existence is totally contingent upon God's loving will. They also share an intrinsic valuation of other creatures according to their natures and a desire to live in harmony with them. However, their approaches to addressing companionship differ, insofar as Sittler and the Himeses reflect theologically about the need for embracing the notion of companionship and for acting companionably with other species, whereas the solitaires demonstrated their companionship as indicated in hagiographies written primarily by their contemporaries. When informed by current scientific findings about the human relatedness to other species and at least a partial genetic predisposition toward affinity with other creatures, the kinship attitudes and actions of the solitaires are worth considering for clues to the kinds of behavior patterns that might be helpful during a time when the diversity of biological life is rapidly declining. Suggestive patterns include acknowledging the genetic and environmental relationships that humans have with other living and nonliving entities that constitute Earth, cherishing the human companionship with nonhumans in the journey of life, appreciating the integral human constituency with other biota within ecosystems, being humble about the human dependency on other species and biological systems, and assuming a posture of piety toward the other-than-human constituents of Earth.

Acknowledging Relationships with Other Living and Nonliving Entities

People who believe God initiated, empowers, and sustains the processes through which life emerged, evolved, and persists will acknowledge their genetic relationships with other living and inanimate beings from and with whom humans emerged over cosmological and biological time. Acknowledging "kinship" in a biological sense is an essential first step. At least broad scientific findings will be taken seriously, and the faithful will accept the place of humans as constituents of the world who are at least distantly related to all life that preceded our species and strives to survive today. As the theologian Sallie McFague urges, we must avoid telling "lies" about ourselves as entities apart from the world in which we live.[210]

Cherishing Human Companionship with Other Species

The faithful will cherish their familial relationships with their other living companions. Knowing the evolutionary and molecular biological connections between *Homo sapiens* and other species should help convince the faithful to cherish these species as creatures who have needs and interests in surviving. Although many people readily show how deeply they cherish their household "pets" with whom they share their space, other animals require protection from human intrusion and disturbances. Companionship with them may be distant—as in wilderness areas, national parks, and vast marine ecosystems—but cherishing them as companions in the web of life is nevertheless warranted if they are to flourish. To walk lightly with these companions, humans must learn about them, desire to protect them, and develop constraints against disturbing their habitats or diminishing the size and quality of the space they need to perpetuate themselves as species.[211]

Valuing the Interrelationships of Other Species and Natural Systems

The faithful will cherish other species for the roles they play in relation to one another in ecosystems, and they will also cherish the ecosystems of which they are constituents. Other species and natural systems will not be viewed merely as objects to study. Interspecies relationships and the natural systems in which they participate will be cherished for the beauty, stability, and integrity that is brought about by their interactions.[212] To cherish them requires knowing as much as possible about their interrelationships and relying upon experts' findings about species' interactions that bring about healthy ecosystems. The faithful will follow informed advice that is aimed at giving interacting species and systems the space they need to maintain themselves.

Acknowledging Human Dependence on Other Creatures

Inspired by the saints' behavior and informed by current scientific findings, the faithful will acknowledge human dependence upon other species, ecosystems, and the biosphere for human health and well-being and will recognize that humans need their companionship to lead healthful lives. That humans are radically dependent upon the air, land, water, minerals, plants, other animals, and other humans to flourish in this life should be self-evident to anyone who eats, breathes, drinks, wears clothing, recreates, and travels anywhere. That humans are radically dependent upon healthy ecosystems in which they function should become increasingly obvious as facts are made known about the adverse effects that polychlorinated byphenals (PCBs), metals, and other toxic chemicals have on human health and well-being as well as the health and well-being of other species. The faithful will recognize and accept their dependence on other species and natural systems with humility and will act toward them in humble, respectful ways.[213]

Demonstrating Piety toward Creatures

The faithful will assume with Saint Francis of Assisi and Saint Bonaventure a posture of *piety* toward all creatures by

- *Loving them for themselves* and not simply for their usefulness to humans.
- *Devoting themselves to their interests* in surviving and flourishing, making sure that they are not impeded in sustaining themselves.
- *Showering them with affection* by tending to and protecting them from human and other intrusions that prevent them from meeting their needs and flourishing.
- *Being kind to them* as travelers in a shared journey of life who need dedicated space to sustain themselves in order to continue their journey.

- *Standing up for and with them before others* when they are threatened individually or as a species.
- *Showing compassion for their suffering,* while understanding that decay, death, and the emergence of new species are characteristics of temporal existence.
- *Acting generously toward them without interfering with their self-expressions* according to their natures.

Conclusion

From their understanding of the world and circumstances of their times, the Christian desert fathers, Celtic wanderers, English hermits, Francis of Assisi, and Anthony of Padua expressed affinity for the animals they encountered and natural places in which they lived while striving for a closer relationship with God. Among these expressions are protecting and feeding wild animals, acting toward them with compassion, love, affection, kindness, devotion, and steadfastness, perceiving animals as reciprocating the holy solitaires' care and compassion, appreciating and preserving the natural environment, and using familial language when referring to the animals and natural phenomena in their surroundings.

When these attitudes are informed by contemporary cosmology and biology, the behavior anticipated from people who believe in God centers on the notion of companionship whereby other animals are considered "kin" in the broadest sense of the term. Recognizing other animals as kin will incline the faithful to acknowledge their genetic relationships with other species from and with whom humans emerged over biological time through God's empowerment; to cherish their familial relationships with their companions in the unfolding of the universe; to value other species and natural systems for themselves according to their natures, their interests in thriving, and their roles in bringing about the integrity of ecosystems; to acknowledge human dependence on other species, ecosystems, and the biosphere for human health and well-being; and, with Saint Francis of Assisi and Saint Bonaventure, to assume a posture of piety toward all creatures by loving them for themselves, devoting ourselves to their interests in surviving and flourishing, showering them with affection, being kind to them, standing up for and with them before others, showing compassion for their suffering, being generous toward them without interfering with their self-expressions, and giving glory to God by identifying ways of interacting companionably with them in the ecosystems we share. In the concept of kinship, which points to companionable behavior, Christians have yet another viable option for charting a course of action.

Notes

1. The term "kinship" is very broadly defined by Roger Keesing, *Kin Groups and Social Structure* (New York: Holt, Rinehart & Winston, 1975), 150, as a relationship based

on a culturally recognized connection between parents and children that is extended to more distant relatives. "Connection" in this definition refers to a common genetic code and elementary features of cell structure as explained in the second part of this chapter, though an even more distant connection can be made between humans and the death of stars out of whose furnaces the heavy elements essential for life were produced and the finite singularity 14 billion years ago that produced helium and hydrogen essential for the formation of stars. "Culture" refers specifically to Christianity as conveyed by the desert fathers, Celtic wanderers, English hermits, Francis of Assisi, and his followers, who expressed affinity with the animals and natural places in which they lived.

2. The term "hagiography," derived from the Greek roots (*hagio* = holy and *graphe* = writing), refers to the full range of Christian literature that concerns the saints, including the various legends and other genres about their lives, sermons, visions, collections of miracle stories, and inquests held into the life of a candidate under consideration for canonization. Often idealizing or idolizing the saints, legends about them and other forms of hagiography have been written from at least the middle of the second century to the present day. This term has also been used most recently as a pejorative reference to the works of biographers and historians who critics think are uncritical and romantically reverential in their treatment of saintly people.

3. Though the foregoing discussion of Francis of Assisi and his followers focuses on their interactions with wild creatures and places, his *Rule,* issued in 1221, allowed for limited consumption of foods, including meat and fish, as well as other necessities of life that were offered to them by others, especially when the mendicants were receiving food for which they begged and, when received, attributed ultimately to God's providence. See Saint Francis of Assisi, "The Earlier Rule," in *Francis of Assisi: Early Documents, Volume 1: The Saint,* ed. Regis J. Armstrong, J. A. Wayne Hellmann, and William J. Short (Hyde Park, NY: New City Press, 1999), 64, 70–71. Also see Roger Sorrell's explanation in *St. Francis of Assisi and Nature: Tradition and Innovation in Western Christian Attitudes toward the Environment* (New York: Oxford University Press, 1988), 75–76, about Francis's complex balancing of injunctions in the Bible about the goodness of creation, human dominion over it, traditional medieval ascetic ideals that included dietary restrictions, his love for creatures, and the beliefs and ascetic practices of the Cathars, who thought that the material creation was created by an evil being. Though the Franciscan *Rule* allowed eating foods offered to the friars, one account by Thomas of Celano, in "The Second Life of St. Francis," in *St. Francis of Assisi: First and Second Life of St. Francis, with Selections from Treatise on the Miracles of Blessed Francis,* trans. Placid Hermann, OFM (Chicago: Franciscan Herald Press, 1963), chap. 48, nos. 78–79, pp. 202–3, indicates that Francis ate a capon offered to him by his host and gave some of the capon to a Cathar who pretended to be a beggar but proceeded unsuccessfully to try to embarrass the saint for not being holy because he ate meat unlike his predecessors among the saintly desert fathers who avoided it for various reasons, as disclosed by Blake Leyerle in "Monks and Other Animals," in *The Cultural Turn in Late Ancient Studies: Gender, Asceticism, and Historiography,* ed. Dale B. Martin and Patricia Cox Miller (Durham, NC: Duke University Press, 2005). See, further, Blake Leyerle, "Monastic Formation and Christian Practice: Food in the Desert," in *Educating People of Faith: Exploring the History of Jewish and Christian Communities,* ed. John Van Engen (Grand Rapids: William

B. Eerdmans, 2004). As shown in this chapter, many hagiographical accounts of Francis's life indicate that he did not consume wildlife given to him, found by him, or rescued by him; he chose instead to care for them and/or set them free.

4. Rufinus of Aquilea, "History of the Monks of Egypt," in *The Desert Fathers,* ed. and trans. Helen Waddell (Ann Arbor: University of Michigan Press, 1957). The distance between the cells was described as "no less great" than the three- or four-mile distance they had to walk to church, as indicated on p. 54. An informative introduction to the desert fathers is provided by Benedicta Ward through Cop Net, the online resources of the Coptic Orthodox Church (the Christian Apostolic Church of Egypt), www.coptic.net/articles/ParadiseOfDesertFathers.txt.

5. In *Life of Antony,* by Athanasius, in *Early Christian Lives,* trans. and ed. Carolinne White (London: Penguin Books, 1998), 15, Athanasius described the devil's taking on "shapes of wild animals and snakes" and instantly filling Antony's cell with "spectres in the form of lions, bulls, wolves, vipers, serpents, scorpions and even leopards and bears," who "made noises according to their individual nature: the lion roared, eager for the kill; the bull bellowed and made menacing movements with his horns; the serpent hissed; the wolves leaped forward to attack; the spotted leopard demonstrated all the different wiles of the one (the devil) who controlled him." After Antony moved to another location in order to have the solitude he desired, "the devil gathered so many packs of wild animals outside his cell," Athanasius reported, and "Antony saw that he was surrounded by all the creatures of the desert. When they snarled at him, threatening to tear his body with their teeth, he understood the cunning of the enemy and said, 'If the Lord has given you permission to attack me, I will give myself up to you for you to devour me; but if you are sent here by demons go away as fast as you can for I am the servant of Christ.' And so it was: at the sound of his command, all the beasts ran away as if they had been whipped by the lash of God's power."

6. Jeffrey Burton Russell, *Satan: The Early Christian Tradition* (Ithaca, NY: Cornell University Press, 1981). At p. 166, Russell recounts legends about the demons that were forced out of the cities by Christian prayer and subsequently congregated in the desert where they challenged the faith of the desert fathers. Monks thought that demons lived in the air and could move long distances at will. In *Life of Antony,* 14, Athanasius recounted that "the devil was afraid that, as time went on, Antony might cause the desert to become inhabited," so the devil endeavored to deter Antony from his goal.

7. Susan Power Bratton, "The Original Desert Solitaire: Early Christian Monasticism and Wilderness," *Environmental Ethics* 10 (Spring 1988): 31–53, at 50: "The monks absorbed the qualities of the desert and developed a strong sense of place. Their treatment of the desert and its creatures was never far from their own spiritual goals; yet they seem to have adjusted well to the environment and to have held both the desert and its animal inhabitants in high regard."

8. Primary among the biblical influences are accounts in the New Testament of Jesus Christ's seeking solitude in the wilderness where he was tempted by Satan (Mk 1:12), went up the mountain to pray (Mk 6:46), and led selected disciples up a mountain where he was transfigured (Mk 9:2). Other influences are noted as stories are identified under the various headings in this section. In *Christianity, Wilderness, and Wildlife: The Original Desert Solitaire* (Scranton, PA: University of Scranton Press, 1993), 27–156, Susan Power Bratton explores poignantly the many references to ex-

periences that the ancient Hebrews to the first Christians had with wildlife and wilderness areas as recounted in the books of Genesis through Revelation, and she notes subsequently how some of these biblical stories probably influenced the desert fathers, Celtic wanderers, and English hermits.

9. Bratton, "Original Desert Solitaire," 46, citing *Griechische Märchen*, ed. Aug. Hausrath and Aug. Marx (Jena: Diederichs, 1913), esp. viii, 74–85.

10. Bratton, "Original Desert Solitaire," 46.

11. In *Christianity, Wilderness, and Wildlife,* 183–84, Bratton stresses the influence the desert fathers had on the Celtic monks. Paul R. Lonigan indicates in *Early Irish Church* (Woodside, NY: Celtic Heritage Press, 1985), 66, that the *Life of Antony* apparently reached Gaul within twenty years after it was written. In 600 CE, Columban wrote a letter to Pope Gregory the Great in which he discussed the writings of Jerome (331–420 CE), one of the most learned of the desert fathers, who wrote about Antony as well as other desert fathers, including saints Paul of Thebes, Hilarion, and Malchus, translated the books of the Old Testament from Hebrew to Latin, and revised the Latin translation of the New Testament.

12. This is explained by Deborah Vess, professor of history and interdisciplinary studies at Georgia College and State University in Milledgeville, at her informative website on Celtic Monasticism (www.faculty.de.gcsu.edu/~dvess/ids/medieval/celtic/celtic.shtml#peregrini). Susan Power Bratton and Christopher Bamford have researched and reflected constructively on the Celtic saints in relation to the natural environment. See Bratton, *Christianity, Wilderness, and Wildlife,* esp. chap. 11, 183–216; and Christopher Bamford, "Ecology and Holiness: The Heritage of Celtic Christianity," lecture to the Lindisfarne Association on Saint Cuthbert's Day, Cathedral of Saint John the Divine, New York City, 1981, in *Celtic Christianity: Ecology and Holiness,* ed. William Parker Marsh (Great Barrington, MA: Lindisfarne Press, 1987).

13. Bratton, *Christianity, Wilderness, and Wildlife,* 182.

14. Eleanor Shipley Duckett, *Wandering Saints of the Early Middle Ages* (New York: W. W. Norton, 1959).

15. Bratton, *Christianity, Wilderness, and Wildlife,* 194.

16. Though some of the early sanctuaries and hermitages were founded on offshore islands, in inaccessible glens, and in other remote areas, the Celtic clerics also built in lowland areas that had previously been forested but little occupied. To these places they brought productive activity by introducing the mould board plow and other innovations that enabled the monks to sustain themselves. See Bratton, *Christianity, Wilderness, and Wildlife,* 213.

17. The influential traditions of the desert fathers, and especially the Celtic saints on medievalists, are overlooked by Roderick Nash, in *Wilderness and the American Mind* (New Haven, CT: Yale University Press, 1982), who insists on p. 19 that Saint Francis of Assisi is the only medieval theologian who had "a posture of humility and respect towards the natural world." As Bratton insists (*Christianity, Wilderness, and Wildlife,* 218), Nash "overlooks the continuous interest of Christian monks in wild nature from the time of Antony through the Middle Ages, a span of nearly one thousand years. Not only did the desert fathers influence the Celts, the Celts in turn influenced the Italians, including the Franciscans." Edward A. Armstrong shows in *Saint Francis: Nature Mystic; The Derivation and Significance of the Nature Stories in the Franciscan Legend* (Berkeley: University of California Press, 1973) that most of the Franciscan legends have precursors in Irish saints' tales and other nature-loving

monks. Nevertheless, writings by and about Francis of Assisi are unparalleled in medieval Christian literature for the flowering and deepening of the companionship
tradition.

18. The Latin term is *pietas*, which has a broader scope than the English "piety"; *pietas*
    includes love, devotion, affection, reverence, kindness, fidelity, and compassion.
    Saint Bonaventure explored Francis of Assisi's piety in chapter 8 of *The Life of St.
    Francis*, in *Bonaventure*, trans. Ewert Cousins, Classics of Western Spirituality Series
    (New York: Paulist Press, 1978), 250 n. 1.

19. Bratton, *Christianity, Wilderness, and Wildlife*, 220. For Bratton, these animals "reflect
    an environment dominated by cultivation and subject to human exploitation." She
    recognizes, however, that the literature includes several accounts of wolves that are
    bothering towns or farmers and are cast by medieval hagiographers as "unrelent-
    ing villains."

20. Armstrong, *Saint Francis*, 31–41. As noted above, Francis's pious actions and famil-
    ial language when addressing other species he encountered were balanced by his
    sense of hospitality and practicality in accepting and allowing his followers to con-
    sume meat and other foods offered to them to sustain their bodily lives. Directions
    for limiting consumption to bodily needs and for fasting are found in the earlier and
    later *Rules*; see *Francis of Assisi: Early Documents*, vol. 1, 63–86, 99–106. Nevertheless,
    that Francis released to freedom or made pets of wild animals (e.g., the pheasant
    as recounted by Thomas of Celano in "Second Life of Francis," II, 129.170, 273–74;
    and by Saint Bonaventure in *The Life of St. Francis*, 8.10, 259), some of which were
    presented to him for his consumption, must be factored into his encounters with
    them and his overall valuing of God's creation as good. See further Sorrell's insight-
    ful discussion on Francis of Assisi's attitudes toward food in *St. Francis of Assisi and
    Nature*, 75–79.

21. Franciscans are at the forefront today promoting attitudes and actions that are com-
    patible with the well-being of all creatures. See, e.g., selections from *Franciscan The-
    ology of the Environment : An Introductory Reader*, ed. Dawn M. Nothwehr (Quincy, MA:
    Franciscan Press, 2002); and Ilia Delio, OSF, *A Franciscan View of Creation: Learning to
    Live in a Sacramental World*, Franciscan Heritage Series, vol. 2 (Saint Bonaventure, NY:
    Franciscan Institute, 2003). Nevertheless, some critics are skeptical about Franciscan
    spirituality for its romanticism and practice of calling nonhuman animals "brothers"
    and "sisters." René Dubos, "Franciscan Conservation versus Benedictine Steward-
    ship," in *Ecology and Religion in History*, ed. David and Eileen Spring (New York: Harper
    & Row, 1974), 129, dismisses Franciscan spirituality in favor of the conservation ap-
    proach taken by the Benedictines and lauds the process that eventually "humanized
    a large percentage of the earth." Of course, the goal of humanizing any percentage
    of Earth would be highly anthropocentric and shortsighted of the place of humans
    in the evolutionary process, as discussed in subsequent parts of this chapter.

22. Pope John Paul II, "S. Franciscus Assisiensis caelestis Patronus oecologiae cultorum
    eligitur," *Acta Apostolicae Sedis—Commentarium Officiale* 71 (1979): 1509–10.

23. Pope John Paul II, "Peace with God the Creator, Peace with All of Creation," Mes-
    sage for the Celebration of the World Day of Peace, January 1, 1990, Vatican City
    State, December 8, 1989.

24. A long rectangle of tartan material hung over the shoulder. For a description, see
    "Highland Dress for Men," Scottish Tartans Authority, www.tartansauthority.com/
    Web/Site/Highland_Dress/Highland_Dress.asp.

25. Carolus Plummer, ed., "Life of Maedoc of Ferns," in *Bethada náem nÉrenn, Lives of Irish Saints,* vol. 2, trans. Carolus Plummer (Oxford: Clarendon Press, 1997), 178. In another version of this legend, at 190–91, Maedoc put his rosary on the stag's horns, the hounds thought the stag was a man, and they ceased pursuing him.

26. Helen Waddell, ed., "St. Kevin and the Wild Boar," in *Beasts and Saints,* trans. Helen Waddell (London: Constable & Co., 1934). Waddell indicates that she translated this legend from Giraldus Cambrensis's *Topigraphia Hibernica* 2.28. Kevin founded a monastery at Glendalough and is honored as one of Ireland's greatest saints.

27. Sister Mary Donatus MacNickle, *Beasts and Birds in the Lives of Early Irish Saints* (Philadelphia: University of Pennsylvania Press, 1934), 146. Patrick picked up the fawn, and followed by the doe, carried it on his shoulders until he reached another spot where he put it down.

28. Waddell, "St. Godric and the Hunted Stag," in *Beasts and Saints,* 90–91.

29. Ibid.

30. Ibid., 87–89.

31. Saint Francis of Assisi, *The Little Flowers of St. Francis,* trans. Raphael Brown (Garden City, NY: Image Books, 1958), 91–92.

32. Thomas of Celano, *St. Francis of Assisi,* 1.21.58–61, 53–56.

33. Bonaventure, *Life of St. Francis,* 8.8, 257.

34. Waddell, "The Hermit's Garden in the Desert" in *Beasts and Saints,* 3–5. Waddell translated this work from Sulpicius Severus's *Dialogues ecclesiasticorum latinorum* 1.13-14 (405 CE); the story had been told by a friend who had been journeying in North Africa late in the fourth century.

35. John Moschus, *Pratum spirituale,* in *The Desert Fathers,* ed. and trans. Helen Waddell (New York: Sheed & Ward, 1942), 166–72. Moschus collected tales about the life and beliefs of monks after observing hermits along the Jordan River and sojourning in Egypt, the Sinai Desert, Cyprus, and Antioch.

36. Ibid., 168.

37. Rufinus of Aquilea, "History of the Monks of Egypt," vi, 46.

38. This tale may reflect the healing of the blind by Jesus Christ, as recorded in Mark 10:46–52 and Matt 20:20–34 (cf. Lk 18:35).

39. "St. Macarius of Alexandria and the Grateful Hyaena," in *Beasts and Saints,* 13–15. Waddell indicates that she translated this story from a French translation by Amélineau, *Monastères de la Basse-Egypte,* 233–25, of the fourth-century Coptic text. In that text, the storyteller recounts a sojourn into the Scete Desert by the thirty-year-old Macarius. He was dubbed by his followers the "aged youth" who rivaled Antony's reputation for prophecy and healing, and eventually became known as "Macarius the Great."

40. Plummer, "Life of Maedoc of Ferns," 189–90.

41. Ibid., 206.

42. Saint Jerome, *Life of Hilarion,* in *Early Christian Lives,* trans. and ed. Carolinne White (London: Penguin Books, 1998), 107. When he discovered that the wild asses had devastated his little subsistence garden, Antony "beat" the sides of the leader ass and demanded to know: 'Why are you eating what you did not sow?' From then on, Jerome reported, "the animals never touched the fruit trees or the vegetables, only the water which they often used to come and drink." Jerome is most well known for translating the books of the Old Testament from Hebrew to Latin and revising the Latin translation of the New Testament; his translation, commonly referred to

as the Latin Vulgate, was pronounced as the authentic and authoritative Latin text of the Catholic Church by the Council of Trent in the sixteenth century.

43. Waddell, "St. Kevin and the Wild Boar," 127–29.

44. Bratton, *Christianity, Wilderness, and Wildlife,* 193.

45. Waddell, "St. Ciaran and the Nesting Bird," in *Beasts and Saints,* 99–100. Waddell translated this legend from Carolus Plummer, *Vitae Sanctorum Hiberniae* (Oxford: Oxford University Press, 1910). Ciaran, a fifth- or sixth-century pagan who is reported as having met Patrick on a road in Italy, converted to Catholicism and eventually became the first bishop of Ossory; he is *not* to be confused with the Ciaran who established a monastery at Clonmacnoise.

46. Waddell, "St. Godric and the Hare," 87–89.

47. Waddell, "St. Cuthbert's Birds and Bartholomew, the Hermit of Farne," in *Beasts and Saints,* 93–95; trans. from *Vita* by Geoffrey, 24–25, in the appendix to the *Historia Dunelmensis Ecclesiae* by Symeon of Durham (Chronicles and Memorials).

48. Waddell, "St. Kevin and the Blackbird," 137; trans. from Giraldus Cambrensis, *Topographia Hibernica,* 2.28.

49. Thomas of Celano, *St. Francis of Assisi,* 1.28.77, 69.

50. Bonaventure, *Life of St. Francis,* 8.1, 250.

51. Francis of Assisi, *The Little Flowers of St. Francis,* 92.

52. Bonaventure, *Life of St. Francis,* 8.8, 257.

53. Ibid., 257.

54. Ibid., 257–58.

55. Ibid., 8.6–11, 254–61.

56. Thomas of Celano, *St. Francis of Assisi,* 1.21.58, 54.

57. Ibid., 1.29.80, 72.

58. Athanasius, *Life of Antony,* 39. The Greek verb used for "fell in love" is a form of *agapao* that implies spiritual or divine love.

59. The description is given by Saint Jerome, *Life of Hilarion,* 106–7.

60. Bratton, "Original Desert Solitaire," 50.

61. Pelagius the Deacon and John the Subdeacon, "The Sayings of the Fathers," in *The Desert Fathers,* ed. Waddell, 129.

62. That God's creation is one book that speaks about God reflects chapter 13 of the Book of Wisdom. This notion became prominent in patristic and medieval theology as demonstrated in the works of eminent theologians (e.g., Augustine, Hugh of Saint Victor, Bonaventure, and Thomas Aquinas). See chapter 3 on the sacramentality of creation and ethics of reverence.

63. Rufinus of Aquilea, "History of the Monks of Egypt," 56.

64. Waddell, "The Mountains That Are Creatures of God," in *Beasts and Saints,* 134–36; trans. Waddell from Plummer, *Vitae Sanctorum Hiberniae.*

65. As Bratton notes in *Christianity, Wilderness, and Wildlife,* 196, to "turn down such a religious honor in favor of preserving the mountains makes Coemgen [Gaelic for Kevin] truly a saint of the wilderness."

66. Lady Isabella Gregory, *A Book of Saints and Wonders Put Down Here by Lady Gregory According to the Old Writings and the Memory of the People of Ireland* (London: J. Murray, 1908), 21.

67. Ibid., 23–24.

68. Carolus Plummer, "Life of Coemgen," in *Bethada náem nÉrenn, Lives of Irish Saints,* vol. 2, trans. Carolus Plummer (Oxford: Clarendon Press, 1997), 123.

69. Carolus Plummer, "Life of Mochuda," in *Bethada náem nÉrenn, Lives of Irish Saints,* vol. 2, trans. Carolus Plummer (Oxford: Clarendon Press, 1997), 283.

70. Plummer, "Life of Maedoc of Ferns," 177.

71. E.g., see Francis of Assisi, *Little Flowers of St. Francis,* 43, 47, 51.

72. Bratton, *Christianity, Wilderness, and Wildlife,* 215.

73. Thomas of Celano, *St. Francis of Assisi,* 124.165, 270.

74. Ibid.

75. Francis of Assisi, *Little Flowers of St. Francis,* 57.

76. Bonaventure, *Life of St. Francis,* 13.1, 303.

77. Thomas of Celano, *St. Francis of Assisi,* 1.29.80, 72.

78. Frank Mitchell, *The Irish Landscape* (London: Collins, 1976), 166, 172. According to F. H. A. Aalen, *Man and Landscape in Ireland* (London: Academic Press, 1978), 102, early monastic settlements in Ireland were "self-supporting institutions economically, producing their own food by farming and fishing. The nationwide spread of monasteries must have brought land clearance and productive activity into many hitherto unsettled areas, especially as many of the early communities deliberately selected sites of extreme remoteness such as off-shore islands and inaccessible mountain glens. Scores of settlements were also built into lowland areas which previously had been forested and little occupied."

79. Bratton, *Christianity, Wilderness, and Wildlife,* 213.

80. Ibid., 194.

81. Aalen, *Man and Landscape in Ireland,* 102.

82. Bratton, "Original Desert Solitaire," 41.

83. Saint Jerome, "Life of Paul of Thebes," in *The Desert Fathers,* ed. Waddell, 80. This story may reflect 1 Kings 17:1–6, wherein the ravens brought bread to Elijah at wadi Kerith.

84. Palladius, *Lausiac History,* trans. Robert Meyer, Ancient Christian Writers, no. 34 (London: Longmans, Green, 1965), 61.

85. Athanasius, *Life of Antony,* 42.

86. Derwas J. Chitty, *The Desert A City: An Introduction to the Study of Egyptian and Palestinian Monasticism under the Christian Empire* (Crestwood, NY: St. Vladimir's Seminary Press, 1966), 106. Bratton notes plausibly, in "Original Desert Solitaire," 41, that "wild horses and asses have been known to excavate for water," so "it is possible that a wild equid could have led Sabas to the site of the spring. The monk was keenly observant and may have known enough about the behavior of wild asses to suspect that the animal might be looking for water."

87. Plummer, "Life of Coemgen," 145.

88. Anonymous Monk of Lindisfarne, "Life of St Cuthbert," in *Two Lives of Saint Cuthbert,* trans. Bertram Colgrave (Cambridge: Cambridge University Press, 1940), 85–87.

89. Venerable Bede, "Life of St Cuthbert," in *Two Lives of Saint Cuthbert,* trans. Bertram Colgrave (Cambridge: Cambridge University Press, 1940), 225–27.

90. Anonymous Monk, "Life of St Cuthbert," 77–79.

91. Bede, "Life of St Cuthbert," 227.

92. Norman Russell, trans., *The Lives of the Desert Fathers: The Historia Monachorum in Aegypto,* (Kalamazoo: Cistercian Press, 1981), 12.7–9, 91. As the story continued, when Abba Helle returned from the other side, he told the animal that "it is better for you to die and make restitution for all the lives you have taken" and the animal immediately "went belly up and died."

93. Waddell, "St. Pachome, Abbot of Tabenne, and the Crocodiles," in *Beasts and Saints*, 17–18.
94. Anonymous Monk, "Life of St Cuthbert," 81.
95. Moschus, *Pratum Spirituale*, 172.
96. MacNickle, *Beasts and Birds*, 144. A similar legend was told about Cainnic (525–99 CE), a hermit and eventually abbot of the monastery of Agahanoe, as indicated on the Patron Saints Index (www.catholic-forum.com/saints/saintc2w.htm).
97. Waddell, "St. Kevin and the Wild Boar," 127–30.
98. Plummer, "Life of Coemgen," 123.
99. MacNickle, *Beasts and Birds*, 144.
100. Waddell, "St. Colman and the Cock, the Mouse, and the Fly," in *Beasts and Saints*, 145–47; Waddell translated this legend from Colgan's *Vitae Sanctorum. . . Hiberniae* 1.244a.
101. Bonaventure, *The Life of St. Francis*, 8.10, 259.
102. Ibid., 259–60.
103. Plummer, "Life of Coemgen," 125.
104. Carolus Plummer, "Life of Abban," in *Bethada náem nÉrenn, Lives of Irish Saints*, vol. 2, trans. Carolus Plummer (Oxford: Clarendon Press, 1997), 8.
105. Russell, *Lives of the Desert Fathers*, 80.
106. Plummer, "Life of Coemgen," 125.
107. Carolus Plummer, "Life of Berach," in *Bethada náem nÉrenn, Lives of Irish Saints*, vol. 2, trans. Carolus Plummer (Oxford: Clarendon Press, 1997), 30–31.
108. Arthur Vööbus, *History of Asceticism in the Syrian Orient: A Contribution to the History of Culture in the Near East, Volume 2: Early Monasticism in Mesopotamia and Syria* (Louvain: Secretariat du Corpus SCO, 1960), 27–28.
109. Plummer, "Life of Coemgen," 145.
110. MacNickle, *Beasts and Birds*, 162.
111. Waddell, "The Abbot Gerasimus and the Lion," in *Beasts and Saints*, 25–29.
112. Jerome, "Life of Paul of Thebes," 83.
113. Bratton, *Christianity, Wilderness, and Wildlife*, 193.
114. Waddell, "St. Ciaran and Brother Fox and Brother Badger," in *Beasts and Saints*, 101–6.
115. Ibid.
116. Bonaventure, *Life of St. Francis*, 8.7, 256.
117. Ibid.
118. Ibid., 8.11, 260–61.
119. Russell, *Lives of the Desert Fathers*, 10, 66. Also see Maureen A. Tilley, "Martyrs, Monks, Insects, and Animals," in *An Ecology of the Spirit: Religious Reflection and Environmental Consciousness*, ed. Michael Barnes, College Theology Society no. 36 (Lanham, MD: University Press of America, 1994), 106.
120. Francis of Assisi, *Little Flowers of St. Francis*, 16, 76–77.
121. Ibid.
122. Thomas of Celano, *St. Francis of Assisi*, 1.29.81, 73; see also 1.29.80, 72, where Celano recounts Francis inviting "all the elements to praise and glorify the Creator of the universe." He continued that Francis was "filled with the spirit of God" and "never ceased to glorify, praise, and bless the Creator and Ruler of all things in all the elements and creatures." Placid Hermann notes on p. 350 that Celano was referring to *The Canticle of Brother Sun* that Francis composed at San Damiano during a long illness in 1225.

123. Thomas of Celano, *St. Francis of Assisi,* 40, 131–33.

124. Waddell, "St. Ciaran and Brother Fox and Brother Badger," in *Beasts and Saints,* 101–6.

125. Bonaventure, *Life of St. Francis,* 8.6, 254–55.

126. Saint Francis, "The Canticle of Brother Sun," in *Francis and Clare: The Complete Works,* trans. Regis J. Armstrong, OFM, and Ignatius C. Brady, OFM; preface by John Vaughn, OFM (New York: Paulist Press, 1982). As Bratton notes in *Christianity, Wilderness, and Wildlife,* 223, the Canticle "expresses human dependence on the rest of the creation and demonstrates Francis's insight into the interdependence of all things. The end of the poem praises bodily death for the righteous as the final divinely ordained member of the universal order." Paul M. and Joan deRis Allen explore the organic relationships between the creatures and the natural world as expressions of God in *Francis of Assisi's Canticle of the Creatures: A New Spiritual Path* (New York: Continuum International, 2000).

127. Bonaventure, *Life of St. Francis,* 8.10, 259.

128. Ibid., 8.9, 258.

129. Ibid., 8.9, 258–59.

130. Ibid., 8.8, 257 n 58.

131. Francis of Assisi, *Little Flowers of St. Francis,* 21, 88–92.

132. Bonaventure, *Life of St. Francis,* 8.6, 255.

133. Ibid.

134. Ibid., 40, 131–33.

135. Bratton refutes this point persuasively in "Original Desert Solitaire," 40: "It is tempting to dismiss these stories as legends or inventions and therefore as poor representations of monastic attitudes toward the wilderness and wild nature. Although some of them are fiction or highly decorated versions of fact, this does not make them less valid as indicators of environmental perception or values. The purpose of these histories was spiritual instruction."

136. Jet Propulsion Laboratory, "Emerging Modern Universe: Understanding How Today's Universe of Galaxies, Stars, and Planets Came to Be," National Aeronautical Space Administration (NASA) (www.origins.jpl.nasa.gov/universe/index.html): "There is growing evidence that star formation began before there were galaxies, and that when these early stars died explosively as supernovae they produced the first spray of heavy elements. But it also appears that the birth of galaxies, by binding the stars and gas together to create these cosmic ecosystems, was crucial to the buildup of heavy elements to a level where planets and life were possible. The emergence of such enormous structures from the near-featureless universe that preceded them, and the manufacture of vast amounts of heavy elements by their stars, were key steps on the road to life."

137. Harold Morowitz, "The First 2 Billion Years of Life," *Origins* 27, no. 34 (February 12, 1998): 577–80, at 578. In a podcast from NASA's Jet Propulsion Laboratory in Pasadena, California, on December 21, 2005, Don Brownlee (the principal investigator of NASA's Stardust Project, in which cosmic dust was collected at the edge of our solar system in order to learn about its early formation) stated: "The relation between humans and stardust, amazingly is that, virtually all the atoms in our bodies were in little grains like the ones we're bringing back from the comet. They were in there before the earth and sun were formed. Stardust, or interstellar grains, form around other stars and they are the vehicle which carry elements like carbon, nitrogen,

silicon, and iron and magnesium from place to place within our galaxy. So when stars in new planetary systems form, they form from gas and dust. Virtually all the elements except hydrogen and helium are in the dust, and we have collected some of that stuff and it will be in our lab just after January 15." The podcast, "The Treasures of Stardust are Heading Home," can be accessed at www.nasa.gov/multimedia/ podcasting/podcast-stardust-20051221.html.

138. Brownlee, "Treasures of Stardust are Heading Home."

139. Morowitz, "First 2 Billion Years of Life," 579. Morowitz continues: "At 500 atmospheres of pressure and 500 degrees centigrade of temperature, reactions occur that seem to have produced the principal molecules that stand at the base of the metabolic chart."

140. Morowitz, "First 2 Billion Years of Life," 579.

141. These are prokaryotes; higher organisms like plants and animals are classified as eukaryotes.

142. The eukaryotic cell has a nuclear membrane, well-defined chromosomes (bodies containing the hereditary material), mitochondria (cellular energy exchangers), a Golgi apparatus (secretory device), an endoplasmic reticulum (a canal-like communication system within the cell), and lysosmes (digestive apparatus within many cell types).

143. Ian Tattersall, "Human Evolution: An Overview," in *An Evolving Dialogue: Theological and Scientific Perspectives on Evolution,* ed. James B. Miller (Harrisburg, PA: Trinity Press International, 2001), 197.

144. David Pilbeam, "The Descent of Hominoids and Hominids," *Scientific American* 250 (March 1984): 84–96. Discovered by Louis Leakey and others, *Homo habilis* was present 2 million years ago, had a larger brain, and chipped stones to make primitive tools.

145. Ibid. Dating from 1.6 million years ago, *Homo erectus* had a much larger brain, lived in long-term group sites, made more complicated tools, and probably used fire. Archaic forms of *Homo sapiens* appeared 500,000 years ago. Ian Barbour, *Religion and Science: Historical and Contemporary Issues* (San Francisco: HarperSanFrancisco, 1997), 254, provides some "broad outlines" of the evolution of the physiology and behavior from nonhuman to human forms and the beginnings of human culture: "Cro-Magnons made paintings on cave walls and performed burial rituals 30,000 years ago, whereas the Neanderthals were in Europe 30,000 years ago. Agriculture goes back only 10,000 years. The earliest known writing, Sumerian, is 6,000 years old. Techniques for melting metallic ores brought the Bronze Age and then, less than 3,000 years ago, the Iron Age."

146. Other hominids not in the direct line of ascent include the first known hominid *Ardipithecus ramidus* (4.4. million years ago), *Australopithecus africanus, Paranthropus aethiopicus, P. Boisei,* and *P. Robustus,* all of who lived contemporaneously on the African continent between 3 and 1 million years ago. *Homo erectus* spread to other continents, with fossil remains found in Indonesia, China, the Middle East, and Europe. Also not ancestral to *Homo sapiens* is *Homo neanderthalensis,* which appeared in Europe about 200,000 years ago and persisted until 30,000 to 40,000 years ago. See Francisco Ayala, "Evolution and the Uniqueness of Humankind," *Origins* 27, no. 34 (February 12, 1998): 565–80, at 565-68.

147. Did the genetic exchange occur from time to time between populations with the species evolving as a single gene pool, or did the first modern humans arise in Africa

or in the Middle East sometime prior to 100,000 years ago and from there spread throughout the world, replacing elsewhere the preexisting populations of *H. erectus* and *archaic H. sapiens*? Ayala asks this lingering question in "Evolution and the Uniqueness of Humankind," 568.

148. Tattersall, "Human Evolution," 209.

149. Ayala, "Evolution and the Uniqueness of Humankind," 569.

150. Paul D. MacLean, "Evolution of the Psychencephalon," *Zygon* 17 (1982): 187–211.

151. Ayala, "Evolution and the Uniqueness of Humankind," 568.

152. Ibid., 565–66.

153. Edward O. Wilson, *Biophilia* (Cambridge, MA: Harvard University Press, 1984), 130. Also see Barbour's supportive discussion in *Religion and Science*, 253–55.

154. Malcolm Ritter, "Scientists Complete Chimpanzee Genome Project," *Science and Theology News*, November 21, 2005 (www.stnews.org/research-2404.htm): "'It's a huge deal,'" said Dr. Francis Collins, director of the National Human Genome Research Institute that supported the project. 'We now have the instruction book of our closest relative,' he concluded."

155. Ayala, "Evolution and the Uniqueness of Humankind," 568.

156. Chimps lack the vocal organs, especially the larynx, necessary for articulated speech, but they can be taught to communicate in sign language or with geometric symbols on a computer keyboard. They can combine these symbols into simple sentences. D. M. Rumbaugh and others have found evidence of elementary abstract thought; see D. M. Rumbaugh, E. S. Savage-Rumbaugh, and J. L. Scanlon, "The Relationship between Language in Apes and Human Beings," in *Primate Behavior*, ed. J. L. Forbes and J. E. King (New York: Academic Press, 1982), 361–85. From a few examples, chimps can form general concepts, such as food or tool, and then assign a new object to the correct conceptual category. They can also express intentions, make requests, and communicate information to other chimps. See also J. de Luce and H. T. Wilder, eds., *Language in Primates* (New York: Springer-Verlag, 1983); and Stephan Walker, *Animal Thought* (London: Routledge & Kegan Paul, 1983).

157. If a chimp sees in a mirror a mark previously placed on its forehead, it will try to remove the mark. See Barbour, *Religion and Science*, 254.

158. Ibid., 254–55. Theodore Dohzhansky is particularly illuminating on these distinct characteristics of humans; see Theodore Dohzhansky, *The Biological Basis of Human Freedom* (New York: Columbia University Press, 1956); and Theodore Dohzhansky, *The Biology of Ultimate Concern* (New York: New American Library, 1967).

159. In insects these patterns are for the most part genetically determined, whereas there is a greater capacity for learning and individuality in higher animals. Primates have elaborate social structures and patterns of dominance and submission, and dolphins form close friendships and engage in playful activity. Information relevant to survival is transmitted socially by the young learning from their parents.

160. Ayala, "Evolution and the Uniqueness of Humankind," 567.

161. Ibid. Ayala concludes that (1) the proclivity to make ethical judgments (e.g., to evaluate actions as either good or evil) is rooted in our biological nature and is "a necessary outcome of our exalted intelligence," whereas (2) the moral codes that guide our decisions as to which actions are good and which ones are evil are products of culture, including social and religious traditions.

162. Barbour, *Religion and Science*, 255.

163. Ayala explains in "Evolution and the Uniqueness of Humankind," 570, that geneticist have long recognized the phenomenon of pleiotrophy—the expression of a gene in different organs or anatomical traits: "It follows that a gene that becomes changed owing to its effects on a certain trait will result in the modification of other traits as well. The changes of these other traits are epigenetic consequences of the changes directly promoted by natural selection. The cascade of consequence may be, particularly in the case of humans, very long and far from obvious in some cases. Literature, art, science and technology are among the behavioral features that may have come about not because they were adaptively favored in human evolution, but because they are expressions of the high intellectual abilities present in modern humans: What may have been favored by natural selection (its 'target') was an increase in intellectual activity rather than each one of those particular activities."

164. The term "culture" denotes a set of human activities and creations that are not strictly biological. Culture includes social and political institutions, ways of doing things, religious and ethical traditions, language, common sense and scientific knowledge, art and literature, technology, and in general all the creations of the human mind. See Ayala, "Evolution and the Uniqueness of Humankind," 569, where he concluded that cultural evolution has become the dominant mode of human evolution over the last few millennia as "a distinctly human mode of achieving adaptations to the environment and transmitting the adaptations through the generation."

165. Ayala, "Evolution and the Uniqueness of Humankind," 569. At 567, Ayala posits two kinds of heredity: (1) biological, based on the transmission of genetic information in human; and (2) cultural, based on the transmission of information by a teaching and learning process that "in principle" is "independent of biological parentage" but "makes possible the cumulative transmission of experience from generation to generation." Cultural heredity is "a swifter and more effective" mode of adaptation to the environment than the biological mode. He continues at 570: "Humans have become the most widespread and abundant species of mammal on earth" due to the "appearance of culture as a superorganic form of adaptation that made mankind the most successful animal species."

166. See, e.g., Marc Bekoff, "Animal Emotions: Exploring Passionate Natures," *BioScience* 50 (2000): 861–70; Marc Bekoff, "Wild Justice and Fair Play: Cooperation, Forgiveness, and Morality in Animals," *Biology & Philosophy* 19 (2004): 489–520; Marc Bekoff, "Animal Reflections," *Nature* 419 (202): 255; "Animal Passions and Beastly Virtues: Cognitive Ethology as the Unifying Science for Understanding the Subjective, Emotional, Empathic, and Moral Lives of Animals," *Zygon* 41.1 (2006): 71–104; Marc Bekoff, *Animal Passions and Beastly Virtues: Reflections on Redecorating Nature* (Philadelphia: Temple University Press, 2005); and Marc Bekoff, *The Cognitive Animal* (Cambridge, MA: MIT Press, 2002). See also William J. Long, Rupert Sheldrake, and Marc Bekoff, *How Animals Talk: And Other Pleasant Studies of Birds and Beasts* (Rochester, VT: Bear & Co., 2005); Marc Bekoff, ed., *The Smile of a Dolphin: Remarkable Accounts of Animal Emotions* (New York: Random House, 2002); and, Marc Bekoff, ed., *Encyclopedia of Animal Behavior* (Westport, CT: Greenwood Press, 2004).

167. Marc Bekoff, *Minding Animals: Awareness, Emotions, and Heart* (Oxford: Oxford University Press, 2002), xvi.

168. Marc Bekoff, *Strolling with Our Kin: Speaking For and Respecting Voiceless Animals* (New York: Lantern Books, 2000).

169. Donna Yarri, "Animals as Kin: The Religious Significance of Marc Bekoff's Work," *Zygon* 41, no. 1 (2006): 21–28.

170. Wilson, *Biophilia*, 1; and Edward O. Wilson, "Biophilia and the Conservation Ethic," in *The Biophilia Hypothesis*, ed. Stephen R. Kellert and Edward O. Wilson (Washington, DC: Island Press, 1993), 31.

171. Wilson, "Biophilia and the Conservation Ethic," 31.

172. Ibid., 32.

173. Ibid., 39.

174. Stephen R. Kellert, *Kinship to Mastery: Biophilia in Human Evolution and Development* (Washington, DC: Island Press, 1997), 5. Kellert develops this perspective in *The Value of Life: Biological Diversity and Human Society* (Washington, DC: Island Press, 1996).

175. Kellert, "The Biological Basis for Human Values of Nature," in *The Biophilia Hypothesis*, ed. Kellert and Edward O. Wilson (Washington, DC: Island Press, 1993).

176. Kellert, *Kinship to Mastery*, 6.

177. Ibid.

178. Ibid., 44.

179. Kellert, *Kinship to Mastery*, 4, pointing to C. Lumsden and E. O. Wilson, *Genes, Mind, and Culture* (Cambridge, MA: Harvard University Press, 1981) and "The Relation between Biological and Cultural Evolution," *Journal of Biological Structure* (1983): 343–59.

180. Kellert, *Kinship to Mastery*, 4, pointing to Lumsden and Wilson, *Genes, Mind, and Culture* and "Relation between Biological and Cultural Evolution."

181. Wilson, "Biophilia and the Conservation Ethic," 32–33.

182. Ibid., 32.

183. Ibid., 35.

184. Kellert, "Biological Basis for Human Values of Nature," 59.

185. Ibid., 64.

186. Ibid., 59.

187. Ibid., 60.

188. Roger S. Ulrich provides a summation of relevant research findings and identifies areas in which research is needed in "Biophilia, Biophobia, and Natural Landscapes," in *Biophilia Hypothesis*, ed. Kellert and Wilson, 73–137.

189. Wilson, "Biophilia and the Conservation Ethic," 40.

190. Ibid., 38. Wilson argues that the diversity of life has immense aesthetic and spiritual value for humans. In addition to this and other well-documented utilitarian potential that diverse wild species have for humans, Wilson continues, biodiversity is the ongoing creation that will draw to its own conclusions, other species are our "kin" literally in light of a common genetic code from which all higher organisms arose, biodiversity of a country is part of its national heritage, and biodiversity is the frontier of the future of life on Earth.

191. Kellert, *Kinship to Mastery*, 106: "Kinship and companionship offer intimacy and friendship, a way of feeling trusted and needed. . . . Separated from other life for prolonged periods of time, we often suffer mental and sometimes physical deterioration. Intimate and secure relationships with other creatures can counter feelings of separation and loneliness."

192. Holmes Rolston III, "Biophilia, Selfish Genes, Shared Values," in *Biophilia Hypothesis*, ed. Kellert and Wilson, 381–414.

193. Ibid., 385.

194. Ibid., 387.

195. Ibid., 413.

196. Ibid., 388.

197. Ibid., 397.

198. Ibid., 413.

199. Ulrich, "Biophilia, Biophobia, and Natural Landscapes," 126.

200. Ibid.

201. The environmental scientist Michael E. Soulé—in "Biophilia: Unanswered Questions," in *Biophilia Hypothesis,* ed. Kellert and Wilson, 441–55, at 454—stresses the need for biophilia to become "a religion-like movement" if it is to be a powerful force for conservation. "Only a new religion of nature, similar but even more powerful than the animal rights movement, can create the political momentum required to overcome the greed that gives rise to discord and strife and the anthropocentrism that underlies the intentional abuse of nature. . . . The social womb for such a "biophilism" could be bioregional communities that recapture tribal-hunter-gatherer-pagan wisdom, integrating it with relevant science, appropriate technology, family planning, and sustainable land use practices."

202. Among the principles that can be offered for applying the concept of the kinship of humans and other creatures to particular problems are the following: (1) Acknowledge the human genetic companionship with the subject from and/or with whom humans emerged over cosmological-biological time through God's sustaining empowerment; (2) cherish the familial relationships that humans have with the subject; (3) cherish the subject for the roles it plays in relation to others in the shared ecosystem; (4) acknowledge with humility and gratitude the radical human dependence humans have for their health and well-being upon the subject and the biological system in which the subject functions; and (5) assume with Saint Francis of Assisi and Saint Bonaventure a posture of piety toward other creatures by (i) *loving them for themselves* and not simply for their usefulness to humans, (ii) *devoting human concern for their interests* in surviving and flourishing, making sure that they can sustain themselves, (iii) *showering them with affection* by tending to and protecting them from human and other intrusions that prevent them from meeting their needs and flourishing, (iv) *being kind to them* as fellow travelers in the journey of life who need dedicated space to meet their needs and to continue their journey alongside humans and other species, (v) *standing up for and with them before others* when they are threatened individually or as a species, (vi) *showing compassion for their suffering,* while understanding the decay, death, and the emergence of newness in the course and web of life, and (vii) *being generous to them without interfering with their self-expressions* according to their natures.

203. Joseph Sittler Jr., "A Theology for Earth," *Christian Scholar* 37 (September 1954): 376–74, at 372.

204. Ibid.

205. Michael J. Himes and Kenneth R. Himes, *Fullness of Faith: The Public Significance of Theology* (New York: Paulist Press, 1993), 112.

206. Ibid.

207. Lazarus Macior, "A Sense of the Sacred in Creation and Natural Science," in *Proceedings of the 13th Convention of the Fellowship of Catholic Scholars,* ed. P. L. Williams (Pittston, PA: Northeast Books, 1990), 101.

208. Himes and Himes, *Fullness of Faith,* 109.

209. Ibid., 111.

210. Sallie McFague, *The Body of God: An Ecological Theology* (Minneapolis: Fortress Press, 1993), 112–29.

211. A group of Christian theologians advocate some practical ways of demonstrating the intrinsic valuing of animals in "Liberating Life: A Report to the World Council of Churches," by Jay McDaniel, John Cobb, Tom Regan, and Charles Birch, in *Good News for Animals,* ed. Charles Pinches and Jay B. McDaniel (Maryknoll: Orbis Books, 1993), 235–52. Among the practical recommendations in this report are: (1) Avoid cosmetics and household products that have been cruelly tested on animals and instead buy cruelty-free items; (2) avoid clothing and other aspects of fashion that have a history of cruelty to animals, particularly products of the fur industry, and instead buy cruelty-free products; (3) avoid buying and eating meat and other animal products that have been produced on factory farms, and instead purchase meats and animal products from sources where animals have been treated with respect, or abstain from these products altogether; (4) avoid patronizing forms of entertainment that treat animals as mere means to human ends, and instead seek benign forms of entertainment or ones nurture a sense of wonder of God's creation and reawaken the duty to live respectfully with all life.

212. Aldo Leopold, *Sand County Almanac: With Essays on Conservation from Round River* (New York: Ballantine Books, 1966), 262.

213. As noted in the previous chapter, the International Joint Commission identified humans as one of the living organisms in the Great Lakes in the *Great Lakes Water Quality Agreement,* Ottawa, November 22, 1978, which was signed by representatives of the United States and Canada.

7

USING CREATION WITH GRATITUDE
AND RESTRAINT

That God provided all living creatures with means to sustain themselves permeates patristic and medieval teachings. Theologians characterized this basic tenet of Christian faith as God's *providence,* upon which the faithful can rely.[1] As indicated in chapter 5, on the integrity of creation, some theologians reflected on God's care for creatures by maintaining a hierarchically ordered world in which nonliving and living creatures serve as sources of sustenance for one another according to their natures.[2] Patristic and medieval theologians reasoned from their understanding of the world that humans are at the top of this instrumental order, primarily because they are endowed by God with the intellectual capacity to make informed decisions on means of sustaining their temporal lives and the freedom to execute their decisions.

As this chapter demonstrates, these patristic and medieval theologians underscored repeatedly that humans should use other creatures restrictively and why. Their teachings have profound significance for humanity today in light of our persistent overconsumption, depletion, and wastefulness of Earth's sources, especially in economically developed countries. The straightforward application of the theologians' teachings suggests a clear trajectory for making decisions about using other species and abiota.

Patristic and Medieval Teachings

When reflecting on the Genesis 1 story of creation, Basil of Caesarea (329–79) explained that God commanded Earth to produce vegetation that could produce seeds, reproduce, and thereby perpetuate the various species. This first command to Earth became "a law of nature" that remained embedded in Earth and accounted for an "infinite variety of growing plants."[3] Plants became useful to other living creatures for their sustenance, while their seeds were allotted to humans for their agricultural use.[4] According to Basil, each plant has a purpose in the orderly scheme of creation, even the poisonous plants that are dangerous and useless to humans, and each is valuable.[5] He considered Earth's ability to perpetuate species as "the marvel of creation"[6] and "a rich treasure" that humans should acknowledge as having been provided by God.[7]

Aquinas (1224/25–74) also contemplated the orderly creation and the use of its constituents in relation to one another. God designed the orderly creation and sustains it through the hierarchical interactivity of creatures, wherein plants act on minerals and mixed elements for nourishment, animals on plants, and humans on other animals.[8] Aquinas referred occasionally to this arrangement as an "order of conservation," in which the higher entity relied on the lower for sustenance.[9] From his medieval understanding of the world, he reasoned that all constituents are needed internally to maintain the cosmos.[10] He configured all entities of the cosmos as constituting an order of users and used, in which every entity God created has a purpose to fulfill according to its position on the hierarchical scale, while all users and used achieve the purpose of the cosmos when functioning as God intended.[11] Blanchette recognizes this corporeal order of instrumentality, but Aquinas's understanding of the order of users and used goes beyond corporeal parameters to encompass the totality of existence with God as the ultimate mover of the instrumental order. The order of users and used begins with God as the primary mover and extends hierarchically to natural entities down to the basic elements of nature—air, water, fire, and earth. Of course, Aquinas taught that God acts in a unique way that has no parallel in the created order.

Because humans are at the apex of the corporeal users in the created order, they are intended to use other creatures—but only in restricted ways, patristic and medieval theologians insisted. They posited several requirements. Humans are supposed to use other created entities (1) by using their ability to reason rather than giving into their irrational desires, (2) by moderating and limiting their intake to the necessities of life, (3) to know God, (4) to gain knowledge about God's creation, and (5) joyfully, as blessings from God.

Use According to Reason

Augustine of Hippo, John Scotus Eriugena, Albertus Magnus, and Thomas Aquinas were among the theologians who stressed the need for humans to use their reasoning capacity to determine how to use other entities. Because the ability to reason and freedom of the will to make informed decision were considered characteristics unique to humans among other corporeal creatures,[12] using that ability to determine how to use God's creation is a natural capacity that is mandatory.

For Augustine (354–430), heretics fail to recognize the goodness of creation and their place in the splendid order of all things God created. They are distressed by fire, cold, wild animals, and other aspects of the natural world that cause inconveniences, and they fail to see how much these same things benefit humans if they make "wise and appropriate use of them." When used wisely and appropriately, even poisons are "turned into wholesome medicines by their proper application," whereas food, drink, and other things that give pleasure to humans are experienced as harmful when used without restraint and in improper ways.[13] The "great artificer" of all natural things wants humans to avoid indulging in "silly complaints" about the natural world and "to take pains" to inquire about the "useful purposes" of things.[14] Clearly, Augustine wanted the members of his flock to use their God-given abilities to reason about the appropriate use of God's creatures.

John Scotus Eriugena (810–ca. 877) followed Augustine in urging the faithful to think carefully about their use of God's creation. Writing to instruct "simple minds" in the faith so they would not be "easy prey" to heretical teachings, Eriugena exhorted them to avoid acting irrationally because God had created them to use their ability to reason. Acting irrationally would mar "their natural beauty" and diminish their dignity as creatures who are made in the image and likeness of God.[15] Their irrational impulses are "diametrically opposed" to the rational nature of humans and must be self-controlled:

> And here no other situation for the cause of the irrational impulse seems more likely than the misuse, contrary to the Laws of God, of the natural goods, which is the characteristic feature of the perverted and unruly desire of the free will, which uses the good in the wrong way. Examples of this misuse are so common that there can be hardly anyone who could not produce a copious supply of them from his own nature.[16]

According to Eriugena, humans are gifted by God with the ability to reason, which will guide them in using natural goods, even the "lowest sensible goods," for the glory and service of God, "the Bestower of all good things." When humans succumb to their irrational impulses to use material goods to gratify their "perverse" desires, they are acting in opposition to their God-given rational natures.[17]

As one committed to the full use of the ability to reason, Albertus Magnus (?1193–1280) taught that humans govern God's creation correctly only if they use their God-given rationality to control their bodies. Humans are not intended to be subject to the world, he taught; God intends them to govern it.[18] However, if they act irrationally, they shed the dignity of their humanity and assume the nature of other animals: "Such a man is likened to a pig because of his wanton behavior, to a dog because of his snarling temper, to a lion because of his rapacity, and similarly to other animals because of his sub-human actions."[19]

When humans persevere in controlling their actions from "the throne of their minds," Albert taught, they master both themselves and the physical world. Those who choose "to shackle" themselves to bodily demands incur the "marks of corruption," because these "accidental qualities of the body wreak changes" in the human soul. When failing to exercise restraint over their bodies, they open "the door to rapid weakening and deterioration, especially through the imagination and passions" that "accelerate the process of bodily corruption."[20] He also demonstrated how to put human reason into practice when identifying a variety of ways to improve the land and crops.[21]

Albertus Magnus's most famous student, Thomas Aquinas, also stressed the need for humans to use their ability to reason when deciding how to use natural entities. He lauded the knowledge humans acquire through their innate capacity to reason, and he distinguished this knowledge from both the knowledge of God that is received through revelation and the perfect knowledge of God that is enjoyed in eternal life.[22] He also lauded the key differences between rational and irrational animals when explaining the term "use." The use of something requires two acts: the act of the will, and the act of reason. Humans' use of other creatures is an act of the will, whereby external things are applied intentionally to an operation (e.g., the use of a horse is to ride, and the use of a stick is to strike),[23] whereas the act of reason assumes the facility to know how to refer an external thing to an operation. Aquinas taught that only a rational animal is capable of these two acts,[24] whereas other animals act according to natural instinct and cannot reason to how an external entity can be applied to an operation.[25] The application of an operation must fit into the natural order of things in relation to one another for their sustenance, and their use cannot be ends in themselves because they are not the ultimate goal of human existence. If humans use natural entities as ends in themselves, their rational power is considered disordered; they have strayed from God's will that they order their actions ultimately in relation to God.[26]

Furthermore, when commenting on the Genesis 1 story of creation, Aquinas taught that humans have a natural dominion over other material creatures, as executors of God's primary dominion over all.[27] They are supposed to use their capacity to reason when exercising their dominion,[28] and their use of other creatures must show their reverence for God as their mutual creator and sustainer.[29]

When using other creatures, Aquinas insisted, humans should conform their wills to God's will to ensure that the common good is sought. God apprehends and wills the good of the entire universe under the aspects of justice and the natural order, and humans know in a general way that God wills good universally. When they choose to seek the common good they are imitating God.[30] However, they may not be able to know God's will in temporal life when willing particular goods, though they should will a particular good with the intention of conforming their wills to God's. Upholding the natural order of things in relation to one another and understanding God's justice should help toward that end.[31] Developing the moral virtues to guide the use of other creatures can also assist humans in using them rationally, as explained in chapter 8.[32]

Thus, according to patristic and medieval theologians, people who believe in God as their creator and sustainer should employ their reasoning ability when using other creatures. If they do not, they shed their unique dignity among the other creatures that constitute the universe and reduce themselves to the level of irrational creatures. Doing so would be contrary to God's intentions that they rely on their own natural abilities when using other entities. This stance leads to exploring more specific directions on how to use other creatures.

Use Moderately for the Necessities of Life

The theological literature during the patristic and medieval periods is replete with admonitions that Christians should use God's creation moderately to provide the necessities of life. Inherent in this teaching is a sense of justice that others should also be able to obtain their material needs in temporal life as they journey toward eternal happiness with God. Among the theologians who wrote instructively on using nonhuman entities to sustain their lives are Tertullian of Carthage, Origen of Alexandria, Gregory of Nyssa, John Chrysostom, Theodoret of Cyrrhus, Augustine of Hippo, Benedict of Nursia, Symeon the New Theologian, Hildegard of Bingen, Albertus Magnus, and Thomas Aquinas.

According to Tertullian (ca. 160–?), God blessed the entirety of creation for "wholesome and advantageous uses" by humankind. He found a "wide difference" between purpose and misuse and between moderation and excess, and he opted for purposeful and moderate use from his faith-based premise that humans are responsible to God for their use of God's creation.[33]

Origen (185–254) insisted that God appointed humankind to rule the natural world as God's partner. Yet humans are needy, he stressed, and more so than irrational animals, who have protective coverings and other natural attributes that humans do not. Using their God-given ability to reason, humans can obtain the necessities of life by developing agricultural, gardening, carpentry, and navigation skills.[34]

After the first humans sinned, John Chrysostom (347–407) contended, God entrusted them and their descendants with control over only those creatures that are essential to sustain human life.[35] God provided many kinds of creatures to share human labor, and he urged humans to use these and other natural goods moderately, to avoid luxuries and excesses of any kind, and to fast. He also cautioned them to maintain control over their ability to reason when seeking and acquiring the necessities of life.[36]

Affirming the value of God's creation, Gregory of Nyssa (ca. 330–95) asserted that humans are intended to satisfy their needs in this life by serving God as masters over creation. He was specific about the use of horses to help humans move more quickly, the use of sheep for clothing, the use of oxen for food, the use of the dog jawbone for knives, and the use of iron for protection.[37]

Theodoret (390–458) depicted the human as a triumphant doer and transformer whose hands and arms serve the mind to plow and sow the land, dig ditches, cut vines, reap the harvest, bind sheaves, and winnow grain. God gave humans the wisdom with which to invent the tools they need for mining, agriculture, and traveling. Through the gift of wisdom, humans can embellish Earth with flowery meadows, rich harvests, spacious woods, and routes over the sea.[38]

Augustine of Hippo reserved the term "use" of God's creation as a means of ensuring that the material needs of temporal life are met while the faithful aim ultimately toward enjoying eternal life.[39] He also urged restraint when using them,[40] and he told his followers to use God's creation as if they were pilgrims in a foreign land:

> A household of human beings whose life is based on faith looks forward to the blessings which are promised as eternal in the future, making use of earthly and temporal things like a pilgrim in a foreign land, who does not let himself be taken in by them or distracted from his course towards God, but rather treats them as supports which help him more easily to bear the burdens of 'corruptible body which weighs heavy on the soul' [Ws 9:15]; they must on no account be allowed to increase the load.[41]

Augustine also encouraged the appropriate use of God's creation according to the nature of the creature used.[42] He argued that all things God created are good and serve useful purposes in the "universal commonwealth," though those purposes may not be obvious to all humans.[43] Heretics especially fail to see the goodness of creatures and, therefore, disparage fire, cold, wild animals, and other natural entities. They not only fail to value them intrinsically, for their positions in "the splendour of the providential order and the contribution they make by their own special beauty to the whole material scheme of the cosmos." They also fail to understand how much those same things contribute to their benefit if they make wise and appropriate use of them. Even poisons that are disastrous when improperly used are turned into wholesome medicines by their proper application, Augustine insisted. By contrast, things that give pleasure—like food, drink, and even light itself—are experienced as harmful when used inappropriately and without restraint.[44] Anyone who wrongly uses these temporal goods, he warned, "shall not receive the blessings of eternal life."[45]

In his rule 34, Benedict of Nursia (ca. 480–547) stipulated the distribution of goods to the monks solely on the basis of need. He recognized that different persons have considerably different needs, so the abbot must use discretion and compassion when dealing with the monks. Frugality was key to running the monasteries under the Benedictine Rule.[46]

Systematically approaching the human use of natural entities, Aquinas stressed throughout his teachings that other living and nonliving creatures serve humans as sustenance for their bodily lives. He repeatedly taught that humans should use other constituents of God's creation for the necessities of life.[47] The necessities of life are things humans need to support their bodies, such as food, clothing, transportation,[48] and those things without which they cannot carry on their lives in appropriate ways as they seek eternal happiness with God.[49] He proscribed the exorbitant use of God's other creatures, describing it as inordinate and wasteful,[50] immoderate,[51] disordered, and vicious.[52] The excessive use of other entities was judged sinful in the scheme of the human desire for eternity with God,[53] because human attention must be centered ultimately on God.

Following this line of reasoning, Aquinas viewed natural goods as instruments of temporal happiness, because humans need them to support their bodily lives as they strive to live virtuously.[54] He taught that humans could pray for the necessities of life that bring about "imperfect happiness," because they assist humans in tending toward eternal life with God, which constitutes "perfect happiness."[55] Humans cannot use other creatures as ends in themselves, according to Aquinas, because their primary end is God.[56]

Furthermore, Aquinas taught, humans should use God's creation in proper ways for the purposes they fulfill in the scheme of creation. Plants exist for animals to eat, animals exist for other animals, and all exist for humans to eat or use in other ways to bring up children, support a family, and meet other bodily needs.[57] Therefore, the human use of plants and animals for the necessities of life is appropriate. Also appropriate is the possession of wealth if it is used to benefit the owner and others.[58] However, an individual who possesses or desires to possess immoderate amounts of material goods sins against another with the sin of avarice, because one individual cannot have an abundance of external riches without other individuals lacking them.[59]

Aquinas also underscored the need for acting justly toward one's neighbor and seeking the temporal common good of one's community. Those who seek to be just would use natural goods in ways that did not interfere with other community members' access to the goods they need to sustain their lives,[60] a point that moral theologian Mary Hirschfeld makes in her study of Aquinas' teachings.[61] Coveting things was proscribed unequivocally.[62]

Symeon the New Theologian (949–1022) was particularly reflective about avoiding the sin of coveting goods when using God's creatures. All natural entities in the world are common to all for their use and enjoyment:

> Like the light and this air that we breathe, as well as the pasture for the dumb animals on the plains and on the mountains. All these things were made for all in common solely for use and enjoyment; in terms of ownership they belong to no one. But covetousness, like a tyrant, has intruded into life, so that its slaves and underlings have in various ways divided up that which the Master gave to be common to all. She has enclosed them by fences and made them secure by means of watchtowers, bolts, and gates. She has deprived all other men of the enjoyment of the Master's good gifts, shamelessly pretending to own them, contending that she has wronged no one.[63]

The "devil" urges hoarding things for ourselves and unjustly depriving others, Symeon cautioned.[64] For this sin, hoarders "owe a debt of penitence to their dying day for all that they so long have kept back and deprived their brothers from using![65] Those who scatter the goods abroad generously to others in need "with joy and magnanimity, not reluctantly or under compulsion," are set free from condemnation of covetousness and are on their way to "eternal life and enjoyment" of God.[66] He also urged other works of mercy to help the hungry and thirsty.[67]

When viewed together, these as well as other patristic to medieval theologians urged their faith-filled followers to use the goods of Earth for the necessities of life, to avoid using them excessively, to use them appropriately according to their natures, and to be conscious of others' needs so they also are able to sustain their lives, the lives of their families, and the members of their larger communities. These normative prescriptions loom large in Christian teachings and can have significance when considering how other species, the air, land, and water are used today.

Use to Know God

Another prevalent teaching that loomed large in Christian theology during the patristic and medieval periods was the use of God's creation as a means of knowing about God. Theologians taught that humans who study the world God created can discern some of God's characteristics—chiefly, God's goodness, power, and wisdom, as discussed in depth in chapter 3. Belief in God is presumed when approaching the world to learn about God.[68] Of course, as underscored in chapter 3, creatures mediate these attributes by being themselves and functioning according to their natures.

Use to Gain Knowledge about God's Creation

Some theologians taught that the physical creation is worth studying in order to gain knowledge about God's creation per se, rather than using it exclusively to discern God's attributes. Augustine, Bernard of Clairvaux, Albertus Magnus, and Aquinas are among these theologians. They reflected on the human ability to learn about the world through their natural God-given capacities from their faith perspective in God as the purposeful creator and sustainer of the world.

Augustine urged his followers to learn about the purposes of natural entities and to avoid indulging in "silly complaints" about any that cause inconveniences or problems. God wants humans "to take pains to inquire what useful purposes are served by things. And when we fail to find the answer, either through deficiency of insight or of staying power, we should believe that the purpose is hidden from us, as it was in many cases where we had great difficulty in discovering it. There is a useful purpose in the obscurity of purpose; it may serve to exercise our humility or to undermine our pride."[69]

Bernard of Clairvaux (1090–1153) questioned the Christian attitude toward living creatures that seemed to be useless to themselves and to humans. Even if they appear useless, he concluded, they are nevertheless beautiful to look at. They are also useful by providing "food for reflection," because they make humans use their ability to reason and learn from the things that God has made. If they are found harmful and even damaging to human salvation, he reasoned optimistically from his belief in a purposeful God, somehow their bodies can work together to achieve good.[70]

As a strong proponent and example of scientific learning during the medieval period, Albertus Magnus explained that he composed *Physica* to satisfy requests, pleas, and prayers from his Dominican colleagues who wanted a book to help them understand the world as portrayed in the corpus of Aristotle, which had been newly translated from Greek into Latin. Yet his primary purpose in writing this impressive text was to praise the omnipotence of God, who is the source of wisdom and the creator, establisher and ruler of nature.[71] In another work, *De Animalibus,* he viewed his scientific endeavors as having been perfected with the help of God.[72] He was strongly convinced, contra Aristotle, that the world God created is perfect and that each creature has a purpose for existing. For his exemplary efforts in distinguishing the differences between religious faith as imparted by God and the natural sciences as discerned through human reason,[73] Albertus Magnus has been designated the patron saint of natural scientists.[74]

Aquinas agreed with his teacher's views on the benefits of studying creatures. They are usefull for perfecting human knowledge,[75] since they serve as means for learning about reality. Furthermore, Aquinas explained, human knowledge about the world constitutes a participation in God's knowledge, which encompasses the totality of reality.[76] On a more practical level, Aquinas taught that humans need experimental knowledge about living creatures so they will know how to manage and use them intelligently for food, clothing, and transportation.[77] In a refrain used occasionally by theologians, he concluded that those who do not take care of the things needed for this life are foolish.[78]

Knowledge of God's creation also serves the purpose of destroying errors about God, Aquinas insisted. If human minds are ignorant of the nature of creatures, they become so perverted that they think nothing exists beyond the realm of visible creatures, attribute to creatures what belongs only to God, fail to recognize God's power in creating and sustaining all things, and think that humans are subject to other creatures.[79] Aquinas was convinced that the study and contemplation of God's creatures will not only correct misconceptions about God, but will also lead the human mind toward God when approached fom a Christian faith perspective.[80]

Use Gratefully as Blessings from God

For Augustine, the world is full of "blessings" for humans to "behold and use." He lamented not being able to adequately describe them:

> How could any description do justice to all these blessings? The manifold diversity of beauty in sky and earth and sea; the abundance of light, and its miraculous loveliness, in sun and moon and stars; the dark shades of woods, the colour and fragrance of flowers; the multitudinous varieties of birds, with their songs and their bright plumage; the countless different species of living creatures of all shapes and sizes, amongst whom it is the smallest in bulk that moves our greatest wonder— for we are more astonished at the activities of the tiny ants and bees than at the immense bulk of whales. Then there is the mighty spectacle of the sea itself, putting on its changing colours like different garments, now green, with all the many varied shades, now purple, now blue. Moreover, what a delightful sight it is when stormy, giving added pleasure to the spectator because of the agreeable thought that he is not a sailor tossed and heaved about on it! Think too of the abundant supply of food everywhere to satisfy our hunger, the variety of flavours to suit our pampered taste, lavishly distributed by the riches of nature, not produced by the skill and labour of cooks! Think, too, of all the resources for the preservation of

health, or for its restoration, the welcome alternation of day and night, the soothing coolness of the breezes, all the material for clothing provided by plants and animals. Who could give a complete list of all these natural blessings?[81]

Augustine also enumerated the blessings that are inherent in human nature:
The ability to procreate and grow; the intellectual capacity to become knowledgeable and absorb wisdom; the disposition to acquire the virtues that equip humans
"to struggle against error and all the evil propensities inherent" in human nature;
and, the desire for peace that consists in "bodily health and soundness," "fellowship" with others, and "everything necessary . . . to safeguard . . . and recover
this peace, . . . including light, speech, air to breathe, water to drink, and whatever is suitable for the feeding and clothing of the body, for the care of the body
and the adornment of the person." He lauded "natural" human abilities "to discover, to learn, and to practice" the various arts, abilities that he attributed to
God's goodness. He also complimented human achievements in many spheres
of life.[82] His list comprised a "compressed pile of blessings," he exclaimed. If these
blessings are so great for sinners, he speculated, the blessings of eternal life would
be even more wondrous.[83]

Basil of Caesarea also relished the splendor of God's creation for its usefulness. He urged his followers to acknowledge their "gratitude for the useful
plants," as well as those that pose hazards to human life. God did not create everything for human stomachs, he cautioned. Plants intended to nourish humans are
readily accessible, and they should discern what is useful and what is injurious
to them. Yet not one plant is without value, he insisted, whether it is useful or
harmful to humans:

> Either it provides food for some animal, or it has been sought out for us by the
> medical profession for the relief of certain diseases. In fact, starlings eat hemlock,
> escaping harm from the poison because of the constitution of their bodies. Since
> they have very tiny passage ways in the heart, they digest the poison swallowed
> before its chilling effect has seized upon the vital organs. Hellebore is food for quails,
> who escape harm because of their peculiar constitution.[84] These same plants are
> sometimes useful to us also. For instance, with mandrake doctors induce sleep and
> with opium they lull violent pains of the body. Some also have already dulled even
> their mad appetites with hemlock, and with hellebore have banished many of the
> long continued sufferings.[85]

Being able to study these plants is "an additional cause for thankfulness."[86] As indicated in chapter 2, on the beauty of creation, the bishop of Caesarea relished
learning about God's creation. Thus, patristic and medieval theologians provide
a basis from which to think carefully about the human use of natural goods: They
are God's blessings, which should be used for the necessities of life and to know
God. They should be used appropriately according to their natures. They should
be used with a sense of justice, so others may also have natural goods available
to meet their needs in life. And the faithful should express gratitude to God for
these blessings.

To what extent are these teachings demonstrated in the consumption of Earth's goods today and in the recent past? A brief examination of the evidence yields a bleak conclusion. The need to call the teachings of patristic and medieval theologians to the attention of faith-filled people is urgent indeed.

Unrestrained Use: An Alarming Contemporary Problem

Statistics regarding the consumption of Earth's sources and the resulting wastes indicate that humans collectively have been living in ways that contrast with the teachings of patristic and medieval theologians. The escalating growth in consumption over the past fifty years has adversely affected the land, waters, air, and other species. As summarized by the American Association for the Advancement of Science, human effects on Earth have reached "a truly massive scale, leaving an ecological 'footprint' that outweighs the impact of all other living species combined."[87] This impact is due to excessive human use and abuse of the land, freshwater, oceans, air, and other species.

The Use and Abuse of the Land

Approximately half the landmass of our planet has been transformed for human use. Around 11 percent is used today for farming, another 11 percent for forestry, 26 percent for pasture, and at least 2 to 3 percent for housing, industry, services, and transportation.[88] The area used for growing crops has increased significantly over the last three centuries, primarily at the expense of forests and woodlands.[89]

Of Earth's original forest cover, about half remains today, and approximately 30 percent of the remaining forests has been fragmented or degraded by the selective removal of valuable trees.[90] Worldwide deforestation escalated from 1990 to 2000, resulting in the loss during that time of more than 4 percent of the planet's forest area.[91] Although losses have occurred in all types of forests,[92] more than 90 percent of losses from 1990 to 2000 were in tropical forests that contain an estimated half or more of the planet's biological diversity,[93] the ramifications of which are discussed in a separate section below. The realization that forests provide many services (e.g., mitigating climate change, conserving biological diversity, maintaining clean and reliable water sources, sustaining and enhancing land productivity, protecting coastal and marine sources, and furnishing renewable wood and nonwood products for human use) has prompted the replanting of forests and restoring of landscapes, and allowed the natural expansion of forests.

These efforts have reduced the net loss of forest area,[94] though losses in the tropics have remained permanent when planting was delayed. Some countries have reported an increase in their areas of primary forests as a result of setting them aside as "no intervention" areas.[95] Although progress has been made toward reversing the overall trend of forest area loss, the Food and Agricultural Organization of the United Nations reported in 2005 that deforestation, including conversion of forests to agricultural land, continues at "an alarmingly high rate. . . . Considerable efforts are needed before the overall trend in extent is positive or stable in all regions."[96]

Grasslands and savannas fare no better, having been subjected to massive transformation by humans. By the second half of the twentieth century, nearly all Earth's temperate grasslands and tropical savannas had been converted for growing crops or grazing, and many of these ecosystems have been degraded by invasive species.[97] Conversions of these lands for grazing and growing crops have led to a greater dependence on water and chemicals to support high yields, which have caused soil erosion and water pollution.[98] Although soils that support crops are generated at rates of inches per millennium, some are being eroded at rates of inches per decade.[99] Converted lands that are prime for growing crops have been lost throughout the world to urbanization, suburbanization, industrialization, roads, and other human activities.[100] Lands that are marginal for crop production and are worked by poor farmers who do not have access to more productive plots are especially susceptible to degradation.

Minerals, sources of energy, and other valuable natural materials are being extracted from the land at alarming rates. Because these sources are not renewable, they will be used up sooner or later. Mechanisms of the market have acted to forestall their depletion—when shortages occur, prices rise, exploration for more sources ensue, research on alternatives is conducted, less expensive substitutes are found, and recycling increases. Nevertheless, the rate at which valuable nonrenewable sources are being used warrants attention. Key among these sources is oil, a mainstay for heating, cooling, transportation, the production of electricity, and the extraction of chemicals for use in a wide array of products that humans need and want.[101] Approximately 35 percent of the oil used in the various sectors of the nation's economy is produced domestically,[102] whereas the remaining amounts are imported from other countries.[103] The demand for oil-based products has been increasing, the amount of oil produced in the United States has been decreasing each year,[104] and the amount of imported oil has been increasing due to consumer demand.[105]

According to recent projections of future oil use in the world, nearly 60 percent of the growth anticipated will occur in the United States, China, and the rest of developing Asia.[106] When the United States will use up its estimated 21.4 billion barrels of reserves or when the world will deplete its estimated 1,277.2 billion barrels of reserves[107] remain questions that are not easily answered. Various proposals have been proffered, often splattered with optimism over technological advances that will make oil production and use more efficient in a growing world economy,[108] to meet the demand from increasing numbers of people.[109] However, as Bent, Orr, and Baker caution,

> Many earlier predictions of oil and other resource production peaks and exhaustion times have been proven wrong because of unforeseen discoveries and technological developments, which during the last two centuries have always been more rapid than resource depletion. But this pattern cannot be expected to continue indefinitely—there are limits to how long nonrenewable resources can last. In the

case of oil, the limit will be reached when the energy required to recover a gallon of oil is greater than the energy content of the oil. It may become economical to switch to substitutes long before that point is reached.[110]

Among the renewable sources to which switches can be made are the sun, wind, and geothermal energy to generate electricity, passive solar power to heat homes, biomass for fuel,[111] and hydrogen for fuel cells. Efforts to tap these renewable energy sources lag.[112]

Throughout the world, wetlands (e.g., marshes, swamps, and bogs) are being used and abused by people in a wide spectrum of activities. However, the amount of wetland loss throughout the world is illusive due to methods used to collect data, the failure to collect data in many areas of the world, and different ways of defining these complex ecosystems that make collecting data difficult.[113] Ecosystems serve valuable internal functions, including improving water quality, controlling floods, diminishing droughts, and stabilizing shorelines. They also harbor species with considerable commercial and recreational value to humans. Before the ecological value of wetlands was recognized in the United States in the 1970s, they were often destroyed indiscriminately for agricultural use, building homes and other structures, and controlling mosquitoes. These uses resulted by the 1980s in the loss of half the wetland area that had existed in the contiguous United States in the 1780s.[114] From 1986 to 1997, the annual rate of wetland loss in the contiguous United States decreased by 77 percent from the previous decade, a drop-off that the National Research Council suspects may be attributable to a federal permit process that deterred developers.[115]

Despite progress in minimizing the loss of wetlands in the past twenty years, the goal of preventing any further loss of wetlands is not being met. From 1993 to 2000, about 24,000 acres of wetlands in the United States were allowed to be filled, and 42,000 acres were required as compensatory mitigation; thus, nearly 2 acres should have been gained for every 1 acre lost. However, required mitigation projects were either uninitiated or projects that had been started were not completed. The full magnitude of this loss is not precisely known because the data on wetland destruction, restoration, and development are insufficient.[116]

The Use and Abuse of Water

Freshwater is vital for humans, other animals, plants, and microbes of ecosystems.[117] Although most freshwater is locked up in ice and snow and in aquifers that are too deep to tap, the rest is unevenly distributed, predominantly in the form of lakes, rivers, and aquifers.[118] Humans have used more than half Earth's available freshwater for a plethora of needs, but the greatest use—70 percent— is for watering crops.[119]

Though essential for health and well-being, bodies of freshwater are polluted variously throughout the world by siltation from soil erosion, farm and industry chemicals, and partially treated or untreated sewage. The flows of approximately two-thirds of the planet's rivers are regulated to human advantage, creating artificial lakes and altering the ecological functioning of existing lakes and river estuaries.[120] Diverting water to more arid locations where people are settling has become a common though sometimes disputed quest.[121] Many deposits of groundwater that accumulated during the ice ages are now being drained, other aquifers are being drawn down faster than they can be replenished by natural recharge, and groundwater is being contaminated by various pollutants, including heavy metals, farm chemicals, and industrial chemicals. Because half the population of the United States depends on wells for drinking water, many are unknowingly exposed directly to these contaminants. The availability of safe water for people to drink is a growing problem in the United States and many other countries,[122] prompting the World Health Organization to rank unsafe water among the top ten global health risks.[123] Chronic and acute water shortages are especially common in countries with rapidly increasing populations, and conflicts have arisen over access to this basic life necessity.[124]

Oceans constitute 70 percent of the planet's surface, and human use and abuse of these ecosystems has been extensive. Two-thirds of the marine fisheries have been exploited to their limits or beyond, and the ecological functioning of a vast array of marine species has been altered. All important oceanic fish stocks are considered seriously depleted or in danger of being depleted,[125] and an estimated 90 percent of large predatory fish have been lost.[126] Many are important sources of human nutrition (e.g., tuna, sharks, cod, and swordfish), and all play important roles in maintaining the functioning of the oceans' ecosystems.[127] Silt, waste oil, and other contaminants are entering near shore waters due to the increasing numbers of people living in coastal areas. Every year, coastal development destroys huge areas of salt marshes and mangrove swamps—ecosystems that serve as nurseries for many ocean fish species.[128] The rapid growth of aquaculture has added risks to wild fish in the oceans by utilizing as feed for farmed fish some species that are not usually marketed for human consumption but are essential to the oceanic food web. Furthermore, farmed fish that escape their enclosures play havoc with naturally occurring fish of their species, furthering the decline of wild species.[129]

Underwater oceanic forests—coral reefs—are also being used and abused by humans both directly and indirectly. These reefs are brittle, sensitive to light, and need pristine, clear, warm, and relatively nutrient-free waters to survive, and they represent some of the most dense, varied, and complex ecosystems of Earth. Though they cover only 0.2 percent of the ocean's floor, scientists estimate that nearly 1 million species of fish, invertebrates, and algae can be found in and around them.[130] Unfortunately, 10 percent of the coral reefs worldwide have been degraded or destroyed, primarily by human expansion and development. As the construction of homes, other buildings, roads, and other paved surfaces escalates in coastal areas, the increased amount of freshwater runoff carries large amounts of sediment from land-clearing areas, high levels of nutrients from agricultural areas and septic systems, and many pollutants, including petroleum products and insecticides. Sedimentation on the reefs and increases in excessive plant nutrients (eutrophication) decrease the amounts of light reaching the corals and bleaches their coloration.[131] Discharges of extremely hot water from large power plants exacerbate coral bleaching, while increases in the amounts of nutrients enhance the growth of other reef organisms (e.g., sponges) that may outcompete the corals for space on crowded reefs.[132]

Also adversely affecting coral reefs is the overfishing of species that are integral to ecosystem functioning and the use of traps to catch small juvenile fish.[133] Leaking fuel from commercial and private vessels, antifouling paints for the bottoms of boats,[134] and emissions of pollutants and toxins are known to adversely affect coral reproduction and growth. Other actions that destroy corals include collecting them as decorations, dropping boat anchors onto the corals, and groundings of large seagoing vessels. Diseases that are carried by ocean currents and flushed through the ballast water of ships are also destructive.[135] According to climate change specialists, corals will be further harmed by the carbon dioxide emitted from burning fossil fuels[136] and by the more frequent tropical storms that are likely to cause greater coastal erosion, sedimentation, and turbidity.[137] Scientists warn that ongoing human stresses will also weaken corals and limit their ability to adapt to climate change.[138] Clearly, the sensitivity of the coral reefs to degradation and the many threats to their survival warrant attention.[139] Although reefs have been monitored for less than twenty years, the latest reports indicate that about 27 percent of monitored reef formations have been lost and 32 percent are at risk of being lost within the next thirty-two years.[140]

The Use and Abuse of the Air

Though radically dependent upon clean air for breathing, humans have been emitting pollutants and toxins into the atmosphere in concentrations high enough to cause serious problems for themselves as well as for other animals, vegetation, ecosystems, and the biosphere. Particularly problematic are the smoke, sulfur dioxide, nitrogen oxides, and carbon dioxide produced when coal, oil, and gas are burned to power internal combustion engines, provide heat for industrial and other processes, and to generate electricity. Also problematic are gases from pesticides, refrigerants, and solvents of various types (e.g., used in dry cleaning).[141]

The increasing volume of these emissions over the last few decades and the persistence of some have resulted in their accumulation in the atmosphere, where they are transformed to cause widespread damage to trees and lakes through acid deposition.[142] These emissions have also precipitated the accumulation of ozone in the lower atmosphere, causing health problems, especially for the very young, the elderly, and people afflicted with upper respiratory diseases.[143] Conversely, ozone in the upper atmosphere is essential to human health, because it absorbs some of the potentially harmful ultraviolet radiation from the sun that can cause skin cancer and damage vegetation. This protection has been thinned at all latitudes, however, by the use of chlorofluorocarbons, halons, and other chlorine and bromine compounds that create "holes" in the upper atmospheres of the two arctic areas for several weeks each spring.[144] International efforts to curtail the use of upper-ozone-depleting chemicals resulted in the Montreal Protocol of 1987, which called for phasing out their production in industrial countries by 1996 and in developing countries by 2009.[145]

Although much more could be written about other chemicals and compounds that are emitted into the air and cause havoc with the biotic and abiotic constituents of Earth, the chemicals with which scientists are currently engrossed are carbon dioxide and methane—key players in the phenomenon of global warming because they trap heat in the atmosphere to create a "greenhouse" effect. Carbon dioxide is a naturally occurring gas that is responsible for maintaining the atmospheric temperature at all levels so organisms can survive, but burning coal, oil, and gas for transportation, industrial processes, and the generation of electricity is estimated to have increased the amount of carbon dioxide in the atmosphere by 30 percent above preindustrial levels (in about 1750), according to the United Nations' Intergovernmental Panel on Climate Change (IPCC).[146] Over the past two hundred years, North America, Europe, and the former Soviet Union, accounting for 20 percent of the world's population, have contributed 80 percent of these emissions.[147] The National Oceanic and Atmospheric Administration of the U.S. Department of Commerce reported in 2008 that the atmospheric concentration of carbon dioxide increased by 0.6 percent in 2007, an increase that equaled the total 2005 measurement—the third-highest since atmospheric measurements were begun in 1958.[148] China became the largest emitter of carbon dioxide in 2008.

The real and projected effects of global warming prompted an international effort launched in Kyoto in 1997 to curb the emission of greenhouse gases.[149] However, the United States, their largest emitter at that time, accounting for approximately 35 percent of emissions worldwide, withdrew from the resulting Kyoto Protocol, claiming that there would be severe consequences for its economy if the protocol were followed. Efforts are under way to identify cost-effective ways to curb the emissions of methane and other greenhouse gases that are contributing to the planet's warming as well as other means of mitigating global warming (e.g., planting trees), but cutting carbon dioxide emissions remains crucial. The IPCC continues to assess the scientific, technical, and socioeconomic data for policymakers.[150]

Scientists predict many physical, ecological, economic, social, and health effects from global warming during this century. Among the physical and ecological effects are high risks for extreme weather; rising sea levels as glaciers and ice sheets melt; thermal expansion of the oceans; increased flooding, especially along coastal areas; the loss of wetlands due to flooding; the destruction of most of the Amazon rainforest; more extensive droughts in some regions and a decrease in freshwater availability in others; and negative consequences for species in their interactions and geographic ranges. The projected socioeconomic effects include displacement of people from coastal areas and river floodplains, more people living in water-stressed areas, a decrease in crop productivity at lower altitudes, and the need to grow different crops. Hunger and malnutrition, an increased frequency of heat strokes and cardiorespiratory diseases, and spreading infectious diseases as people move and adjust to new regions are among the human health effects anticipated.[151] As the IPCC's chairman noted when issuing its 2007 report, "It is the poorest of the poor in the world, and this includes poor people even in prosperous societies, who are going to be the worst hit." Addressing global warming has become "a global responsibility."[152] The U.S. Catholic bishops have been alerting the faithful to this responsibility for several years,[153] and Pope Benedict XVI has expressed concern about human-induced climate change on several occasions.[154]

The Use and Abuse of Other Species

That species are in danger of becoming extinct appears too frequently in both the popular news and in scholarly reports and bulletins issued by scientific, environmental, and government organizations. Though the extinction of species is a natural occurrence in the evolutionary process, the rate of extinction of animal and plant species has accelerated rapidly as humans have used and abused other species for human purposes, modified their habitats, and disturbed the functioning of the ecosystems of which they are constituents. The introduction of "invasive" species to an ecosystem of which they are not natural constituents has been particularly vexing.

Identifying the exact number of species that have become endangered or extinct by human actions is illusive. However, according to the entomologist E. O. Wilson, experts who have used several indirect methods of analysis agree that the rate of species extinction on land and in freshwater is "very roughly" a hundred times higher today than before the emergence of *Homo sapiens* approximately one hundred fifty thousand years ago.[155] The paleontologist Richard E. Leakey and the anthropologist Roger Lewin estimate that thirty thousand species are "wiped out by human agency every year," threatening the entire complex fabric of life on Earth, including the species at fault."[156] The International Union for Conservation of Nature maintains a "Red List" enumerating 16,306 species that are at risk for extinction,[157] whereas the United States Fish and Wildlife Service lists daily the number and types of threatened and endangered species.[158]

Scientists link the loss of species to human population growth and economic development.[159] Wilson coined the acronym HIPPO to list the decline of Earth's biodiversity in an order that corresponds with their rank in destructiveness: habitat loss, invasive species, pollution, overpopulation by humans, and overharvesting.[160] He considers human overpopulation to be the root cause of the other four factors. These human actions have resulted in the loss, degradation, and conversion of species habitats to other uses, the overexploitation of biological sources, and the loss of genetic diversity. One of the most ambitious efforts to assess the status of species, *The Global Biodiversity Assessment,* urges taking immediate steps to stem the loss and degradation of biological diversity or forever forgo opportunities through which its full potential can be derived.[161] The signatory nations of the Convention on Biological Diversity that was initiated at the 1992 Earth Summit held in Rio de Janeiro identified in 2002 the goal of achieving significant reduction in the current rate of biodiversity loss at global, regional, and national levels. When signing the convention, the nations recognized that biological diversity is also about people, especially poor people, and their need for food security, medicines, fresh air and water, shelter, and a clean and healthy environment in which to live.[162]

One of the direct derivatives of biological diversity is better health for humans through medical research and treatment. If biological diversity continues to decline, researchers insist, a new generation of antibiotics, new treatments for thinning bone disease and kidney failure, and new cancer treatments will be lost. Endangered species hold secrets to the development of safer and more powerful painkillers, treatments for macular degeneration, diagnostic testing, and ways of regrowing lost tissues and organs. To ensure these possibilities, saving species of baby frogs in the Australian rainforests, "denning" bears in Asia, cone snails in coral reefs, sharks in the oceans, and many other endangered species identified by medical researchers is vital to improving human health.[163]

Overconsumption and Waste

As concluded by the United Nations Development Program, the growth in consumption during the twentieth century was unprecedented in both scale and diversity. More people are better fed and housed than ever before. Living standards rose to enable hundreds of millions to enjoy housing with hot and cold water, warmth, and electricity, transportation to and from work, comfortable homes, and time for recreation and leisure.[164] Some live in huge homes[165] and have second homes in ski or other recreational areas that deplete metals, require the manufacture of more concrete, and use electric power for heating. Some drive sport utility vehicles and other high-priced, high-performance vehicles that guzzle gasoline.[166]

Globally, 20 percent of the world's people in the highest-income countries account for 86 per cent of total private consumption expenditures. They consume 45 percent of all meat and fish, 58 percent of total energy, and 84 percent of all paper. They also own 87 percent of the world's vehicle fleet and use 74 percent of all telephone lines.[167] If everyone in the world were to live as the relatively wealthy in the United States live, the eminent botanist Peter H. Raven insists, three more planets comparable to Earth would be needed to support their consumption.[168]

Overconsumers have put great strains on the environment by depleting nonrenewable sources for construction materials and energy, accelerating the rate of species extinction by degrading and destroying their habitats for space, emitting pollutants and persistent toxins into the air and flushing them into bodies of water to dispose of their waste products, and interfering with the internal functioning of ecosystems by not living as responsible constituents.[169] In addition to wastes emitted and flushed into Earth's systems, overconsumers also produce huge quantities of all kinds of solid wastes—high-, intermediate-, and low-level radioactive wastes from the generation of electricity, from weapons production, and from medical treatment; hazardous wastes from industrial, commercial, and domestic products;[170] wastes from the production of materials;[171] and relatively benign but immense quantities of nonhazardous wastes from all sectors of the economy.[172] Recycling waste products has been attempted but is not keeping pace with the increasing amounts of wastes.[173]

Studies indicate that poor people consume little of Earth's sources and waste little of whatever they have available to use. According to the United Nations Development Program, the poorest 20 percent of the world's population accounts for 1.3 percent of private consumption expenditures. The poorest fifth consume 5 percent of all meat and fish, less than 4 percent of the energy, and 1.1 percent of paper. They use 1.5 percent of all telephone lines and less than 1 per cent of the world's vehicle fleet.[174] The World Health Organization estimates that half the people of the world are malnourished at some level and that one in four people survives on less than a dollar per day.[175] Yet poor people are most affected by environmental degradation and, according to climate change studies, will be most gravely affected by global warming.[176] The inequalities between the rich and the poor are staggering.[177]

The overuse and abuse of terrestrial ecosystems, bodies of water, atmospheric air, and plant and animal species are rampant throughout the world. All aspects of human behavior that have prompted these dire conditions need to be addressed. To what extent can the teachings of patristic and medieval theologians be helpful?

Restraining the Use and Abuse of God's Creation

Patristic and medieval theologians urge the faithful to recognize God's creation as blessings from God that should be used gratefully with restraint.[178] Their teachings transcend time and cultures. Their instructions can be helpful during this age of widespread ecological degradation, when some humans are overconsuming and abusing other species, lands, waters, and airways. When appropriating and applying their teachings, faith-filled people will acknowledge Earth with its diverse species, airways, lands, and waters as blessings from God to whom gratitude should be expressed. They will accept their accountability to God for their use of these natural blessings. They will think carefully about why and how these blessings from God are to be used and plan to use them appropriately according to their natures. They will limit their use of other species, the air, land, and water to amounts needed, not wanted. They will strive to assure the availability of these natural blessings to future generations as well as to other species who need them to survive and flourish. And they will use them joyfully to gain knowledge about God's creation and to know God.

Acknowledging and Thanking God for the Blessings of Earth

Earth and its diverse species, lands, airways, and waters are blessings from God, to whom the faithful will express deep gratitude. Whereas the faithful thank God for the food they eat, the clothing they wear, and the amenities of life that are available to them, they will look beyond finished products to the natural blessings from which they were fabricated. The faithful will recognize that these blessings rely upon their symbiotic relationship with other natural blessings for their flourishing over time and space. They will realize that these natural blessings evolved into existence from and with other matter over time and expanding space through a remarkable process empowered and sustained by God, and they will be grateful to God for providing for the necessities of life for all species through this process. They will be grateful to God for the ability humans have to use other biota and abiota for meeting their needs in life, for the needs they meet in the lives of other species, and for the natural functioning of ecosystems through which needs are met. They will be grateful for the human capacity to know how to meet their needs and to flourish physically, culturally, and economically through meeting them. They will express gratitude to God for the use of these natural blessings at all steps involved in appropriating, handling, and consuming them, for being able to discern ways of recycling waste products, and for disposing of remaining wastes in environmentally sound ways.

Recognizing Human Accountability to God

The faithful will accept their responsibility to God for their use of the many natural blessings that God has empowered into existence—forests, grasslands, savannas, wetlands, agricultural lands, freshwater, oceans, coral reefs, air in the troposphere to the stratosphere, and the biologically diverse species whose numbers are dwindling from overuse and abuse. They will recognize their accountability to God for every stage of their use to recycling whatever is not usable to the safe disposal of whatever cannot be recycled. They will recognize their role in governing the use of these natural blessings with others and accountability to God for their governance. Because the ultimate end to which believers are striving is eternal happiness with God, they will view their use from the perspective of having to account to God at the end of their lives for their cumulative use of these blessings and for their cooperation with others in governing their use.[179]

Reasoning Carefully about Appropriate Use

The faithful will strive to reason carefully about how they should use God's material blessings and choose to use them in the most appropriate ways. They will deliberate on the use of blessings that are renewed naturally and take steps to ensure that they are renewed. They will be especially cautious in reasoning to the appropriate uses of nonrenewables and take steps to minimize their use at all levels of social, economic, and political life to what is needed and can be used efficiently, with a view to making alternatives available. They will phase out inefficient and inappropriate uses of these blessings. They will develop their intellectual capabilities and apply them to the task of identifying appropriate and efficient uses of these blessings from God.

Developing and nurturing the intellectual and moral dimensions of the virtue of prudence will help toward reaching this goal. The faithful will investigate all possibilities for arriving at the most appropriate use of God's material blessings, consider all circumstances pertinent to them—including environmental, economic, and social aspects—to avoid injustices to vulnerable groups of people, especially the poor, and exercise foresight about future supplies and needs. And the faithful will execute their prudent decisions with determination.[180]

Limiting Use to the Necessities of Life

Limiting the use of God's blessings to the necessities of life is indeed a serious challenge in a society of overconsumers of goods, abusers of other species and their habitats directly and indirectly, and producers of immense quantities of many different wastes. Popes and bishops have called the attention of the faithful to the ongoing problem of excessive consumption and wastefulness, especially in the economically developed countries of the world.[181] Heeding both these prelates and the teachings of patristic and medieval theologians, the faithful will distinguish between the necessary and unnecessary uses of other animals and plants, lands, and waters. They will choose to use only what they need to sustain their temporal lives as they aim for eternal life with God. They will avoid excessive patterns of living in their homes, in their modes of transportation, and in their recreational choices. They will avoid the excessive use of material goods and will minimize wastefulness in their places of employment. As executives, they will make decisions geared toward using natural sources wisely and efficiently, recycling any postproduction materials, and carefully disposing of what cannot be recycled. They will be leaders in demonstrating lives in which minimal goods are consumed. They will heed and be stimulated by the many teachings that the Catholic bishops have issued on consumption, with particular concern for how overconsumption affects poor people.[182]

How one lives in relation to others is significant when thinking about using God's blessings of Earth's goods, because loving one's neighbor and wishing one's neighbor the blessings of life both temporally and eternally are imperative to demonstrating their love for God, as patristic and medieval theologians instructed (see chapter 9). Thus, the faithful will ensure that others have access to the goods they need to sustain their bodily lives. They will be alert to their neighbors' needs, seek private ways to help the neediest, and, following the principle of subsidiarity,[183] advocate help for those in need at the next level of economic and political activity to ensure that the needs of their neighbors are met.

Also significant is the need to protect the health of one's neighbors—especially the poor, the very young and old, and the sick—from the adverse effects of excessive use and abuse of material goods. Embracing the poor has been a basic principle of Catholic social teaching for centuries, and poor people must be cared about and embraced with determination during this age of overconsumption, abuse, and waste by some. Steps will be taken by the faithful to ensure that the poor are protected and that adverse effects on them are minimized.

Ensuring Availability for Future Human Use

In addition to ensuring that their contemporaries' needs are met, the faithful will strive to ensure the availability of natural blessings to future generations. While using nonrenewables only for the necessities of life should prolong their availability in the future, they are nevertheless finite blessings that eventually will have to be replaced by alternatives. The faithful will phase environmentally compatible alternatives into their lives where possible before nonrenewables are available, and they will pressure decision makers to engage in researching and testing potential alternatives that are environmentally compatible and making them available before nonrenewables are depleted.

Also key to the welfare of future humans and other species is taking steps to minimize the adverse effects that the use of environmentally harmful nonrenewables inflict on other species, the air, land, and water. The faithful will be motivated to minimize those adverse effects in their daily lives and to pressure decision makers at incremental levels to take steps to minimize them.

Using to Gain Knowledge about God's Creation

As Albertus Magnus, Thomas Aquinas, and other patristic and medieval theologians encouraged, God's creation should be used to acquire knowledge about it. Gaining knowledge about other species, the air, land, and water, about the ecosystems they constitute, about the marginal areas around and between the ecosystems that bridge them, and about the biosphere is essential today for knowing how to act toward them and how to function within them. Especially poignant is Wilson's plea to build an "Encyclopedia of Life" that will record all the species of Earth.[184] Thus far, estimates of species extinction is based on one-fourth of all *known* species, whereas full knowledge of all species is needed not only for the sake of knowing, a desirable and laudable goal in itself, but also for the benefits this knowledge can bring to human health and well-being directly and indirectly. The faithful will demand the accumulation and consolidation of knowledge about all species, and they will demand knowing practical ways in which the loss of biological diversity can be minimized and prevented.

Using to Know God

Reflecting from a sacramental view of God's creation, as examined in chapter 3, patristic and medieval theologians prescribed using the sensible world to gain a glimpse of God's character. They dwelled on the divine attributes of goodness, wisdom, and power from their prescientific understanding of the world. Following this practice, the faithful will use the physical world as a way of discerning God's attributes informed by the current scientific understanding of the world (e.g., empowering, generous, patient, caring, freedom giving, and humble). This "use" of God's creation qualifies the instrumental significance of the term to convey a reverential beholding of the sensible world as it is and as it functions in a web of relationships. Even a glimpse of God's character requires understanding species and their habitats, the functioning of the ecosystem and biosphere, and cosmic bodies as they exist in expanding space, as they interrelate, and as they are grounded by the laws of physics, chemistry, and biology.

However, the faithful will think more deeply about God's creation. They will think beyond what is observed or observable scientifically to refer to God, the ultimate grounding for all that scientists can observe. The scientific knowledge that the faithful gain will enable them to speak more cogently about God, to speak more comprehensively about the physical, visible world in relation to God, and to reflect on the human role in relation to the world that is sustained and called to completion by God.

Conclusion

Many patristic and medieval theologians taught that God's creation should be used moderately and appropriately for the necessities of life, cognitively to gain knowledge about the world, and reverentially to know God. These uses of God's creation are God's blessings to us. They require expressions of gratitude to God for their use. Their teachings have significance for today as the rate of species extinction is accelerating, biological diversity is declining, the functioning of the ecosystem is being disrupted, and nonrenewable goods are being depleted.

An examination of patristic-medieval teachings suggests a pattern of behavior that points to at least seven ways of using God's creation. The faithful will acknowledge Earth with its diverse constituents as blessings from God. They will recognize their responsibility to God for how they use God's creation. They will reason carefully about how to use God's blessings appropriately according to their natures. They will use God's blessings for the necessities of life and share them with others so they also can meet their needs, and they will use them with a view to assuring their availability for future generations to meet their needs. They will use God's blessings of creation to gain empirical knowledge about the world and to know something about God's character. In these uses, the faithful will be thankful to God for the many blessings of species, land, water, and air that God empowers forth from the cosmological-biological evolutionary process and calls to completion.

The instructions patristic and medieval theologians gave for using God's blessings transcend time and cultures. Obviously, their teachings present serious challenges to the ways in which too many humans are over-using, over-consuming, and wasting the goods of Earth today.

Notes

1. Patristic and medieval teachings about God's governing and caring for creation have many precursors in the Old and New testaments. Consider, e.g., Ps 104 (especially vv. 10–21), 145:16, 147:8–9; Jb 38, 39:1–8; Dt 11:14–17; and Mt 6:25–34.

2. God's providence is a particularly significant focus by Thomas Aquinas, *Summa contra Gentiles,* third book. Therein, Aquinas stressed God's care for all creatures by providing for an order of conservation through which the universe can be sustained internally.

3. Saint Basil, *On the Hexaemeron,* in *Exegetic Homilies,* trans. Sister Agnes Clare Way, CDP (Washington, DC: Catholic University of America Press, 1963), 5.1, 67.

4. Ibid., 5.2, 68.

5. Ibid., 5.4, 71–72.

6. Ibid., 5.2, 69.

7. Ibid., 5.4, 71.

8. Aquinas, *Summa theologiae,* 1.47.2. This article serves as one of many examples of Aquinas's teachings about the instrumental order of all entities that constitute the universe. That everything God created has a purpose to fulfill in the integral whole and all are related to one another in a hierarchical order to achieve their purposes as well as the purpose of the whole cosmos was constant in his works. See also Aquinas, *Summa contra Gentiles,* 3.20, 45, 71.

9. See Aquinas, *Summa contra Gentiles,* 3.22. See also Aquinas, *Summa theologiae,* 2|2.66.2.

10. Aquinas, *Summa theologiae,* 1.65.2. According to Aquinas, each creature exists for its own proper act and perfection, the lower on the hierarchical scale exists for the higher, but every creature exists for the perfection of the universe which is ordained toward God, inasmuch as it imitates and shows forth the divine goodness to the glory of God; see also 2|2.64.1, wherein Aquinas established the lawfulness of humans' killing plants to feed animals and animals to feed themselves.

11. Oliva Blanchette, *The Perfection of the Universe According to Aquinas: A Teleological Cosmology* (University Park: Pennsylvania State University Press, 1991), 256. Also see Aquinas, *Summa theologiae,* 1.47.2; and Aquinas, *Summa contra Gentiles,* 3.20, 45, 71.

12. Saint Augustine, *The Trinity,* Fathers of the Church, vol. 45, trans. Stephen McKenna (Washington, DC: Catholic University of America Press, 1963), 11.5.8, 326–28. Humans are images of God, Augustine taught, because they participate in God and derive some sense of God by virtue of their rational souls. Their souls make them closer to God through an ability to respond to God's call, to turn to God, and to be formed and made beautiful by God.

13. Augustine, *Concerning the City of God against the Pagans,* trans. Henry Bettenson; introduction by John O'Meara (London: Penguin Books, 1984), 11.22, 453–54.

14. Ibid.

15. John Scotus Eriugena, *Periphyseon* (The Division of Nature), trans. I. P. Sheldon-Williams (Washington, DC: Dumbarton Oaks, 1987), 5, 657–58. The *Periphyseon*—Eriugena's magnum opus and one of the most original works of the early Middle Ages—was written between 864 and 866. Before that time, he translated the entire corpus of Pseudo-Dionysius (*The Divine Names, Mystical Theology, The Celestial Hierarchy,* and *The Ecclesiastical Hierarchy*), Maximus the Confessor's *Ambiguities,* Gregory of Nyssa's *The Making of the Human,* and Epiphanius' *Sermon on Faith.*

16. Eriugena, *Periphyseon*, 5, 659.
17. This was a common teaching among patristic and medieval theologians.
18. Albertus Magnus, *Man and the Beasts (De animalibus, Books 22–26)*, trans. James J. Scanlan (Binghamton: Medieval & Renaissance Texts & Studies, 1987), 65.
19. Ibid.
20. Ibid.
21. Albertus Magnus, *De vegetabilibus libri VII: Historiae naturalis* (Frankfurt: Minerva GMBH, 1982), 7.1.1. Clarence J. Glacken offers a brief but astute evaluation of Albertus Magnus's efforts to improve upon nature in *Traces on the Rhodian Shore: Nature and Culture in Western Thought from Ancient Times to the End of the Eighteenth Century* (Berkeley: University of California Press, 1967), 314–15.
22. See Aquinas, *Summa contra Gentiles* 4.1. See also Aquinas, *Summa theologiae*, 1.12.13.
23. Aquinas, *Summa theologiae*, 1 | 2.16.1.
24. Ibid., 1 | 2.16.2.
25. Ibid., 1 | 2.16.2 ad 2. Also see *Summa theologiae* 2 | 2.64.1 ad, where he elaborated on the natural impulses of plants and animals that indicate their natural enslavement and accommodation to being used by others.
26. Aquinas, *Summa theologiae*, 1 | 2.71.1–2, 74.5.
27. Ibid., 2 | 2.66.1–2.
28. Ibid., 1.96.1 ad 2, 1 | 2.74.3. Also see Aquinas, *Summa contra Gentiles*, 3.128–29.
29. Aquinas, *Summa contra Gentiles*, 3.121.
30. Aquinas, *Summa theologiae*, 1 | 2.19.9–10.
31. Ibid., 1 | 2.19.10 ad 2.
32. See, e.g., Aquinas, *Summa theologiae*, 1 | 2.58.3, 62.1, 64.1, 66.3, 68.8, 100.1, 2 | 2.47.6, 161.5. An exploration on how developing the moral virtues can aid humans when relating to the other living and nonliving constituents of Earth appears in chapter 8. See also Aquinas, *Summa contra Gentiles*, 3.121, wherein he indicated that both the inner feelings and the use of corporeal things should be regulated by reason.
33. Tertullian, *Adversus Marcionem*, ed. and trans. Ernest Evans (Oxford: Clarendon Press, 1972), 1.29, 81–85.
34. Origen, *Contra Celsum*, trans. Henry Chadwick (Cambridge: Cambridge University Press, 1953), 4.76, 244–45.
35. Saint John Chrysostom, *Homilies on Genesis 1-17, Volume 74, Fathers of the Church*, trans. Robert C. Hill (Washington, DC: Catholic University of America, 1986), 9.11, 123–24. Whereas God gave mastery over all creatures before the first humans "fell" away from God, God removed from human control those unnecessary to the wellbeing of humans (e.g., wild animals).
36. Ibid., 135–36.
37. Gregory of Nyssa, *The Great Catechism*, in *A Select Library of Nicene and Post-Nicene Fathers of the Christian Church*, Series 2, vol. 5, ed. Philip Schaff (Grand Rapids: William B. Eerdmans Publishing, 1956), 471–509.
38. Theodoret, *Discours sur la Providence*, trans. Yvan Azéma (Paris: Les Belles Lettres, 1954), 30–32. See also Étienne Gilson, *History of Christian Philosophy in the Middle Ages* (New York: Random House, 1955), 596–97.
39. In Augustine's thinking, "use" refers to willing what is appropriate to temporal life as *means to an end* (e.g., maintaining one's life on Earth), whereas "enjoy" refers to willing what is appropriate to eternal life as an end in itself. See William Riordan O'Connor, "The *Uti/Frui* Distinction in Augustine's Ethics," *Augustinian Studies* 14

(1983): 45–62. Also see Tarsicius van Bavel, OSA, "Creator and the Integrity of Creation," *Augustinian Studies* 21 (1991): 1–19.

40. Augustine, *Concerning the City of God,* 11.22, 453.

41. Ibid., 19.17, 877. In sec. 14, Augustine explained that the human is a pilgrim in a foreign land since he or she has not yet passed into an eternal status of immortality with God in Heaven—the ultimate end. His emphasis is on God's providence by providing what is needed in temporal life as the human seeks eternal life with God.

42. Ibid., 11.22, 453.

43. Ibid. Augustine urged his readers to inquire about the purposes natural entities serve instead of indulging in "silly complaints" about them.

44. Ibid.

45. Ibid., 19.13, 872.

46. Saint Benedict, Abbot of Monte Cassino, *The Rule of Benedict: A Guide to Christian Living,* commentary and trans. George Holzherr, Monks of Glenstal Abbey (Dublin: Four Courts Press, 1994), rule 34, 187–88.

47. See, e.g., Aquinas, *Summa theologiae,* 1 | 2.4.6–7, 114.10, 2 | 2.76.2, 83.6, 118.1, Supp. 91.1; Aquinas, *Summa contra Gentiles,* 3.22; and Aquinas, *Compendium theologiae,* 173.

48. See Aquinas, *Summa theologiae,* 2 | 2.141.6; and see 2 | 2.64.1, 83.6, Supp. 91.1 Also see Aquinas, *Summa contra Gentiles,* 3.22, 121, 129, 131. The prescription that humans are intended to use only what is needed to sustain their lives and not what is desired beyond the necessities of life resounds throughout his works.

49. Aquinas, *Summa theologiae,* 1 | 2.4.7; see also 2 | 2.83.6, 118.1, 141.6.

50. Ibid., 2 | 2.83.6.

51. Ibid., 2 | 2.169.1. For his understanding of the appropriate use of things by humans, see *Summa contra Gentiles* 3.129. Some uses for the necessities of life are naturally fitting, he taught, whereas as immoderate uses are naturally unfitting in the scheme of the integrity of the universe and, ultimately, in the human quest for God.

52. Aquinas, *Summa contra Gentiles,* 4.83.

53. Aquinas, *Summa theologiae,* 2 | 2.118.1; see, further, 2 | 2.83.6.

54. Ibid., 1 | 2.4.7.

55. Ibid., 2 | 2.83.6, 179.2 ad 3. See also Aquinas, *Summa contra Gentiles,* 3.22, 121.

56. Aquinas, *Summa contra Gentiles,* 3.127.

57. Ibid. For Aquinas, creatures interact for mutual benefit to meet their needs within the orderly creation God established; see, e.g., Aquinas, *Summa theologiae,* 1.11.3, 13.7; Aquinas, *Summa contra Gentiles,* 2.41, 3.22, 69; and Aquinas, *Compendium theologiae,* 148.

58. Aquinas, *Summa contra Gentiles,* 3.121.

59. Aquinas, *Summa theologiae,* 2 | 2.118.1.

60. Ibid., 2 | 2.58.5–9; also see 1 | 2.19.10.

61. Mary Hirschfeld, "Standard of Living and Economic Virtue: Forging a Link between St. Thomas Aquinas and the Twenty-First Century," *Journal of the Society of Christian Ethics* 26 (Spring–Summer 2006): 61–78.

62. Aquinas, *Summa theologiae,* 2 | 2.118.1.

63. Symeon the New Theologian, *The Discourses,* trans. C. J. deCatanzaro (New York: Paulist Press, 1980), 9.4, 152–53.

64. Symeon, *Discourses,* 9.6, 155.

65. Ibid., 9.4, 153.

66. Ibid., 9.7, 156–57.

67. Ibid., 9.8, 157–58.
68. This approach is properly categorized as a theology of nature rather than a natural theology because faith in God is presumed when striving to discern God's attributes. As demonstrated in chapter 3 on the sacramentality of creation, with its companion behavioral trajectory of reverencing the world because it mediates God's presence and attributes, God's attributes are reconstructed and new attributes are discerned when informed by our current scientific understanding of the world.
69. Augustine, *Concerning the City of God,* 11.22, 453–54.
70. Saint Bernard of Clairvaux, *Selected Writings,* trans. G. R. Evans (New York: Paulist Press, 1987), sermon 5.1.3, 229.
71. Albertus Magnus, *Physica,* ed. Paul Hossfeld (Münster: Aschendorff, 1987), 1.1.1, 4–6.
72. Albertus Magnus, *On Animals: A Medieval Summa Zoologica,* trans. Kenneth F. Kitchell Jr. and Irven Michael Resnick (Baltimore: Johns Hopkins University Press, 1999), 21.51, 1439.
73. The claim that religious faith and the natural sciences conflict has been addressed in considerable depth over the last forty years by outstanding scholars, including Ian Barbour, *Religion and Science: Historical and Contemporary Issues* (San Francisco: HarperSanFrancisco, 1997); John F. Haught, *Science & Religion: From Conflict to Conversation* (New York: Paulist Press); Arthur Peacocke, *Theology for a Scientific Age: Being and Becoming—Natural, Divine and Human* (London: SCM Press, 1993); and John C. Polkinghorne, *Belief in God in an Age of Science* (New Haven, CT: Yale University Press, 1998). An impressive bibliography of books on the religion-science dialogue—grouped into basic, intermediate, and research levels—can be accessed from the Center for Theology and the Natural Sciences (www.ctns.org/books_bio.html).
74. Pope Pius XII conferred this status on Albertus Magnus in 1941.
75. Aquinas, *Summa contra Gentiles,* 3.22.8. See, further, Aquinas, *Summa theologiae,* 2│2.167.
76. Aquinas, *Summa contra Gentiles,* 2.2; also see 3.22.8, 47.8–9. See, further, Aquinas, *Summa theologiae,* 2│2.180.4–6, Supp. 91.1.
77. Aquinas, *Summa theologiae,* 1.96.1 ad 3. Here Aquinas refers to the Genesis 2 story of creation, in which God is depicted as leading the animals to the first human who was told to name them (v. 20). See also *Summa contra Gentiles,* 3.75.
78. Aquinas, *Summa contra Gentiles,* 3.75.
79. Ibid., 2.3.
80. Ibid.
81. Augustine, *Concerning the City of God,* 22.24, 1075.
82. Ibid., 22.24, 1072–73.
83. Ibid., 22.24, 1075. Centuries later, the Lutheran theologian Joseph Sittler extended Augustine's thinking about the many blessings that God provides for humans to use and for which they should be grateful. In "The Care of the Earth," in *The Care of the Earth and Other University Sermons* (Philadelphia: Fortress Press, 1964), 97, Sittler insisted on a graced use of God's creation wherein natural entities are used "rightly" with joy in them for themselves.
84. Hellebore is a plant that derives its generic name from the Greek *elein* (to injure) and *bora* (food), indicating its poisonous nature. Black hellebore was used as a purgative in mania more than a thousand years before Jesus Christ. A varied explanation is provided at usually reliable Botanical.com (www.botanical.com/botanical/mgmh/h/helbla14.html).

85. Hippocrates described the effects of hellebores in *Aphorisms*, 4.13–16: "Persons who are not easily purged upward by the hellebores, should have their bodies moistened by plenty of food and rest before taking the draught. When one takes a draught of hellebore, one should be made to move about, and indulge less in sleep and repose. . . . When you wish the hellebore to act more, move the body, and when to stop, let the patient get sleep and rest. Hellebore is dangerous to persons whose flesh is sound, for it induces convulsions." See also "Hellebores," Botanical.com (www.botanical.com/botanical/mgmh/h/helbla14.html).

86. Basil, *On the Hexaemeron*, 5.4, 72.

87. Paul Harrison and Fred Pearce, eds., *AAAS Atlas of Population and Environment* (Berkeley: University of California Press for American Association for the Advancement of Science, 2000), 3.

88. Ibid.

89. B. L. Turner, William C. Clark, Robert W. Kates, John F. Richards, Jessica T. Mathews, and William B. Meyer, eds., *The Earth as Transformed by Human Action: Global and Regional Changes in the Biosphere over the Past 300 Years* (Cambridge: Cambridge University Press, 1990). See also William B. Meyer, *Human Impact on the Earth* (New York: Cambridge University Press, 1996).

90. World Resources Institute, *World Resources 2000–2001* (Washington, DC: World Resources Institute, 2000). Also see Dirk Bryant, Daniel Nielsen, and Laura Tangley, *The Last Frontier Forests: Ecosystems and Economies on the Edge* (Washington, DC: World Resources Institute, 1997). Measurement of loss is complicated by the differing methods of calculating forest cover and loss that are used by international agencies.

91. Dirk Bryant, *Vital Signs 2002: Trends That Are Shaping Our Future* (New York: W. W. Norton for Worldwatch Institute, 2002).

92. These types of forests are tropical, subtropical, Mediterranean (also located in California, Chile, and Western Australia), temperate, coniferous, and montane. Among forests decreasing at alarming rates are mangroves—salt-tolerant forest ecological systems that are commonly found along sheltered coastlines, in deltas, and along riverbanks in the tropics and subtropics. These trees and shrubs have developed morphological adaptations to tidal environments, such as aerial roots, salt excretion glands and, in some species, seeds that grow and bloom while attached to the mother plant, an example of vivipary. The total area of mangroves is estimated at 15.2 million hectares as of 2005, down from 18.8 million hectares in 1980. See Food and Agricultural Organization, *Global Forest Resources Assessment 2005: Progress Toward Sustainable Forest Management*, FAO Forestry Paper 147 (Rome: Food and Agricultural Organization, 2006), 28–29.

93. This is commonly referred to as "biodiversity," to describe the complexity of life. Biodiversity is measured generally at three levels—the variety of species, the genetic diversity found within members of the same species, and the diversity of the ecosystems within which species live. All levels are intricately connected. According to the Food and Agricultural Organization's *Global Forest Resources Assessment 2005*, 13, South America suffered the largest net loss of forests from 2000 to 2005, about 4.3 million hectares a year, followed by Africa, which lost 4.0 million hectares annually. North and Central America and Oceania each had a net loss of about 350 000 hectares, while Asia, which had a net loss of some 800,000

hectares per year in the 1990s, reported a net gain of 1 million hectares a year from 2000 to 2005, primarily as a result of large-scale afforestation reported by China.

94. Food and Agricultural Organization, *Global Forest Resources Assessment 2005*, 13. Net global change in forest area in the period 2000–5 is estimated at −7.3 million hectares a year, an area about the size of Panama, down from −8.9 million hectares a year in the period 1990–2000.

95. These areas are in Japan and some European countries. See Food and Agricultural Organization, *Global Forest Resources Assessment 2005*, 38–39.

96. Food and Agricultural Organization, *Global Forest Resources Assessment 2005*, 14.

97. Species that are not native to an area but are transported to one primarily by humans for their use (e.g., goats in the Galápagos Islands).

98. Paul R. Ehrlich and Anne H. Ehrlich, *One with Nineveh: Politics, Consumption, and the Human Future* (Washington, DC: Island Press, 2004), 34.

99. Vaclav Smil, *Feeding the World: A Challenge for the Twenty-First Century* (Cambridge, MA: MIT Press, 2000).

100. Gary Gardner, *Shrinking Fields: Crop Loss in a World of Eight Billion*, Worldwatch Paper 131 (Washington, DC: Worldwatch Institute, 1996); and M. L. Imhoff, D. Stutzer, W. T. Lawrence, and C. Elvidge, "Assessing the Impact of Urban Sprawl on Soil Resources in the United States Using Nighttime "City Lights" Satellite Images and Digital soil maps," in *Perspectives on the Land Use History of North America: A Context for Understanding Our Changing Environment*, Biological Sciences Report USGS/BRD-1998-0003, ed. T. D. Sisk (Springfield, VA: U.S. Geological Survey, 1998).

101. Energy Information Administration, *Annual Energy Review*, Report DOE/EIA-0384 (Washington, DC: U. S. Department of Energy, 2005), www.eia.doe.gov/emeu/aer/pecss_diagram.html. According to these data, oil accounted for 40.1 percent of the energy consumed in the United States in 2005, with the remaining consumption in 2005 from natural gas (22.6 percent), coal (22.9 percent), nuclear electric power (8.1 percent), and renewable energy—hydropower, wood, waste, alcohol, geothermal, solar, and wind (6.1 percent). Approximately 68 percent of the 40.1 percent of the energy from oil was used for transportation, 24 percent for combined heat and power for industrial processes, 6 percent for residential and commercial heating and power, and 3 percent for generating electricity. When viewing the contributions that all resources made to energy consumption, petroleum accounted for 98 percent of all energy used in the transportation sector, 46 percent in the industrial sector, 21 percent in the residential and commercial sector, and 3 percent for electric power. Paul Hesse, information specialist with the U.S. Department of Energy's Energy Information Administration, was particularly helpful in guiding me through the maze of tables and other pertinent information that is accessible from the administration's website, www.eia.doe.gov.

102. Energy Information Administration, "Table 3.2a Crude Oil Overview: Supply," *Monthly Energy Review* (U.S. Department of Energy), July 2006, www.eia.doe.gov/emeu/mer/pdf/pages/sec3_6.pdf.

103. Energy Information Administration, "Crude Oil and Total Petroleum Imports Top 15 Countries," U.S. Department of Energy, July 28, 2006, www.eia.doe.gov/pub/oil_gas/petroleum/data_publications/company_level_imports/current/import.html.

104. Ibid.
105. Ibid. The top sources of U.S. crude oil imports for May 2006, in barrels per day, were Canada (1.868 million), Mexico (1.576 million), Saudi Arabia (1.457 million), Venezuela (1.169 million), Nigeria (1.075 million), Iraq (0.666 million), Angola (0.379 million), Algeria (0.350 million), Russia (0.255 million), and Ecuador (0.239 million). Total crude oil imports averaged 10.247 million barrels per day in May 2006, an increase of 0.415 million barrels per day from April 2006.
106. Ibid.
107. Energy Information Administration, "Table 11.4, World Crude Oil and Natural Gas Reserves," U.S. Department of Energy, January 1, 2005, www.eia.doe.gov/emeu/ aer/pdf/pages/sec11_9.pdf. See also Energy Information Administration, "Table 8.1, World Crude Oil and Natural Gas Reserves," in *International Energy Annual 2005*, U.S. Department of Energy, January 1, 2005, www.eia.doe.gov/pub/international/ iea2004/table81.xls.
108. E.g., see John H. Wood, Gary R. Long, and David F. Morehouse, "Long-Term World Oil Supply Scenarios: The Future Is Neither as Bleak or Rosy as Some Assert," Energy Information Administration, U.S. Department of Energy, August 18, 2004, www.eia.doe.gov/pub/oil_gas/petroleum/feature_articles/2004/worldoilsupply/o ilsupply04.html. See also Daniel Yergin, "Long-Term World Oil Supply Scenarios," *Washington Post*, July 31, 2005, www.washingtonpost.com/wp-dyn/content/arti- cle/2005/07/29/AR2005072901672.html.
109. Earth Trends Environmental Information, "July 2006 Monthly Update: World Population Growth—Past, Present, and Future," Earth Trends, www.earthtrends.wri .org/updates/node/61. The growing number of humans on the planet (from approximately 1 billion people in about 1800, 3 billion in 1960, and another 1 billion every twelve to fourteen years) had reached an approximate total of 6.5 billion by 2006. Nearly all this growth is occurring within developing countries. By 2050, the total population is expected to reach 9.1 billion (a medium projection at the current growth rate of 1.1 percent annually).
110. Robert Bent, Lloyd Orr, and Randall Baker, eds. *Energy: Science, Policy, and the Pursuit of Sustainability* (Washington, DC: Island Press, 2002), 3.
111. Developing this alternative fuel source has become problematic as agribusiness has begun diverting the growing of corn and other crops from food production.
112. Renewable resources (hydropower, wood, waste, alcohol, geothermal, solar, and wind) accounted for 6.1 percent of the energy consumed in the United States in 2005, whereas oil accounted for 40.1 percent of the energy consumed in the United States in 2005, with the remaining consumption from natural gas (22.6 percent), coal (22.9 percent), and nuclear electric power (8.1 percent).
113. The National Research Council stresses the urgency of adopting criteria to facilitate standard wetlands measures. Among the criteria cited are where a wetland starts and finishes and how often an area must be flooded before it is classified as a wetland. The U.S. National Wetlands Inventory conducted the most comprehensive study that is valued for its rigorous scientific approach to the identification and description of wetland habitats, standardized protocols for data collection and interpretation, and comprehensive coverage of all wetland habitats across the entire country. This system was developed over two decades and cost millions of dollars, an investment that is outside the immediate reach of most other countries. National Research Council, *Compensating for Wetland Losses under the Clean Water Act* (Washington, DC:

National Academies Press, 2001), www8.nationalacademies.org/onpinews/news item.aspx?RecordID=10134.

114. Ibid.

115. Ibid.

116. Ibid.

117. As underscored by Harrison and Pearce, *AAAS Atlas of Population and Environment,* 3, the surface of Earth is mainly ocean with an estimated 97 percent of all water as salty and thereby useless for drinking and agriculture. Thus, freshwater is a much more limited resource upon which many demands are being made; supplies are decreasing, while degradation is increasing.

118. Ibid., 24.

119. Sandra L. Postel, "Water for Food Production: Will There Be Enough in 2020?" *Bioscience* 48 (1998): 629–36. According to Postel, the controlled water supply from irrigation more than doubles crop yields.

120. Peter M. Vitousek, Harold A. Mooney, Jane Lubchenco, and Jerry M. Melillo, "Human Domination of Earth's Ecosystems," *Science* 277 (July 25, 1997): 494–99, at 494.

121. Water-rich states bordering the Great Lakes have initiated the Great Lakes Compact, which restricts water diversion out of the basin. Also see Dean E. Murphy, "California Report Supports Critics of Water Diversion," *New York Times,* January 7, 2003; and Ehrlich and Ehrlich, *One with Nineveh,* 30.

122. Peter Gleick, *The World's Water 2002–2003: The Biennial Report on Freshwater Resources* (Washington, DC: Island Press, 2002).

123. Gro Harlem Brundtland, "Overview," in *World Health Report 2002: Reducing Risks and Promoting Health Life* (Geneva: World Health Organization, 2002), 7. Peter Gleick of the Pacific Institute for Studies in Development, Environment, and Security estimated in 2002 that more than 100 million people will die from water-related diseases by 2020 as a consequence of lack of clean water unless much more is done to improve the situation; see "Table 3: Access to Safe Drinking Water, by Country, 1970 to 2002" with an update at Pacific Institute's "The World's Water," www.world water.org/data20062007/Table3.pdf. As many as 1.2 billion people, one in every five worldwide and nearly all developing regions, have no access to safe drinking water, and some 2.4 billion lack adequate sanitation.

124. Harrison and Pearce, *AAAS Atlas of Population and Environment,* 51.

125. World Resources Institute, *World Resources 1998–99* (New York: Oxford University Press, 1998). Also see Food and Agricultural Organization, *The State of the World Fisheries and Aquaculture* (Rome: Food and Agricultural Organization, 1997).

126. Ehrlich and Ehrlich, *One with Nineveh,* 42.

127. Vitousek et al., "Human Domination of Earth's Ecosystems."

128. Ehrlich and Ehrlich, *One with Nineveh,* 42.

129. Because fish farms are most inexpensively and easily maintained in areas natural to the species, farms are often located off the shore of natural migratory rivers and streams. Studies of salmon farms indicate that approximately 3 million fish escape their cages annually, breed with wild salmon, and alter the gene pool of wild fish in destructive ways (e.g., impairing their mating behavior and making it difficult for them to swim upstream to spawn). They also spread diseases for which wild salmon have little or no immunity. Uneaten feed and excrement in coastal areas lead to harmful algae and dead zones in coastal waters. See Kenneth Black, *Environmental Impacts of Aquaculture* (Boca Raton, Fl: CRC Press, 2001), 66.

130. John Weier, "Mapping the Decline of Coral Reefs," *Earth Observatory*, March 12, 2001, www.earthobservatory.nasa.gov/Study/Coral/.

131. B. E. Brown and J. C. Odgen, "Coral Bleaching," *Scientific American* 269 (1993): 64–70. See also Fisheries Institute, "Eutrophication (Nutrient Pollution)," Experimental Lakes Area, University of Manitoba, www.umanitoba.ca/institutes/fisheries/eutro.html. Humans add excessive amounts of plant nutrients (primarily phosphorus, nitrogen, and carbon) to streams and lakes in various ways. Other sources of nutrients include runoff from agricultural fields, field lots, urban lawns, and golf courses and untreated or partially treated sewage. Sewage was also a source of phosphorus in lakes when detergents contained large amounts of phosphates that acted as water softeners to improve the cleaning action but also stimulated algal growth when the phosphates were flushed into lakes, depleted oxygen, caused native fish to disappear, and fouled beaches and shorelines. See also P. W. Glynn, "Coral Reef Bleaching in the 1980s and Possible Connections with Global Warming," *Trends in Ecology & Evolution* 6, no. 6 (1991): 175–79; Tom Goreau, Tim McClanahan, Ray Hayes, and Al Strong, "Conservation of Coral Reefs after the 1998 Global Bleaching Event," *Conservation Biology* 14, no. 1 (February 2000): 5–15; and T. J. Goreau and R. L. Hayes, "Coral Bleaching and Ocean 'Hot Spots,'" *Ambio* 23 (1994): 176–80.

132. James J. Bell and David K.A. Barnes, "The Influences of Bathymetry and Flow Regime upon the Morphology of Sublittoral Sponge Communities," *Journal of the Marine Biological Association of the UK* 80, no. 4 (2000): 707–18.

133. R. H. Richmond, "Coral Reefs: Present Problems and Future Concerns Resulting from Anthropogenic Disturbance," *American Zoologist* 33 (1993): 524–36.

134. R. S. Henderson, "Marine Microcosm Experiments on Effects of Copper and Tributyltin-Based Antifouling Paint Leachates," CSA Guide to Discovery, md1.csa.com/partners/viewrecord.php?requester=gs&collection=ENV&recid=2995225&q=&uid=788579802&setcookie=yes. See also "Alternative Antifouling Bottom Paints Workshop," Santa Barbara, CA, August 24, 2004, www.cdpr.ca.gov/docs/sw/caps/sb_works090904.pdf#search=percent22anti-fouling percent20bottom percent22.

135. International Society for Reef Studies, "Statement on Diseases on Coral Reefs," www.fit.edu/isrs/council/disease.htm. Three coral diseases—"white-band," "black-band," and "plague"—were first reported in the Caribbean in the 1970s. The first documented, regional-scale epizootic, however, affected the long-spined sea urchin, *Diadema antillarum*. In 1983–84, a disease carried by ocean currents, and possibly in the ballast water of ships, killed more than 95 percent of the urchin throughout the Caribbean Sea region, clearly demonstrating that diseases can have major effects on reef ecology. Before its mass mortality, *Diadema* was an important herbivore that ate fast-growing fleshy algae (seaweeds), keeping space free for corals to survive and grow. After the urchins died, algae increased dramatically on many Caribbean reefs, colonizing corals that had been killed by hurricanes and by diseases, particularly the white-band variety. Since that time, algal growth has been so rapid on some reefs that the surviving corals have been unable to continue growing, and small, newly settled corals are simply being overgrown and killed.

136. Juliet Eilperin, "Growing Acidity of Oceans May Kill Corals," *Washington Post*, July 5, 2006, www.washingtonpost.com/wp-dyn/content/article/2006/07/04/AR2006070400772.html. In-depth studies are provided by Clive Wilkinson, ed., *Status of Coral Reefs of the World: 2004*, 2 vols. Australian Institute of Marine Science, www.aims.gov.au/pages/research/coral-bleaching/scr2004. As ocean

warming coincides with sea level rise due to more frequent tropical storms, coral reefs are likely to experience greater coastal erosion, sedimentation, and turbidity, all of which would add to their demise.

137. G. Hodgson, "A Global Assessment of Human Effects on Coral Reefs," *Marine Pollution Bulletin* 38 (1999): 345–55. L. A. Nurse, R. F. McLean, and A. G. Suarez, "Small Island States," in *The Regional Impacts of Climate Change: An Assessment of Vulnerability*, ed. R. T. Watson, M. C. Zinyowera, and R. H. Moss (Cambridge: Cambridge University Press, 1998), 331–54. Union of Concerned Scientists, "Global Warming: Early Warning Signs: Coral Reef Bleaching," www.ucsusa.org/global_warming/science/early-warning-signs-of-global-warming-coral-reef-bleaching.html.

138. Weier, "Mapping the Decline of Coral Reefs."

139. Ibid.

140. Ibid.

141. Other persistent pollutants (e.g., dichloro-diphenyl-trichloroethane, DDT, and polychlorinated biphenyls, PCBs) are recognized as accumulating globally at some-times higher concentrations than when they were first released and cause disruptions to the hormone systems of humans and wildlife. Though the use of persistent pollutants is falling, their presence in Arctic ecosystems continues to rise and concentrations in the diets of some Arctic inhabitants exceed tolerable daily intakes. Negotiations are under way to phase out some persistent pollutants and tightly control others. Harrison and Pearce, *AAAS Atlas on Population and Environment*, 95, 98.

142. Commonly dubbed "acid rain," this phenomenon occurs when sulfur dioxide and nitrogen oxide both acidify water droplets in the air. The resulting rain, fog, or snow may fall locally or travel long distances in clouds to acidify soils and leach metals from them, thereby poisoning trees and making lakes and streams too acidic for some fish. See Harrison and Pearce, *AAAS Atlas of Population and Environment*, 95. In the middle of the twentieth century, increased fossil fuel burning precipitated the first internationally recognized case of transboundary air pollution that pointed to German, British and Polish emissions causing acid deposition that caused the death of fish in Scandinavia; J. L. Stoddard, "Regional Trends in Aquatic Recovery from Acidification in North America and Europe," *Nature* 401 (October 7, 1999): 575–78.

143. "Smog" is caused when nitrous oxides react with hydrocarbons in sunlight to create a new range of photochemical pollutants in the lower atmosphere that is dangerous to human health and crops. See Harrison and Pearce, *AAAS Atlas of Population and Environment*, 95; and United Nations Environment Program, *Global Environment Outlook 2000*, www.unep.org/GEO/. The very young, the very old, and people with lung and heart conditions are most adversely affected by smog; "ozone alerts" are issued in the United States when ozone levels are high, especially in hot, humid weather. Smog occurs regularly in northern Chinese and Indian cities. According to the United Nations Environment Program, *Global Environment Outlook 2000*, China's smog causes more than 50,000 premature deaths and 400,000 new cases of chronic bronchitis a year in eleven of its largest cities. Conditions are worst in thin air at higher altitudes, especially when the air is trapped inside a valley (e.g., Mexico City, where smog alerts close factories and force cars off streets several times a year). The American Academy of Family Physicians sponsors FamilyDoctor.org to educate people on the health effects of air pollution; see www.familydoctor.org/online/famdocen/home/common/asthma/triggers/085.printerview.html. See also

the U.S. Environmental Protection Agency, "Why Should You Be Concerned About Air Pollution?" www.epa.gov/air/caa/peg/concern.html.

144. United Nations Environment Program, *Global Environment Outlook 2000.*

145. Harrison and Pearce, *AAAS Atlas of Population and Environment,* 98.

146. John T. Houghton, L. G. Meiro Filho, B. A. Callander, N. Harris, A. Kattenberg, and K. Maskell, eds., *Climate Change 1995: The Science of Climate Change,* Contribution of Working Group I to the Second Assessment Report of the Intergovernmental Panel on Climate Change (Cambridge: Cambridge University Press, 1996). Carbon is also present in the second most important anthropogenic greenhouse gas, methane, produced in agricultural activities such as rice paddies, the domestication of ruminants, and the clearance of natural vegetation. The industrial age has seen a 145 percent rise in methane concentrations in the atmosphere, according to the World Resources Institute, *World Resources 1998–99: Environmental Change and Human Health* (New York: Oxford University Press, 1999). See also Anne Simon Moffat, "Global Nitrogen Overload Problem Grows Critical," *Science* 279 (February 13, 1998): 988–89, at 988.

147. Harrison and Pearce, *AAAS Atlas of Population and Environment,* 99–100.

148. National Oceanic and Atmospheric Administration, "Carbon Dioxide, Methane Rise Sharply in 2007," April 23, 2008, www.noaa.gov/stories2008/20080423_methane.html.

149. Most industrial nations agreed at Kyoto in 1997 to cut emissions of six greenhouse gases by around 5 percent by 2012. Mechanisms for reaching these goals are flexible, allowing the nations to invest in emissions reduction or "carbon-sink enhancing projects," such as planting trees in other countries. Harrison and Pearce, *AAAS Atlas of Population and Environment,* 99–100.

150. The activities and reports of the Intergovernmental Panel on Climate Change are accessible from is website, www.ipcc.ch.

151. Harrison and Pearce, *AAAS Atlas of Population and Environment,* 99–102.

152. Environmental News Service, "UN Climate Change Impact Report: Poor Will Suffer Most," quoting Rajendra Pachauri of India on April 6, 2007, www.ens-newswire.com/ens/apr2007/2007-04-06-01.asp.

153. United States Conference of Catholic Bishops, *Global Climate Change: A Plea for Dialogue, Prudence, and the Common Good* (Washington, DC: USCCB Publications, 2001), www.usccb.org/sdwp/international/globalclimate.shtml#sidebar. An overview of efforts that religious organizations have taken to address global warming is provided by Jame Schaefer, "Quest for the Common Good: A Collaborative Public Theology for a Life-Sustaining Climate," in *Cultural Landscapes: Religion & Public Life,* ed. Gabriel R. Ricci (New Brunswick, NJ: Transaction, 2007), vol. 35, 1–22.

154. Statements by the pope on July 14 and September 2, 6, and 16, 2008, can be found on the Vatican News Agency's website (www.zenit.org) by searching for articles on climate change. Another source for papal statements is the Vatican website (www.vatican.va).

155. E. O. Wilson, *The Creation: An Appeal to Save Life on Earth* (W. W. Norton, 2006), 79. In a chapter cleverly titled "The Pauperization of Earth," 73–81, Wilson laments the endangerment and extinction of species.

156. Richard E. Leakey and Roger Lewin, *The Sixth Extinction: Patterns of Life and the Future of Humankind* (New York: Doubleday, 1995). Similar conclusions are reached by the Secretariat of the Convention on Biological Diversity, *Global Biodiversity Outlook 2* (Montreal: Convention on Biological Diversity, 2006), www.biodiv.org/GBO2.

157. International Union for Conservation of Nature, "Red List," www.iucnredlist.org. The Red List, a strongly scientifically based and authoritative guide to the status of biological diversity, constitutes the world's most comprehensive inventory of the global conservation status of plant and animal species. The International Union for Conservation of Nature uses a set of criteria to evaluate the extinction risk of thousands of species and subspecies and conveys the urgency and scale of conservation problems to the public and policymakers to motivate the global community to pay attention to the ongoing problem of species extinction and loss of biological diversity. See Environmental Literacy Council, "Threatened and Endangered Species," www.enviroliteracy.org/article.php/33.html.

158. U.S. Fish and Wildlife Service, "Threatened and Endangered Species System," www.ecos.fws.gov/tess_public/TessStatReport. At the time of writing, this report listed 1,353 endangered or threatened species. It also enumerates species in the United States that are proposed for listing, species that have designated critical habitats, candidate species, and habitat conservation plans that have been approved.

159. See especially Harrison and Pearce, *AAAS Atlas on Population and Environment,* for an illuminating explanation that includes impressive graphics of the available data.

160. Wilson, *The Creation,* 75.

161. V. H. Heywood, ed., *The Global Biodiversity Assessment* (Cambridge: Cambridge University Press for United Nations Environment Program, 1995).

162. Iraq, Somalia, and the United States are not parties to the Convention on Biological Diversity. See www.cbd.int/countries/and Wilson's discussion in *The Creation,* 93. Some nations have amended their constitutions to include the charge to protect the ecological systems within their borders.

163. Eric Chivian and Aaron Bernstein, eds., *Sustaining Life: How Human Health Depends on Biodiversity* (Oxford: Oxford University Press, 2008).

164. United Nations Development Program, *Human Development Report 1998: Consumption for Human Development* (New York: Oxford University Press, 1998), 1.

165. The size of the American home built in the United States almost doubled in the last half of the twentieth century, according to R. H. Frank in *Luxury Fever: Why Money Fails to Satisfy in an Era of Excess* (New York: Free Press, 1999), 3. Though the average household size has been shrinking, larger homes and more households per 1,000 people mean more environmental impact, primarily in the forms of increased resource consumption per person and more destruction of biodiversity; J. Liu, G. C. Daily, P. R. Ehrlich, and G. W. Luck, "Effects of Household Dynamics on Resource Consumption and Biodiversity," *Nature* 421 (2003): 530–33.

166. Frank, *Luxury Fever,* 3.

167. United Nations Development Program, *Human Development Report 1998,* 2.

168. Peter H. Raven, "Foreword," in *AAAS Atlas of Population and Environment,* x. Many studies and reports address perceptively the perils of overconsumption; see Thomas Princen, Michael Maniates, and Ken Conca, eds., *Confronting Consumption* (Cambridge, MA: MIT Press, 2002); Philip J. Cafaro, Richard B. Primark, and Robert L. Zimdahl, "The Fat of the Land: Linking American Food Overconsumption, Obesity, and Biodiversity Loss," *Journal of Agricultural and Environmental Ethics* 19, no. 6 (2006): 541–61; Bill Barnes, "The Ecological Economics of Consumption," *Journal of Economic Issues* 40, no. 3 (September 2006): 830–32; Jan Otto Andersson, "Our Full, Unequal World," *Inroads* 17 (Summer 2005): 48–57; and Alan Durning, "How Much Is Enough?" *Technology Review* 94, no. 4 (May–June 1991): 56–63.

169. United Nations Development Program, *Human Development Report 1998*, 2.
170. Harrison and Pearce, *AAAS Atlas of Population and Environment*, 21.
171. One study found that about 93 percent of materials used in production end up as waste, whereas 80 percent of products are discarded after a single use. See Harrison and Pearce, *AAAS Atlas of Population and Environment*, 25.
172. The amount of municipal waste generated in a country is related to the rate of urbanization, the types and patterns of consumption, household revenue, and lifestyles. Though municipal waste is only one part of total waste generated, its management and treatment often absorbs more than one-third of the public sector's financial efforts to abate and control pollution, as explained by the Organization for Economic Cooperation and Development, *Environmental Outlook to 2030* (Paris: Organization for Economic Cooperation and Development, 2008), www.titania.sourceoecd.org/vl=3747995/cl=15/nw=1/rpsv/factbook/080202.htm. In the mid-1990s the rich countries belonging to the Organization for Economic Cooperation and Development produced 1.5 billion tons of industrial waste and 579 million tons of municipal waste, an annual total of almost 2 tons of waste for every person. See Raven, "Foreword."
173. Whereas poor communities recover every valuable item from waste (e.g., Asian recyclers use rubber from scrap tires to make shoes and flatten cans to make metal sheets for roofing) and recyclables are shipped distances to developing countries, a shortage of reprocessing capacity and the cost of collecting small quantities of materials from many locations has not always been resource efficient. See Harrison and Pearce, *AAAS Atlas of Population and Environment*, 110.
174. United Nations Development Program, *Human Development Report 1998*, 2.
175. Harrison and Pearce, *AAAS Atlas of Population and Environment*, 110.
176. United Nations Development Program, *Human Development Report 1998*, 1.
177. Ibid. See also Andersson, "Our Full, Unequal World; and Ehrlich and Ehrlich's discussion in *One with Nineveh*, 86, where they describe the vast differences between the rich nations (Australia, Canada, Japan, New Zealand, the United States, and the Western European countries) and the poor. Ehrlich and Ehrlich note that these rich nations, with less than 15 percent of the world's population, account for nearly 80 percent of the world's income. With 4.6 percent of the world's people, the United States accounts for nearly 29 percent of the world's income. The 2.6 billion people in middle-income countries share 17 percent of the world's income, but the low-income countries, with 2.4 billion people, have access to less than 3.5 percent of the world's income. Even when large differences in purchasing power are taken into account, the average U.S. citizen has about seventeen times the income of a person in a low-income nation.
178. Among the principles that are useful for application to ecological problems researched are (1) Acknowledge the subject of the problem, species, air, land and water as blessings from God to whom gratitude should be expressed; (2) recognize accountability to God for their use; (3) think carefully about why and how the subject of the ecological problem should be used and plan to use the subject appropriately according to its nature in specific ways; (4) limit using the subject of the problem to what is needed, not wanted; and (5) assure the availability of the subject to future humans and other species and/or abiota who need them for their sustenance.
179. E.g., see Saint Augustine, *Concerning the City of God*, 11.22, 453; Aquinas, *Summa contra Gentiles*, 3.141; and Aquinas, *Summa theologiae*, 2|2.83.6.

180. Chapter 8, on living virtuously, explores in more depth the virtue of prudence and its significance for addressing environmental concerns.

181. See, e.g., Pope John Paul II, *Ecclesia in America,* Apostolic Exhortation to the Bishops, Priests and Deacons, Men and Women Religions, and All the Lay Faithful, Mexico City, January 22, 1999, www.vatican.va/holy_father/john_paul_ii/apost_exhortations/documents/hf_jp-ii_exh_22011999_ecclesia-in-america_en.html; and U. S. Catholic Conference of Bishops, *Renewing the Earth: An Invitation to Reflection and Action on Environment in Light of Catholic Social Teaching* (Washington, DC: USCCB Publications, 1991), www.usccb.org/sdwp/ejp/bishopsstatement.shtml.

182. For teachings that relate consumption to the natural environment, see Pope Benedict XVI, "The Human Family, A Community of Peace," World Day of Peace Message, January 1, 2008, no. 8, where he teaches the need to "sense" that Earth is "our common home," to have a "greater conviction about the need for responsible cooperation," to "reassess the high levels of consumption" of resources, to "search for alternative sources of energy and for greater energy efficiency," and to assure that the needs of emerging countries are met without humiliating them in light of the facts that they are poor, have insufficient infrastructures, and "are forced to undersell the energy resources they do possess." This statement is available at www.vatican.va/holy_father/benedict_xvi/messages/peace/documents/hf_ben-xvi_mes_20071208_xli-world-day-peace_en.html. Also see United States Conference of Catholic Bishops, *Renewing the Earth,* section III-H; National Conference of Catholic Bishops, *Economic Justice for All: Pastoral Letter on Catholic Social Teaching and the U.S. Economy,* November 13, 1986, no. 217, www.usccb.org/sdwp/international/EconomicJusticeforAll.pdf; an overview of the Environmental Justice Program of the United States Conference of Catholic Bishops that focuses on educating and motivating Catholics to a deeper respect for the natural environment and engaging parishes in dealing with environmental problems that especially affect the poor, which can be found at www.usccb.org/sdwp/ejp/overview.shtml; and Monsignor Charles Murphy, "The Good Life from a Catholic Perspective: The Problem of Consumption," www.usccb.org/sdwp/ejp/background/articles/consumption.shtml.

183. An insightful overview of this principle is provided by Benjamin S. Llamzon, "Subsidiarity: The Term, Its Metaphysics and Use," *Aquinas* 21 (January–April, 1978): 44–62. The principle of subsidiarity, which was first explicitly articulated by Pope Pius XI in *Quadragesimo Anno,* had its basis in Aquinas's teachings. See the multiplicity of entries on the principle of subsidiarity in *Compendium of the Social Doctrine of the Church,* by Pontifical Council for Justice and Peace (Washington, DC: United States Conference of Catholic Bishops, 2005).

184. Wilson, *The Creation,* 120.

8

LIVING VIRTUOUSLY WITHIN
THE EARTH COMMUNITY

Recent scholarly interest in the moral virtues[1] prompts this exploration into the possibilities for addressing ecological concerns. Although some patristic and medieval theologians eschewed basing moral theology on pagan theories,[2] others adapted them to Christianity.[3] Foremost among the adapters was Thomas Aquinas (ca. 1224/25–74) who explored the *limited* happiness that humans can achieve in temporal life by practicing the moral virtues that Aristotle described as naturally acquirable. Whereas *limited* happiness can be achieved in one's lifetime, Aquinas taught, *unlimited* happiness occurs in eternal life,

This chapter explores Aquinas's teachings on the chief moral virtues through an ecological lens to determine the extent to which they can be cogent, relevant, and helpful. In the first section, his teachings on prudence, justice, temperance, and fortitude are examined. Scientific findings on one ecosystem—the Great Lakes Basin—are explored subsequently to serve as a test case for identifying human actions that have caused its degradation. The third section focuses on how living virtuously in the ecosystem as individuals and as communities of faith will facilitate its cleanup and conservation for multiple purposes.

Aquinas on the Moral Virtues

Aquinas taught that humans should be guided by the virtues when acting on other creatures.[4] Whereas the intellectual virtues perfect the power of reason in the human mind and the theological virtues unite the human being to God,[5] the moral virtues[6] incline the human will to follow the dictates of reason in their temporal lives while aiming for eternal happiness with God. The moral virtues are only innate to the individual potentially.[7] They are like seeds that are naturally present in human reason and must be cultivated.[8] Once perfected in the individual, the moral virtues confer an aptness—a prompt will—to act correctly.[9]

Prudence, temperance, justice, and fortitude are the cardinal virtues that incline rational beings to act morally toward one another within God's creation.[10]
More specifically, prudence provides the rationale for acting on other living and
nonliving beings in appropriate ways,[11] whereas justice, temperance, and fortitude incline the human to act according to what prudence dictates. These four
virtues and their subvirtues have significance for living appropriately during this
age of ecological degradation.

Prudence

According to Aquinas, prudence is the habit of being discreet.[12] A prudent person chooses means of acting on other living and inanimate entities through a
process of taking counsel, forming a good judgment, and commanding correctly.[13]

Taking counsel is an act of inquiry aimed at discovering the appropriate means
for achieving a goal.[14] Both the private good of the individual and the common
good of those groups to which the individual belongs are considered when seeking counsel. The good of the individual is impossible, Aquinas argued, unless the
common good of others is assured.[15] Thus, the prudent individual considers
what is good for one's self by being prudent about what is good for many.[16] In
the process of taking counsel from informed sources, the human discerns what
is needed to sustain one's life, the life of one's neighbor, and the community to
which one belongs.

Judgment is made subsequently on the best means of relating to others that
is most appropriate to achieving the goal of sustaining human life. The choice
is made among the possibilities identified when seeking counsel.[17]

Command, the chief and final act in prudent decision making, requires three
considerations that have special significance for environmental ethics today: foresight, circumspection, and caution.[18] Foresight ensures that whatever is commanded in the present is fitting for the future.[19] Circumspection facilitates the
choice of suitable means to an end in light of a combination of circumstances
that may arise.[20] Caution is required to avoid evil through a firm understanding
of good.[21]

Though this step-by-step process does not absolutely ensure that the action
chosen will be successful for the reasons intended, Aquinas explained, the habit
of making prudent decisions lessens the uncertainty of the outcome.[22] To habitually choose correct means of acting requires the development of this virtue
through instruction and experience over a long period of time.[23] This framework
for the exercise of prudence offers a systematic approach to addressing environmental problems.

Temperance

The virtue of temperance inclines the human to act according to what prudence
dictates by curbing irrational desires and passions for bodily pleasures and material goods that are contrary to reason.[24] Because God intends that they serve

as means for sustaining human life while aiming ultimately toward eternal happiness with God, Aquinas taught, the individual should not take excessive pleasure in them for themselves apart from God or they will distract the individual from their path toward God.[25]

These temporal needs fall into two categories: (1) Things without which humans as individuals and as a species cannot survive, and (2) things without which humans cannot carry on their lives in appropriate ways.[26] Survival needs for bodies are understandable from Aquinas's teachings, and they coincide well with his notions about the internal consumptive order of all entities in relation to one another to bring about the internal sustainability of the universe, as discussed in chapter 5, on the integrity of creation. Exactly what he means by things beyond these necessities is somewhat obscure. They go beyond purely physical requirements and extend to the ownership of external things, including a moderate amount of material wealth that is determined when considering the place, time, and manners of the circumstances in which the person lives.[27]

However, in light of Aquinas's emphasis on the virtue of temperance as a guide toward controlling one's desire for material goods and sensual pleasures, excessive standards of living would seem to be precluded in any setting in order to avoid deflecting attention from the ultimate desire for eternal happiness with God. He embraced poverty for himself as a Dominican while endorsing it cautiously with restrictions for others, because he thought it was an extraordinary way to perfect one's life as a Christian. He also insisted that a person who adopts poverty should retain the ability to secure the necessities of life in a lawful manner.[28] Obviously, the virtue of temperance would incline the faithful toward living more moderately in the world in ways that contrast with the overconsumption and waste that is rampant, especially in industrially developed countries.

The subvirtues of temperance also have significance for addressing environmental problems today. For example, the subvirtue of *continence* can avoid the will's succumbing to immoderate self-desires. The subvirtue of *humility* can restrain the inordinate desire to acquire nonnecessities of life and positively condition human attitudes toward other-than-human creatures when informed by scientific findings about their interrelationship and interdependency.[29]

Opposing humility in Aquinas's teachings is the vice of *pride*. This vice is twofold from his perspective: An inordinate sense of excellence that a person has for himself or herself that overrules the person's reason by excess or default,[30] and an influence on other vices by directing them toward the person's inordinate sense of excellence. Thus, pride is both a special sin and a general sin,[31] the root of which is failure to subject oneself to God and God's rule.[32] Pride is always contrary to the love of God, inasmuch as proud persons do not subject themselves to living the God-oriented lives that God intends. Sometimes pride is contrary to the love of neighbor by setting oneself inordinately above one's neighbor,[33] evidence for which abounds today as some people overconsume and abuse the goods of Earth while others struggle to survive in environmentally impoverished areas.

Other vices related to temperance that have relevance for living in an ecologically endangered age include *insensibility*—not making use of one's senses when reasoning about the appropriate use of natural goods,[34] *intemperance*—being childlike by unchecked self-desires for natural goods,[35] gluttony—succumbing to inordinate desires for natural goods,[36] and *cowardice*—failing to recognize the dangers of death and to preserve life.[37] Cowardice is an especially intriguing vice to explore in light of the declining biological diversity in rainforests, coral reefs, wetlands, and other ecosystems. These losses are due to their overuse and abuse by humans who fail to recognize the dangers their actions cause not only to the species but also to the ecosystems of which they are integral parts.

Justice

The virtue of justice inclines humans to relate to one another in ways that are conducive to achieving their temporal common good as they seek their eternal common good with God.[38] All members of a community stand in relation to it as parts to the whole, Aquinas taught repeatedly, and the good of the individual should be directed to the common good of that community.[39] Because the community's temporal good is to have sufficient means through which its members can sustain their lives, the person would be inclined by the virtue of justice to relate to living and inanimate constituents of Earth in ways that ensure their availability to meet the needs of all humans in that community.[40] An individual who possesses or desires to possess immoderate amounts of material goods sins against another, he insisted, because one individual cannot have an abundance of external riches without other individuals lacking them.[41]

Because Aquinas thought about humans as members of various kinds of communities—households, states, and the universe,[42] his thinking provides an opening for construing the virtue of justice as inclining humans to use goods of Earth in ways that ensure their availability to meet the needs of other humans now and in the future. Furthermore, because the common good of the human community would be jeopardized by the degradation of the air, land, and water, the accelerated rate of species extinction, the destruction of habitats, and damage to the biosphere,[43] the virtue of justice could be construed today as inclining humans individually and collectively to relate to other biota and abiota in ways that do not jeopardize the functioning of natural systems in the interests of human communities near and far, now and in the future.

A more expansive and ecologically sensitive role for justice is suggested by Aquinas's teaching that the more comprehensive the good envisaged by the human, the more the human will corresponds to the will of God, who wills the good of the whole universe.[44] God is the exemplar for humans to follow by acting in ways that are geared toward the good of the world.[45] As creatures endowed with intellectual capacities to discern appropriate actions and to choose to act accordingly, humans would be inclined by the virtue of justice to act for the common good of the entire corporeal world. Of course, because the human is, according to Aquinas, the end of all corporeal things in the orderly universe,[46] acting primarily in the interest of the common good of the universe would concurrently be acting in the interests of the human species.

One type of particular justice has significance for addressing environmental concern—distributive justice. When habitual in an individual, this kind of justice would incline the person individually and people collectively to ensure that others receive their fair share of goods held in common by that community[47] in order to sustain their lives. Distributive justice would also incline the individual and the community to take steps to ensure that people in the future will have access to the goods of Earth for their needs. When this virtue is expanded to include all types of biological life and abiota, human communities would take steps to ensure that all species and abiota are able to meet their needs for surviving—needs for nourishment, space, and integrity.

Fortitude

The virtue of fortitude inclines the individual to persevere in relating appropriately to other living and nonliving entities despite impediments that may weaken the individual's efforts to cooperate with them.[48] Fortitude reinforces justice to incline humans individually and collectively to seek the good of other humans now and into the future. Fortitude supports temperance so it inclines humans to use other corporeal things for the necessities of life and to know God rather than for pure pleasure or pride of ownership.[49] Because fortitude is directed toward the common good, especially when thinking about the protection of others, this virtue would incline individuals to be steadfastly protective of the good of all humans.[50] Fortitude strengthens prudence to persist in inclining humans in their efforts to discern the best ways of relating to other living and nonliving entities that constitute Earth.

Fortitude can be appropriated today as the virtue that will strengthen the faithful to persist in using the goods of Earth minimally with the aim of ensuring the internal sustainability of ecosystems and the biosphere. This point is especially important to stress among the middle-income to affluent faithful in both industrially developed and developing countries. Though Aquinas considered this virtue as inclining humans to be steadfast, despite fear and other passions that may impede their acting according to the dictates of prudence,[51] fortitude could also be construed today as fortifying human resolve to take protective and remedial actions for fear of the real or potentially adverse effects of human actions on other species and their habitats and on ecosystems.

How promising are the chief moral virtues and their subvirtues for application to ecological problems today? The plight of one ecosystem serves as a basis for testing the extent to which Aquinas's teachings can be helpful.

A Degraded Ecosystem

Comprising one-fifth of Earth's freshwater and 80 percent of the freshwater on the North American continent, the Great Lakes of Ontario, Erie, Huron,

Michigan, and Superior[52] were once dubbed "the sweet seas" by early explorers who could drink directly from them without becoming ill.[53] Today, their waters are no longer safe for drinking without disinfection, many of their beaches are too polluted for swimming, and much of their fish and waterfowl are too contaminated to eat. The native fish populations of the Great Lakes are overfished, and the introduction of exotic fish and other organisms foreign to the area further debilitate its fisheries.[54]

Many other problems that persist in the Great Lakes are caused by activities in the drainage basin that encompasses their waters. Among these problematic activities are the filling of wetlands and other spawning areas that thwart the flourishing of native marine life, the leveling of most of the basin's forests that serve invaluable climatic and water-cycle control services, and the flushing of sewage from households and other sources into the lakes and their tributaries that wash up on the beaches and prompt their closing. Also highly troublesome is the runoff of nutrients from agricultural areas, storm water conduits, urban development, fertilized yards and gardens, failing septic systems, land clearing, municipal and industrial wastewater, construction projects, and recreational activities. Nutrients that contain high amounts of nitrogen and phosphorus accelerate the growth of algae, which depletes oxygen, leads to fish kills, thwarts the growth of other plants, causes taste and odor problems in water and fish desired for human consumption, clogs the filters of wastewater treatment plants, and inhibits the aesthetic appeal of the lakes.[55]

One of the most significant and alarming abuses of the Great Lakes centers on the pollutants and toxicants that reach their waters from municipal, agricultural, and industrial activities throughout the basin. Tons of toxic chemicals enter the lakes directly and indirectly every day from among the approximately 13,000 factories in the basin that refine petroleum and make plastics, chemicals, paints, iron, steel, cars, pulp, and paper. Some factories dump their chemical wastes directly into the lakes, whereas others are sent through the municipal sewage treatment systems, where toxicants are collected in sewage sludge and others are released into the lakes or tributary rivers.[56] Trace amounts of radioactive nuclides are emitted periodically into the lakes and vented into the atmosphere by the thirty-nine nuclear generators operating in the basin.[57] Toxic wastes seep into the lakes and their tributaries from landfills near their shorelines; runoff reaches them from farm fields, lawns and gardens, construction sites, and urban areas;[58] and polluting particles fall into them from industrial smokestacks and incinerators located both in and outside the basin.[59]

Many of these toxicants break down very slowly in the aquatic environments into which they are deposited. They accumulate at higher levels in the food chain, where they become increasingly dangerous to living beings.[60]

Hundreds of the more stable chemicals and metals have been detected in the Great Lakes, including its water, sediments, fish, reptiles, waterfowl, and mammals. Many fish are highly contaminated with industrial metals, pesticides, transformer fluids, and other chemical wastes.[61] Some of the birds and other wildlife that feed on contaminated fish have become ill (e.g., thyroid and liver abnormalities in herring gulls), have suffered reproductive problems (e.g., embryo mortality in Caspian terns and the inability of bald eagles to reproduce naturally), and have produced offspring with birth defects (e.g., crossed bills and club feet in cormorants).[62]

Humans have not escaped the effects of these toxicants. Studies indicate that children whose mothers consumed contaminated fish were born with lower weights and smaller head sizes and, by the age of four years, had poorer verbal skills and shorter-term memories than children whose mothers had not eaten contaminated fish.[63] Other studies show that toxic substances increase the risk of cancer, birth defects, sterility, mutations, and nerve damage; attack the nervous system and various organs of the body; and change body chemistry.[64]

Considerable debate has ensued within the scientific community about the specific amounts of toxicants that cause human health problems, to what extent chronic diseases can be attributed to environmental pollution in light of the many variables that must be taken into consideration, and what the synergistic effects of chemicals on living beings may be.[65] However, at least one conclusion has few disputants: Infants and young children are considered more highly susceptible to the toxic effects of chemicals. This is because the very young have high metabolic rates through which their bodies assimilate more airborne toxicants and because they lack the fully developed natural barriers that protect adults from some toxicants.[66] The future of a healthy human species may be contingent upon making every possible effort to prevent chemical exposure from the uterine stage through the age of puberty.

Specific kinds of atmospheric toxicants emitted from land-based facilities in the Great Lakes Basin are causing some of the most perplexing problems whose effects go beyond the region. Among these is acid rain, which occurs when sulfur and nitrogen compounds emitted from burning fossil fuels mix with moisture in the atmosphere and cause deleterious effects on lakes, streams, groundwater, forests, agricultural production, buildings, and human health.[67] Holes in the ozone layer of the upper atmosphere, resulting from the use of chlorofluorocarbons in aerosol sprays, plastic foams, refrigeration systems, and dry cleaning facilities, are cited as causing increased incidences of skin cancers.[68] Also highly problematic are large quantities of ozone emitted from gasoline-burning vehicles and other sources of volatile organic compounds that accumulate in the lower atmosphere. These pollutants threaten public health in general and the health of the very young, the elderly, and people with upper respiratory problems in particular.

Furthermore, the effects of global warming on the Great Lakes Basin looms as a major concern. Scientists predict that rising temperatures will increase the evaporation of water from the lakes and rivers in the basin, lower their water levels, warm the waters, and exacerbate existing problems pertaining to water quality, fisheries, navigation, hydropower, and ongoing controversies over water diversion from the lakes.[69] As the historian of medieval technology Lynn

White lamented: "All forms of life modify their contexts. . . . [But] surely no creature other than [the human being] has ever managed to foul its nest in such short
order."[70]

Realizing that a coordinated and cooperative effort must be expended to address the plethora of problems affecting the Great Lakes, the governments of the
United States and Canada signed the Great Lakes Water Quality Agreement in
1972, in which they declared their determination and commitment to "restore
and enhance water quality in the Great Lakes System," including the international
section of the Saint Lawrence River through which the lakes drain. Through a
new agreement in 1978, the two governments made a clear commitment to "restore and maintain the chemical, physical, and biological integrity of the waters
of the Great Lakes Basin Ecosystem" and agreed that "the discharge of any or
all persistent toxic substances be virtually eliminated."[71] This agreement has
been revised twice to address the ongoing problems in the Great Lakes under
the direction of the International Joint Commission that was established by the
United States and Canada.

Though the commission reported in 2006 that "some impressive progress has
been made over the past 34 years, particularly during the 1980s and 1990s," when
pollution from industrial and municipal sources were reduced, the commission
recognized that "significant challenges persist and new ones are emerging."
Among the persisting challenges are: The increase in beach closures, advisories
on limiting fish consumption, very slow progress in remediating the forty-three
Areas of Concern designated in the late 1980s for cleanup,[72] outputs of toxic substances from contaminated sediment, air, and other sources, polluted runoff
from farmlands and urban surfaces, an inadequate capacity to collect and treat
sewage, increasing numbers of chemical spills,[73] and alien invasive species. Urban sprawl, shoreline development, new chemicals and personal care products,
globally airborne pollution, and climate change are among the emerging issues
that the commission must address. All issues are complicating efforts to restore
the quality of the lakes.[74]

A dramatic reduction in the amounts of some gross pollutants has occurred
since the binational agreement was signed. Among the measures that have
brought about this reduction are the construction of more effective sewage
treatment plants, the prohibition of a number of chemicals such as dichloro-
diphenyl-trichloro-ethane (DDT) and polychlorinated byphenals (PCBs), and
restrictions on direct discharge of chemicals, metals, radiological waste, and
other substances into the water.[75]

Despite these achievements, early decreases in some persistent toxicants have
leveled out above designated targets,[76] contaminants endure in the sediments,
waters, and various organisms of the Great Lakes, and tons continue to be
added annually. Some fish and waterfowl are so contaminated with PCBs, pesticides, mercury, and other toxic substances that governmental warnings about
eating them are issued annually.[77] Ozone alerts are sounded during hot, humid
months. Many areas in the region are plagued with extremely high concentra-

tions of toxicants, but only forty-three of them have been prioritized as "Areas of Concern," for which remediation planning is required.[78] If and when these highly contaminated areas are remediated, there is little probability that the toxicants can be removed completely.[79] According to specialists who have studied the problems involved in remediating toxicants and methods of preventing them from entering the Great Lakes, "it is far easier and more cost-effective to avoid a problem than to react after its manifestation."[80] Both remediation and "zero discharge" of contaminants are essential to protect the integrity of the Great Lakes.[81]

However, the commitment of the two nations to the virtual elimination of toxicants and other problems in the Great Lakes may be merely rhetorical, as the commission lamented: "Despite the significance of the Great Lakes and the collective rhetoric to restore and enhance them, we as a society continue to mortgage their future by poisoning, suffocating and otherwise threatening them. . . . What our generation has failed to realize is that, what we are doing to the Great Lakes, we are doing to ourselves and to our children."[82]

To address ongoing and emerging problems more effectively, the commission recommended to the governments of Canada and the United States that the Great Lakes Water Quality Agreement be replaced with one that is "more action-oriented" and makes "a bold and convincing statement of commitment" by the two governments to "address a broader array of stressors that impact on the quality of the waters of the Great Lakes Basin ecosystem."[83]

Assistance for addressing global warming was initiated by the World Meteorological Organization and the United Nations Environment Program through the establishment in 1988 of the Intergovernmental Panel on Climate Change. The panel is charged with assessing the scientific, technical, and socioeconomic information relevant for understanding climate change, its potential effects, and options for adaptation and mitigation. Among the panel's periodic report on the current state of knowledge about the phenomenon are several on regional effects,[84] including those on the Great Lakes,[85] human health risks,[86] emission scenarios,[87] and effects on society and the economy.[88]

In light of the many problems ongoing in the Great Lakes and efforts to address them, drawing from theological resources that may guide the faithful is warranted. Among these sources are Aquinas's teachings on the moral virtues.

Living Virtuously in the Great Lakes Ecosystem

Aquinas's teachings about the moral virtues have significance for living in the Great Lakes Basin today.[89] By following his teachings, the faithful will be guided to live prudently, justly, moderately, and courageously as responsible constituents. The extent of ecological degradation and the need for collaboration to address the many problems cause by human actions requires thinking about more than virtuous individuals. Also needed are virtuous communities made up of virtuous individuals who are grounded in their shared faith in God, their purposeful creator and sustainer.

Living Prudently

The faithful will be guided by the virtue of prudence when living with the other species, the water, the land, and the ambient area that constitute the Great Lakes ecosystem. Individually and collectively, the faithful will follow the principle of subsidiarity,[90] by which they will act incrementally at appropriate levels of governance to which they belong to choose the best possible approach for mitigating the adverse effects of human actions on the Great Lakes. All available sources of information on possible strategies for action will be sought upon which to form a sound judgment about the best means to restore and maintain the lakes for the mutual well-being of all constituents of the ecosystem. Action will be taken expeditiously to implement the judgment that is made.

In the process of taking counsel from informed sources, the needs of humans and other biota to sustain their lives now and in the future will be considered. Crucial to this process is discerning how these needs can be met while making as minimal an impact as possible on the ecosystem's functioning. The faithful will recognize that its well functioning is essential to the well-being of not only humans but also of the other mammals and the fish, waterfowl, reptiles, plants, sediments, waters, and air that constitute the Great Lakes Basin.

A retrieval of Aquinas's thinking in its most altruistic sense and its application to the Great Lakes ecosystem will be all encompassing of the present and the future. The needs of people in and peripheral to the basin will be considered, as also will the needs of future generations who will inhabit the area. Among the factors that will be considered are the carrying capacity of the Great Lakes system, the quality of water, and the point and nonpoint (diffused) sources from which pollutants and toxicants are emitted into the air and enter the water. Steps will be taken to ensure the availability of clean water, air, and land for present and future residents.

Prudent individuals will collaborate in their faith-grounded communities to exercise foresight when discerning the appropriate means to use in order to provide the necessities of life that will sustain humans now and into the future as eternal happiness with God is sought. Because the use of constituents of the Great Lakes Basin affect other constituents, the functioning of the whole ecosystem, other ecosystems, and the entire biosphere, Aquinas's view of the virtue of prudence will be extended to encompass an understanding of global prudence. Global prudence will be essential to making decisions about how human life can be sustained while concurrently avoiding interference with the integrity of the ecosystem and with the biosphere.

Prudent individuals working independently and in collaboration with one another in their faith-based communities will press tenaciously to expedite the remediation of the forty-two most polluted Areas of Concern around the Great Lakes.[91] Though they will recognize some success in determining the best means for remediating these areas, their recognition that judgments have been slow will spur them to be persistent.[92] They will also press for attention to other looming problems including invasive species, water pollution, acid rain, holes in the ozone layer of the upper atmosphere, the accumulation of ozone in the lower atmosphere, and human activities that are forcing changes in the global climate. Where the causes of these problems can be identified locally, plans of action to address them will be developed and implemented.

Living Moderately

When Aquinas's teachings are applied to human functioning throughout the Great Lakes Basin, severe restrictions will be placed on the human use of other biota and the water, land, and ambient air. They will not be used as ends in themselves. They will be used as means through which human existence can be sustained as eternal happiness with God is sought, and as means leading to knowledge about God and participating in God's knowledge.

The Great Lakes ecosystem and its constituents will serve as means through which knowledge of God can be acquired, though this knowledge can only be a mere glimpse—a feeble knowledge of God in temporal life. When appropriating Aquinas's teachings about the sacramentality of creation and updating his thinking to reflect contemporary human understanding of the world,[93] the Great Lakes ecosystem and its parts will be understood as means through humans can admire God's creative and sustaining power and God's wisdom in giving the world the freedom to become and self-organize over eons of time into an orderly ecosystem in which the air, land, water, and biota interact to constitute one ecosystem.

The Great Lakes ecosystem will also inspire reverence for God in the human heart and elicit love for God as the source of all the goodness that is distributed so variously among the parts of the ecosystem. The goodness, beauty, and delightfulness of the ecosystem and its constituents will be so alluring to the faithful that their minds will be drawn to God. Of course, the ecosystem and its constituents will not serve as means of knowing about God unless they function as themselves, so the faithful will strive to ensure their capacity to function according to their natures.

By using ecosystems and their parts as means for sustaining human life and knowing God, the faithful will achieve some measure of temporal happiness. They will recognize that happiness in this life is only possible when they order the use of all things toward achieving eternal happiness with God.

Through Aquinas's lens, the human authority to use the various biota, water, land, and ambient air will be understood as authority given gratuitously by God to humans. Thus the human power to use them will not be perceived as absolute. The human use of ecosystem constituents will be understood as subservient to God's absolute power, because God continuously retains the absolute sovereignty over all things used by humans, and humans are accountable to God for how they use the various components of ecosystems.

Nor will the use of ecosystems and their parts be understood as ending absolutely with humanity. The faithful will understand that the absolute end of all things is God. Therefore, the air, land, waters, and diverse species of the Great Lakes ecosystem will be used with the intention of serving as means for sustaining temporal life while striving to achieve finality in God. This teleological intent for the use of things will be recognized as right and appropriate.

Although the faithful will ensure that the constituents of the Great Lakes ecosystem are used as means to sustain life while seeking eternal happiness with God, the virtue of temperance would curb immoderate consumption of the fish, waterfowl, water, and other ecosystem constituents. That other biota and the air, land, and water of the ecosystem will be used only to the extent that they are essential to sustain human life is an especially poignant message to impress upon economically wealthy nations such as the United States, where such a high percentage of the world's resources are used by a small percentage of the world's population and where a tremendous amount of waste is generated when using both renewable and nonrenewable resources. The need and means whereby constituents of other ecosystems can be used moderately will also be important to impress upon developing nations so they can avoid the problems precipitated by the economically developed nations. The example of successfully using the Great Lakes ecosystem's water, air, land, and biota with restraint will serve as a testimony to others of a commitment to moderate living.

The habit of living moderately will also curb individual and corporate dumping of sewage, hazardous wastes, PCBs, street salt, metals, and other toxicants and pollutants into the Great Lakes. Self-control will reign to prevent thoughtless or careless actions that cause havoc to the Great Lakes ecosystem.

Although the virtue of temperance will guide the actions of the faithful when nurtured in and by them, nurturing the subvirtues can also contribute significantly to living virtuously in ecosystems like the Great Lakes. The subvirtue of *humility* will restrain the inordinate desire for acquiring nonnecessities of life, but this subvirtue can do much more when informed by scientific findings about the interrelationship and interdependency of humans and other creatures. A nurtured inclination toward humility will allow informed reason to prevail regarding humanity's relatedness with other species and humans' dependence on them and on the air, land, and water that constitute the Great Lakes ecosystem and will positively condition human attitudes accordingly. The nurturing of humility will counter tendencies toward the vice of pride so the faithful will recognize themselves in their utter dependency on the health and well-being of the area's other people, species, and abiota for their own well-being. The faithful will recognize the human place in the functioning of the ecosystem and will seek to act humbly in cooperation with the ecosystem's other constituents to ensure its sustainability. By thinking and acting humbly, the faithful will be subjecting themselves to God, who calls all natural constituents of the ecosystem to function cohesively according to their natures.

Nurturing the virtue of moderation will counter other vices that must be avoided. The faithful will avoid the vice of *insensibility* by being sensitive to the needs that native marine species have for surviving in their environment, that the air has for remaining free of particulate matter and volatile organic compounds that adversely affect human and other species that live within the Great Lakes area, that the shoreline and beaches have for remaining uncluttered with human trash and other debris, that the lakes and their tributaries have for being restored to their integrity, and that other humans have when desiring to recreate sensitively and appropriately in the lakes. The faithful will avoid the vice of *intemperance* by checking their self-gratifying demands on the lakes with their various species of fish and wildlife and by disposing of toxic materials in hazardous waste depositories. The faithful will avoid the vice of *gluttony* by curbing their appetites for fish in a lake and its tributaries. And the faithful will avoid the vice of *cowardice* by recognizing the dangers that persistent toxicants pose when emitted into the air, flushed into waterways, and spread on the land of the ecosystem. They will clamor publicly for remediation of the Areas of Concern identified by the International Joint Commission for the Great Lakes, for the minimization of toxicants leading to the goal of zero discharge, and for addressing the many other problems that prevail in the ecosystem.

Living Justly

Although the virtue of prudence retrieved from Aquinas's works provides a step-by-step method for discerning how to relate to other constituents of the Great Lakes ecosystem and the virtue of temperance curtails inordinate desires for ecosystem constituents and their abuse, appropriation of the virtue of justice will aim to ensure that all humans now and into the future will be able to sustain themselves as they seek their mutual end in God. The various types of mammals, fish, waterfowl, reptiles, plants, sediments, water, and air of the Great Lakes ecosystem will be viewed as held in common by the basin's residents to be shared with one another in the present and in the future. Their overuse and abuse will be avoided, and regulations will be established to prevent their overuse and abuse by those who are not guided by the moral virtues. The integrity of the Great Lakes—upon which humans are so dependent for their livelihoods, recreation, and daily living—will be protected so that the common good of all can be served.

Exercising the virtue of justice individually and collectively as people who believe in God will lead to mitigating the ongoing injustice that afflicts the poor and minority residents of the Great Lakes ecosystem, who are vulnerable to pollutants, toxicants, and hazardous materials in and around their neighborhoods and who are least able to defend and protect themselves from harmful effects. Virtuously just people collaborate in defending and protecting vulnerable people so they are no longer adversely affected by environmental degradation. Virtuously just people will demand the cleanup of areas that cause injury to the vulnerable and aid them in becoming empowered to speak for themselves and to have their voices heard.

Some voices cannot be empowered or heard because they are voices of future generations, so the faithful who practice justice will advocate on the behalf of people who will live in the area in the future and be affected adversely by its degraded condition. Just people will demand the remediation of contaminated areas so they do not harm the health and well-being of future residents of the area or become their financial burden to remediate.

The faithful will recognize that extensions of Aquinas's teachings on the virtue of general justice and distributive justice are warranted today in light of contemporary scientific findings about the human place in the cosmological-biological continuum and the radical human dependence on other-than-humans for sustenance. Justice will be accorded generally to other species and the abiota that constitute the Great Lakes ecosystem as essential parts of the community of Earth whose interests in functioning should be considered when adjudicating actions. The faithful's extension of Aquinas's teachings about distributive justice will ensure that humans will recognize and respect the needs of other species, the abiota, and the ecosystem as a whole for their survival.

Living Courageously

Finally, the virtue of fortitude will be understood as enabling the faithful to be steadfast and courageous when functioning prudently, justly, and moderately in the Great Lakes ecosystem. Fortitude will curb fear and other irascible passions that deter them from following the dictates of reason when living in the ecosystem. Supported by members of the virtuous community, virtuous individuals will be able to endure the difficulties they may encounter and the criticism that may be leveled against the practice and promotion of virtuous living in the Great Lakes area. The faithful will be fortified to persevere in seeking the common good for all, to withstand the lures of excessive living and the throwaway mindset that prevails in the United States and other economically developed nations, and to persistently seek means of functioning in the Great Lakes ecosystem that will ensure its integrity.

When appropriated and practiced, the virtue of fortitude will also strengthen the faithful individually and collectively to encourage, support, and cooperate with agencies and groups that work assiduously on behalf of the Great Lakes ecosystem, including the International Joint Commission,[94] the Great Lakes Commission,[95] the Alliance for the Great Lakes,[96] and Great Lakes United.[97] These and other governmental agencies and groups at the local, state/provincial, regional, and international levels will be recognized and appreciated for having persisted in dedicating time, energy, and money to attend to problems that continue to plague the area. These agencies and groups will be strongly urged by the faithful to forge ahead with plans for remediating the heavily polluted Areas of Concern around the Great Lakes, mitigating human-forced climate change, and resolving the many other problems that plague the ecosystem.

As the faithful exercise of the virtue of fortitude, both individually and collectively, they will avoid ignorance, misguided fanaticism, and uncontrolled anger. They will be strengthened to use the process of prudent decision making when striving to live virtuously in the Great Lakes region.

Motivation for Virtuous Living

Following Aquinas's thinking, the theological virtue of love infused in individuals by God and developed in church communities will motivate the practice of living prudently, justly, moderately, and courageously in the Great Lakes ecosystem. The faithful will live virtuously out of love for God, their mutual creator, sustainer, and ultimate end, with whom they wish to spend eternal life. They will also live virtuously out of love for one another, whom they wish will also enjoy happiness with God forever. A full exploration of this theological virtue appears in the next chapter.

The faithful can demonstrate their love individually and collectively by living virtuously in the Great Lakes ecosystem to the maximum possible extent, by watching over and caring about their shared ecosystem for themselves and future generations, by managing themselves so they do not adversely affect the area, by cleaning up and preventing further pollution, and by conserving the air, land, water, and biota of the Great Lakes Basin so they can give glory and honor to God. Other species, the land, water, and air can also be cared about by the faithful out of gratitude to God for their beauty, for their manifestation of God's overflowing goodness, and for their sacramentality in pointing to God, who created, sustains, and beckons all creatures to their self-expressions, interactions, and consummation.

Conclusion

Aquinas's teachings on the chief moral virtues suggest fruitful ways of thinking about how to live prudently, justly, moderately, and courageously within ecosystems. The development and practice of prudence should guide virtuous individuals and virtuous communities to act on other living and nonliving entities that constitute ecosystems through a step-by-step process of discovering ways to achieve a goal, selecting one way that best meets the goal, and taking action to achieve it when considering the current circumstances, having foresight about future occurrences, and remaining cautious about achieving goals.[98] Developing and practicing justice, temperance, and fortitude should incline the faithful to act according to what prudence dictates. Through Aquinas's lens, the faithful should be able to understand that God has gratuitously instilled in their human nature the capacity to develop habits that prompt their wills to relate to other living beings, water, land, and air in virtuous ways. The theological virtue of charity should motivate virtuous living out of the desire to share eternal happiness with God and to wish the same for others.

The ideal of living virtuously in relation to other species and the natural environment differs radically from the ways in which they are plundered mindlessly, greedily, excessively, wastefully, and irreverently by people throughout the world, especially in economically developed countries. Appropriating and applying Aquinas's teachings should be helpful toward countering these prevailing attitudes and actions among people who profess the Catholic, Christian faith.

Notes

Parts of this chapter are revised from Jame Schaefer, "The Virtuous Cooperator: Modeling the Human in an Age of Ecological Degradation," which appeared in *Worldviews: Environment, Culture, Religion* 7, nos. 1–2 (March 2003): 171–95.

1. Jean Porter, *Moral Action and Christian Ethics* (New York: Cambridge University Press, 1995); and Jean Porter, *The Recovery of Virtue: The Relevance of Aquinas for Christian Ethics* (Louisville: Westminster/John Knox Press, 1990); Romanus Cessario, *The Virtues, Or, the Examined Life* (New York: Continuum International, 2002); Stephen R. L. Clarke, *Biology and Christian Ethics* (New York: Cambridge University Press, 2000); Gilbert C. Meilaender, ed., *Working: Its Meaning and Its Limits* (Notre Dame, IN: University of Notre Dame Press, 2000); Roger Crisp and Michael Slote, eds., *Virtue Ethics* (New York: Oxford University Press, 1997); Stephen Darwell, *Virtue Ethics* (Malden, MA: Blackwell, 2003); Thomas L. Carson and Paul K. Moser, eds., *Morality and the Good Life* (New York: Oxford University Press, 1997).

2. E.g., Augustine scoffed at thinking that Christians could learn morality from the pagans in theory or practice, in the first part of *Concerning the City of God against the Pagans,* trans. Henry Bettenson (London: Penguin Books, 1984), esp. chaps. 2 and 5. Virtues that serve the end of human glory are "shameful" (5.20, 214), whereas true virtues are gifts given by God to pious people "in response to their wish, their faith, and their petition" (5.19, 214).

3. Augustine's mentor, Ambrose of Milan (ca. 340–97), anticipated adapting Cicero's Stoic-inspired account of virtue to the Christian quest for eternal happiness with God. Saint Martin of Braga (ca. 520–80) wrote influential moral tracts based closely on works by Seneca, the Roman Stoic (ca. 4 BCE–65 CE). The Cistercian Abbot Ailred of Rievaulx (1109–66) modeled his *De spirituali amicitia* (On spiritual friendship) on Cicero's *De amicitia* (On friendship). And Peter Abelard (1079–1142), drew on commentaries Cicero and Boethius wrote on Aristotle's *Categories* in which he defined natural virtues as dispositions that are acquired through human powers and transformable into Christian virtues aimed toward eternal happiness with God. See the overview by Jill Kraye, "Philosophy, Moral: Medieval and Renaissance," in *New Dictionary of the History of Ideas,* ed. Maryanne Horowitz, vol. 4 (New York: Charles Scribner's Sons, 2005), 1790–92.

4. Thomas Aquinas, *Summa contra Gentiles,* 1.92.

5. E.g., see Aquinas, *Summa theologiae*, 1 | 2.58.3, 62.1, 66.3, 68.8; also see 2 | 2.161.5.

6. Aquinas attributed the term *moralis* to these four virtues, a term he derived from *mos* in the sense of a natural or quasi natural inclination to perform some particular action; see Aquinas, *Summa theologiae*, 1 | 2.58.1. He sometimes characterized the four moral virtues as cardinal virtues (*virtutes cardinales*), as in his introduction to these virtues in the *secunda sedundae* of the *Summa theologiae* before question 47.

7. Aquinas, *Summa theologiae*, 1 | 2.58.1; also see 50.3, 63.1

8. Ibid., 1 | 2.63.1; also see 55.1–3, 56.4.

9. Ibid., 1 | 2.56.3; also see 68.3.

10. On the role of the virtues in relation to informed decision making, see Aquinas, *Summa theologiae*, 1 | 2.58.3, 62.1, 64.1, 66.3, 68.8, 100.1, 2 | 2.47.6, 161.5.

11. Aquinas, *Summa theologiae*, 1 | 2.57.4–6; see also 1 | 2.58.4, 2 | 2.47.7.

12. Ibid., 1 | 2.61.2.

13. Ibid., 1 | 2.65.1; see also 1 | 2.57.4–6, 2 | 2.47.2, 8.

14. Ibid., 1 | 2.14.1, 57.6; see also 2 | 2.47.1–2, 8.

15. Ibid., 2 | 2.47.10.

16. Ibid., 2 | 2.47.10; also see 1.22.1, where Aquinas discusses God's providence as prudence by ordering all things in the universe to their ends, which serves to underscore the need for humans to reason correctly by ordering all their actions toward their ultimate end in God.

17. Aquinas, *Summa theologiae*, 2 | 2.47.8, 1 | 2.57.6.

18. Ibid., 2 | 2.47.8; also see 1 | 2.57.6, 2 | 2.47.9.

19. Ibid., 2 | 2.49.6 and 55.7.

20. Ibid., 2 | 2.49.7.

21. Ibid., 2 | 2.49.8.

22. Ibid., 2 | 2.49.5.

23. Aquinas, *Summa contra Gentiles*, 3.122. Any person who has the ability to reason is competent to have prudence in proportion to the person's rationality, he explained in *Summa theologiae*, 2 | 2.47.12.

24. Aquinas, *Summa theologiae*, 1 | 2.65.1, 60.5. This does not mean that Aquinas thought that the passions are evil. As stipulated in *Summa theologiae*, 2 | 2.141.6, passions are good aspects of being human so long as they are controlled by the dictates of reason; see, further, 2 | 2.141.1–5.

25. Ibid., 2 | 2.141.5–6.

26. Ibid., 2 | 2.141.6.

27. Ibid.

28. See Aquinas, *Summa contra Gentiles*, 3.132–33; and Aquinas, *Summa theologiae*, 2 | 2.184.3–4, 7, 186.3. Aquinas chose poverty as a way of life when joining the fledgling Dominican Order of Preachers and leaving behind his family's relatively wealthy lifestyle, as explained by James Weisheipl, *Friar Thomas D'Aquino: His Life, Thought, and Work* (Garden City, NY: Doubleday, 1974), 131.

29. Aquinas, *Summa theologiae*, 2 | 2.143.1.

30. Ibid., 2 | 2.162.1; Aquinas quoted Augustine in *Concerning the City of God*, 14.13, in which the patristic theologian explained that a prideful person imitates God inordinately and wishes to usurp God's dominion over "fellow-creatures."

31. Ibid., 2]2.162.2.

32. Ibid., 2 | 2.162.5.

33. Ibid.

34. Ibid., 2 | 2.142.1.

35. Ibid., 2 | 2.142.2.

36. Ibid., 2 | 2.148.1–6.

37. Ibid., 2 | 2.142.3.

38. Ibid., 2 | 2.61.2, 58.5.

39. Ibid., 2 | 2.58.5–9, 1 | 2.19.10.

40. Symeon the New Theologian proscribed covetousness, as indicated in *The Discourses,* trans. C. J. deCatanzaro (New York: Paulist Press, 1980), 9, "On Works of Mercy," § 4, 152–53; § 6, 155–56; and §7, 156–57. In section 4, he warned that "covetousness, like a tyrant, has intruded into life, so that its slaves and underlings have in various ways divided up that which the Master gave to be common to all. She has enclosed them by fences and made them secure by means of watchtowers, bolts, and gates. She has deprived all other men of the enjoyment of the Master's good gifts, shamelessly pretending to own them, contending that she has wronged no one." Those who covet "owe a debt of penitence to their dying day for all that they so long have kept back and deprived their brothers from using!" In section 7, he instructed Christians to distribute their goods with "cheerfulness" that consists in regarding the goods as having been "entrusted to us by God for the benefit of our fellow-servants, . . . scattering them abroad generously with joy and magnanimity, not reluctantly or under compulsion."

41. Aquinas, *Summa theologiae,* 2 | 2.118.1.

42. Aquinas, *De potentia Dei,* 5.6.

43. E.g., see Aquinas, *Summa contra Gentiles,* 3.64.

44. Aquinas, *Summa theologiae,* 1 | 2.19.10. See also *Summa contra Gentiles,* 3.24, where he explains that the more perfect something is in its capabilities to act, the more it desires and acts for the common good. Creatures that are incapable of making informed decisions tend to seek their own individual good whereas the more perfect act for the good of their species, the even more perfect act for the good of their genus, and God, the most perfect, who acts for the good of the entire created world.

45. Aquinas, *Summa contra Gentiles,* 3.24, 2.45–46.

46. See, e.g., Aquinas, *Summa theologiae,* 1.47.2, 1.76.3, 1.48.2, Supp. 91.5. Also see Aquinas, *Summa contra Gentiles,* 2.68, 3.71.

47. Aquinas, *Summa theologiae,* 2 | 2.61.1.

48. Ibid., 2 | 2.123.2–3; see, further, 123.11, 141.3, 1 | 2.61.4.

49. Ibid., 1 | 2.68.4.

50. Ibid., 2 | 2.142.3.

51. Ibid., 1 | 2.61.2.

52. U.S. Environmental Protection Agency, "Great Lakes," www.epa.gov/glnpo/factsheet.html. See also Wisconsin Sea Grant, "Gifts of the Glaciers," www.seagrant .wisc.edu/Communications/greatlakes/GlacialGift/map.html.

53. William Ashworth, *The Late, Great Lakes: An Environmental History* (New York: Alfred A. Knopf, 1986), 4; Harlan Hatcher and Erich A. Walter, *A Pictorial History of the Great Lakes* (New York: Bonanza Books, 1963).

54. Great Lakes Water Quality Board, *Cleaning Up Our Great Lakes* (Windsor: International Joint Commission for the Great Lakes, 1991), 11; and Sea Grant Institute, *The Fisheries of the Great Lakes* (Madison: Sea Grant Institute, University of Wisconsin, 1988).

55. Descriptions of the various types of algae, their beneficial roles in marine systems, and causes of their accelerated growth are available through the National Museum of Natural History, "Algae Research," Smithsonian Institution, www.nmnh.si.edu/botany/projects/algae/. See also V. L. Lougheed and R. J. Stevenson, "Exotic Marine Algae Reaches Bloom Proportions in a Coastal Lake of Lake Michigan," *Journal of Great Lakes Research* 30, no. 4 (2004)): 538–44; and, further, Michigan State University, "Exotic Marine Algae Blooms in Great Lakes," www.msu.edu/~algaelab/Ent_webpage/ent.htm.

56. Great Lakes Water Quality Board, *Cleaning Up Our Great Lakes* (Windsor: International Joint Commission for the Great Lakes, 1991), 11; Henry Regier, "Remediation and Rehabilitation of the Great Lakes," in *Perspectives in Ecosystem Management for the Great Lakes,* ed. Lynton K. Caldwell (Albany: State University of New York Press, 1988), 169–89, at 180–81.

57. Great Lakes Science Advisory Board, *Report to the International Joint Commission* (Windsor: International Joint Commission, 1991), 80–81.

58. Philip A. Meyers, "Petroleum Contaminants in the Great Lakes," in *Toxic Contaminants in the Great Lakes,* ed. Jerome O. Nriagu and Milagros S. Simmons (New York: John Wiley & Sons, 1984), 147–62; and Regier, "Remediation and Rehabilitation of the Great Lakes," 180–81.

59. Nriagu and Milagros, *Toxic Contaminants in the Great Lakes;* and Great Lakes Water Quality Board, *Cleaning Up Our Great Lakes,* 11–12.

60. Ann Misch, "Assessing Environmental Health Risks," in *State of the World, 1994: A Worldwatch Institute Report on Progress Toward a Sustainable Society,* project director Lester R. Brown, ed. Linda Starke (New York: W. W. Norton, 1994), 117–36, at 117. The Agency for Toxic Substances and Disease Registry of the U.S. Department of Health and Human Services provides updated information about health risks from pollutants and toxicants in the Great Lakes and other areas of the country, which is accessible from www.atsdr.cdc.gov/icbkmark.html#3.

61. Great Lakes Science Advisory Board, *Report to the International Joint Commission,* 20, 24–28.

62. Milagros S. Simmons, "PCB Contamination in the Great Lakes," in *Toxic Contaminants in the Great Lakes,* ed. Nriagu and Simmons, 287–310; and Great Lakes Science Advisory Board, *Report to the International Joint Commission,* 19–20.

63. Greta G. Fein, Joseph L. Jacobson, Sandra W. Jacobson, Pamela M. Schwartz, and Jeffrey K. Dowler, "Prenatal Exposure to Polychlorinated Biphenyls: Effects on Birth Size and Gestational Age," *Journal of Pediatrics* 105 (1984): 315–20; Joseph L. Jacobson, Sandra W. Jacobson, and H. E. B. Humphrey, "Effects of Exposure to PCBs and Related Compounds in Growth and Activity in Children," *Neurotoxicology and Teratology* 12 (1990): 319–26; and Joseph L. Jacobson, Sandra W. Jacobson, and H. E. B. Humphrey, "Effects of *In Utero* Exposure to Polychlorinated Biphenyls and Related Contaminants on Cognitive Functioning in Young Children," *Journal of Pediatrics* 116 (1990): 38–45.

64. Pascale Krumm, "PCBs: Measuring the Danger," *Journal of Environmental Health* 64, no. 10 (June 2002): 31, 34; William C. Sonzogni and Wayland R. Swain, "Perspectives on Human Health Concerns from Great Lakes Contaminants," in *Toxic Contaminants in the Great Lakes,* ed. Nriagu and Simmons, 1–30; and Great Lakes Science Advisory Board, *Report to the International Joint Commission,* 39–40. See the compilation of many studies from 1996 to 2005 regarding health effects on fish eaters by

Daniel Hryhorczuk, MD, MPH, "Anthropogenic Chemicals in the Great Lakes Basin: Human Health Effects," U.S. Environmental Protection Agency, www.epa.gov/glnpo/solec/solec_2006/.

65. Ann Misch, "Assessing Environmental Health Risks," in *State of the World, 1994: A Worldwatch Institute Report on Progress Toward a Sustainable Society,* ed. Linda Starke (New York: W. W. Norton, 1994), 117–36, at 117, 133; Edward Calabrese, *Multiple Chemical Interactions* (Chelsea, MI: Lewis Publishers, 1991).

66. Krumm, "PCB's: Measuring the Danger"; Misch, "Assessing Environmental Health Risks," 127; Jacobson, Jacobson, and Humphrey, "Effects of Exposure to PCBs"; National Research Council, *Pesticides in the Diets of Infants and Children* (Washington, DC: National Academies Press, 1993).

67. William S. Fyfe, "Our Planet Observed: The Assault by *Homo Sapiens,*" in *Planet under Stress: The Challenge of Global Change,* ed. Constance Mungall and Digby J. McLaren, Royal Society of Canada (Toronto: Oxford University Press, 1990), 3–27, at 23; and Regier, "Remediation and Rehabilitation of the Great Lakes," 180–81.

68. See Peter Weber, "Safeguarding the Oceans," in *State of the World, 1994,* 41–60, at 50; and National Research Council, *Pesticides in the Diets of Infants and Children,* 19–20. Also see Gordon A. McKay and Henry Hengeveld, "The Changing Atmosphere," in *Planet under Stress,* ed. Mungall and McLaren, 46–79, at 57–58.

69. Intergovernmental Panel on Climate Change, *Climate Change 2007: Impacts, Adaptation, and Vulnerability—Contribution of Working Group II to the Fourth Assessment Report of the Intergovernmental Panel on Climate Change,* ed. M. M. Parry, O. F. Canziani, J. P. Palutikof, P. J. van der Linden, and C. E. Hanson (Cambridge: Cambridge University Press, 2007).

70. Lynn White Jr., "The Historical Roots of Our Ecologic Crisis," *Science* 155 (March 10, 1967): 1203–7, at 1203–4.

71. United States and Canada, "Great Lakes Water Quality Agreement," Ottawa, November 22, 1978.

72. Only three Areas of Concern have been remediated and delisted, while two others are in the "recovering" stage. See International Joint Commission, *Status of Restoration Activities in Great Lakes Areas of Concern: A Special Report* (Ottawa and Washington: International Joint Commission, 2003), 6; also at www.ijc.org/php/publications/pdf/ID1500.pdf. See, further, the maps and other graphics made available online by the Great Lakes Information Network, www.great-lakes.net/infocenter/restoration.html.

73. International Joint Commission for the Great Lakes, *Report on Spills in the Great Lakes Basin with a Special Focus on the St. Clair–Detroit River Corridor* (Ottawa and Washington: International Joint Commission, 2006), 1. The report indicates that the number of polluting spills of chemicals, oils and other hydrocarbons, and wastes to the Great Lakes and the Saint Lawrence River had been on the decline since the mid-1990s, but spills from a chemical plant in Canada and from a sewage treatment facility in the United States occurred in 2003, when a massive power outage crippled the northeastern part of North America for several days. Another spill occurred in February 2004 when a leak in a heat exchanger released two chemicals (methyl ethyl ketone and methyl isobutyl ketone) into the Saint Clair River, and several other spills into that river were reported, all of which caused increasing public alarm. A "spill" is defined at 2 as accidental or illicit discharge of substances (i.e., oils and hydrocarbons, chemicals, and wastes) that cause or may cause harm to the

environment or to humans. The International Joint Commission, *12th Biennial Report on the Great Lakes Water Quality* (Ottawa and Washington: International Joint Commission, 2004), expressed concern about the apparent increase in major spills into the channel that connects Lake Huron to Lake Erie and committed to explore the issue further.

74. International Joint Commission, *Status of Restoration Activities in Great Lakes Areas of Concern,* 6. Emerging issues are discussed by International Joint Commission for the Great Lakes, *Expert Consultation on Emerging Issues of the Great Lakes in the 21st Century,* ed. Peter Boyer, Allan Jones, and Deborah Swackhamer, Papers Submitted to Great Lakes Science Advisory Board of International Joint Commission at Wingspread, Racine, WI, February 5–7, 2003 (Ottawa and Washington: International Joint Commission, 2006). See also International Joint Commission, *Report on Spills in the Great Lakes Basin with a Special Focus on the St. Clair–Detroit River Corridor.*

75. Great Lakes Water Quality Board, *Report on Great Lakes Water Quality* (Windsor: International Joint Commission for the Great Lakes, 1987); Great Lakes Water Quality Board, *Report on Great Lakes Water Quality* (Windsor: International Joint Commission, 1989); Douglas McTavish, "Public Comments Sought on Strategy to Virtually Eliminate Persistent Toxic Substances," *Focus* 18 (1993): 1–2.

76. International Joint Commission, *Fifth Biennial Report under the Great Lakes Water Quality Agreement of 1978 to the Governments of the United States and Canada and the State and Provincial Governments of the Great Lakes Basin,* 2 vols. (Washington and Ottawa: International Joint Commission, 1990), 3.

77. Richard W. Hatch, Stephen J. Nepszy, Kenneth M. Muth, and Carl T. Baker, "Dynamics of the Recovery of the Western Lake Erie Walleye (*Stizostedion Vitreum Vitreum*) Stock," *Canadian Journal of Fishery Aquatic Science* 44 (1984): 15–22.

78. Great Lakes Science Advisory Board, *Report to the International Joint Commission* (Windsor: International Joint Commission, 1991), 43.

79. Virtual Elimination Task Force, *Persistent Toxic Substances: Virtually Eliminating Inputs to the Great Lakes* (Windsor: International Joint Commission, 1991), 21.

80. Ibid.

81. Ibid. See, further, International Joint Commission, *Fifth Biennial Report,* 7–10.

82. International Joint Commission, *Fifth Biennial Report,* 6. See also International Joint Commission, *12th Biennial Report,* esp. chap. 2 on biological integrity and chap. 3 on the chemical integrity of the Great Lakes; www.ijc.org/php/publications/html/12br/english/report/.

83. International Joint Commission, *Advice to Governments on Their Review of the Great Lakes Water Quality Agreement: A Special Report to the Governments of Canada and the United States* (Ottawa and Washington: International Joint Commission, 2006), 1.

84. Intergovernmental Panel on Climate Change, *Climate Change 2007: The Physical Science Basis* (Cambridge: Cambridge University Press, 2007). According to the promotional materials, this report is written by the world's leading experts to provide the "most comprehensive and balanced assessment of climate change available" for researchers, students, and policymakers and serve as "the standard reference works for policy decisions for government and industry worldwide." See "Climate Change 2007," Intergovernmental Panel on Climate Change, available at www.ipcc.ch/.

85. Intergovernmental Panel on Climate Change, "The Regional Impacts of Climate Change," in *IPCC Special Report on The Regional Impacts of Climate Change,* www.grida.no/climate/ipcc/regional/196.htm.

86. World Health Organization, World Meteorological Organization, and the United National Environment Program, *Climate Change and Human Health: Risks and Responses,* www.who.int/globalchange/climate/en/ccSCREEN.pdf.

87. See, e.g., Working Group III Technical Support Unit, "Workshop on New Emission Scenarios, 29 June–1 July 2005, Laxenburg, Austria," Intergovernmental Panel on Climate Change, Bilthoven, The Netherlands, August 2005.

88. See, e.g., James P. Bruce, *From Climate to Weather: Impacts on Society and Economy, Natural Disasters Roundtable, Washington, DC, 28 June 28 2002* (Washington, DC: National Academies Press, 2003), available at www.nap.edu. Bruce is realistic about modeling efforts to date, finding it "not very reliable" in particular parts of the world (e.g., Africa). One key issue with which scientists are struggling is how global warming and seasonal and also intraseasonal variations are connected to one another. Scientific sources used to prepare "The Regional Impacts of Climate Change," prepared by Intergovernmental Panel on Climate Change, www.grida.no/climate/ipcc/regional/324.htm.

89. Principles to apply to ecological problems as addressed by the faithful individually and collectively as members of their religious communities: (1) Act prudently when addressing the problem by following the steps for prudent decision making stipulated by Aquinas—(i) seeking counsel for the best means through which action can be taken to achieve a purpose, (ii) deciding the best route of action when having foresight about the future outcome, considering all possible circumstances/circumspection, and being cautious to make sure that good is achieved and evil avoided, and (iii) employing the activity chosen while being open to corrections as further information becomes available; (2) act justly through general, distributive, and universal justice toward humans, other species and systems; (3) act moderately by taking what is needed to sustain human life, other biota, and the systems of which they are constituents and by being guided by appropriate subvirtues (insensibility, intemperance, gluttony, and cowardice); and (4) be courageously steadfast in acting prudently, justly, and moderately to address the problem.

90. Ad Leys provides an overview of the historical development of the principle of subsidiarity; Ad Leys, *Ecclesiological Impacts of the Principle of Subsidiarity* (Kampen: Kok, 1995), part 1. J. Verstraeten explores the principle of subsidiarity in relation to the notion of solidarity; J. Verstraeten, "Solidarity and Subsidiarity," in *Principles of Catholic Social Teaching,* ed. David. A. Boileau (Milwaukee: Marquette University Press, 1998), 133–48. Individuals should be cognizant of the need to work with one another to bring about collective virtuous activity at appropriate levels of communities to which they belong, from family, neighborhood, municipality, county, state, federal, and international agencies, and not remand to the next collective level what can be accomplished on a more local level in keeping with the principle of subsidiarity.

91. Great Lakes Areas of Concern are severely degraded geographic areas within the Great Lakes Basin. They are defined by the U.S.-Canada Great Lakes Water Quality Agreement (Annex 2 of the 1987 Protocol) as "geographic areas that fail to meet the general or specific objectives of the agreement where such failure has caused or is likely to cause impairment of beneficial use of the area's ability to support aquatic life."

92. Great Lakes National Program Office, "Great Lakes Areas of Concern," U.S. Environmental Protection Agency, www.epa.gov/glnpo/aoc/.

93. See chapter 3 on the sacramentality of creation.
94. The International Joint Commission is an independent binational organization established by the Boundary Waters Treaty of 1909 between Canada and the United States. The commission's purpose is to help prevent and resolve disputes relating to the use and quality of boundary waters and to advise the two countries on related issues. Background information is available at www.ijc.org/en/home/main_accueil.htm.
95. The Great Lakes Commission is a binational agency that promotes the orderly, integrated, and comprehensive development, use, and conservation of the water and related natural resources of the Great Lakes Basin and Saint Lawrence River. Its members include the eight Great Lakes states with associate member status for the Canadian provinces of Ontario and Quebec. Each jurisdiction appoints a delegation of three to five members comprised of senior agency officials, legislators and/or appointees of the governor or premier. For more information, go to www.glc.org/.
96. Alliance for the Great Lakes, www.lakemichigan.org/.
97. Great Lakes United, www.glu.org/english/index.html.
98. Aquinas, *Summa theologiae*, 1|2.57.4–6; see also 1|2.58.4, 2|2.47.7.

9
LOVING EARTH

Although patristic and medieval theologians reflected on God's love for the world, few wrote about the love that humans should have for God's creation. Among those who did were Augustine, John Chrysostom, Boethius, Dionysius the Aeropagite, John Scotus Eriugena, Thomas Aquinas, and Julian of Norwich. Aquinas especially reflected on God's love for creation and on ways in which humans can also love the world that God created and sustains in existence.

Explored in the first section of this chapter are the theologians' reflections on God's love for all creatures and God's superior love for the entirety of creation. The second section focuses on types of human love for God's creation—other humans, other creatures, and natural phenomena. Closing the chapter is a digression on how the faithful can love more than human creatures when informed by the current scientific understanding of the world.

God's Love for Creation

That God loves all creatures surfaces explicitly in the Book of Wisdom. God's love can best be understood within the context of the sage's recounting for Jews in Alexandria God's love, powerful care, and generous steadfastness throughout the history of their ancestors' covenant with God. According to Wisdom 11:24–25, God loves all creatures God has made, and God lovingly sustains them in existence. This loving care warrants the faithful to worship the one and only God.

Patristic theologians appropriated and elaborated upon biblical notions about God's providential care as indications of God's love. For example, when delivering a homily on the Genesis 1 story of creation, John Chrysostom (347–407) pointed to God's care for all creatures by ordering them to one another to constitute an internally sustainable universe. Furthermore, God entrusts the control of creation to humankind out of God's loving-kindness, a kindness that is shown by providing food for both tame and wild beasts to prevent human distress when having to nourish them.[1]

As the Christian philosopher Roland Teske concludes from his impressive study of works by Augustine of Hippo (354–430), God was motivated by love to create all things out of nothing, God created freely, not out of necessity; God's love for creation is totally gratuitous.[2] Furthermore, Augustine explained that God governs the world in a loving way that allows creatures to function according to their innate powers,[3] while "brooding" over the totality of creation in a nurturing way with the warmth of the Holy Spirit—like a mother bird resting on her nest.[4]

The Roman philosopher Boethius (ca. 480–525) also attributed to God's love God's care of all creatures through an order of relationships.[5] In his renowned *Consolation of Philosophy,* most likely written from his jail cell when awaiting judgment on his political views, Boethius praised God's providence as evident throughout the orderly universe—in the sun, the oceans, the times of day, the primary elements, and the seasons. God created rules to govern this order of things in relation to one another, the philosopher contended, and God rules them from "on High" with "Lordly might" as "their law and judge" who acts through a "powerfull love" that is "common unto all."[6]

Early in the sixth century, the Christian Neoplatonist Dionysius the Areopagite (Pseudo-Dionysius) reflected on the loving care that God has for everything created. He wrote that God is beguiled by the goodness of creatures. God loves and yearns for them. God is enticed away from the divine dwelling place to "abide with all things," while simultaneously remaining within the divine self through a "supernatural and ecstatic capacity."[7] A strong sense of God's immanence within the world persists that does not diminish Pseudo-Dionysius's belief in God's transcendence of the world. The panentheism of Pseudo-Dionysius further resounds in his thinking about God's unifying and commingling power, a power that moves the internal self-sustainability of the world's diverse constituents and lifts them to God's self as the Yearner, Lover, Good, and Beautiful One.[8]

John Scotus Eriugena (810–ca. 877) built upon Pseudo-Dionysius's thinking about the unifying action of God's love. Also exhibiting a panentheistic perspective of God in relation to the world, Eriugena defined God's love as "a bond and chain by which the totality of all things is bound together in ineffable friendship and indissoluble unity."[9] God's love is both immanent in creatures and transcendent of them. God's love is immanent by permeating them with divine love and serving as "the end and quiet resting place of the natural motion of all things that are in motion." God's love is also transcendent—beyond all creation, where no motion of any creature extends.[10] Creatures are attracted to God according to their God-given natures, Eriugena contended, likening the God–creature attraction to a magnet that attracts iron.[11] When unifying all creatures, God brings about an "inseparable bond of love and desire to those who are receptive" without obliterating their identities.[12] They remain uniquely themselves according to their natures. In his thinking about God's immanence and transcendence, Eriu-gena found considerable agreement with Pseudo-Dionysius[13] and with Maximus the Confessor.[14]

Aquinas (ca. 1224/25–74) addressed God's love for all creation systematically from his medieval understanding of the world. For Aquinas, God's love is twofold: (1) The love of desire—*amor/amare;* and (2) the love of friendship—*amicitiae/ caritas.* With a loving desire, God loves all types of creatures and the entire cre-ated universe.[15] God's love for them is a creative love that is the first movement of God's will, through which God wills good to others, the basic good of which is existence,[16] and God's willing this and other goods to them binds them to God,[17] who is goodness itself.[18] As Gilson stressed, Aquinas understood God's love as "the unfathomable source of all causality."[19] God also cares equally for all created entities by loving them with one simple act of the will and by admin-istering them with the same wisdom and goodness.[20]

However, while loving and caring equally for all creatures by creating and sus-taining them, Aquinas explained, God also wills a greater good to some more than to others.[21] He described their different levels of goodness in Aristotelian terms as primary elements (air, water, fire, and earth), mixed bodies, ascending order of elements, minerals, plants, irrational animals, and humans[22] and other times according to their operations or capacities for acting as elements, mixed bodies, plants, irrational animals, and rational creatures.[23] As indicated in chap-ter 1, on the goodness of creation, these diverse creatures constitute grades of goodness on a hierarchical scale, with humans as the apex of corporeal creatures. Humans have this status, according to Aquinas, because of their intellectual ca-pability to transcend bodily conditions,[24] act voluntarily through reason and will rather than by instinct,[25] know that ultimate purpose is to be with God forever, and aim for that end throughout temporal life by using the abilities with which humans have been endowed by God.[26]

On occasion, Aquinas characterized creatures metaphorically as constituting a ladder of forms,[27] with each rung of the ladder representing a grade of good-ness that is higher, more perfect, or more complete than the lower rung due to their natures and capacities to act accordingly. On this "ladder," created and sus-tained by God, creatures are ordered in relation to one another for their suste-nance, while all creatures are ordered in relation to humans for their sustenance during their temporal lives.[28] Yet despite their various grades of goodness, God loves all creatures with the love of desire, does not love one type of creature more than another type with the love of desire, and, of all corporeality, loves best the entirety of the universe in which all entities are ordered in relation to one an-other as God intended when creating them.[29]

In addition to loving humans with the love of desire, God also loves them with a second kind of love—the love of friendship. This kind of love is reserved per se for those who are capable of transcending their corporeal natures and enjoy-ing eternal happiness with God.[30] Humans also receive a special kind of care from God in the form of grace, through which they can be aided in ordering their wills and actions toward eternal happiness with God.[31] Moreover, God so loved and cared about humans that God assumed human nature as Jesus Christ to help humans remedy their tendencies to stray from God.[32]

Though reserving God's love of friendship for humans who can enjoy eternal life with God, Aquinas extends the love of friendship *indirectly* to other creatures. They are loved by God with the love of friendship as entities that humans can use to sustain themselves during their temporal lives.[33] Clearly, this kind of love is instrumental and consistent with the order of instrumentality that persists throughout Aquinas's thinking.[34]

Julian of Norwich (1342–ca. 1416) meditated on God's love for all creatures. She gazed at something that she described as "no bigger than a hazelnut" lying in the palm of her hand and wondered how it could last. "It lasts and always will," she concluded, "because God loves it" and all creatures that exist. She envisioned three properties in the little creature in her hand: God made it, God loves it, and God preserves it. For Julian, "God is the Creator and protector and the lover" of all created things.[35]

Human Love for God's Creation

Although celebrating God's love for the entirety of creation, some pointing to different kinds of love according to the natures of creatures, patristic and medieval theologians also reflected on human love. Their reflections centered primarily on the biblically based commandment to love one's neighbor and the demonstration of that love through the life, dying, and resurrection of Jesus Christ. Yet some theologians also considered human love for other creatures and even for natural phenomena. Paralleling their reflections on God's love, they specified different kinds of love that humans can have for other natural entities.

Human Love for One's Human Neighbor

The Old and New testaments are replete with exhortations to love one's neighbor out of love for God. For example, in Leviticus 19:18, when God is depicted as continuing to tell Moses what to say to the Israelites, God proscribed revenge and grudges against members of one's nation. God commanded the Israelites to love God and love other Israelites as they love themselves. In Matthew 5:43, Jesus extends love of neighbor to include one's enemies and exhorts his listeners to pray for those who persecute them. In Mark 12:30–31, Jesus identifies love of God and love of neighbor as the first- and second-greatest commandments. Matthew 22:38–39 embellishes the greatest commandment to read that you should love God with all your heart, soul, and mind, whereas the second-greatest commandment is to love your neighbor as yourself. When asked by a scholar of the law what he should do to inherit eternal life, as recorded in Luke 10:27–28, Jesus is depicted as asking the scholar how he reads the law; the scholar repeats the two love commandments, and Jesus tells him that he has answered correctly and will live if he follows these commandments. For Saint Paul, in Romans 13:9–10, all commandments are summed up in the command to love one's neighbor as oneself. Because love does no evil to one's neighbor, love fulfills the law.[36]

Patristic and medieval theologians followed the scriptures by urging their listeners and readers to love their neighbors. Especially significant are Aquinas's reflections on the love of friendship that humans are capable of extending to one another. Humans can love one another with the love of friendship because they can return love to their neighbor, communicate with them on their experiences of life, wish that their neighbor love God and live in ways that aim toward eternal happiness with God, and share in the intellectual and beatific life of God.[37] When loving one's neighbor with the love of friendship, God is loved simultaneously. This is because one's neighbors are loved with the wish that they order their lives toward eternal happiness with God, who is their common good and goal.[38] From this perspective, love of one's neighbor is the same act whereby God is loved.[39]

Human Love for Other Creatures and Natural Phenomena

Although patristic and medieval theologians exhorted their followers to love their human neighbors, some encouraged them to also love the other creatures and natural phenomena that God created. For example, Augustine attempted an exhaustive list of God's creation that humans should love:

> Certainly you love only the good, because the earth is good by the height of its mountains, the moderate elevation of its hills, and the evenness of its fields; and good is the farm that is pleasant and fertile; and good is the house that is arranged throughout in symmetrical proportions and is spacious and bright; and good are the animals, animate bodies; and good is the mild and salubrious air; and good is the food that is pleasant and conducive to health; and good is health without pains and weariness; and good is the countenance of man with regular features, a cheerful expression, and a glowing color; and good is the soul of a friend with the sweetness of concord and the fidelity of love; and good is the just man; and good are riches because they readily assist us; and good is the heaven with its own sun, moon, and stars; and good are the angels by their holy obedience; and good is the lecture that graciously instructs and suitably admonishes the listener; and good is the poem with its measured rhythm and the seriousness of its thoughts.[40]

According to Aquinas, the goodness of creatures calls forth the love of desire that humans should have for them. Love for their goodness should direct human actions toward preserving the good that creatures have (their existence and their natures) and receiving the good that they do not have (whatever they need to sustain their existence). The love of desire that humans are supposed to have for other creatures differs considerably from the love of desire that only God could have for them as their creator and sustainer, Aquinas insisted. Following Augustine, Aquinas explained that God freely created out of love and infused goodness into all things created.[41] Humans do not have this kind of creative ability.

Whereas humans can and should demonstrate their love of desire toward other creatures, humans cannot love them for themselves with the love of friendship.

This is because nonhuman creatures are incapable of freely exercising their natures, returning love to others, regulating their lives and communicating to others
through the use of reason, and transcending their corporeal natures to enjoy eternal happiness with God.[42]

Loving Other Creatures Indirectly with the Love of Friendship

Nevertheless, according to Aquinas, there are two ways in which humans can love
nonhuman creatures indirectly with the love of friendship: They can be loved as
good things humans wish to preserve for God's honor and glory, and they can
be loved in order to be used to sustain themselves in temporal life as they seek
eternal happiness with God.[43] When loving nonhuman entities as good things
desired for one's neighbor in temporal life, they are not loved intrinsically for
themselves. Instead, they are loved instrumentally for their use to other humans
when ordering their lives to God.[44] As explained in depth in chapter 7 of this volume, Aquinas and other theologians clearly restricted the human use of other
creatures to the necessities of life.

Loving other creatures so they are preserved for God's honor and glory reflects the faith perspective of Aquinas and other theologians of his time that
creatures manifest God's character, particularly God's goodness, wisdom, and
power.[45] Loving nonhuman creatures with the love of friendship accords well
with this sacramentality of creation concept, as explored in chapter 3. Humans
can love other creatures with the highest kind of love so they can continue to
give honor and glory to God.

Aquinas also taught that the entire universe can be loved with the love of
friendship. He reasoned to this position when reflecting on the order of creatures
in relation to one another that culminates in humans.[46] Because they can achieve
eternal life with God, humans can love with the love of friendship the orderly
universe that is loved by God.[47] Aquinas's thinking is consistent with the order
of instrumentality that permeates his understanding of how God designed the
world to function, as explained in chapters 1 and 5.[48]

Finally, the love of friendship motivates the human to act morally. As the theological virtue that God infuses in rational creatures, the love of friendship disposes them to acquire moral virtues that incline them toward temporal goods
in prudent, just, temperate, and courageous ways. Living in these virtuous ways
in relation to temporal good orients humans toward their ultimate end in God.[49]

Blanchette concludes from Aquinas's reflections that "for the medieval theologian . . . to speak of something as lovable out of charity was to raise it to the highest level of goodness and esteem."[50] One dimension of Aquinas's thinking about
human love *ex caritate* for other-than-human creatures does not appear to raise
them to the highest level of goodness and esteem, whereas the other dimension
does. Human love for other-than-human creatures so they can be used to sustain
the bodily lives of other humans qualifies as instrumental love, a love through
which other creatures are not valued intrinsically in themselves for themselves.
Thus instrumental love does not attribute the highest kind of value to any entity.

However, to love other creatures *ex caritate* as good things that should be preserved for God's honor and glory places the highest possible value on them. As themselves and in themselves, they give glory and honor to God. They should be loved *ex caritate* by preserving them for this purpose. From this perspective, love *ex caritate* has significance for addressing ecological problems today.

Acting Lovingly in an Age of Ecological Degradation

What basic behavior would be demonstrated by those who ascribe to these various teachings in which the faithful are exhorted to love God's creation?[51] Informed by our current scientific understanding of the world, the faithful will love other species and abiota by striving to image God's love, to give glory and honor to God, and to show love for one's neighbor now and in the future.

Imaging God's Love for the World

Those who believe that God loves the world will love Earth with its various species, ecosystems, and the biosphere as a way of striving to image God's love for them. Because God loves them with the love of desire, having willed the possibility of their existence, empowering their emergence through the cosmological-biological process, and sustaining their ability to function within that process, the faithful will strive to image God's love by avoiding actions that disrupt their self-development and functioning. The faithful will strive to image God's love by ensuring that human and other species are not thwarted from obtaining the sustenance they need to flourish, from having the space in which to flourish, and from relating to others for their mutual well-being as a community of Earth.

Aware of the evolutionary process from which *Homo sapiens* emerged with other species as they interacted in their developing abiotic environment, the dependence humans have on other species and abiota for human life and well-being, and the ability of other species and systems to function without humans, the faithful will focus on *managing themselves,* not on managing other species and systems. The faithful will curtail their own actions to avoid degrading and destroying other species and systems within which humans function. The faithful will also collaborate with others to discern and avoid actions that disrupt the functioning of ecological systems and the biosphere.

Loving Creation for God's Honor and Glory

The faithful will also preserve other species and biological systems for God's honor and glory. They will ensure that the manifestations of God's loving, caring, generous giving, empowering, and freedom-giving attributes through biota and abiota are not thwarted. They will ensure that the best manifestation of God's character—the well functioning of the orderly universe—is not dulled by causing biological systems to malfunction. They will value other species and systems for their intrinsic goodness, whereby they give glory and honor to God by being themselves according to their natures in relation to the other entities that constitute Earth.

Showing Love for One's Neighbor

Out of love for one's neighbor, the faithful will ensure that the manifestations of God's loving, caring, generous giving, empowering, and freedom-giving attributes that are discernible when studying biota and abiota are not thwarted by human actions. The faithful will recognize that other species and biological systems give glory to God by being themselves, and the faithful will work to preserve these capacities so other humans now and in the future may also have the opportunity to recognize them.

Also out of love for one's neighbor, the faithful will limit their use of the goods of Earth to the necessities of life, with the aim of ensuring that their families, their neighbors, and future generations will have what they need to sustain their lives. The faithful will ensure that their neighbors have unpolluted air to breathe, water to drink, and land on which to live now and in the future. The faithful will show their love by conserving natural goods at the local level, seeking protection for them when necessary at higher levels of decision making, and implementing sound decisions that ensure the availability of the necessities of life for other human neighbors.

Infused by God with the theological virtue of love and motivated by love *ex caritate,* faithful people will be aided by God's grace to live morally in relation to other species and biological systems. They will live prudently by knowing about them, what they need to flourish, what can be done to ameliorate their degradation, and actions that should be avoided to prevent additional degradation or total destruction. The faithful will live moderately by limiting their encounters with sensitive and endangered biological systems so others can have opportunities to enjoy them. They will live justly by respecting the needs of other species and systems for unencumbered space in which to flourish and nondegrading ways in which people who live in these areas can interact with them. And the faithful will live courageously by standing firm for measures that protect species and systems out of love for them as needed by their neighbors in this life.

Conclusion

The patristic-medieval theme of loving creation holds promise for addressing ecological concerns. Connections are evident between this theme and others in the Catholic tradition, especially the goodness, functional unity, and sacramentality of creation as well as the restrained and grateful use of God's creation. Yet the loving creation theme tends to raise to new heights the quest for thinking about and acting toward other humans, other species, ecosystems, and the biosphere. To love them is an intimate act that links them intricately to love of God and love of one's neighbor. As Rahner explained centuries after Aquinas, these two loves cannot be separated because they are one and the same act of human willing that ends ultimately in eternal happiness with God.[52] Enfolding love for God's creation into the God–neighbor relationship elevates the physical world's status into a triad of love, within which one love cannot be separated from other loves. Attention must be paid to human loving of God's creation as a dimension of one's salvation.[53]

The theological virtue of love has practical implications for how humans function. Love will motivate the faithful to develop and practice the moral virtues. Love will motivate the faithful to live prudently by knowing about the species and biological systems in which they function and acting to remediate and protect them from further degradation. Love will motivate the faithful to live moderately by limiting their intake of Earth's goods and their interactions with fragile biological systems so they can sustain themselves. Love will motivate the faithful to live justly by respecting the needs of indigenous peoples to sustain themselves within the biological systems in which they function. And love will motivate the faithful to courageously stand firm on measures that remediate and protect these systems.

Another way in which to love Earth with its various species, abiota, and systems is to consider them as "neighbors." Going beyond the traditional understanding of neighbor, the faithful will love Earth and its constituents for themselves, for the usefulness of constituents to one another within their dynamic communities, and for their capacity to manifest God for God's honor and glory. This love is indeed expansive and altruistic. This is a love that is greatly needed during our age of ecological degradation.[54]

One exercise that can demonstrate inclusive and altruistic love is to reconfigure 1 Corinthians 13:4–8 to refer to other species and systems of Earth. How can we think of love as patient, kind, not jealous, not pompous, not inflated, not rude; as rejoicing in the truth; and as believing, enduring, and hoping all things? How can we think of human love for Earth, its species, its systems, and its biosphere as never failing and always persisting?

Notes

1. Saint John Chrysostom, *Homilies on Genesis 1–17, Volume 74, Fathers of the Church,* trans. Robert C. Hill (Washington, DC: Catholic University of America Press, 1986), homily 10.11, 135–36.

2. Roland J. Teske, "The Motive for Creation According to Saint Augustine," *The Modern Schoolman* 65 (May 1988): 245 n53, at 53.

3. Saint Augustine, *Concerning the City of God Against the Pagans,* trans. John O'Meara (London: Penguin Books, 1972), 7.30, 292.

4. Augustine, *The Literal Meaning of Genesis,* trans. John Hammond Taylor (New York: Newman Press, 1982), 1.18.36, 41.

5. Anicius Manlius Severinus Boethius, *The Consolation of Philosophy,* trans. William Anderson (Carbondale: Southern Illinois University Press, 1963).

6. Ibid., 4.6, 100–2.

7. Pseudo-Dionysius, *The Divine Names* in *The Complete Works,* trans. Colm Luibheid; notes and trans. collab. Paul Rorem; intro. Jaroslav Pelikan, Jean LeClerq, and Karlfried Froehlich (New York: Paulist Press, 1987), 4.13–15, 82–83.

8. Ibid. 4.17, 84.

9. John Scotus Eriugena, *Periphyseon/Division of Nature,* trans. I. P. Sheldon-Williams; rev. John J. O'Meara (Washington, DC: Dumbarton Oaks, 1987), 1.519B, 117. Eruigena's discussion spans 1.518c-522d, 116–21.

10. Ibid., 1.519b, 117.

11. Ibid., 1.520b-c, 118–19.

12. Ibid., 1.520c, 119.

13. Ibid., 1.519c, 117.

14. Ibid., 1.520c, p. 119.

15. Thomas Aquinas, *Summa theologiae,* 1.20.4 ad 1.

16. Ibid., 1.20.2; see also 1.5.3, 6.3, 65.2.

17. Aquinas, *Summa theologiae,* 1.20.1 ad 3.

18. Ibid., 1.44.4, 47.1. See also Aquinas, *Summa contra Gentiles,* 4.20; Aquinas, *Compendium theologiae,* 73; and Aquinas, *De Potentia Dei,* 3.16—where Aquinas taught that God created to communicate divine goodness. See Aquinas, *Compendium theologiae,* 102; Aquinas, *Summa contra Gentiles,* 1.38; and Aquinas, *Summa theologiae,* 1.6—where Aquinas taught that God's goodness is the foundation for the goodness of all created things. And see Aquinas, *Compendium theologiae,* 100, where Aquinas taught that all good is a certain imitation of the supreme good that is God.

19. Etienne Gilson, *The Christian Philosophy of St. Thomas Aquinas,* trans. L. K. Shook (New York: Random House, 1956; reprint, New York: Octagon, 1983), 183. See also Josef Pieper, "Of the Goodness of the World," *Orate Fratres* 25 (September): 433–37; at 434.

20. Aquinas, *Summa theologiae,* 1.20.3.

21. Ibid.

22. Ibid., 1.47.2.

23. Aquinas, *Summa contra Gentiles,* 2.68; see also 3.71. See, further, Aquinas, *Summa theologiae,* 1.48.2, 76.3.

24. Aquinas, *Summa theologiae,* 2 | 2.2.3. See also Aquinas, *Compendium theologiae,* 79.

25. Aquinas, *Summa theologiae,* 1.78.4; also see 1 | 2.1.1. See, further, Aquinas, *Summa contra Gentiles,* 2.23.

26. Aquinas, *Summa theologiae,* 1.22.2, 65.2. See, further, *Summa contra Gentiles,* 3.3, 111; and Aquinas, *De veritate,* 5.3.2.

27. Aquinas, *Summa contra Gentiles,* 2.68.

28. Aquinas, *Summa theologiae,* 1.20.2.

29. Aquinas, *De caritate,* 7 ad 5.

30. Aquinas, *Summa theologiae,* 1.20.3.

31. Ibid., 1.20.4; see also 1.49.3 ad 5, where Aquinas explained that evil is a majority occurrence among humans because they do not seek good according to reason as intended by God but, rather, seek good through their senses.

32. Aquinas, *Summa theologiae,* 1.20.4 ad 2. Aquinas identified a disordered will as a culpable evil for which humans are responsible.

33. Ibid., 2 | 2.25.3. Of course, Aquinas's thinking about God's loving other-than-human creatures for human use is an instrumental and anthropocentric love, a love that as-

sumes restrictions placed on human use of other creatures for the purpose of sustaining bodily life while aiming for eternal life with God.

34. Aquinas, *Summa theologiae,* 1.47.2. I explore his order of instrumentality in chapter 1, on the goodness of creation.

35. Julian of Norwich, *Showings,* trans. Edmund Colledge and James Walsh (New York: Paulist Press, 1978), 184.

36. See, further, Gal 5:14 and James 2:8.

37. Aquinas, *Summa theologiae,* 1.20.2 ad 3.

38. Ibid., 2 | 2.25.1 ad 2. Aquinas continued in his reply to objection 3 that love of neighbor must not end in one's neighbor; a neighbor is loved for God's sake. Centuries later, the theologian Karl Rahner insisted that humans can only love God by loving their neighbors. Love of neighbor is an act of love of God, even if one's love of neighbor is not explicitly considered to be love of God. See Karl Rahner, "Reflections on the Unity of the Love of Neighbour and the Love of God," *Theological Investigations, Volume 6, Concerning Vatican Council II,* trans. Karl-H. Kruger and Boniface Kruger (New York: Crossroad, 1982), 231–49, at 236–37.

39. Aquinas, *Summa theologiae,* 2 | 2.25.1.

40. Augustine, *The Trinity,* 8.3.4, 247.

41. Aquinas, *Summa theologiae,* 1.20.2.

42. Ibid., 2 | 2.25.3. Also see Aquinas, *De caritate,* 7 ad 8.

43. Aquinas, *Summa theologiae,* 2 | 2.25.2–3; also see 83.7.

44. Aquinas, *De caritate,* 4, 7.

45. Aquinas, *Summa theologiae,* 2 | 2.25.3. See also Aquinas, *De caritate,* 7.

46. Aquinas, *De caritate,* 7.

47. Ibid.

48. Aquinas, *Summa theologiae,* 2 | 2.25.3.

49. Ibid., 1 | 2.65.2.

50. Oliva Blanchette, *The Perfection of the Universe According to Aquinas: A Teleological Cosmology* (University Park: Pennsylvania State University Press, 1992), 317.

51. Among the principles that can be particularized when addressing ecological problems are the following: (1) Love the subject because God loves them and desires their existence for themselves and their relationships to others. (2) Love the subject by using it with restraint for the necessities of life out of love for one's human neighbors so they can meet their needs for sustenance and well-being in temporal life while questing eternal life with God. (3) Love the subject with restraint out of altruistic love for neighbors near and far, now and into the future who need the subject for their health and well-being. (4) Love the subject by preserving it so it can continue to give honor and glory to God. And (5) applying 1 Cor 13 to the subject in ways that are pertinent, describe how to love the subject by being (a) patient and kind; (b) not jealous, pompous, or inflated; (c) not rude; (d) not seeking self-interests; (e) not quick-tempered or brooding over injury; (f) rejoicing with the truth and not rejoicing over wrongdoing; (g) bearing, believing, hoping for, and enduring all things; and (h) never failing.

52. Rahner, "Reflections on the Unity of the Love of Neighbour and the Love of God," 236–37.

53. The relationship between focusing on both heaven and Earth and loving Earth as a Catholic joy was discussed by Pope Benedict XVI when meeting with 400 Italian priests in July 2007. As reported by the Vatican news bureau in "Benedict XVI Urges

Loving the Human and Divine," *Zenit,* July 25, 2007 (www.zenit.org), the Pope urged living "with our feet on the ground and our eyes fixed on heaven." "Loving the beauty of this earth . . . is not just very human, but also very Christian and quite Catholic," the pontiff taught. "Everyone according to their own gifts and their own charism loves the earth and the beautiful things the Lord has given us," he continued, "but to also be grateful for the light of God that shines on the earth, that gives splendor and beauty to everything else. Let us live in this Catholicity joyously."

54. At least one order of religious women expanded its charism to love "the dear neighbor without distinction" to love "for all creation," as indicated in the "Directional Statement" adopted by the Sisters of Saint Joseph of Baden, Pennsylvania, at its 1993 chapter. Sister Anne Clifford, CSJ, shared this document with the author; it can be obtained through www.stjoseph-baden.org/contactus.asp.

10

MODELING THE HUMAN IN AN AGE
OF ECOLOGICAL DEGRADATION

Several models of the human have been proffered by theologians in the twentieth century to address ecological concerns. Among these are various interpretations of *imago Dei* from Genesis 1,[1] *homo faber* from Teilhard de Chardin,[2] the U.S. Catholic bishops' "cocreator" and "stewards" duo,[3] Philip Hefner's "created cocreator,"[4] and Michael Himes and Kenneth Himes's "companionship."[5]

Models also surface from the nine concepts appropriated from patristic and medieval texts, reconstructed to reflect current scientific findings about the world, and probed for behavior patterns they suggest. The goodness of creation concept suggests a model of the human as an *intrinsic-instrumental valuer* of species, systems, and the biosphere. The beauty of creation concept yields the *aesthetic appreciator* of the beautiful constituents of Earth and their harmonious interactions to constitute the planet. The human is a *reverencer* of Earth when following the behavioral trajectory suggested by the sacramentality concept that God is self-disclosing in presence and character through the world. Creation's praise for God leads to the human as *respecter* of all natural entities to praise God according to their unique "voices." The human person is a *cooperator* with other species and abiota when viewed from the perspective of the functional integrity of creation. From the kinship concept surfaces the human as a *companion* with other species and systems in the ongoing dynamic web of existence. The human is modeled as a *restrained and grateful user* from the timeless teachings of patristic and medieval theologians. Motivated by love of God and one's neighbor, the human person becomes a *virtuoso* who lives prudently, justly, moderately, and courageously in his or her temporal life while aiming for eternal happiness with God, and the faithful who collaborate in acting virtuously become a model for virtuous communities. Finally, the human is modeled as a *lover* of Earth.

Each of these models suggests a general way of acting based on the premise of the concept. How might a faith-filled person act if he or she believed that God's creation is good? That God's creation is beautiful? That it has a sacramental character? That all creatures praise God in their own "voices" while the totality praises God as a chorus? That the world is gifted by God as a unity with integrity? That creatures are related to one another? That the faithful are intended by God to use God's creation with gratitude and restraint? That the faithful should live virtuously in relation to other creatures? That the faithful should love other species and biological systems? The initial answers to these questions are admittedly modest. They provide a beginning framework for addressing the plethora of ecological problems that loom today.

A model can be chosen for various reasons, including its practicality, appeal to a person's imagination, an intuitive sense of a particular model's "feeling right," or the motivation it imparts. When required to use criteria that conform to those used to test scientific theories and expressions of religious faith,[6] a relatively rigorous examination of various model options is required.

In this concluding chapter, five criteria for modeling the human for our age of ecological degradation are identified and explained. One model combines two concepts that have been explored in previous chapters. How this exemplar meets the criteria for modeling the human today is explained subsequently. In the conclusion is a reflection on all nine models as constituting an overarching model of a faith-filled person who responds to God's call to live authentically in the world.

Criteria for Modeling the Human in an Age of Ecological Degradation

Several criteria are pertinent to the task of developing a model of the human that is responsive to our ecologically destructive age.[7] For a theological model, the first and foremost criterion is that it should be rooted in a religious faith tradition so it can be recognized, embraced with confidence, and applied by people who profess that faith. The more deeply embedded the model is in that religion's primary texts, doctrines, and teachings by eminent theologians, the more likely the faithful may find the model appealing.

A second criterion for modeling the human for our time is the need to be consistent with broad scientific findings about the physical world. Theological discourse regarding the human must cohere with knowledge gained through other modes of inquiry or run the risk of being irrelevant and meaningless. When informed by the contemporary sciences, a model of the human will assume that the possibility for our species to emerge occurred approximately 14 billion years ago when heavy elements essential for the formation of bodies were produced in the interiors of stars. This ensuing process enabled the formation of at least one planet with the chemical composition, temperature, and radiation emission to bring about replicating molecules that led eventually to complex and diverse beings.[8] Among them emerged one species with the ability to reflect on the history of its emergence from and with other species and to recognize the radical human connection with all living and inanimate entities that constitute Earth.[9]

That the model should be positively relational to other species and physical systems is a third criterion. Although an understanding of the interconnection of humans and other past and present entities surfaces when ensuring the model's consistency with contemporary scientific findings, a metaphysical understanding of this relationship is also crucial. A model of the human for our time must avoid dualistic thinking that places humans over or apart from other entities and views them merely as instruments to be used for whatever purposes a human desires. Conversely, a model for our ecologically endangered times must incorporate re-gard for humans as integral actors with nonhumans in ecosystems, respect for their mutual interests in and needs for surviving, valuing of the distinct contri-butions they make to the functioning of ecosystems, and appreciation for the de-pendence humans have on the health and well-being of other species, the air, the land, and waters.

A fourth criterion is that the model should outline at least broadly the kind of behavior that is needed today. The more descriptive the normative language is, the more effective the model will be for guiding human actions.

Finally, the model should point to the motivation for bringing about a change in the way people who profess a religious faith think about and act toward the more-than-human others that constitute Earth. This is a pivotal criterion because a model will most likely fail unless the ultimate theological reason for bringing about a transformation in attitude and behavior is explicit. From my experience as a teacher with a past and present in environmental advocacy, this standard has been crucial for the students in environmental ethics classes at Marquette Uni-versity and for the activists with whom I have been working over the past three decades.

The Virtuous Cooperator

The virtuous cooperator is one model of the human that surfaces from reflec-tions by Thomas Aquinas during the medieval period. Examining the substance of this model in some depth is warranted before proceeding to test its promise for appropriation during our age of ecological degradation. Aquinas's multifac-eted notion of cooperation is explored in this section and integrated with his teachings on the virtuous ways in which humans are intended to cooperate.

Informed by a medieval understanding of the world as a geocentric organism with fixed species created and ordered hierarchically in relation to one another by God,[10] Aquinas reflected on the cooperation among creatures and their co-operation with God. He used variations of *cooperator* to convey four distinct but related types of cooperation:[11] (1) Creatures cooperate by acting or being acted upon according to their God-given natures for their individual and common good in conformity with the orderly world God created and sustains in exis-tence;[12] (2) living creatures cooperate with God, their primary cause for existing, by acting as secondary agents on other creatures to carry out God's plan for the universe;[13] (3) God both operates on and cooperates with humans for their temporal and eternal good;[14] and (4) humans cooperate with God's grace by acting virtuously on others in ways that achieve good in temporal life as they seek their eternal good, which is happiness with God.[15]

The Intercooperation of Creatures

Aquinas's teachings that creatures cooperate by acting or being acted upon according to their natures reflected his understanding that God created all animate and inanimate beings with specific capabilities of fulfilling their purposes in relation to one another. From his medieval perspective, the ascending order of creatures with some material composition consisted of the four primary elements of air, earth, water and fire; minerals and other mixed elements, plants, irrational animals, and humans.[16] Primary elements serve as the basic substrata for mixed elements, mixed elements provide nourishment for plants, plants provide food for animals, and animals as well as plants supply the physical needs of humans. Aquinas referred to this arrangement as an order of conservation, within which creatures cooperate to internally sustain the universe that God created and maintains in existence.[17] At least implicitly, this arrangement also constitutes an order of instrumentality, in which humans use plants and animals, animals use plants, and plants use mixed elements for their sustenance.[18]

Aquinas lavished with superlatives his descriptions of this orderly universe of cooperators, each of which contributes something essential to the perfection of the universe and all of which cooperate to achieve its internal common good.[19] Although he considered some cooperators qualitatively better than others, primarily because of their natures and capacities to act, and he thought that humans are superior to other material beings, because of the innate human capacity to make informed decisions and act freely on them, he concluded that the whole universe of cooperators is better than one or several types of creatures.[20]

Of course, Aquinas's depictions of the physical world's functioning were limited by his knowledge of the world informed by the natural philosophy of his time. There are no inklings in his works about the evolution of species that in turn account for the human connection with other species over eons of time, about their molecular similarities, or about the complex makeup and synergistic effects of abiota and biota within ecosystems. Nor did he convey any anticipation that human activities could accelerate the extinction of species, destroy habitats, degrade ecosystems, or threaten the integrity of the biosphere. Foundational to his thirteenth-century thinking was his faith that God created and sustains the world's capacity to maintain itself physically according to the natural laws that God established to ensure its functioning.[21]

Creatures' Cooperation with God

That living creatures cooperate with God by acting on other creatures has its basis in Aquinas's thinking about God as the primary cause of the universe of many diverse entities, some of which are secondary causes that act on others according to their natures.[22] As the primary cause of their existence, God endowed living creatures with capacities to act on others to achieve their respective purposes as God intends.[23] God's cooperators are, Aquinas taught, plants acting on minerals and other mixed elements for their nourishment, animals acting on plants for their food, and humans acting on plants and animals for their temporal needs. They act instrumentally on others to acquire what they need for their sustenance, and they act together to maintain the internal functioning of the universe.[24] By acting on others, secondary actors enable those upon which they act to achieve their God-endowed purposes for existing in the universe.

Secondary agents are also God's cooperators in a sacramental sense by manifesting God's goodness and wisdom.[25] They manifest God's goodness and wisdom as individual types of creatures that actively achieve their temporal purposes according to their natures in relation to others as God intends. However, the best manifestation of God's goodness and wisdom is the functioning of all secondary agents and those acted upon as God intends.[26]

As cooperators among many different cooperators, humans cooperate with God by acting freely according to the dictates of reason to achieve what is good in their temporal lives, which are supposed to be geared toward achieving their eternal happiness with God.[27] Whereas other living creatures operate by instinct in determined patterns through principles innate to their species,[28] Aquinas reasoned from his medieval understanding of the world, humans have the unique ability among creatures to act by making informed decisions about how they ought to be living in the world and to exercise their free wills in deciding whether or not to act accordingly.[29] Their decisions and actions are supposed to be conducive to the quest for eternal life in God's presence.[30]

Aquinas stressed repeatedly that humans should restrict their actions on other creatures to acquiring the necessities of life and knowing God as they seek their eternal goal.[31] When acting on other creatures in these two ways that are appropriate to the functioning of the universe, humans are God's cooperators.[32]

The necessities of life are things humans need to support their bodies, such as food, clothing, transportation,[33] and those things without which they cannot carry on their lives in appropriate ways as they seek eternal happiness with God.[34] Aquinas proscribed the exorbitant use of God's other creatures, describing it as inordinate and wasteful,[35] immoderate,[36] disordered, and vicious.[37] As noted in chapter 8, on the moral virtues, the excessive use of other entities was judged sinful in the scheme of the human desire for eternity with God.[38]

Aquinas's teachings that humans can use other creatures to know God reflect his sacramental perception of the physical world as a means through which God's goodness, wisdom, power, and other attributes can be contemplated.[39] This teaching also reflects his optimism that humans have been gifted by God with the capacity to rise gradually from the world to limited knowledge of God, though he expressed his sacramental view of the world in ways less emotive than found in works by Augustine, Hugh of Saint Victor, Bonaventure, and Francis of Assisi.[40] Physical entities can lead humans to God, Aquinas contended, referring occasionally to Romans 1:20 and Wisdom 13:1–5, as long as they start from their faith perspective that the world is God's creation and approach it as a means of knowing and loving God.[41]

That humans often fail to cooperate concerned Aquinas. Whereas other living and nonliving entities do not deviate from God's intentions, defective behavior occurs extensively among humans.[42] Their behavior is defective when they do not orient their actions toward their temporal common good,[43] with a view to their eternal good, who is God.[44] For Aquinas, the more comprehensive the good envisaged by the human, the more the human will corresponds to the will of God, who wills the good of the orderly universe[45] and loves it with the highest kind of love.[46] To show humans how to live a God-centered life, God became incarnate in the person of Jesus Christ.[47]

God's Grace Operating on and Cooperating with Humans

To help individuals make and act on decisions to acquire temporal goods in ways that cohere with the quest for eternal happiness, God provides special care to individuals by giving them grace.[48] God's grace both operates on and cooperates with humans toward their ultimate goal,[49] without interfering in the human exercise of making and carrying out their decisions freely.[50] God's grace operates lovingly on the human, working on the human spirit to think about and act in ways that are conducive to achieving eternal life.[51] God's grace cooperates with the human by actively sustaining the innate human capacity to make informed decisions and to choose to act accordingly. God's grace also operates on and cooperates with humans to develop moral virtues that will aid them in exercising their wills appropriately in this life because they are motivated to achieve eternal life with God.[52]

Human Cooperation with God's Grace: Living Virtuously

According to Aquinas, God created humans with the potential for developing moral virtues that will assist them in acting appropriately as God intends,[53] and God offers grace to humans to develop and practice these virtues. Prudence, justice, temperance, and fortitude are the chief moral virtues about which he wrote and from which he identified an extensive system of subvirtues motivated by the theological virtue of love for God and desire to enjoy eternal happiness with God,[54] as discussed in chapter 9. The moral virtues are innate to the individual potentially.[55] Like seeds in the ground, they are naturally present in the human reason and must be cultivated.[56] Humans cooperate with God's grace by developing the virtues in themselves. Once perfected, they confer an aptness to act correctly without hesitation.[57]

Motivated by love *ex caritate,* the faithful will develop the virtues through which they can live morally in relation to other species and the various constituents of the ecosystems within which humans function. The faithful will develop and practice the virtue of prudence so they are able to discern how to act through a process of discovering the facts, choosing a means of acting that avoids or at least minimizes the potential of adversely affecting others, and implementing that means cautiously with foresight, circumspection, and openness to correction. The faithful will develop and practice the virtue of temperance so they are able to live moderately, taking from the goods of Earth what is *needed* for their lives, not what is desired, excessive, or superfluous, and to live with humility before other species and abiota with whom humans are interrelated in space and time and upon whom humans are utterly dependent for their health and well-being. The faithful will develop and practice the virtue of justice so they can strive to ensure that other humans, especially the poor and vulnerable, are able to provide for their necessities of life unencumbered by adverse environmental conditions in their neighborhoods and the ecosystems in which they function. The faithful will develop and practice the virtue of fortitude so they are able to stand firmly for prudent, moderate, and just ways of living in relation to others, ultimately out of a love for them that is inseparable from their love for God. The faithful are able to develop and practice these virtues because God offers them the grace to do so and because they wish to cooperate with God by functioning cooperatively with the other creatures whose existence God facilitated through the cosmological-biological process, whose cooperative existence God sustains, and, whose cooperative development God empowers while calling it to completion.

To what extent is the virtuous cooperator model helpful for addressing environmental concerns? Can it meet the five criteria for modeling the human during our time when the rate of species extinction is accelerating, wastes of all types are increasing and piling up, signs of changes in the global climate are identifiable, and a plethora of other environmental problems are plaguing Earth?

Testing the Virtuous Cooperator Model

The virtuous cooperator model meets the five criteria for modeling the human during our age of ecological degradation. It is deeply rooted in the Catholic tradition, consistent with contemporary scientific findings, positively relational to other species and physical systems, descriptive of the type of behavior humans should demonstrate, and provides a strong motivation for acting appropriately. How is each of these criteria met by the virtuous cooperator model?

Rooted in the Religious Tradition

Thinking about the human as a virtuous cooperator is rooted in the Catholic faith, as indicated in the works of Aquinas, one of the Church's most eminent theologians. Whereas the notion of human cooperation has a long history in theological reflections and magisterial teachings,[58] this model should be retrieved for consideration by the faithful at a time when appropriate behavior toward other species, ecosystems, and Earth must be discerned and practiced. Finding this model in Aquinas's works should command the attention of many within the Christian and other traditions who value his outstanding contributions to theological discourse. His appeal may be especially strong for Roman Catholics because he is revered as a "doctor of the universal Church," as a saint who may have been the first person canonized for being a theologian and teacher, as a scholar and priest whose methods, doctrines, and principles were required by the *Codex Juris Canonica* to be taught to candidates for the priesthood,[59] and as a profound thinker who stimulated numerous strains of systematic theology. As Karl Rahner remarked about Aquinas's overall appeal: "I believe that even today Thomas still remains, in a quite special and *unique* sense, a theologian of such magnitude that he must not cease to have a place in our discussions."[60] His notions about the human as a virtuous cooperator should be considered when searching for a meaningful and relevant way of responding to the ongoing degradation of God's creation.

Support from the Catholic tradition for thinking about humans as cooperating with God's grace can also be found in the theological conclusions of the Council of Trent (1545–63). In the context of the Reformation and Martin Luther's teachings about justification by faith alone, the council explained the need for individuals to consent to and cooperate with God's grace in the process of seeking eternal salvation.[61] More recent support was given by the late Pope John Paul II, who lamented the failure of humans to cooperate with God's grace[62] and urged their collaboration to avoid development strategies that fail to respect other beings or jeopardize the planet's integrity.[63]

Retrieving the virtuous cooperator model from Aquinas's teachings also has the advantage of distinguishing between God's activity and human activity, a criticism leveled against the "cocreator" model.[64] For the monotheistic traditions, the use of terminology to exemplify how we ought to act must avoid confusing or misleading the faithful about their role in relation to God's unparalleled role.

Consistent with Contemporary Scientific Findings

Although Aquinas's understanding of the physical world differs vastly from the current scientific understanding, there is some resonance between his metaphysical thinking about humans as cooperators among many other cooperators that internally sustain the physical world and ecologists' findings about the cooperative interactions of the air, land, water, and living beings that sustain ecosystems. So, too, does his hierarchical thinking about humans as cooperators among various cooperators who act on others for their sustenance cohere generally with scientific observations about the food chain.[65] Some consistency may also be found between contemporary scientific findings about the intellectual capacity of the human and Aquinas's understanding of the human as a rational cooperator who can contemplate various courses of action, make informed decisions, and choose among them. These parallels in thinking follow the natural law tradition that Pope Benedict XVI finds appealing today for determining how humans should function within the natural environment.[66]

Of course, Aquinas's thirteenth-century works do not convey, nor should they be expected to, any inkling of scientific evidence obtained centuries later that the human species emerged out of and with other species in a cosmological-biological continuum, that the DNA compositions of humans and other species account in part for affinities and disparities in their actions, or that the interconnections and interdependencies of species, the air, land, and water are highly complex ecosystems of which humans are parts. However, his faith perspective that God created, empowers, and sustains the internally self-maintaining world does not conflict with these contemporary scientific findings,[67] though his metaphysical framework for thinking about species as "fixed" from the beginning of time is implausible today.

Modeling the human as a virtuous cooperator is also consistent with ongoing discussions about the sustainability of the planet among natural and social scientists and leaders of nations and nongovernmental organizations. They have been striving for two decades to define "sustainable development" in order to identify realistic ways in which Earth's dynamic physical systems can be sustained while developing countries strive to industrialize their economies and industrialized countries continue to advance their economic wealth.[68] How humans ought to use other species and the air, land, and water is crucial to this discussion.

Positive Relation to Other Species and Physical Systems

The virtuous cooperator model developed from Aquinas's thinking is positively relational to other species, their habitats, and ecosystems. Grounded physically in the mutual needs of all beings to sustain themselves and thereby sustain the functioning of ecosystems and the biosphere, virtuous cooperators will assume a posture of humility before other-than-humans for the late arrival of the human species in the unfolding universe, the dependence humans have on other beings for human health and well-being, the havoc that humans have caused to other species and ecosystems, and the technological power with which humans are equipped to destroy Earth. Virtuous cooperators will aim to manage human activities so they are not degrading or destroying other species, their habitats, ecosystems, or the greater biosphere, because the virtuous cooperator would recognize that nonhuman entities and systems are capable of managing themselves. Virtuous cooperators will view other entities as cooperators essential to the functioning of the systems of which they are parts. Virtuous cooperators will be concerned about the interests that other species, habitats, ecosystems, and the biosphere have for surviving and strive to avoid impeding their efforts. Virtuous cooperators will be ecologically centered in their daily activities because they are centered ultimately on God who created, empowers, sustains, and beckons forth the further unfolding of the universe to its completion. Virtuous cooperators will also appreciate their distinctive capabilities in relation to other cooperators and accept responsibility for functioning in relation to them in ways that are conducive to their well-being.

In addition to this positive relational attitude toward other species and physical systems, the virtuous cooperator model provides a unique aesthetic dimension. Clothed in a sacramental sensitivity toward the physical world that Aquinas shared with other theologians before, during, and after his time, virtuous cooperators will be inclined to revere other humans, members of other species, their habitats, the wider ecosystems within which they function, and the fragile biosphere that encompasses Earth. They will not be considered sacred in themselves, however, as held by some world religions. Instead, virtuous cooperators will relate reverently to other physical beings because they mediate God's presence and character.

Descriptive of Behavior

The virtuous cooperator model provides a framework for behavior that is needed during this age of ecological degradation. Being habitually prudent, just, moderate, and courageous are the basic behavioral characteristics of the virtuous cooperator. Each virtue should be encouraged in young children and developed by the individual until virtuous behavior becomes consistently characteristic of that person. Individual cooperators should be cognizant of the need to cooperate with one another to bring about collective virtuous activity at appropriate levels of communities to which they belong—family, neighborhood, municipality, county, state, federal, and international—not remanding to the next collective level what can be accomplished on a more local level, in keeping with the principle of subsidiarity.[69]

Guided by the virtue of prudence, virtuous cooperators will make informed decisions and act accordingly in relation to individuals of other species, the air, the land, and the bodies of water in their mutual interests of sustaining themselves, sustaining the dynamic functioning of the ecosystems of which they are parts, and maintaining the integrity of Earth. Virtuous cooperators will apply a step-by-step process of discovering the best possible courses of action based on the data that are available, choosing one that is compatible with the well-being of all affected in the present and future, and enacting that decision cautiously when considering the circumstances and contingencies that could arise. Virtuous cooperators will be open to appropriating and applying the "precautionary principle" that was adopted at the United Nations Conference on Environment and Development in 1992 and calls upon governments to institute protective measures even when a definitive cause–effect relationship on a problem has not been identified.[70] Virtuous cooperators, grounded in their faith in God and open to receiving God's grace, will collaborate in making and carrying out informal decisions, particularly regarding environmental problems in their locales, while remaining cognizant of other problems on the planet that their locales may be exacerbating and should be mitigating.

Furthermore, virtuous cooperators will be guided by the virtue of temperance to limit the use of other species and abiota to the necessities of life, cognizant of their needs for flourishing as essential, interacting components of ecosystems.

Virtuous cooperators will concurrently approach them as means through which God's presence can be experienced and God's character can be contemplated. From this sacramental perspective, virtuous cooperators will cautiously encounter individuals of other species, their habitats, and vistas of land, sea, and sky to avoid degrading their capacities to mediate God; will endeavor to preserve species and ecosystems so they can continue to mediate God's presence and character in the future; will react with restraint when individuals of other species threaten the health and domiciles of humans; and will work to enable the identification and implementation of rationales for relating to ecosystems and the larger biosphere so their harmonious functioning can reflect God's empowering character.

Informed by the natural sciences and particularly by evolutionary biology and ecology, virtuous cooperators will develop temperance's subvirtue of humility[71] and act humbly before other species and constituents of Earth. Incorporating humility into a model of the human is essential to recognize that humans had their bodily possibilities begun in the furnaces of stars, emerged from and with other entities in the cosmological-biological continuum, and are radically dependent upon other types of animate and inanimate beings for their bodily well-being.

So, too, will virtuous cooperators avoid vices that counter temperance. The virtuous cooperator will avoid the vice of insensitivity by striving to be sensitive to the needs of other species and the air, land, and water as they cooperate in their ecosystems. Virtuous cooperators will avoid the vice of gluttony by curbing their appetites for Earth's goods. And virtuous cooperators will avoid the vice of cowardice by recognizing the danger in human activities that extinguish species, degrade ecosystems, and threaten the integrity of the biosphere, and they will act to counteract and correct these damaging human activities.

Guided by the virtue of justice, virtuous cooperators will use the goods of Earth in ways that ensure their availability to meet the needs of other humans near and far, now and in the future. The needs of the most vulnerable and powerless will be met. Nonrenewable resources will not be depleted by some at the expense of others. The functioning of natural systems will not be degraded or destroyed to avoid adverse effects on others in the present and future. Personal property will be managed in ways that make it possible to aid others who do not have sufficient goods with which to meet their needs in life.

Virtuous cooperators will also be open to extending Aquinas's notion of justice from acting justly toward other humans within the human community to acting justly toward all biota, recognizing their needs for sustaining themselves within their habitats. Virtuous cooperators will also be just toward all constituents of ecosystems to avoid activities that disrupt or inhibit their interactions. Virtuous cooperators will work with other virtuous cooperators at social, economic, and political levels, following the principle of subsidiarity, to bring about justice for all species and ecosystems.[72]

Finally, the virtue of fortitude will guide virtuous cooperators in remaining steadfastly prudent, temperate, and just when relating to other species and ecosystems, despite fatigue, cynicism, failure to bring about immediate change, and

social rebuffs when deviating from self-centered societal values. Virtuous cooperators will also be propelled to stand firm in opposing the loss of biodiversity,
the degradation and destruction of ecosystems, and the damage to the ozone
layer due to fear of present and future consequences.

Identification of Religious Motivation

Because the motivation behind acting virtuously in this life is love for God and
the desire to spend eternal happiness in God's presence, the virtuous cooperator model meets the final criterion for modeling the human in our ecologically
endangered age. Those who profess faith in God, and believe in the promise of
everlasting happiness with God, are offered a compelling model in the virtuous
cooperator. Appropriated from Aquinas's works and extended to reflect contemporary scientific findings about the world, this model explains why humans
should act prudently, justly, and moderately with firm resolve. Modeling the human as a virtuous cooperator also points to the ultimate goal toward which temporal life aims.

    Moreover, this model of the human ensures that individuals will have divine
assistance to become virtuous cooperators. In Aquinas's thinking, God offers humans the grace they need to develop the moral virtues until their aptness to act
prudently, justly, and moderately is habitual. God provides this supernatural aid
out of love for humans and for the whole world that God loves with the highest
kind of love. God's grace operates on humans to facilitate their resolve to live in
ways that are geared ultimately toward their goal of everlasting happiness in
God's presence. The grace of God also cooperates with humans so they can use
their capacities to the fullest possible extent to develop virtuous behavior toward
the more-than-humans that constitute God's Earth.

Conclusions

Aquinas's teachings about cooperation and the chief moral virtues provide
some basic components for constructing the virtuous cooperator as a model for
the human that is needed during our ecologically endangered age. When appropriated within an evolutionary view of the world and informed by contemporary scientific findings, the virtuous cooperator meets the five criteria posited
for modeling the human today. The virtuous cooperator is rooted in the Christian faith tradition, with special significance for Roman Catholics and others who
respect Aquinas's synthesis of Judeo-Christianity and Greek philosophy. The
virtuous cooperator coheres with broad scientific findings about the physical
world when acknowledging the cooperative interactions of diverse biota and
abiota that constitute ecosystems, the food chain through which species feed hierarchically on one another to sustain themselves, and the human place in the
biological-cosmological continuum. The virtuous cooperator is positively relational to other species and physical systems by positing humans as integral ac-

tors within ecosystems, rather than over or apart from them, and by celebrating the unique human capacities to identify, reflect upon, and choose to implement options for acting responsibly on other-than-humans. The virtuous cooperator outlines the kind of human behavior that is helpful today by acting prudently through a stepwise process of making informed decisions, using other goods of Earth moderately for actual needs and for thinking about God, acting justly by considering the needs of other humans now and in the future and ensuring that their needs are met within the context of achieving the common good of all beings, and remaining steadfast about living virtuously despite fears of social pressures and in light of fears of ecological destruction that will affect humans now or in the future. Finally, the virtuous cooperator stipulates the religious motivation for acting virtuously in relation to more than humans, a motivation that is no less than love for God and desire to spend eternity in God's presence.

The virtuous cooperator is one of several models of the human person in the Catholic tradition that is plausible, relevant, and helpful for addressing ecological concerns. Among others suggested in this text are:

- The *intrinsic-instrumental valuer* of the good creation;
- The *aesthetic appreciator* of the beautiful and harmonious creation;
- The *reverencer* of the sacramental creation, through which God's presence and character can be sensed;
- The *respecter* of ways in which creatures and the totality of creation praise God;
- The *companion* of entities that have emerged from the cosmological-biological continuum;
- The *restrained user* of creation out of gratitude to God's generosity; and
- The *lover* of creation for human well-being in temporal life and God's glory.

Criteria used widely in theological and scientific circles to test statements of faith and theories can also test the extent to which these and other models are plausible, relevant, and helpful during our age of environmental injustice, loss of biodiversity, degradation of ecosystems, and threats to the integrity of the biosphere.

In the end, the choice rests with the individual or group selecting and appropriating a model. Perhaps it "fits" well or "feels right," as my students often remarked when identifying one that motivates them personally. Perhaps a particular model works best for convincing and showing others how to act because the model is more realistic than others and does not require an imaginative stretch, as may the respecter of creation's praise for God.

Although each model offers a unique perspective and one or two may resonate more than others, these nine models may be viewed as a composite of how the faithful may be fully responsive to God's call to live authentically as human creatures in relation to other entities that constitute our shared temporal home. The faithful can be fully responsive to God's call by valuing the constituents of Earth both intrinsically and instrumentally, by appreciating their beauty and harmony, by reverencing their manifestations of God's presence and character, by respecting their unique voices that praise God and adding the human voice to that praise, by cooperating with them to ensure our mutual sustainability, by treating them companionably in the journey of life, by using them while recognizing their usefulness to one another, by living virtuously in relation to other humans and constituents of Earth, and by loving them for themselves and for their vital relationships out of love for one's neighbor and love for God. That these models are drawn from the Catholic theological tradition warrants their consideration by the faithful today as they strive to respond to God's call to participate in the advancement of the universe to its completion.

Notes

This chapter has been revised from Jame Schaefer, "The Virtuous Cooperator: Modeling the Human in an Age of Ecological Degradation," *Worldviews: Environment, Culture, Religion* 7, nos. 1–2 (2003): 171–95.

1. Among the most notable efforts to define *imago Dei* as recorded in Genesis 1 and to make the model meaningful and relevant for our ecological age are Douglas John Hall, *Imaging God: Dominion as Stewardship* (Grand Rapids: William B. Eerdmans, 1986); and Colin Gunton, "Trinity, Ontology and Anthropology: Towards a Renewal of the Doctrine of the *Imago Dei*," in *Persons, Divine and Human*, ed. Christoph Schwööbel and Colin Gunton (Edinburgh: T & T Clark, 1991), 47–61.

2. Problems with the *homo faber* model in an age of technological abuse are identified perceptively by several scholars, including the Teilhardian scholar Thomas Berry, *Teilhard in the Ecological Age* (Chambersburg, PA: Anima Press, 1982); and the moral theologian William C. French, "Subject-Centered and Creation-Centered Paradigms in Recent Catholic Thought," *Journal of Religion* 70 (January 1990): 48–72.

3. On the "cocreator" and "steward" models juxtaposed, see United States Catholic Conference of Bishops, *Renewing the Earth: An Invitation to Reflection and Action on Environment in Light of Catholic Social Teaching*, November 14, 1991 (Washington, DC: United States Catholic Conference, 1992); and Benedict M. Ashley, "Ethics of Co-Creative Stewardship," in *Theologies of the Body: Humanist and Christian* (Saint Louis: Pope John Center, 1985), 415–28. For reactions to the cocreator model as appropriated by some authors from Pope John Paul II's early writings, see some helpful essays in *Co-Creation and Capitalism: John Paul II's Laborem Exercens*, ed. John W. Houck and Oliver Williams, CSC (Lanham, MD: University Press of America, 1983). Among the many explorations of the "steward" model, especially well grounded and developed is the one by Douglas John Hall, "Stewardship of the Earth in the Old Testament," in *Tending the Garden: Essays on the Gospel and the Earth*, ed. Wesley Granberg-Michaelson (Grand Rapids: William B. Eerdmans, 1987), 50–64.

4. Philip J. Hefner developed this impressive model in part to distinguish human from divine activity; see his *The Human Factor: Evolution, Culture, and Religion* (Minneapolis: Fortress Press, 1993), esp. 255–75.

5. Michael J. Himes and Kenneth R. Himes, "The Sacrament of Creation: Toward an Environmental Theology" in *Readings in Ecology and Feminist Theology,* ed. Mary Heather MacKinnon and Moni McIntyre (Kansas City: Sheed & Ward, 1995), 270–83.

6. An overview of the criteria for assessing scientific theories and expressions of religious faith is given by Ian Barbour, *Religion and Science: Historical and Contemporary Issues* (San Francisco: HarperSanFrancisco, 1997), 113, 158–59). These criteria are consistent with the criteria for theological statements given by Thomas Rausch, *The College Student's Introduction to Theology* (Collegeville: Michael Glazier Books, 1993), 19–20.

7. Ibid.

8. See the synopsis given by John Polkinghorne, *One World: The Interaction of Science and Theology* (Princeton, NJ: Princeton University Press, 1987), 56.

9. Sallie McFague summarizes poignantly our "common creation story" with all beings: "At some level and in a remote or intimate way, everything is related to everything else. We are distant relatives to the stars and kissing cousins with the oceans, plants, and other creatures on the earth." Sallie McFague, *The Body of God: An Ecological Theology* (Minneapolis: Fortress Press, 1993), 27.

10. Among the pertinent texts are Thomas Aquinas, *Summa theologiae,* 1.47.2, 76.3; and Aquinas, *Summa contra Gentiles,* 2.68, 3.71. Aquinas reasoned from his faith perspective that God created and ordered the many diverse, essential, and valuable types of beings to one another because they are ordered ultimately to God, an arrangement that he described as a twofold order of beings in *De veritatis,* 5.1, 3. Also see Aquinas, *De potentia Dei,* 3.7.9; Aquinas, *Summa theologiae,* 1.21.1; Aquinas, *Summa contra Gentiles,* 3.112; Aquinas, *Compendium theologiae,* 148; and the insightful exploration by John Wright, *The Order of the Universe in the Theology of St. Thomas Aquinas* (Rome: Gregorian University, 1957).

11. Wright, *Order of the Universe,* 30–113. *Index Thomisticus* identifies 286 entries of these usages of *cooperator:* 20 regarding the cooperation of creatures, 106 on their cooperation with God, 45 in which humans cooperate freely with God or God's grace, and 115 on divine grace operating on humans and cooperating with human actions.

12. See, e.g., Aquinas, *Summa theologiae,* 1.61.3, 111.2, 1 | 2.9.1, 19.10; Aquinas, *De veritate,* 9.2, 27.5; Aquinas, *Compendium theologiae,* 124; and Aquinas, *Summa contra Gentiles,* 1.70, 3.21, 69–70.

13. When God works through secondary causal agents, Aquinas taught (e.g., in *Summa theologiae* 1.105.5), the innate efficacy of their causal powers is left absolutely intact. God's activity in them does not displace or obviate their actions; it sustains and guides their actions lovingly toward their ultimate end. Aquinas perceived God's employing secondary causes to govern other creatures as a way of communicating the dignity of causality to creatures as indicated, e.g., in *Summa theologiae,* 1.23.8, and explained by Etienne Gilson, *The Christian Philosophy of St. Thomas Aquinas,* trans. L. K. Shook (New York: Random House, 1956), 184. In *Summa contra Gentiles,* 3.21, Aquinas cites Pseudo-Dionysius and 1 Cor 3:9 to support his thinking that creatures operating on others according to the innate characteristics given to them by God are *Dei cooperatorem.*

14. E.g., see Aquinas, *De veritate,* 27.5. Also see Aquinas, *Summa theologiae,* 1.105.4–5, for Aquinas's understanding of God's will acting on rational creatures.

15. According to Aquinas, *De veritate,* 24.11, 27.5, God offers grace to humans to enable their cooperation with God's intention that they seek the temporal good in this life while aiming for eternal happiness.

16. Aquinas, *Summa theologiae,* 1.47.2. Also see *Summa contra Gentiles,* 2.68, where Aquinas graded creatures according to their operations or capacities for acting, beginning with inanimate elements followed by mixed bodies, and the animate souls of plants, irrational animals, and rational animals. In *Summa theologiae,* 1.48.2, he graded creatures according to their incorruptible to corruptible properties as heavenly bodies, angels, humans, animals, plants, minerals and mixed bodies, and the primary elements; see also Aquinas, *Summa theologiae* Supp. 91.5; and Aquinas, *Summa contra Gentiles,* 3.71. In *Summa contra Gentiles* 2.68, he described the grades of creatures metaphorically as a ladder of forms.

17. Aquinas, *Summa contra Gentiles,* 3.22.

18. Oliva Blanchette recognizes in Aquinas's work an order of instrumentality among corporeal beings; Oliva Blanchette, *The Perfection of the Universe According to Aquinas: A Teleological Cosmology* (University Park: Pennsylvania State University Press, 1992), 256. However, Aquinas's thinking seems more expansive and inclusive of the totality of reality because he also considered God's providential actions as somewhat instrumental when moving beings toward their end in God (e.g., *Summa contra Gentiles,* 3.100, and *De potentia Dei,* 3.7 and 5.9) and humans' using one another (e.g., *Summa contra Gentiles,* 3.128, *Summa theologiae,* 1.96.4, 2 | 2.47.10). See also James Weisheipl, *Friar Thomas D'Aquino: His Life, Thought, and Work* (Garden City, NY: Doubleday, 1974), 206.

19. In *Summa contra Gentiles,* 2.39, 44, Aquinas described this orderly arrangement as the greatest good of the universe, in *Summa theologiae,* 1.15.2, as its highest good; in *Summa contra Gentiles,* 2.45, 102, as the ultimate and noblest perfection; and in *Summa contra Gentiles,* 3.71, as the highest beauty. John Wright summarizes Aquinas's thinking about the universe as "God's masterpiece"; see Wright, *Order of the Universe,* 87. See also the indispensable philosophical analysis of Aquinas's thinking given by Blanchette, *Perfection of the Universe According to Aquinas.*

20. E.g., see Aquinas, *Summa contra Gentiles,* 1.85; Aquinas, *De potentia Dei,* 1.6.1; and Aquinas, *Summa theologiae,* 1.103.7.

21. As F. C. Copleston explained, the medieval theologian believed that every finite entity depends existentially on God at every moment of its existence; if the divine conserving or sustaining activity were withdrawn, it would immediately cease to exist; F. C. Copleston, *Aquinas: An Introduction to the Life and Work of the Great Medieval Thinker* (London: Penguin Books, 1955), 142. That God sustains the natural world by laws is one dimension of Aquinas's discussion of divine providence, and human creatures have the intellectual ability to seek to know natural laws and determine ways to assure that they actions are conducive to these laws imposed by God's eternal law on God's creation; Aquinas, *Summa theologiae,* 1 | 2.93.5. Pope Benedict XVI's recent statement about "the inner laws of creation, of this earth" that all people should strive discern, "respect" and "obey" in order "to survive" in an era of widespread environmental degradation indicates his interest in the natural law tradition. See John L. Allen, "Benedict on Going Green," *National Catholic Reporter,* July 27, 2007, www.ncrcafe.org/node/1241.

22. E.g., see the discussions by Aquinas, *Summa theologiae,* 1.105.5; Aquinas, *Summa contra Gentiles,* 3.67; and Aquinas, *De potentia Dei,* 3.7.

23. See Aquinas, *Summa theologiae,* 1.44.3–4, 47.1; and Aquinas, *Summa contra Gentiles,* 3.16–20. For his understanding of God's primary activity and creatures secondary

causality, see *Summa contra Gentiles* 3.17, 103, 123–24. In *Summa contra Gentiles*, 3.69, he described the actions of secondary agents as a likeness to God who communicates goodness to creatures, and he taught in (e.g., in *Compendium theologiae*, 124) that goodness proliferates in the universe when the more richly endowed creature cooperates to procure the good of many.

24. Aquinas taught in *Summa theologiae*, 1.61.3, and *Summa contra Gentiles*, 1.70, 3.69, that the interactions of creatures in the orderly universe benefit the entire universe.

25. E.g., see Aquinas, *Summa theologiae*, 1.65.2; and Aquinas, *Summa contra Gentiles*, 2.45.

26. See, e.g., Aquinas, *Summa theologiae*, 1.47.1; Aquinas, *Summa contra Gentiles*, 2.45; and Aquinas, *De potentia Dei*, 3.16.

27. E.g., see Aquinas, *Summa theologiae*, 1|2.3.6–8, 1|2.180.4. See, further, Aquinas, *Summa contra Gentiles*, 4.55, on his teachings that the ultimate end of humans is their eternal union with God, a union that is enabled by God's incarnation, death, and resurrection in the person of Jesus Christ.

28. Aquinas, *Compendium theologiae*, 74, 127, 148; Aquinas, *Summa contra Gentiles*, 3.7, 111–12; Aquinas, *Summa theologiae*, 1.96.1.

29. Aquinas, *Summa contra Gentiles*, 3.78; Aquinas, *Summa theologiae*, 2|2.64.2.

30. E.g., see Aquinas, *Summa contra Gentiles*, 1.92, 3.17–25, 145; Aquinas, *Summa theologiae* 2|2.118.1; and Aquinas, *Compendium theologiae*, 173.

31. See Aquinas, *Summa theologiae*, Supp. 91.1; also see 1|2.4.6–7, 114.10, 2|2.76.2, 83.6, 118.1. See, further, Aquinas, *Summa contra Gentiles*, 3.22; and Aquinas, *Compendium theologiae*, 173.

32. Aquinas considered the human use of other creatures for the necessities of life and knowing God as an exercise of natural dominion; e.g., see Aquinas, *Summa theologiae*, 2|2.66.1–2; Aquinas, *Compendium theologiae*, 74, 127, 148; and Aquinas, *Summa contra Gentiles*, 3.78, 111–12. In *Summa theologiae*, 2|2.66.1, he insisted that God retains absolute dominion over both users and used.

33. See Aquinas, *Summa theologiae*, 2|2.141.6; see also Supp. 91.1, 2|2.64.1, 83.6. See, further, Aquinas, *Summa contra Gentiles*, 3.22, 121, 129, 131. The prescription that humans are intended to use only what is *needed* to sustain human life and not what is *desired* beyond the necessities of life resounds throughout his works.

34. See Aquinas, *Summa theologiae*, 1|2.4.7; also see 2|2.83.6, 118.1, 141.6.

35. Ibid., 2|2.83.6.

36. Ibid., 2|2.169.1. For his understanding of the appropriate human use of natural entities, see Aquinas, *Summa contra Gentiles*, 3.129. Some uses for the necessities of life are naturally fitting, he taught, whereas as immoderate uses are naturally unfitting in the scheme of the integrity of the universe and, ultimately, in the human quest for God.

37. Aquinas, *Summa contra Gentiles*, 4.83.

38. See Aquinas, *Summa theologiae*, 2|2.118.1; see also 2|2.83.6. See, further, Aquinas, *Summa contra Gentiles*, 4.83.

39. Aquinas, *Summa contra Gentiles*, 2.2.

40. E.g., see Aquinas, *Summa contra Gentiles*, 4.1, 3.47; and Aquinas, *Summa theologiae*, 1.65.l, 2|2.180.4.

41. See Aquinas, *Summa theologiae*, 1.65.1; see, further, 2|2.180.4, Supp. 91.1.

42. Ibid., 1.49.3.

43. See ibid., 1|2.109.3; see also 1|2.77.4, 87.3. See, further, Aquinas, *Summa contra Gentiles*, 3.6, 9; Aquinas, *De potentia Dei*, 3.6; and Aquinas, *De veritate*, 24.11.

44. See Aquinas, *Summa theologiae,* 1.49.1–3; see also 1 | 2.19.10, 87.3. See, further, Aquinas, *Summa contra Gentiles,* 3.6, 9; Aquinas, *De malo,* 1.1; and Aquinas, *De potentia Dei,* 3.6.

45. See Aquinas, *Summa theologiae,* 1 | 2.19.10; also see 1.115.3. See, further, Aquinas, *Summa contra Gentiles,* 3.94; and Aquinas, *De potentia Dei,* 1.6.1.

46. Aquinas, *De caritate,* 7. Aquinas taught that God loves the orderly universe through which all creatures are ordered ultimately to God more than God loves the human or any other type of creature. In *Summa contra Gentiles,* 3.64, he explained that, among created beings, God cares most for the order of things established in relation to one another to constitute the universe.

47. Aquinas, *Summa theologiae,* 3.1–5.

48. See ibid., 1.22.2. See, further, Aquinas, *Summa contra Gentiles,* 3.112–13; and Aquinas, *De veritate,* 1.5.6–7. According to Aquinas, God's special care is needed for individual humans, who have the capacity to think about how to act and to choose to act, capacities that humans often misuse. This special divine care for individual humans contrasts with God's general care for other species because they do not have intellectual capabilities or free will with which to deviate from God's intentions. God's care for individual humans and other species should be considered in relation to Aquinas's teaching in *Summa contra Gentiles,* 3.64, that among God's creation God cares most for the order of all things that constitute the universe.

49. Aquinas, *De veritate,* 24.11, 27.5.

50. This follows his rationale that God governs all things to their end through God's eternal law, which God imposed on the universe in the form of natural law; e.g., see Aquinas, *Summa theologiae,* 1 | 2.91.1, 93.1–5; and Aquinas, *De veritate,* 5.1.6. On his thinking about rational creatures who are ruled by eternal law and are rulers of themselves to whom God gives grace to seek their ultimate end, see *Summa theologiae,* 1 | 2.109.1, and *Summa contra Gentiles,* 3.1.

51. Aquinas, *Summa theologiae,* 1 | 2.110.1.

52. E.g., see Aquinas, *Summa theologiae,* 1.111.2; and Aquinas, *De veritate,* 27.5.

53. See Aquinas, *Summa theologiae,* 1 | 2.63.1; see also 1 | 2.55.1–3, 56.4.

54. For Aquinas's understanding of the theological virtue of love *ex caritate* as motivating the moral virtues, see, e.g., *Summa theologiae,* 2 | 2.23–25; and *De caritate,* 3, 7.

55. See Aquinas, *Summa theologiae,* 1 | 2.58.1; also see 1 | 2.50.3, 63.1.

56. See ibid., 1 | 2.63.1; also see 1 | 2.55.1–3.

57. Ibid., 1 | 2.56.3. Also pertinent is his discussion in *Summa theologiae,* 1 | 2.68.3–4, on the gifts of the Holy Spirit as habits whereby the human is perfected to obey the Holy Spirit readily in comparison with the moral virtues that dispose the human to obey what reason dictates.

58. As noted in chapter 5, on the integrity of creation, the notion of cooperation among humans has a long history of applications in the Church as indicated by the Pontifical Council for Justice and Peace, *Compendium of the Social Doctrine of the Church* (Washington, DC: United States Conference of Catholic Bishops, 2007). Thomas Aquinas's thinking facilitates thinking beyond humans to encompass the totality of creation.

59. Josef Pieper, *Guide to Thomas Aquinas,* trans. Richard Winston and Clara Winston (San Francisco: Ignatius Press, 1962), 18.

60. Karl Rahner, "On Recognizing the Importance of Thomas Aquinas," *Theological Investigations* , vol. 13, trans. David Bourke (New York: Crossroad Publishing, 1983), 3–12.

61. Council of Trent, *Canons and Decrees of the Council of Trent,* ed. and trans. H. J. Schroeder, OP (Saint Louis: Herder & Herder, 1941), 31–34.

62. E.g., see John Paul II, *Centesimus annus: Encyclical on the 100th Anniversary of Pope Leo XIII's Rerum Novarum,* Rome, May 1, 1991, no. 37.

63. John Paul II, *Centesimus annus,* no. 37.

64. Edward Vacek, SJ, clarifies Pope John Paul II's understanding of the human as God's cooperator through labor; see his essay "John Paul II and Cooperation with God," in *The Annual of the Society of Christian Ethics,* ed. D. M. Yeager (Knoxville: Society of Christian Ethics, 1990), 81–107. See also the essays taking various views on the pope's thinking about humans in *Co-Creation and Capitalism: John Paul II's Laborem Exercens,* ed. Houck and Williams; and John T. Pawlikowski, "Co-Creators with a Compelling God," *Ecumenism* 134 (1998): 8–11.

65. See R. V. O'Neill, D. L. DeAngelis, J. B. Waide, and T. F. H. Allen, eds., *A Hierarchical Concept of Ecosystems* (Princeton, NJ: Princeton University Press, 1986); and Anthony W. King, "Considerations of Scale and Hierarchy," in *Ecological Integrity and the Management of Ecosystems,* ed. Stephen Woodley, James Kay, and George Francis (Delray Beach, FL: St. Lucie Press, 1993), 19–46.

66. In "Benedict on Going Green," Allen points to Pope Benedict XVI's discussion of the "secular path" open to both religious and nonreligious people, whereby they use their intellectual abilities to learn how the natural environment functions and to discern through the faculty of conscience how humans should act responsibly in order to avoid destroying the foundation of human existence. "Existence itself, our earth, speaks to us," the pope is quoted as saying, "and we have to learn to listen."

67. As Aquinas taught in *Summa theologiae,* 1.1.1, followed by scholars working in the burgeoning field of religion and science contend today, theology and the natural sciences do not conflict when they are practiced according to their distinct data, methods, purviews and limitations. Together they provide a more comprehensive understanding of issues at their boundaries that neither can address exclusively. See the discussion by Barbour, *Religion and Science,* 77–98; and see John F. Haught, *Science and Religion: From Conflict to Conversation* (New York: Paulist Press, 1995), 9–26.

68. United Nations, *Report of the World Summit on Sustainable Development, Johannesburg, South Africa, 26 August–4 September 2002* (New York: United Nations Environment Program, 2002). This conference followed up the United Nations Conference on Environment and Development in June 1992 in Rio de Janeiro, during which agreements were negotiated and enumerated under Agenda 21. An earlier international endeavor to define the term "sustainability" is the United Nations World Commission on Environment and Development, *Our Common Future* (New York: Oxford University Press, 1987). Also see Noel J. Brown and Pierra Quiblier, eds., *Ethics & Agenda 21: Moral Implications of a Global Consensus* (New York: United Nations Environment Program, 1994).

69. An overview of the historical development of the principle of subsidiarity is given by Ad Leys, *Ecclesiological Impacts of the Principle of Subsidiarity* (Kamen: Kok, 1995), part 1. The principle of subsidiarity in relation to the notion of solidarity is given by J. Verstraeten, "Solidarity and Subsidiarity," in *Principles of Catholic Social Teaching,* ed. David. A. Boileau (Milwaukee: Marquette University Press, 1998), 133–48.

70. See the essays in *Protecting Public Health and the Environment: Implementing the Precautionary Principle,* ed. Carolyn Raffensperger and Joel Tickner (Washington, DC: Island Press, 1999).

71. Aquinas, *Summa theologiae,* 2 | 2.161.1, 6.

72. The principle of subsidiarity has had wide application to concerns among humans, as indicated by the Pontifical Council for Justice and Peace, *Compendium of the Social Doctrine of the Church.* Applying the principle to ecological concerns widens its scope and significance, especially when recognizing that damage to the natural environment usually transcends political boundaries.

BIBLIOGRAPHY

PRIMARY SOURCES

Albertus Magnus. *Man and the Beasts (De animalibus, Books 22–26),* trans. James J. Scanlan. Binghamton: Medieval & Renaissance Texts & Studies, 1987.

———. *On Animals: A Medieval Summa Zoologica,* trans. Kenneth F. Kitchell Jr. and Irven Michael Resnick. Baltimore: Johns Hopkins University Press, 1996.

———. *Physica,* ed. Paul Hossfeld. Münster: Aschenforff, 1987.

Alan of Lille. *The Plaint of Nature,* trans. James J. Sheridan. Toronto: Pontifical Institute of Mediaeval Studies, 1980.

Anonymous Monk of Lindisfarne. *Two Lives of Saint Cuthbert,* trans. Bertram Colgrave. Cambridge: Cambridge University Press, 1940.

Aquinas, Thomas. *Compendium theologiae,* trans. Cyril Vollert, SF, STD, from Leonine Edition. Saint Louis: Herder, 1952. (Past Masters [electronic resource]; Charlottesville: InteLex Corp., 1996.)

———. *On Charity* (De caritate), trans. Lottie H. Kendzierski. Mediaeval Philosophical Texts in Translation 10. Milwaukee: Marquette University Press, 1960. (Past Masters [electronic resource]; Charlottesville: InteLex Corp., 1996.)

———. *On Evil* (De malo), trans. Robert W. Mulligan, SJ, from Leonine Edition. Chicago: Henry Regnery, 1952. (Past Masters [electronic resource]; Charlottesville: InteLex Corp., 1996.)

———. *On the Power of God* (De potentia Dei), trans. English Dominican Fathers from Leonine Edition. London: Burns, Oates & Washbourne, 1932. (Past Masters [electronic resource]; Charlottesville: InteLex Corp., 1996.)

———. *On Truth* (De veritate), trans. Robert W. Mulligan, SJ, from Leonine Edition. Chicago: Henry Regnery Publishing, 1952. (Past Masters [electronic resource]; Charlottesville: InteLex Corp., 1996.)

———. *Summa contra Gentiles,* trans. English Dominican Fathers from Leonine Edition. New York: Benziger Brothers, 1924. (Past Masters [electronic resource]; Charlottesville: InteLex Corp., 1996.)

———. *Summa theologiae,* trans. English Dominican Fathers from Leonine Edition. New York: Benziger Brothers, 1924. (Past Masters [electronic resource]; Charlottesville: InteLex Corp., 1996.)

Athanasius, Saint. *Contra Gentes,* edited and trans. Robert W. Thomson. Oxford: Clarendon Press, 1971.

————. *Life of Antony.* In *Early Christian Lives,* ed. and trans. Carolinne White. London: Penguin Books, 1998.

————. *On the Incarnation,* trans. and ed. a Religious of CSMV. Crestwood, NY: St. Vladimir's Seminary Press, 1978.

Augustine, Saint. *Concerning the City of God against the Pagans,* trans. John O'Meara. London: Penguin Books, 1972.

————. *The Confessions of St. Augustine,* trans. John K. Ryan. Garden City, NY: Image Books, 1960.

————. *The Enchiridion: On Faith, Hope, and Love,* trans. J. F. Shaw; ed. Henry Paolucci. Chicago: Regnery Gateway, 1961.

————. *Expositions on the Book of Psalms,* vol. 5. Oxford: John Henry Parker, 1853.

————. *Letters,* vol. 3, trans. Sister Wilfrid Parsons, SND. New York: Fathers of the Church, 1953.

————. *The Literal Meaning of Genesis,* trans. John Hammond Taylor. New York: Newman Press, 1982.

————. *The Nature of the Good against the Manichees* (De natura boni). In *Augustine: Earlier Writings,* trans. and ed. J. H. S. Burleigh. Philadelphia: Westminster Press, 1953.

————. *On Free Will.* In *Augustine: Earlier Writings,* trans. John H. S. Burleigh. Philadelphia: Westminster Press, 1953.

————. *On the Psalms.* Ancient Christian Writers 29. New York: Newman Press, 1960.

————. *The Trinity* (De Trinitate), trans. Stephen McKenna, CSSR. Washington, DC: Catholic University of America Press, 1963.

Basil, Saint. *On the Hexaemeron.* In *Exegetic Homilies,* trans. Sister Agnes Clare Way. Washington, DC: Catholic University of America Press, 1963.

Bede, Venerable. "Life of St Cuthbert." In *Two Lives of Saint Cuthbert,* ed. and trans. Bertram Colgrave. Cambridge: Cambridge University Press, 1940.

Benedict, Saint. *The Rule of Benedict: A Guide to Christian Living,* with commentary by George Holzherr; trans. Monks of Glenstal Abbey. Dublin: Four Courts Press, 1994.

Bernard of Clairvaux, Saint. *Selected Writings,* trans. G. R. Evans. New York: Paulist Press, 1987.

Boethius, Anicius Manlius Severinus. *The Consolation of Philosophy,* trans. William Anderson. Carbondale: Southern Illinois University Press, 1963.

Bonaventure, Saint. *The Life of St. Francis.* In *Bonaventure,* trans. Ewert Cousins. New York: Paulist Press, 1978.

————. *The Soul's Journey into God* (Itinerarium mentis in Deum). In *Bonaventure,* trans. Ewert Cousins. New York: Paulist Press, 1978.

Clement of Alexandria, Saint. *Stromateis,* trans. John Ferguson. Washington, DC: Catholic University of America Press, 1991.

Ephrem, Syrus, Saint. *Hymnen de ecclesia,* trans. Edmund Beck. Louvain: Secrétariat du Corpus SCO, 1960.

————. *Hymnen de fide,* trans. Edmund Beck. Louvain: L. Durbecq, 1955.

————. *Hymns,* trans. Kathleen E. McVey. New York: Paulist Press, 1989.

————. *Hymns on Paradise,* trans. Sebastian Brock. Crestwood, NY: St. Vladimir's Seminary Press, 1998.

————. *Selected Prose Works,* trans. Edward G. Matthews Jr. and Joseph P. Amar; ed. Kathleen McVey. Washington, DC: Catholic University of America Press, 1994.

Eriugena, John Scotus. *Periphyseon* (The Division of Nature), trans. I. P. Sheldon-Williams. Washington, DC: Dumbarton Oaks, 1987.

Francis of Assisi, Saint. "The Canticle of Brother Sun." In *Francis and Clare: The Complete Works,* trans. Regis J. Armstrong, OFM, and Ignatius C. Brady, OFM. New York: Paulist Press, 1982.

———. *Francis of Assisi: Early Documents,* ed. Regis J. Armstrong, J. A. Wayne Hellmann, and William J. Short. Hyde Park, NY: New City Press, 1999.

———. *The Little Flowers of St. Francis,* trans. Raphael Brown. Garden City, NY: Image Books, 1958.

Gregory, Lady Isabella. *A Book of Saints and Wonders Put Down Here by Lady Gregory According to the Old Writings and the Memory of the People of Ireland.* London: J. Murray, 1908.

Gregory of Nyssa, Saint. *The Great Catechism.* In *A Select Library of Nicene and Post-Nicene Fathers of the Christian Church,* vol. 5, ed. Philip Schaff. Grand Rapids: William B. Eerdmans, 1956.

Hildegard of Bingen, Saint. *Book of Divine Works,* ed. Matthew Fox; trans. Robert Cunningham. Santa Fe: Bear & Co., 1987.

———. *Symphonia: A Critical Edition of the Symphonia armonie celestium revelationum,* 2nd edition, ed. and trans. Barbara Newman. Ithaca, NY: Cornell University Press, 1998.

Hugh of Saint Victor. "The Three Days of Invisible Light" (De tribus diebus invisibilis lucis). In *Eruditionis didascalicae libri septum,* book 7, trans. Roland J. Teske, SJ. Milwaukee: Marquette University Press, 1996.

International Union for Conservation of Nature. "Red List." www.iucnredlist.org/.

Jerome, Saint. *Life of Hilarion.* In *Early Christian Lives,* ed. and trans. Carolinne White. London: Penguin Books, 1998.

———. "Life of Paul of Thebes." In *Early Christian Lives,* ed. and trans. Carolinne White. London: Penguin Books, 1998.

John Chrysostom, Saint. *Homilies on Genesis 1–17,* trans. Robert C. Hill. Washington, DC: Catholic University of America Press, 1986.

———. "Homilies on the Statues." In *Saint Chrysostom: The Priesthood; Ascetic Treatists; Select Homilies and Letters,* vol. 9, Select Library of the Nicene and Post-Nicene Fathers of the Christian Church, ed. Philip Schaff. Grand Rapids: William. B Eerdmans, 1956.

John of the Cross, Saint. "The Spiritual Canticle." In *The Collected Works of St. John of the Cross,* trans. Kieran Kavanaugh, OCD, and Otilio Rodriguez, OCD. Washington, DC: ICS Publications, 1973.

John of Damascus, Saint. *On the Divine Images: Three Apologies against Those Who Attack the Divine Images,* trans. David Anderson. Crestwood, NY: St. Vladimir's Seminary Press, 1980.

Julian of Norwich. *Showings,* trans. Edmund Colledge and James Walsh. New York: Paulist Press, 1978.

Moschus, John. *Pratum spirituale.* In *The Desert Fathers,* ed. and trans. Helen Waddell. New York: Sheed & Ward, 1942.

Origen. *Contra Celsum,* trans. Henry Chadwick. Cambridge: Cambridge University Press, 1953.

Palamas, Gregory, Saint. *The Triads,* ed. John Meyendorff; trans. Nicholas Gendle. New York: Paulist Press, 1983.

Palladius. *Lausiac History,* trans. Robert Meyer. Ancient Christian Writers, no. 34. London: Longmans, Green, 1965.

Plummer, Carolus, ed. *Bethada náem nÉrenn, Lives of Irish Saints,* vol. 2. Oxford: Claren-
    don Press, 1997.

Pseudo-Dionysius. *The Divine Names.* In *The Complete Works,* trans. Colm Luibheid with
    notes and collaboration by Paul Rorem. New York: Paulist Press, 1987.

Rufinus of Aquilea. "History of the Monks of Egypt." In *The Desert Fathers,* ed. and trans.
    Helen Waddell. Ann Arbor: University of Michigan Press, 1957.

Symeon the New Theologian. *The Discourses,* trans. C. J. deCatanzaro. New York: Paulist
    Press, 1980.

Tertullian. *Adversus Marcionem,* edit. and trans. Ernest Evans. Oxford: Clarendon Press,
    1972.

Theodoret, Bishop of Cyrrhus. *Discours sur la Providence,* trans. Yvan Azéma. Paris: Les
    Belles Lettres, 1954.

Thomas of Celano. *St. Francis of Assisi: First and Second Life of St. Francis, with Selections
    from Treatise on the Miracles of Blessed Francis,* trans. Placid Hermann, OFM. Chicago:
    Franciscan Herald Press, 1963.

Unknown. "Description of the Position and Site of the Abbey of Clairvaux." In *Life and
    Works of Saint Bernard,* vol. 2, ed. Dom John Mabillon; trans. Samuel J. Eales. Lon-
    don: Burns & Oates, 1889.

Unknown. *The Lives of the Desert Fathers: The Historia Monachorum in Aegypto,* trans. Nor-
    man Russell. Kalamazoo: Cistercian Press, 1981.

Waddell, Helen, ed. *Beasts and Saints,* trans. Helen Waddell. London: Constable & Com-
    pany, 1934.

———. *The Desert Fathers,* trans. Helen Waddell. New York: Sheed and Ward, 1942.

SECONDARY SOURCES

Aalen, F. H. A. *Man and Landscape in Ireland.* London: Academic Press, 1978.

Abram, David. "The Perceptual Implications of Gaia." *The Ecologist* 15, no. 3 (1985): 96–103.

———. *The Spell of the Sensuous: Perception and Language in a More-than-Human World.* New
    York: Pantheon Books, 1996.

Adams, Douglas G. "Sacramental Worship for Creation Consciousness." In *Cry of the En-
    vironment,* ed. Philip N. Joranson and Ken Butigan. Santa Fe: Bear & Co., 1984.

Alliance for the Great Lakes. "Ensuring a Living Resource for All Generations." Alliance
    for the Great Lakes, www.lakemichigan.org.

Allen, John L. "Benedict on Going Green." *National Catholic Reporter,* July 27, 2007,
    http://ncrcafe.org/node/1241.

Allen, Paul M., and Joan deRis Allen. *Francis of Assisi's Canticle of the Creatures: A New Spir-
    itual Path.* New York: Continuum International, 2000.

Ambrose, Roma. "Insight: Canada Maps Out New Position on Kyoto Protocol." *Environ-
    mental News Service,* June 21, 2006, www.ens-newswire.com/ens/ju2006/2006-06-21-
    insamb.asp.

Anderson, Bernard W. *From Creation to New Creation: Old Testament Perspectives.* Minneapo-
    lis: Fortress Press, 1994.

Andersson, Jan Otto. "Our Full, Unequal World." *Inroads* 17 (Summer 2005): 48–57.

Armstrong, Edward A. *Saint Francis: Nature Mystic; the Derivation and Significance of the
    Nature Stories in the Franciscan Legend.* Berkeley: University of California Press, 1973.

Armstrong, H. Hilary. "Negative Theology, Myth, and Incarnation." In *Neoplatonism and
    Christian Thought,* ed. Dominic J. O'Meara, 213–22. Norfolk: International Society for
    Neoplatonic Studies, 1982.

Ashley, Benedict M. *Theologies of the Body: Humanist and Christian.* Saint Louis: Pope John Center, 1985.

Ashworth, William. *The Late, Great Lakes: An Environmental History.* New York: Alfred A. Knopf, 1986.

Ayala, Francisco. "Evolution and the Uniqueness of Humankind." *Origins* 27, no. 34 (February 12, 1998): 565–80.

Ayres, Robert U., Joreon C. J. M. van den Bergh, and John M. Gowdy. "Strong Versus Weak Sustainability: Economics, Natural Sciences, and 'Consilience.'" *Environmental Ethics* 23 (2001): 155–68.

Bamford, Christopher. "Ecology and Holiness: The Heritage of Celtic Christianity." In *Celtic Christianity: Ecology and Holiness,* ed. William Parker Marsh. Great Barrington, MA: Lindisfarne Press, 1987.

Barbour, Ian G. *Ethics in an Age of Technology.* San Francisco: HarperSanFrancisco, 1993.

———. "Five Models of God and Evolution." In *Evolutionary and Molecular Biology: Scientific Perspectives on Divine Action,* ed. Robert John Russell, William R. Stoeger, SJ, and Francisco J. Ayala. Vatican City: Vatican Observatory, 1998.

———. *Religion and Science: Historical and Contemporary Issues.* San Francisco: HarperSanFrancisco, 1997.

Barlow, Connie, and Tyler Volk. "Gaia and Evolutionary Biology." *BioScience* 42, no. 9 (October 1992): 686–93.

Barnes, Bill. "The Ecological Economics of Consumption." *Journal of Economic Issues* 40, no. 3 (September 2006): 830–32.

Beckerman, Wilfred. "Sustainable Development: Is It a Useful Concept?" *Environmental Values* 3 (1994): 191–209.

Begon, Michael, John L. Harper, and Colin R. Townsend. *Ecology: Individuals, Populations, and Communities,* 3rd ed. Boston: Blackwell Scientific Publications, 1996.

Bekoff, Marc. "Animal Emotions: Exploring Passionate Natures." *BioScience* 50 (2000): 861–70.

———. "Animal Passions and Beastly Virtues: Cognitive Ethology as the Unifying Science for Understanding the Subjective, Emotional, Empathic, and Moral Lives of Animals." *Zygon* 41, no. 1 (2006): 71–104.

———. *Animal Passions and Beastly Virtues: Reflections on Redecorating Nature.* Philadelphia: Temple University Press, 2005.

———. "Animal Reflections." *Nature* 419 (202): 255.

———. *The Cognitive Animal.* Cambridge, MA: MIT Press, 2002.

———, ed. *Encyclopedia of Animal Behavior.* Westport, CT: Greenwood Press, 2004.

———. *Minding Animals: Awareness, Emotions, and Heart.* Oxford: Oxford University Press, 2002.

———, ed. *The Smile of a Dolphin: Remarkable Accounts of Animal Emotions.* New York: Random House, 2002.

———. *Strolling with Our Kin: Speaking For and Respecting Voiceless Animals.* New York: Lantern Books, 2000.

———. "Wild Justice and Fair Play: Cooperation, Forgiveness, and Morality in Animals." *Biology & Philosophy* 19 (2004): 489–520.

Bell, James J., and David K. A. Barnes. "The Influences of Bathymetry and Flow Regime upon the Morphology of Sublittoral Sponge Communities." *Journal of the Marine Biological Association of the UK* 80, no. 4 (2000): 707–18.

Benedict XVI, Pope. *Deus caritas est*. Encyclical Letter on Christian Love, Vatican City State, December 25, 2005.

———. "Faith, Reason and the University: Memories and Reflections." Lecture at Meeting with the Representatives of Science, University of Regensburg, September 12, 2006.

———. "The Human Family, A Community of Peace of Pope Benedict." World Day of Peace Message, January 1, 2008.

Benestad, Brian J. "How the Catholic Church Serves the Common Good." In *The Battle for the Catholic Mind: Catholic Faith and Catholic Intellect in the Work of the Fellowship of Catholic Scholars, 1978–95*, ed. William E. May and Kenneth D. Whitehead. South Bend, IN: St. Augustine Press, 2001.

Bent, Robert, Lloyd Orr, and Randall Baker, eds. *Energy: Science, Policy, and the Pursuit of Sustainability*. Washington, DC: Island Press, 2002.

Berg, Linda R., and Peter H. Raven. *Environment*, 3rd ed. San Antonio: Harcourt College Publishers, 2001.

Berry, Thomas. "Teilhard in the Ecological Age," in *Teilhard in the 21st Century*, ed. Arthur Fabel and Donald St. John, 57–76 (Maryknoll, NY: Orbis Books, 2005).

Birch, Charles, and John B. Cobb Jr. *The Liberation of Life: From the Cell to the Community*. Denton, TX: Environmental Ethics Books, 1990.

Black, Kenneth. *Environmental Impacts of Aquaculture*. Boca Raton, FL: CRC Press, 2001.

Blanchette, Oliva. *The Perfection of the Universe According to Aquinas: A Teleological Cosmology*. University Park: Pennsylvania State University Press, 1991.

Blumenthal, H. J., and R. A. Markus, eds. *Neoplatonism and Early Christian Thought: Essays in Honour of A. H. Armstrong*. London: Variorum Publications, 1981.

Booth, Douglas E. *Biocentric Environmental Values and Support for the Ecological Restoration of an Urban Watersheds*. Milwaukee: Institute for Urban Environmental Risk Management, Marquette University, 2000.

Booth, Edward. "St. Augustine's 'notitia sui' Related to Aristotle and the Early Neoplatonists." *Augustiniana* 27 (1977):70–132.

Bosveld, Jane. "Life According to Gaia: Cooperation, Not Competition, May Drive Evolutionary Diversity on Earth." *Omni* 14, no. 1 (October 1991): 66–70.

Boulding, Kenneth E. "What Went Wrong, If Anything, Since Copernicus?" *Science and Public Affairs* 30 (January 1974): 17–23.

Boyd, Brian, and Kurt Johnson. "Nabokov, Scientist." *Natural History* 108 (July–August 1999): 46–50.

Brady, Jules M. "Augustine's Theory of Seminal Reasons." *The New Scholasticism* 38 (1964): 141–58.

Bratton, Susan Power. *Christianity, Wilderness, and Wildlife: The Original Desert Solitaire*. Scranton, PA: University of Scranton Press, 1993.

———. "The Original Desert Solitaire: Early Christian Monasticism and Wilderness." *Environmental Ethics* 10 (Spring 1988): 31–53.

Brock, Sebastian P. "Humanity and the Natural World in the Syriac Tradition." *Sobernost* 12, no. 2 (1990): 131–42.

———. *The Luminous Eye: The Spiritual World Vision of Saint Ephrem*. Kalamazoo: Cistercian Publications, 1992.

Brown, B. E., and J. C. Odgen. "Coral Bleaching." *Scientific American* 269 (1993): 64–70.

Brown, Noel J., and Pierre Quiblier, eds. *Ethics & Agenda 21: Moral Implications of a Global Consensus*. New York: United Nations Environmental Program, 1994.

Bruce, James P. *From Climate to Weather: Impacts on Society and Economy, Natural Disasters Roundtable, Washington, DC, June 28, 2002.* Washington, DC: National Academies Press, 2003.

Brundtland, Gro Harlem. "Overview." In *World Health Report 2002: Reducing Risks and Promoting Health Life.* Geneva: World Health Organization, 2002.

Bryant, Dirk. *Vital Signs 2002: Trends That Are Shaping Our Future.* New York: W. W. Norton for Worldwatch Institute, 2002.

Bryant, Dirk, Daniel Nielsen, and Laura Tangley. *The Last Frontier Forests: Ecosystems and Economies on the Edge.* Washington, DC: World Resources Institute, 1997.

Bundy, David D. "Language and Knowledge of God in Ephrem Syrus." *Patristic and Byzantine Review* 5 (1986): 91–103.

Bunyard, Peter. "The Gaia Hypothesis and Man's Responsibility to the Earth." *The Ecologist* 13, no. 5 (1983): 158–59.

Buttell, F. H. "Social Science and the Environment: Competing Theories." *Social Science Quarterly* 57 (1976): 307–23.

Cafaro, Philip J., Richard B. Primark, and Robert L. Zimdahl. "The Fat of the Land: Linking American Food Overconsumption, Obesity, and Biodiversity Loss." *Journal of Agricultural and Environmental Ethics* 19, no. 6 (2006): 541–61.

Calabrese, Edward. *Multiple Chemical Interactions.* Chelsea, MI: Lewis Publishers, 1991.

Callicott, J. Baird. *Beyond the Land Ethic: More Essays in Environmental Philosophy.* Albany: State University of New York Press, 1999.

———. "The Case against Moral Pluralism." *Environmental Ethics* 12 (1990): 99–124.

———. *In Defense of the Land Ethic: Essays in Environmental Philosophy.* Albany: State University of New York Press, 1989.

———. "Holistic Environmental Ethics and the Problem of Ecofascism." In *Environmental Philosophy: From Animal Rights to Radical Ecology,* 3rd edition, ed. J. Baird Callicott, Michael E. Zimmerman, George Sessions, Karen J. Warren, and John Clark. Upper Saddle River, NJ: Prentice Hall, 2001.

———. "Intrinsic Value in Nature: A Metaethical Analysis." In *Beyond the Land Ethic: More Essays in Environmental Philosophy,* ed. J. Baird Callicott. Albany: State University of New York Press, 1999.

———. "Intrinsic Value, Quantum Theory, and Environmental Ethics." *Environmental Ethics* 7, no. 3 (1985): 257–75.

———. "Moral Monism in Environmental Ethics Defended." *Journal of Philosophical Research* 90 (1994): 51–60.

———. "On the Intrinsic Value of Nonhuman Species." In *The Preservation of Species,* ed. Bryan G. Norton. Princeton, NJ: Princeton University Press, 1986.

———. "The Wilderness Idea Revisited: The Sustainable Development Alternative." *The Environmental Professional* 13 (1991): 235–47.

Carlson, Allen. "Nature, Aesthetic Appreciation, and Knowledge." *Journal of Aesthetics and Art Criticism* 53 (Fall 1995): 393–400.

Carroll, Noël. "On Being Moved by Nature: Between Religion and Natural History." In *Landscape, Natural Beauty and the Arts,* ed. S. Kemal and I. Gaskell. Cambridge: Cambridge University Press, 1993.

Carson, Thomas L., and Paul K. Moser, eds. *Morality and the Good Life.* New York: Oxford University Press, 1997.

Catton, William R., Jr., and Riley E. Dunlap. "A New Ecological Paradigm for Post-Exuberant Sociology." *American Behavioral Scientist* 24 (September–October 1980): 15–47.

Cessario, Romanus. *The Virtues, Or, the Examined Life.* New York: Continuum International, 2002.

Chapman, J. L., and M. J. Reiss. *Ecology: Principles and Applications.* New York: Cambridge University Press, 1992.

Chenu, M.-D., OP. *Toward Understanding Saint Thomas,* trans. A.-M. Landry and D. Hughes, OP. Chicago: Henry Regnery, 1964.

Chitty, Derwas J. *The Desert a City: An Introduction to the Study of Egyptian and Palestinian Monasticism under the Christian Empire.* Crestwood, NY: St. Vladimir's Seminary Press, 1966.

Chivian, Eric, and Aaron Bernstein, eds. *Sustaining Life: How Human Health Depends on Biodiversity.* Oxford: Oxford University Press, 2008.

Christie, W. J., M. Becker, J. W. Cowden, and J. R. Vallentyne. "Managing the Great Lakes as a Home." *Journal of Great Lakes Research* 12 (1986): 2–17.

Cizewski, Wanda. "Reading the World as Scripture: Hugh of St Victor's *De Tribus Diebus.*" *Florilegium* 9 (1987): 65–88.

Clarke, Stephen R. L. *Biology and Christian Ethics.* New York: Cambridge University Press, 2000.

Clarke, W. Norris, SJ. "Is a Natural Theology Still Possible Today?" In *Physics, Philosophy, Theology: A Common Quest for Understanding,* ed. Robert John Russell, William R. Stoeger, SJ, and George V. Coyne, SJ. Vatican City: Vatican Observatory, 1997.

Commons, Mick, and Charles Perrings. "Towards an Ecological Economics of Sustainability." *Ecological Economics* 6 (1992): 7–34.

Congar, Yves M.-J. *Tradition and Traditions: An Historical and a Theological Essay.* London: Burns & Oates, 1966.

Cooke, Bernard. *Sacraments and Sacramentality.* Mystic, CT: Twenty-Third Publications, 1989.

Cooper, William. "Scenes from Science: Who's for Gaia?" *The Spectator,* March 3, 1990, 23.

Copleston, F. C. *Aquinas: An Introduction to the Life and Work of the Great Medieval Thinker.* London: Penguin Books, 1955.

Council of Trent. *Canons and Decrees of the Council of Trent,* ed. and trans. H. J. Schroeder, OP. Saint Louis: Herder Press, 1941.

Crisp, Roger, and Michael Slote, eds. *Virtue Ethics.* New York: Oxford University Press, 1997.

Darwell, Stephen. *Virtue Ethics.* Malden, MA: Blackwell, 2003.

Davies, Paul. *The Cosmic Blueprint.* New York: Simon & Schuster, 1988.

———. *The Mind of God.* New York: Simon & Schuster, 1992.

Davis, Steven M., and John C. Ogden. *Everglades: The Ecosystem and Its Restoration.* Delray Beach, FL: St. Lucie Press, 1994.

Deane-Drummond, Celia. *Biology and Theology Today: Exploring the Boundaries.* London: SCM Press, 2001.

———. *A Handbook in Theology and Ecology.* London: SCM Press, 1996.

de Broglie, Louis. *Heisenberg's Uncertainties and the Probabilistic Interpretation of Wave Mechanics,* trans. Alwyn vander Merwe. Boston: Kluwer Academic Publishers, 1990.

Delio, Ilia, OSF. *A Franciscan View of Creation: Learning to Live in a Sacramental World.* Franciscan Heritage Series, vol. 2. Saint Bonaventure, NY: Franciscan Institute, 2003.

de Luce, J., and H. T. Wilder, eds. *Language in Primates.* New York: Springer-Verlag, 1983.

Devall, Bill, and George Sessions. *Deep Ecology: Living as If Nature Mattered.* Salt Lake City: Gibbs Smith, 1985.

———. "The Development of Nature Resources and the Integrity of Nature." *Environmental Ethics* 6 (1984): 293–322.

Diamond, Jared. *The Third Chimpanzee: The Evolution and Future of the Human Animal.* New York: HarperPerennial, 1992.

Dillard, Annie. *Pilgrim at Tinker Creek.* New York: Harper's Magazine Press, 1974.

Dohzhansky, Theodore. *The Biological Basis of Human Freedom.* New York: Columbia University Press, 1956.

———. *The Biology of Ultimate Concern.* New York: New American Library, 1967.

Douglas, Marjory Stoneman. *The Everglades: River of Grass.* Sarasota, FL: Pineapple Press, 1988.

Dryer, J. L. E. "Medieval Cosmology." In *Theories of the Universe: From Babylonian Myth to Modern Science,* ed. Milton K. Munitz. New York: Macmillan, 1957.

Dubos, René. "Franciscan Conservation versus Benedictine Stewardship." In *Ecology and Religion in History,* ed. David and Eileen Spring. New York: Harper & Row, 1974.

Duckett, Eleanor Shipley. *Wandering Saints of the Early Middle Ages.* New York: W. W. Norton, 1959.

Dunlap, Riley E., and Kent D. Van Liere. "Land Ethic or Golden Rule." *Journal of Social Issues* 33 (1977): 200–207.

———. "The 'New Environmental Paradigm': A Proposed Measuring Instrument and Preliminary Results." *Journal of Environmental Education* 9 (1978): 10–19.

Durning, Alan. "How Much Is Enough?" *Technology Review* 94, no. 4 (May–June 1991): 56–63.

Dusseault, Maurice B. Untitled. www.tpao.gov.tr/spe/meetings/dusseaultabs.htm.

Dworkin, Ronald. *Life's Dominion: An Argument about Abortion, Euthanasia, and Individual Freedom.* New York: Alfred A. Knopf, 1993.

Earth Trends Environmental Information. "July 2006 Monthly Update: World Population Growth—Past, Present, and Future." Earth Trends, www.earthtrends.wri.org/updates/node/61.

Eco, Umberto. *The Aesthetics of Thomas Aquinas,* trans. Hugh Bredin. Cambridge, MA: Harvard University Press, 1988.

Ehrlich, Paul R., and Anne H. Ehrlich. *One with Nineveh: Politics, Consumption, and the Human Future.* Washington, DC: Island Press, 2004.

Ehrlich, Paul R., and Jonathan Roughgarden. *The Science of Ecology.* New York: Macmillan, 1987.

Eilperin, Juliet. "Growing Acidity of Oceans May Kill Corals." *Washington Post,* July 5, 2006.

Elliot, Robert. "Intrinsic Value, Environmental Obligation and Naturalism." *The Monist* 75 (1992): 138–60.

Energy Information Administration. *Annual Energy Review.* Report DOE/EIA-0384. Washington, DC: U.S. Department of Energy, 2005.

———. "Crude Oil and Total Petroleum Imports Top 15 Countries." U.S. Department of Energy. July 28, 2006, www.eia.doe.gov/pub/oil_gas/petroleum/data_publications/company_level_imports/current/import.html.

———. "Table 3.2a Crude Oil Overview: Supply." *Monthly Energy Review* U.S. Department of Energy, July 2006, www.eia.doe.gov/emeu/mer/pdf/pages/sec3_6.pdf.

———. "Table 8.1 World Crude Oil and Natural Gas Reserves." In *International Energy Annual 2005,* U.S. Department of Energy, January 1, 2005, www.eia.doe.gov/pub/international/iea2004/table81.xls.

———. "Table 11.4 World Crude Oil and Natural Gas Reserves." U.S. Department of Energy, January 1, 2005, www.eia.doe.gov/emeu/aer/pdf/pages/sec11_9.pdf.

Environment Defense Fund. "Recent Studies: A Summary of Research: Science Tightens the Link between Storms and Climate Change," May 10, 2008, www.environmentaldefense.org/article.cfm?contentid=5316&campaign=486.

Environmental Literacy Council. "Threatened and Endangered Species," May 8, 2008. www.enviroliteracy.org/article.php/33.html.

Environmental News Service. "UN Climate Change Impact Report: Poor Will Suffer Most," April 6, 2007. www.ens-newswire.com/ens/apr2007/2007-04-06-01.asp.

Evans, Joseph Claude. *With Respect for Nature: Living as Part of the Natural World*. Albany: State University of New York Press, 2005.

Fein, Greta G., Joseph L. Jacobson, Sandra W. Jacobson, Pamela M. Schwartz, and Jeffrey K. Dowler. "Prenatal Exposure to Polychlorinated Biphenyls: Effects on Birth Size and Gestational Age." *Journal of Pediatrics* 105 (1984): 315–20.

Food and Agricultural Organization. *Global Forest Resources Assessment 2005: Progress Toward Sustainable Forest Management*. FAO Forestry Paper 147. Rome: Food and Agricultural Organization, 2006.

———. *The State of the World Fisheries and Aquaculture*. Rome: Food and Agricultural Organization, 1997.

Fisheries Institute. "Eutrophication (Nutrient Pollution." Experimental Lakes Area, University of Manitoba. www.umanitoba.ca/institutes/fisheries/eutro.html.

Frank, R. H. *Luxury Fever: Why Money Fails to Satisfy in an Era of Excess*. New York: Free Press, 1999.

French, William C. "Catholicism and the Common Good of the Biosphere." In *An Ecology of the Spirit: Religious Reflection and Environmental Consciousness,* ed. Michael H. Barnes. Lanham, MD: University Press of America, 1994.

———. "Subject-Centered and Creation-Centered Paradigms in Recent Catholic Thought." *Journal of Religion* 70 (1990): 48–72.

Fretheim, Terence E. "Nature's Praise of God in the Psalms." *Ex Auditu* 3 (1987): 16–30.

Frye, Marilyn. *The Politics of Reality: Essays in Feminist Theory.* Trumansburg, NY: Crossing Press, 1983.

Fyfe, William S. "Our Planet Observed: The Assault by Homo Sapiens." In *Planet under Stress: The Challenge of Global Change,* ed. Constance Mungall and Digby J. McLaren, Royal Society of Canada. Toronto: Oxford University Press, 1990.

Gardner, Gary. *Shrinking Fields: Crop Loss in a World of Eight Billion*. Worldwatch Paper 131. Washington, DC: Worldwatch Institute, 1996.

George, Robert P. "Natural Law, the Common Good, and American Politics." In *The Battle for the Catholic Mind: Catholic Faith and Catholic Intellect in the Work of the Fellowship of Catholic Scholars, 1978–95,* ed. William E. May and Kenneth D. Whitehead. South Bend, IN: St. Augustine Press, 2001.

Gilby, Thomas. "Introduction." In *Summa theologiae* by Thomas Aquinas, vol. 8, trans. Blackfriars. New York: McGraw-Hill, 1964.

Gilson, Etienne. *The Christian Philosophy of St. Thomas Aquinas,* trans. L. K. Shook. New York: Random House, 1956.

Glacken, Clarence L. *Traces on the Rhodian Shore: Nature and Culture in Western Thought from Ancient Times to the End of the Eighteenth Century.* Berkeley: University of California Press, 1967.

Gleick, Peter. *The World's Water 2002–2003: The Biennial Report on Freshwater Resources.* Washington, DC: Island Press, 2002.

Glynn, P. W. "Coral Reef Bleaching in the 1980s and Possible Connections with Global Warming." *Trends in Ecology & Evolution* 6, no. 6 (1991): 175–79.

Godlovitch, Stan. "Icebreakers: Environmentalism and Natural Aesthetics." *Journal of Applied Philosophy* 11 (1994): 15–30.

Golley, Frank B. *A History of the Ecosystem Concept in Ecology.* Princeton, NJ: Princeton University Press, 1994.

Goodenough, Ursula. *The Sacred Depths of Nature.* New York: Oxford University Press, 1998.

Goodman, David C., ed. *Science and Religious Belief 1600–1900.* Dorchester, U.K.: Open University, 1973.

Goodpaster, Kenneth. "From Egoism to Environmentalism." In *Ethics and Problems of the 21st Century,* ed. K. E. Goodpaster and K. M. Sayre. Notre Dame, IN: Notre Dame University Press, 1979.

———. "On Being Morally Considerable." In *Ethics and the Environment,* ed. Donald Scherer and Thomas Attig. Englewood Cliffs, NJ: Prentice Hall, 1983.

Goreau, T., J. Goreau, and R. L. Hayes. "Coral Bleaching and Ocean 'Hot Spots.'" *Ambio* 23 (1994): 176–80.

Goreau, Tom, Tim McClanahan, Ray Hayes, and Al Strong. "Conservation of Coral Reefs after the 1998 Global Bleaching Event." *Conservation Biology* 14.1 (February 2000): 5–15.

Gould, Stephen J. *Wonderful Life: The Burgess Shale and the Nature of History.* New York: W. W. Norton, 1989.

Great Lakes Information Network. "Remedial Action Plans for the Great Lakes Areas of Concern." Great Lakes Information Network. www.great-lakes.net/envt/pollution/rap.html.

Great Lakes National Program Office. "Great Lakes Areas of Concern." U.S. Environmental Protection Agency. www.epa.gov/glnpo/aoc/.

Great Lakes Science Advisory Board. *The Ecosystem Approach: Scope and Implications of an Ecosystem Approach to Transboundary Problems in the Great Lakes Basin.* Windsor: International Joint Commission, 1978.

———. *Report to the International Joint Commission.* Windsor: International Joint Commission, 1991.

Great Lakes United. "Who We Are." www.glu.org/english/index.html.

Great Lakes Water Quality Board. *Cleaning Up Our Great Lakes.* Windsor: International Joint Commission, 1991.

———. *Report on Great Lakes Water Quality.* Windsor: International Joint Commission, 1987.

Gregersen, Nels. "Critical Realism and Other Realisms." In *Fifty Years in Science and Religion: Ian G. Barbour and His Legacy,* ed. Robert John Russell. Burlington, VT: Ashgate, 2004.

Gunton, Colin. "Trinity, Ontology and Anthropology: Towards a Renewal of the Doctrine of the *Imago Dei.*" In *Persons, Divine and Human,* ed. Christoph Schwööbel and Colin Gunton. Edinburgh: T & T Clark, 1991.

Gustafson, James M. *Ethics from a Theocentric Perspective: Theology and Ethics,* vol. 1. Chicago: University of Chicago Press, 1981.

Hall, Douglas John. *Imaging God: Dominion as Stewardship.* Grand Rapids: William B. Eerdmans, 1986.

———. "Stewardship of the Earth in the Old Testment." In *Tending the Garden: Essays on the Gospel and the Earth,* ed., Wesley Granberg-Michaelson. Grand Rapids, MI: William B. Eerdmans, 1987), 50–64.

Hamilton, Calvin J. "Earth from Space: Quotes from Astronauts." www.solarviews.com/eng/earthsp.htm#quote.

Hardin, Garrett. "The Tragedy of the Commons." *Science* 162 (December 13, 1968): 1243–48.

Hargrove, Eugene C. *Foundations of Environmental Ethics.* Englewood Cliffs, NJ: Prentice Hall, 1989.

———. "Weak Anthropocentric Intrinsic Value." *The Monist* 75, no. 2 (1992): 183–212.

Harrison, Carol. *Beauty and Revelation in the Thought of Saint Augustine.* Oxford: Clarendon Press, 1992.

Harrison, Paul, and Fred Pearce, eds. *AAAS Atlas of Population and Environment.* Berkeley: University of California Press for American Association for the Advancement of Science, 2000.

Hart, John. *Sacramental Commons: Christian Ecological Ethics.* Lanham, MD: Rowman & Littlefield, 2006.

Hatch, Richard W., Stephen J. Nepszy, Kenneth M. Muth, and Carl T. Baker. "Dynamics of the Recovery of the Western Lake Erie Walleye (*Stizostedion Vitreum Vitreum*) Stock." *Canadian Journal of Fishery Aquatic Science* 44 (1984): 15–22.

Hatcher, Harlan, and Erich A. Walter. *A Pictorial History of the Great Lakes.* New York: Bonanza Books, 1963.

Haught, John F. *The Promise of Nature: Ecology and Cosmic Purpose.* New York: Paulist Press, 1993.

———. *Science and Religion: From Conflict to Conversation.* New York: Paulist Press, 1995.

Hawking, Stephen. *A Brief History of Time: From the Big Bang to Black Holes.* New York: Bantam Books, 1988.

Heat Island Group. "Evapotranspiration," Laurence Berkeley National Laboratory, http://eetd.lbl.gov/HeatIsland//LEARN/Evapo.

Hefner, Philip J. *The Human Factor: Evolution, Culture, and Religion.* Minneapolis: Fortress Press, 1993.

Heisenberg, Werner. *The Physicist's Conception of Nature,* trans. Arnold J. Pomerans. New York: Harcourt Brace, 1958.

Henderson, R. S. "Marine Microcosm Experiments on Effects of Copper and Tributyltin-Based Antifouling Paint Leachates." CSA Guide to Discovery, md1.csa.com/partners/viewrecord.php?requester=gs&collection=ENV&recid=2995225&q=&uid=788579802&setcookie=yes.

Heywood, V. H., ed. *The Global Biodiversity Assessment..* Cambridge: Cambridge University Press for United Nations Environment Program, 1995.

Himes, Michael J., and Kenneth R. Himes. *Fullness of Faith: The Public Significance of Theology.* New York: Paulist Press, 1993.

———. "The Sacrament of Creation: Toward an Environmental Theology." In *Readings in Ecology and Feminist Theology,* ed. Mary Heather MacKinnon and Moni McIntyre. Kansas City: Sheed & Ward, 1995.

Hirschfeld, Mary. "Standard of Living and Economic Virtue: Forging a Link between St. Thomas Aquinas and the Twenty-First Century." *Journal of the Society of Christian Ethics* 26 (Spring–Summer 2006): 61–78.

Hodgson, G. "A Global Assessment of Human Effects on Coral Reefs." *Marine Pollution Bulletin* 38 (1999): 345–55.

Holling, Crawford S. "Resilience and Stability of Ecological Systems." *Annual Review of Ecological Systems* 4 (1973): 1–24.

Houck, John W., and Oliver Williams, CSC., eds. *Co-Creation and Capitalism: John Paul II's Laborem Exercens.* Lanham, MD: University Press of America, 1983.

Houghton, John T., L. G. Meiro Filho, B. A. Callander, N. Harris, A. Kattenberg, and K. Maskell, eds. *Climate Change 1995: The Science of Climate Change.* Contribution of Working Group I to the Second Assessment Report of the Intergovernmental Panel on Climate Change. Cambridge: Cambridge University Press, 1996.

Hryhorczuk, Daniel. "Anthropogenic Chemicals in the Great Lakes Basin: Human Health Effects." U.S. Environmental Protection Agency. www.epa.gov/glnpo/solec/solec_2006/.

Huggett, Richard J. *Climate, Earth Processes, and Earth History.* New York: Springer, 1991.

Imhoff, M. L., D. Stutzer, W. T. Lawrence, and C. Elvidge. "Assessing the Impact of Urban Sprawl on Soil Resources in the United States Using Nighttime 'City Lights' Satellite Images and Digital Soil Maps." In *Perspectives on the Land Use History of North America: A Context for Understanding Our Changing Environment,* ed. T. D. Sisk. Biological Sciences Report USGS/BRD-1998-0003. Springfield, VA: U.S. Geological Survey, 1998.

Intergovernmental Panel on Climate Change, *Climate Change 2007: Impacts, Adaptation, and Vulnerability—Contribution of Working Group II to the Fourth Assessment Report of the Intergovernmental Panel on Climate Change,* ed. M. M. Parry, O. F. Canziani, J. P. Palutikof, P. J. van der Linden, and C. E. Hanson. Cambridge: Cambridge University Press, 2007.

———. *Climate Change 2007: The Physical Science Basis.* Cambridge: Cambridge University Press, 2007.

———. "Summary for Policymakers." In *The Regional Impacts of Climate Change: An Assessment of Vulnerability,* ed. R. T. Watson, M. C. Zinyowera, and R. H. Moss. Cambridge: Cambridge University Press, 1998. www.ipcc.ch/ipccreports/sres/regional/512.htm.

International Joint Commission. *Advice to Governments on Their Review of the Great Lakes Water Quality Agreement: A Special Report to the Governments of Canada and the United States.* Ottawa and Washington: International Joint Commission, 2006.

———. *Beacons of Light/Des Lumièères dans la Nuit.* March 1998. www.ijc.org/boards/annex2/beacon/beacon.html.

———. *Expert Consultation on Emerging Issues of the Great Lakes in the 21st Century,* ed. Peter Boyer, Allan Jones, and Deborah Swackhamer. Papers Submitted to Great Lakes Science Advisory Board of International Joint Commission at Wingspread, Racine, WI, February 5–7, 2003. Ottawa and Washington: International Joint Commission, 2006.

———. *Fifth Biennial Report under the Great Lakes Water Quality Agreement of 1978 to the Governments of the United States and Canada and the State and Provincial Governments of the Great Lakes Basin.* 2 vols. Ottawa and Washington: International Joint Commission, 1990.

————. "Great Lakes Water Quality Agreement." Ottawa, November 22, 1978.

————. *Report on Spills in the Great Lakes Basin with a Special Focus on the St. Clair–Detroit River Corridor.* Ottawa and Washington: International Joint Commission, 2006.

————. *Status of Restoration Activities in Great Lakes Areas of Concern: A Special Report.* Ottawa and Washington: International Joint Commission, 2003. www.ijc.org/php/publications/pdf/ID1500.pdf.

————. *12th Biennial Report on the Great Lakes Water Quality.* Ottawa and Washington: International Joint Commission, 2004.

International Society for Reef Studies. "Statement on Diseases on Coral Reefs." www.fit.edu/isrs/council/disease.htm.

International Union for Conservation of Nature. "Red List." www.iucnredlist.org/.

Irvin, Kevin W. "Sacrament." In *The New Dictionary of Theology.*, ed. Joseph A. Komonchak, Mary Collins, and Dermot A. Lane. Collegeville, MN: Liturgical Press, 1987.

Jacobs, Jürgen. "Diversity, Stability and Maturity in Ecosystems Influenced by Human Activities." In *Unifying Concepts in Ecology: Report of the Plenary Sessions of the First International Congress of Ecology, The Hague, The Netherlands, September 8–14, 1974,* ed. W. H. van Dobben and R. H. Lowe-McConnell. The Hague: Dr. W. Junk BV, 1975.

Jacobson, Joseph L., Sandra W. Jacobson, and H. E. B. Humphrey. "Effects of Exposure to PCBs and Related Compounds in Growth and Activity in Children." *Neurotoxicology and Teratology* 12 (1990): 319–26.

Jacobson, Joseph L., Sandra W. Jacobson, and H. E. B. Humphrey. "Effects of *In Utero* Exposure to Polychlorinated Biphenyls and Related Contaminants on Cognitive Functioning in Young Children." *Journal of Pediatrics* 116 (1990): 38–45.

Jet Propulsion Laboratory. "Emerging Modern Universe: Understanding How Today's Universe of Galaxies, Stars, and Planets Came to Be." National Aeronautical Space Administration. http://origins.jpl.nasa.gov/universe/index.html.

John Paul II. *Centesimus Annus: Encyclical on the 100th Anniversary of Pope Leo XIII's Rerum Novarum.* Rome, May 1, 1991.

————. *Ecclesia in America.* Apostolic Exhortation to the Bishops, Priests and Deacons, Men and Women Religions, and All the Lay Faithful, Mexico City, January 22, 1999.

————. "The Ecological Crisis: A Common Responsibility." Vatican City, January 1, 1990.

————. "S. Franciscus Assisiensis caelestis Patronus oecologiae cultorum eligitur." *Acta Apostolicae Sedis—Commentarium Officiale* 71 (1979): 1509–10.

————. "Peace with God the Creator, Peace with All of Creation." Message for the Celebration of the World Day of Peace, January 1, 1990. Vatican City, December 8, 1989.

Johnson, Lawrence E. *A Morally Deep World: An Essay on Moral Significance and Environmental Ethics.* New York: Cambridge University Press, 1991.

————. "Toward the Moral Considerability of Species and Ecosystems." *Environmental Ethics* 14 (1992): 145–57.

Joseph, Lawrence E. *Gaia: The Growth of an Idea.* New York: St. Martin's Press, 1990.

Kadavil, Mathai. *The World as Sacrament: Sacramentality of Creation from the Perspectives of Leonardo Boff, Alexander Schmermann, and Saint Ephrem.* Louvain: Peeters, 2005.

Kaiser, Christopher B. *Creational Theology and the History of Physical Science: The Creationist Tradition from Basil to Bohr.* New York: Brill Academic Publishers, 1997.

Kavanaugh, John F., SJ. "Intrinsic Value, Persons and Stewardship." In *The Challenge of Global Stewardship: Roman Catholic Responses,* ed. Maura A. Ryan and Todd David Whitmore. Notre Dame, IN: University of Notre Dame Press, 1997.

Keenan, James F. "Goodness and Rightness in Aquinas's *Summa Theologiae.*" *The Thomist* 58 (1994): 342–48.

Keesing, Roger. *Kin Groups and Social Structure.* New York: Holt, Rinehart & Winston, 1975.

Kelleher, Margaret Mary, OSU. "Ritual." In *The New Dictionary of Theology.*, ed. Joseph A. Komonchak, Mary Collins, and Dermot A. Lane. Collegeville, MN: Liturgical Press, 1987.

Kellert, Stephen R. "The Biological Basis for Human Values of Nature." In *The Biophilia Hypothesis,* ed. Stephen R. Kellert and Edward O. Wilson. Washington, DC: Island Press, 1993.

———. *Kinship to Mastery: Biophilia in Human Evolution and Development.* Washington, DC: Island Press, 1997.

———. *The Value of Life: Biological Diversity and Human Society.* Washington, DC: Island Press, 1996.

Kerr, Richard A. "No Longer Willful, Gaia Becomes Respectable." *Science* 240 (April 22, 1988): 393–95.

King, Anthony W. "Considerations of Scale and Hierarchy." In *Ecological Integrity and the Management of Ecosystems,* ed. Stephen Woodley, James Kay, and George Francis. Delray Beach, FL: St. Lucie Press, 1993.

Kraye, Jill. "Philosophy, Moral: Medieval and Renaissance." In *New Dictionary of the History of Ideas,* vol. 4, ed. Maryanne Horowitz. New York: Charles Scribner's Sons, 2005.

Krumm, Pascale. "PCBs: Measuring the Danger." *Journal of Environmental Health* 64, no. 10 (June 2002): 31, 34.

Leakey, Richard E., and Roger Lewin. *The Sixth Extinction: Patterns of Life and the Future of Humankind.* New York: Doubleday, 1995.

Ledoux, Arthur O. "A Green Augustine: On Learning to Love Nature Well." *Theology and Science* 3 (November 2005): 331–44.

Lee, Keekok. "The Source and Locus of Intrinsic Value: A Reexamination." *Environmental Ethics* 18 (1996): 297–309.

Legrand, Joseph. *L'univers et l'homme dans la philosophie de Saint Thomas.* 2 vols. Brussels: L'Édition Universelle, 1946.

Lenton, Timothy M. "Gaia and Natural Selection." *Nature* 394 (1998): 439.

Leopold, Aldo. *Sand County Almanac: With Essays on Conservation from Round River.* New York: Ballantine Books, 1966.

Levin, Simon A. "Self-Organization and the Emergence of Complexity in Ecological Systems." *Bioscience* 55, no. 12 (December 2005): 1075–79.

Leyerle, Blake. "Monastic Formation and Christian Practice: Food in the Desert." In *Educating People of Faith: Exploring the History of Jewish and Christian Communities,* ed. John Van Engen. Grand Rapids: William B. Eerdmans, 2004.

———. "Monks and Other Animals." In *The Cultural Turn in Late Ancient Studies: Gender, Asceticism, and Historiography,* ed. Dale B. Martin and Patricia Cox Miller. Durham, NC: Duke University Press, 2005.

Leys, Ad. *Ecclesiological Impacts of the Principle of Subsidiarity.* Kampen: Kok, 1995.

Lindberg, David C. "Science and the Early Church." In *God and Nature: Historical Essays on the Encounter between Christianity and Science,* ed. David C. Lindberg and Ronald L. Numbers. Berkeley: University of California Press, 1986.

Liu, J., G. C. Daily, P. R. Ehrlich, and G. W. Luck. "Effects of Household Dynamics on Resource Consumption and Biodiversity." *Nature* 421 (2003): 530–33.

Llamzon, Benjamin S. "Subsidiarity: The Term, Its Metaphysics and Use." *Aquinas* 21 (January–April 1978): 44–62.

Lock, Patricia D. "EOS and Terra: Seeing Earth as a System." *Odyssey* 13, no. 2 (February 2004): 14–15.

Lodge, David. "From the Balance to the Flux of Nature: The Power of Metaphor in Cross-Discipline Conversations." *Worldviews: Environment, Culture, Religion* 7 (2003): 1–4.

Lodge, Thomas E. *The Everglades Handbook: Understanding the Ecosystem*. Boca Raton: St. Lucie Press, 1998.

Long, William J., Rupert Sheldrake, and Marc Bekoff. *How Animals Talk: And Other Pleasant Studies of Birds and Beasts*. Rochester, VT: Bear & Co., 2005.

Longwood, Merle. "The Common Good: An Ethical Framework for Evaluating Environmental Issues." *Theological Studies* 34 (1973): 468–80.

Lonigan, Paul R. *The Early Irish Church*. Woodside, NY: Celtic Heritage Press, 1985.

Lougheed, V. L., and R. J. Stevenson. "Exotic Marine Algae Reaches Bloom Proportions in a Coastal Lake of Lake Michigan." *Journal of Great Lakes Research* 30, no. 4 (2004): 538–44.

Louisia, S., M. Stromboni, A. Meunier, L. Sedel. "Coral Grafting Supplemented with Bone Marrow." *Journal of Bone and Joint Surgery* 81, no. 4 (July 1999): 719–24.

Lourie, Peter. *Everglades: Buffalo Tiger and the River of Grass*. New York: Boyds Mills Press, 1994.

Lovejoy, Arthur O. *The Great Chain of Being: A Study of the History of an Idea*. Cambridge, MA: Harvard University Press, 1957.

Lovelock, James. *The Ages of Gaia : A Biography of Our Living Earth*. New York: W. W. Norton, 1989.

———. *Gaia: A New Look at Life on Earth*. New York: Oxford University Press, 1979.

———. *Gaia and the Theory of the Living Planet*. Eastbourne, U.K.: Gardners Books, 2005.

———. *Homage to Gaia: The Life of an Independent Scientist*. New York: Oxford University Press, 2000.

———. "The Living Earth." *Nature* 426 (2003): 769–80.

———. "Nuclear Power Is the Only Green Solution." *The Independent*, May 24, 2004. www.ecolo.org/media/articles/articles.in.english/love-indep-24-05-04.htm.

———. "What Is Gaia?" Environmentalists for Nuclear Energy. www.ecolo.org/lovelock/what_is_Gaia.html.

Lovelock, James, and Michael Allaby. *The Greening of Mars*. New York: St. Martin's Press, 1984.

Macior, Lazarus. "A Sense of the Sacred in Creation and Natural Science." In *Proceedings of the 13th Convention of the Fellowship of Catholic Scholars*, ed. P. L. Williams. Pittston, PA: Northeast Books, 1990.

MacLean, Paul D. "Evolution of the Psychencephalon." *Zygon* 17 (1982): 187–211.

MacNickle, Sister Mary Donatus. *Beasts and Birds in the Lives of Early Irish Saints*. Philadelphia: University of Pennsylvania Press, 1934.

Maguire, Daniel C. *The Moral Core of Judaism and Christianity: Reclaiming the Revolution*. Minneapolis: Fortress Press, 1993.

Margulis, Lynn. *Slanted Truths: Essays on Gaia, Symbiosis, and Evolution*. New York : Copernicus Press, 1997.

———. *Symbiotic Planet: A New Look at Evolution*. New York: Basic Books, 1998.

Margulis, Lynn, Clifford Matthews, and Aaron Haselton, eds. *Environmental Evolution: Effects of the Origin and Evolution of Life on Planet Earth,* 2nd ed. Cambridge, MA: MIT Press, 2000.

Maritain, Jacques. *The Person and the Common Good,* trans. John J. Fitzgerald. New York: Charles Scribner's Sons, 1947.

Martin, James Alfred. *Beauty and Holiness: The Dialogue between Aesthetics and Religion.* Princeton, NJ: Princeton University Press, 1990.

Martin, Ronald E. "Gaia Out of Equilibrium?" *Bioscience* 55, no. 9 (September 2005): 799–81.

Martos, Joseph. *Doors to the Sacred: A Historical Introduction to Sacraments in the Catholic Church.* Tarrytown, NY: Triumph Books, 1991.

Matarasso, Pauline, ed. *The Cistercian World: Monastic Writings of the Twelfth Century,* trans. Pauline Matarasso. New York: Penguin Books, 1993.

McDaniel, Jay, John Cobb, Tom Regan, and Charles Birch. "Liberating Life: A Report to the World Council of Churches." In *Good News for Animals: Christian Approaches to Animal Well-Being,* ed. Charles Pinchs and Jay B. McDaniel. Maryknoll, NY: Orbis Books, 1993.

McFague, Sallie. *The Body of God: An Ecological Theology.* Minneapolis: Fortress Press, 1993.

McGrath, Alister E. *The Re-enchantment of Nature: Science, Religion and the Human Sense of Wonder.* London: Hodder & Stoughton, 2003.

McKay, Gordon A., and Henry Hengeveld. "The Changing Atmosphere." In *Planet under Stress,* ed. Constance Mungall and Digby J. McLaren, Royal Society of Canada. Toronto: Oxford University Press, 1990.

McTavish, Douglas. "Public Comments Sought on Strategy to Virtually Eliminate Persistent Toxic Substances." *Focus* 18 (1993): 1–2.

McVey, Kathleen. "General Introduction." In *St. Ephrem the Syrian, Selected Prose Works,* trans. Edward G. Mathews Jr. and Joseph P. Amar; ed. Kathleen McVey. Washington, DC: Catholic University of America Press, 1994.

Meijering, E. P. *Athanasius: Contra Gentes.* Leiden: Brill Academic Publishers, 1984.

Meilaender, Gilbert C., ed. *Working: Its Meaning and Its Limits.* Notre Dame, IN: University of Notre Dame Press, 2000.

Merchant, Carolyn. *The Death of Nature: Women, Ecology and the Scientific Revolution.* San Francisco: Harper & Row, 1980.

Meyendorff, John. *A Study of Gregory Palamas.* trans. George Lawrence. Crestwood, NY: St. Vladimir's Seminary Press, 1998.

Meyer, William B. *Human Impact on the Earth.* New York: Cambridge University Press, 1996.

Meyers, Philip A. "Petroleum Contaminants in the Great Lakes." In *Toxic Contaminants in the Great Lakes,* ed. Jerome O. Nriagu and Milagros S. Simmons. New York: John Wiley & Sons, 1984.

Michigan State University. "Exotic Marine Algae Blooms in Great Lakes." www.msu.edu/~algaelab/Ent_webpage/ent.htm.

Minteer, Ben A. "Intrinsic Value for Pragmatists." *Environmental Ethics* 22 (Spring 2001): 57–75.

Misch, Ann. "Assessing Environmental Health Risks." In *State of the World, 1994: A Worldwatch Institute Report on Progress toward a Sustainable Society,* ed. Linda Starke. New York: W. W. Norton, 1994.

Mitchell, Frank. *The Irish Landscape.* London: Collins, 1976.

MIT Energy Research Council. "Issues Report." http://web.mit.edu/erc/news.

Moffat, Anne Simon. "Global Nitrogen Overload Problem Grows Critical," *Science* 279 (February 13, 1998): 988–89.

Morowitz, Harold. "The First 2 Billion Years of Life." *Origins* 27, no. 34 (February 12, 1998): 577–80.

Morrison, D. E. "Growth, Environment, Equity and Scarcity." *Social Science Quarterly* 57 (1976): 292–306.

Murphy, Charles. "The Good Life from a Catholic Perspective: The Problem of Consumption." United States Conference of Catholic Bishops. www.usccb.org/sdwp/ejp/background/articles/consumption.shtml.

Murphy, Dean E. "California Report Supports Critics of Water Diversion." *New York Times,* January 7, 2003.

Murray, Robert, SJ. *Symbols of Church and Kingdom: A Study in Early Syriac Tradition.* Cambridge: Cambridge University Press, 1975.

———. The Theory of Symbolism in St. Ephrem's Theology." *Parole de l'Orient* 6–7 (1975–76): 1–20.

Naess, Arne. "The Deep Ecological Movement: Some Philosophical Aspects." *Philosophical Inquiry* 8 (1986): 10–31.

———. "A Defense of the Deep Ecology Movement." *Environmental Ethics* 6 (1984): 265–70.

Nash, Roderick Frazier. *The Rights of Nature: A History of Environmental Ethics.* Madison: University of Wisconsin Press, 1989.

———. *Wilderness and the American Mind.* New Haven, CT: Yale University Press, 1982.

National Conference of Catholic Bishops. *Economic Justice for All: Pastoral Letter on Catholic Social Teaching and the U.S. Economy.* Washington, DC: NCCB Publications, 1986.

National Institutes of Health. "Ozone Alerts." www.niehs.nih.gov/oc/factsheets/ozone/ozonevalu.htm.

National Museum of Natural History. "Algae Research." Smithsonian Institution. www.nmnh.si.edu/botany/projects/algae/.

National Oceanic and Atmospheric Administration. "Carbon Dioxide, Methane Rise Sharply in 2007." April 23, 2008. www.noaa.gov/stories2008/20080423_methane.html.

National Research Council. *Compensating for Wetland Losses under the Clean Water Act.* Washington, DC: National Academies Press, 2001.

———. *Global Environmental Change: Understanding the Human Dimensions,* ed. Paul C. Stern, Oran R. Young, and Daniel Druckman. Washington, DC: National Academies Press, 1992.

———. *Pesticides in the Diets of Infants and Children.* Washington, DC: National Academies Press, 1993.

Natural Resources Defense Council. "Transportation: Clean Air and Energy." www.nrdc.org/air/transportation/default.asp.

Nebel, Bernard J. *Environmental Science: The Way the World Works,* 3rd ed. Englewood Cliffs, NJ: Prentice Hall, 1990. 4th edition, 1993, with Richard T. Wright.

Norton, Bryan G. "Environmental Ethics and Weak Anthropocentrism." *Environmental Ethics* 6 (1984): 131–48.

Norton, Bryan. "Sustainability, Human Welfare and Ecosystem Health." *Environmental Values* 1 (1992): 97–111.

———. "Why I Am Not a Nonanthropocentrist: Callicott and the Failure of Monistic Inherentism." *Environmental Ethics* 17 (1995): 341–58.

Nothwehr, Dawn M., ed. *Franciscan Theology of the Environment: An Introductory Reader,* ed. Dawn M. Nothwehr. Quincy, MA: Franciscan Press, 2002.

Nriagu, Jerome O., and Milagros S. Simmons, eds. *Toxic Contaminants in the Great Lakes.* New York: John Wiley & Sons, 1984.

Nurse, L. A., R. F. McLean, and A.G. Suarez. "Small Island States." In *The Regional Impacts of Climate Change: An Assessment of Vulnerability,* ed. R. T. Watson, M. C. Zinyowera, and R. H. Moss. Cambridge: Cambridge University Press, 1998.

O'Connor, June. "Sensuality, Spirituality, Sacramentality." *Union Seminary Quarterly Review* 40 (1985): 59–70.

O'Connor, William Riordan. "The Uti/Frui Distinction in Augustine's Ethics." *Augustinian Studies* 14 (1983): 45–62.

Odum, Eugene C. *Fundamentals of Ecology.* Philadelphia: Saunders, 1953.

———. "Historical Review of the Concepts of Energy Flow in Ecosystems." *American Zoology* 8 (1968): 11–18.

———. "The Strategy of Ecosystem Development." *Science* 164 (April 18, 1969): 262–70.

———. *Systems Ecology: An Introduction.* New York: John Wiley & Sons, 1983.

O'Meara, Dominic J. "Introduction." In *Neoplatonism and Christian Thought,* ed. O'Meara. Norfolk: International Society for Neoplatonic Studies, 1982.

O'Neill, R. V., D. L. DeAngelis, J. B. Waide, and T. F. H. Allen. *A Hierarchical Concept of Ecosystems.* Princeton, NJ: Princeton University Press, 1986.

Organization for Economic Cooperation and Development. *Environmental Outlook to 2030.* Paris: Organization for Economic Cooperation and Development, 2008.

Palmer, Clare. "An Overview of Environmental Ethics." In *Environmental Ethics: An Anthology,* ed. Andrew Light and Holmes Rolston III. Malden, MA: Blackwell, 2003.

Pawlikowski, John T. "Co-Creators with a Compelling God." *Ecumenism* 134 (1998): 8–11.

Peacocke, Arthur. *Theology for a Scientific Age: Being and Becoming—Natural, Divine and Human.* London: SCM Press, 1993.

Pearce, Fred. "A Hero for the Greens?" *New Scientist* 123 (September 23, 1989): 63.

Perrings, Charles. "Resilience in the Dynamics of Economy-Environment Systems." *Environmental and Resource Economics* 11 (1998): 503–20.

Pickett, Steward, Tom Parker, and Peggy Fiedler. "The New Paradigm in Ecology: Implications for Conservation Biology above the Species Level." In *Conservation Biology: The Theory and Practice of Nature Conservation, Preservation, and Management,* ed. Peggy L. Fiedler and Subodh K. Jain. New York: Chapman & Hall, 1992.

Pieper, Josef. *Guide to Thomas Aquinas,* trans. Richard and Clara Winston. San Francisco: Ignatius Press, 1962.

———. "Of the Goodness of the World." *Orate Fratres* 25 (September 1951): 433–37.

Pilbeam, David. "The Descent of Hominoids and Hominids." *Scientific American* 250 (March 1984): 84–96.

Polkinghorne, John C. *Belief in God in an Age of Science.* New Haven, CT: Yale University Press, 1998.

———. *One World: The Interaction of Science and Theology.* Princeton, NJ: Princeton University Press, 1987.

Pontifical Council for Justice and Peace. *Compendium of the Social Doctrine of the Church.* Washington, DC: United States Conference of Catholic Bishops, 2004.

Porter, Jean. *Moral Action and Christian Ethics.* New York: Cambridge University Press, 1995.

———. *The Recovery of Virtue: The Relevance of Aquinas for Christian Ethics.* Louisville: Westminster/John Knox Press, 1990.

Postel, Sandra L. "Water for Food Production: Will There Be Enough in 2020?" *Bioscience* 48 (1998): 629–36.

Primavesi, Anne. *Gaia's Gift: Earth, Ourselves, and God after Copernicus.* New York: Routledge, 2003.

———. *Sacred Gaia : Holistic Theology and Earth System Science.* New York: Routledge Publishing, 2000.

Possekel, Ute. *Evidence of Greek Philosophical Concepts in the Writings of Ephrem the Syrian.* Lovanii: Peeters, 1999.

Princen, Thomas, Michael Maniates, and Ken Conca, eds. *Confronting Consumption.* Cambridge, MA: MIT Press, 2002.

Purves, William K., David Sadava, Gordon H. Orians, and H. Craig Heller. *Life: The Science of Biology,* 7th ed. Sunderland, MA: Sinauer Associates and W. H. Freeman, 2003.

Quesnell, Quentin. "Ritual." In *The New Dictionary of Theology,* ed. Joseph A. Komonchak, Mary Collins, and Dermot A. Lane. Collegeville, MN: Liturgical Press, 1987.

Raffensperger, Carolyn, and Joel Tickner, eds. *Protecting Public Health and the Environment: Implementing the Precautionary Principle.* Washington, DC: Island Press, 1999.

Rahner, Karl. "The Body in the Order of Salvation." In *Theological Investigations, Volume 17, Jesus, Man, and the Church,* trans. Margaret Kohl. New York: Crossroad, 1981.

———. "Natural Science and Reasonable Faith." In *Theological Investigations: Science and Christian Faith 21,* trans. Hugh M. Riley, 16–55. New York: Crossroad, 1988.

———. "On Recognizing the Importance of Thomas Aquinas." *Theological Investigations* 13, trans. David Bourke. New York: Crossroad Publishing, 1983.

———. "Reflections on the Unity of the Love of Neighbour and the Love of God." In *Theological Investigations, Volume 6, Concerning Vatican Council II,* trans. Karl-H. Kruger and Boniface Kruger. New York: Crossroad, 1982.

Rahner, Karl, and Herbert Vorgrimler. "Grace." In *Dictionary of Theology,* rev. ed. New York: Crossroad, 1990.

Raines, Diane. *Ward, Water Wars: Drought, Floor, Folly, and the Politics of Thirst.* New York: Riverhead Books, 2002.

Rambler, Mitchell B., Lynn Margulis, and René Fester, eds. *Global Ecology: Towards a Science of the Biosphere.* New York: Academic Press, 1989.

Rasmussen, Larry L. *Earth Community, Earth Ethics.* Maryknoll, NY: Orbis Books, 1996.

Rausch, Thomas. *The College Student's Introduction to Theology.* Collegeville, MN: Michael Glazier, 1993.

Raven, Peter H. "Foreword." In *AAAS Atlas of Population and Environment,* ed. Paul Harrison and Fred Pearce. Berkeley: University of California Press for American Association for the Advancement of Science, 2000.

Regier, Henry. "Remediation and Rehabilitation of the Great Lakes. "In *Perspectives in Ecosystem Management for the Great Lakes,* ed. Lynton K. Caldwell. Albany: State University of New York, 1988.

Richmond, R. H. "Coral Reefs: Present Problems and Future Concerns Resulting from Anthropogenic Disturbance." *American Zoologist* 33 (1993): 524–36.

Ricklefs, Robert E. *Ecology,* 3rd ed. New York: W. H. Freeman, 1990.

Ritter, Malcolm. "Scientists Complete Chimpanzee Genome Project." *Science and Theology News,* November 21, 2005. www.stnews.org/research-2404.htm.

Roglich, Daniel. "Homily 34 of Saint Gregory Palamas." *Greek Orthodox Theological Review* 33, no. 2 (1988): 135–66.

Rolston, Holmes, III. "Aesthetic Experience in Forests." *Journal of Aesthetics and Art Criticism* 56 (1998): 157–66.

———. "Biophilia, Selfish Genes, Shared Values." In *The Biophilia Hypothesis*, ed. Stephen R. Kellert and Edward O. Wilson. Washington, DC: Island Press, 1993.

———. "Disvalues in Nature." *The Monist* 75 (1992): 250–80.

———. "Does Aesthetic Appreciation of Landscapes Need to Be Science-Based?" *British Journal of Aesthetics* 33 (October 1995): 374–86.

———. *Environmental Ethics: Duties to and Values in Nature.* Philadelphia: Temple University Press, 1988.

———. *Philosophy Gone Wild.* Buffalo: Prometheus Press, 1989.

———. "Value in Nature and the Value of Nature." In *Environmental Ethics: An Anthology*, ed. Rolston. Malden, MA: Blackwell, 2003.

Ruether, Rosemary Radford. *Gaia & God: An Ecofeminist Theology of Earth Healing.* San Francisco: HarperSanFrancisco, 1992.

Rumbaugh, D. M., E. S. Savage-Rumbaugh, and J. L. Scanlon. "The Relationship between Language in Apes and Human Beings." In *Primate Behavior*, ed. J. L. Forbes and J. E. King. New York: Academic Press, 1982.

Runyon, Theodore. "The World as the Original Sacrament." *Worship* 54 (November 1980): 495–511.

Russell, Jeffrey Burton. *Satan: The Early Christian Tradition.* Ithaca, NY: Cornell University Press, 1981.

Russell, Robert John, Nancey Murphy, and C. J. Isham, eds. *Quantum Cosmology and the Laws of Nature: Scientific Perspectives on Divine Action.* Vatican City: Vatican Observatory, 1996.

Russell, Robert John, Nancey Murphy, Theo C. Meyering, and Michael A. Arbib, eds. *Neuroscience and the Person: Scientific Perspectives on Divine Action.* Vatican City: Vatican Observatory, 1999.

Russell, Robert John, Nancey Murphy, and Arthur R. Peacocke, eds. *Chaos and Complexity: Scientific Perspectives on Divine Action.* Vatican City: Vatican Observatory, 1995.

Russell, Robert John, William R. Stoeger, SJ, and Francisco J. Ayala, eds. *Evolutionary and Molecular Biology: Scientific Perspectives on Divine Action.* Vatican City: Vatican Observatory, 1998.

Russell, Robert John, William R. Stoeger, SJ, and George V. Coyne, eds. *Physics, Philosophy, and Theology: A Common Quest for Understanding.* Vatican City: Vatican Observatory, 1998.

Sagan, Dorion, and Lynn Margulis. "Gaia and the Ethical Abyss: A Natural Ethic Is a G[o]od Thing." In *The Good in Nature and Humanity: Connecting Science, Religion, and Spirituality with the Natural World*, ed. Stephen R. Kellert and Timothy J. Farnham. Washington, DC: Island Press, 2002.

Sanders, Robert. "Ethanol Can Replace Gasoline with Significant Energy Savings, Comparable Impact on Greenhouse Gases." *UC Berkeley News*, January 26, 2006. www.berkeley.edu/news/media/releases/2006/01/26_ethanol.shtml.

Santmire, H. Paul. *The Travail of Nature: The Ambiguous Ecological Promise of Christian Theology.* Philadelphia: Fortress Press, 1985.

Schaefer, Jame. "Acting Reverently in God's Sacramental World." In *Ethical Dilemmas in the New Millennium II,* ed. Francis A. Eigo. Villanova, PA: Villanova University Press, 2001.

———. "Appreciating the Beauty of Earth." *Theological Studies* 62 (March 2001): 23–52.

———. "Grateful Cooperation: Cistercian Inspiration for Ecological Ethics." *Cistercian Studies Quarterly* 37, no. 2 (2002): 187–203.

———. "Intrinsic-Instrumental Valuing of Earth: A Theological Framework for Environmental Ethics." *Theological Studies* 66, no. 4 (2005): 783–814.

———. "Quest for the Common Good: A Collaborative Public Theology for a Life-Sustaining Climate." In *Cultural Landscapes,* ed. Gabriel Ricci. New Brunswick, NJ: Transaction, 2006.

———. "The Virtuous Cooperator: Modeling the Human in an Age of Ecological Degradation." *Worldviews: Environment, Culture, Religion* 7, nos. 1–2 (March 2003): 171–95.

Schmitz-Moormann, Karl. *Theology of Creation in an Evolutionary World.* In collaboration with James Salmon. Cleveland: Pilgrim Press, 1997.

Schmucki, Oktavian, OFM. "Le 'Lodi per Ogni Ora': Un Invitatorio Francescano alla Celebrazione dell' Ufficio Divino." In *Preghiera Liturgica secondo l'Esempio c l'Inscgnamcnto di San Franecsco d'Assisi: Seconda edizione accresciuta.* Rome: Conferenza Italiana Superiori Provinciali Cappuccini, 1979.

Schneider, Stephen. "Debating Gaia." *Environment* 32 (May 1990): 4–9, 29–32.

———. *Scientists Debate Gaia: The Next Century.* Cambridge, MA: MIT Press, 2004.

———. "What Gaia Hath Wrought: The Story of a Scientific Controversy." *Technology Review* 92, no. 5 (July 1989): 54–61.

Schneider, Stephen H., and Penelope J. Boston, eds. *Scientists on Gaia.* Cambridge, MA: MIT Press, 1991.

Sea Grant Institute. *The Fisheries of the Great Lakes.* Madison: Sea Grant Institute, University of Wisconsin, 1988.

———. "Gifts of the Glaciers." Sea Grant Institute, University of Wisconsin. www.seagrant.wisc.edu/Communications/greatlakes/GlacialGift/map.html.

Sen, Samanta. "Environment: A People's Move to Be Heard at Johannesburg Summit." *Global Information Network,* March 29 2002. Available at www.globalinfo.org/.

Simmons, Milagros S. "PCB Contamination in the Great Lakes." In *Toxic Contaminants in the Great Lakes,* ed. Jerome O. Nriagu and Milagros S. Simmons. New York: John Wiley & Sons, 1984.

Sittler, Joseph. *The Care of the Earth and Other University Sermons.* Philadelphia: Fortress Press, 1964.

———. "Ecological Commitment as Theological Responsibility." *Zygon* 5 (June 1970): 172–81.

———. "A Theology for Earth." *Christian Scholar* 37 (September 1954): 376–74.

Smil, Vaclav. *Feeding the World: A Challenge for the Twenty-First Century.* Cambridge, MA: MIT Press, 2000.

Sobosan, Jeffrey G. *Romancing the Universe: Theology, Science and Cosmology.* Grand Rapids: William B. Eerdmans, 1999.

Solar Views. "Earth from Space: Quotes from Astronauts." www.solarviews.com/eng/earthsp.htm#quote.

Sonzogni, William C., and Wayland R. Swain. "Perspectives on Human Health Concerns from Great Lakes Contaminants." In *Toxic Contaminants in the Great Lakes,* ed. Jerome O. Nriagu and Milagros S. Simmons. New York: John Wiley & Sons, 1984.

Sorrell, Roger D. *St. Francis of Assisi and Nature: Tradition and Innovation in Western Christian Attitudes toward the Environment.* New York: Oxford University Press, 1988.

Soulé, Michael E. "Biophilia: Unanswered Questions." In *The Biophilia Hypothesis,* ed. Stephen R. Kellert and Edward O. Wilson. Washington, DC: Island Press, 1993.

Stammer, Larry B. "Harming the Environment Is Sinful, Prelate Says." *Los Angeles Times,* November 2, 1997.

Stenmark, Mikael. *Environmental Ethics and Policy-Making.* Burlington, VT: Ashgate, 2002.

Stoddard, J. L. "Regional Trends in Aquatic Recovery from Acidification in North America and Europe." *Nature* 401 (October 1999): 575–78.

Stone, Christopher. *Earth and Other Ethics: The Case for Moral Pluralism.* New York: Harper & Row, 1987.

———. "Moral Pluralism and the Course of Environmental Ethics." *Environmental Ethics* 10 (1988): 139–54.

Stutz, Bruce. "Divine Details." *Natural History* 108 (July–August 1999): 6.

Tanner, Katherine. "Creation, Environmental Crisis, and Ecological Justice." In *Reconstructing Christian Theology,* ed. Rebecca S. Chopp and Mark Lewis Taylor. Minneapolis: Fortress Press, 1994.

Tansley, Arthur G. "The Use and Abuse of Vegetational Concepts and Terms." *Ecology* 16 (1935): 284–307.

Tattersall, Ian. "Human Evolution: An Overview." In *An Evolving Dialogue: Theological and Scientific Perspectives on Evolution,* ed. James B. Miller. Harrisburg, PA: Trinity Press International, 2001.

Taylor, Jerome. "Introduction." In *Didascalicon: A Medieval Guide to the Arts,* by Hugh of Saint Victor; trans. Jerome Taylor. New York: Columbia University Press, 1961.

Taylor, Paul. *Respect for Nature: A Theory of Environmental Ethics.* Princeton, NJ: Princeton University Press, 1986.

Temple, William. *Readings in St John's Gospel.* London: Macmillan, 1939.

Teske, Roland J. "The Motive for Creation According to Saint Augustine." *Modern Schoolman* 65 (May 1988): 245–53.

Thomas, R. L., J. R. Vallentyne, K. Ogilvie, and J. D. Kingham. "The Ecosystems Approach: A Strategy for the Management of Renewable Resources in the Great Lakes Basin." In *Perspectives on Ecosystem Management for the Great Lakes,* ed. Lynton K. Caldwell. Albany: State University of New York Press, 1988.

Tilley, Maureen A. "Martyrs, Monks, Insects, and Animals." In *An Ecology of the Spirit: Religious Reflection and Environmental Consciousness,* ed. Michael Barnes. College Theology Society 36. Lanham, MD: University Press of America, 1994.

Torrance, Thomas F. *The Christian Frame of Mind.* Colorado Springs: Helmers & Howard, 1989.

Turner, B. L., William C. Clark, Robert W. Kates, John F. Richards, Jessica T. Mathews, and William B. Meyer, eds. *The Earth as Transformed by Human Action: Global and Regional Changes in the Biosphere over the Past 300 Years.* Cambridge: Cambridge University Press, 1990.

Ulrich, Roger S. "Biophilia, Biophobia, and Natural Landscapes." In *The Biophilia Hypothesis,* ed. Stephen R. Kellert and Edward O. Wilson. Washington, DC: Island Press, 1993.

United Nations. *Report of the World Summit on Sustainable Development, Johannesburg, South Africa,* 26 August–4 September 2002. New York: United Nations Environmental Programme, 2002.

United Nations Development Program. *Human Development Report 1998: Consumption for Human Development.* New York: Oxford University Press, 1998.

United Nations Environment Program. *Global Environment Outlook 2000.* London: Earthscan, 2000.

United States and Canada. *Great Lakes Water Quality Agreement.* Ottawa, November 22, 1978.

United States Conference of Catholic Bishops. *Global Climate Change: A Plea for Dialogue, Prudence, and the Common Good.* Washington, DC: USCCB Publications, 2001.

———. *Renewing the Earth: An Invitation to Reflection and Action on Environment in Light of Catholic Social Teaching.* Washington, DC: USCCB Publications, 1991. www.usccb.org/sdwp/ejp/bishopsstatement.shtml.

Updike, John. *Lectures on Literature,* ed. Fredson Bowers. New York: Harcourt Brace Jovanovich, 1980.

U.S. Environmental Protection Agency, "Great Lakes." www.epa.gov/glnpo/factsheet.html.

———. "Why Should You Be Concerned about Air Pollution?" www.epa.gov/air/caa/peg/concern.html.

U.S. Fish and Wildlife Service. "Threatened and Endangered Species System." www.ecos.fws.gov/tess_public/TessStatReport.

Vacek, Edward, SJ. "John Paul II and Cooperation with God." In *The Annual of the Society of Christian Ethics,* ed. D. M. Yeager. Knoxville: Society of Christian Ethics, 1990.

Van Bavel, Tarsicius, OSA. "The Creator and the Integrity of Creation in the Fathers of the Church, Especially in Saint Augustine." *Augustinian Studies* 21 (1990):1–33.

Vaney, Neil. "Biodiversity and Beauty." *Pacifica* 8 (1995): 335–45.

Van Till, Howard J. "Basil, Augustine, and the Doctrine of Creation's Functional Integrity." *Science and Christian Belief* 8 (1996): 21–38.

Verstraeten, J. "Solidarity and Subsidiarity." In *Principles of Catholic Social Teaching,* ed. David. A. Boileau, 133–48. Milwaukee: Marquette University Press, 1998.

Vess, Deborah. "Celtic Monasticism." Georgia College and State University. www.faculty.de.gcsu.edu/~dvess/ids/medieval/celtic/celtic.shtml#peregrini.

Virtual Elimination Task Force. *Persistent Toxic Substances: Virtually Eliminating Inputs to the Great Lakes.* Windsor: International Joint Commission for the Great Lakes, 1991.

Vitousek, Peter M., Harold A. Mooney, Jane Lubchenco, and Jerry M. Melillo. "Human Domination of Earth's Ecosystems." *Science* 277 (July 25, 1997): 494–99.

Volk, Tyler. *Gaia's Body: Toward a Physiology of Earth.* Cambridge, MA: MIT Press, 2003.

Vööbus, Arthur. *History of Asceticism in the Syrian Orient: A Contribution to the History of Culture in the Near East.* Vol. 2, *Early Monasticism in Mesopotamia and Syria.* Louvain: Secretariat du Corpus SCO, 1960.

Walker, Stephan. *Animal Thought.* London: Routledge & Kegan Paul, 1983.

Wallis, R. T. "Divine Omniscience in Plotinus, Proclus, and Aquinas." In *Neoplatonism and Early Christian Thought,* ed. H. J. Blumenthal and R. A. Markus, 223–35. London: Variorum Publications, 1981.

Ward, Benedicta. "The Paradise of the Desert Fathers." In *Christian Apostolic Church of Egypt.* www.coptic.net/articles/ParadiseOfDesertFathers.txt.

Warden, Duane. "All Things Praise Him (Psalm 148)." *Restoration Quarterly* 35 (1993): 101–8.

Weber, Peter. "Safeguarding the Oceans." In *State of the World, 1994: A Worldwatch Institute Report on Progress toward a Sustainable Society,* ed. Linda Starke. New York: W. W. Norton, 1994.

Weier, John. "Mapping the Decline of Coral Reefs." *Earth Observatory,* March 12, 2001. www.earthobservatory.nasa.gov/Study/Coral/.

Weisheipl, James A., ed. *Albertus Magnus and the Sciences: Commemorative Essays.* Toronto: Pontifical Institute of Mediaeval Studies, 1980.

———. *Friar Thomas D'Aquino: His Life, Thought, and Work.* Garden City, NY: Doubleday, 1974.

Weston, Anthony. "Forms of Gaian Ethics." *Environmental Ethics* 9 (Fall 1987): 217–30.

Westra, Laura. *An Environmental Proposal for Ethics: The Principle of Integrity.* Lanham, MD: Rowman & Littlefield, 1994.

———. "Why Norton's Approach is Insufficient for Environmental Ethics." *Environmental Ethics* 19 (1997): 279–97.

White, Lynn, Jr.. "The Historical Roots of Our Ecologic Crisis." *Science* 155 (March 10, 1967): 1203–7.

Whitney, Elspeth. "Lynn White, Ecotheology, and History." *Environmental Ethics* 15 (Summer 1993): 151–69.

Wildiers, N. Max. *The Theologian and His Universe: Theology and Cosmology from the Middle Ages to the Present.* New York: Seabury Press, 1982.

Wilkinson, Clive, ed. *Status of Coral Reefs of the World 2004.* Australian Institute of Marine Science. www.aims.gov.au/pages/research/coral-bleaching/scr2004.

Williams, George Ronald. "Gaian and Nongaian Explanations for the Contemporary Level of Atmospheric Oxygen." In *Scientists on Gaia,* ed. Stephen H. Schneider and Penelope J. Boston. Cambridge, MA: MIT Press, 1993.

———. *The Molecular Biology of Gaia.* New York: Columbia University, 1996. www.netlibrary.com.libus.csd.mu.edu/Reader/.

Wilson, Edward O. *Biophilia.* Cambridge, MA: Harvard University Press, 1984.

———. "Biophilia and the Conservation Ethic." In *The Biophilia Hypothesis,* ed. Stephen R. Kellert and Edward O. Wilson. Washington, DC: Island Press, 1993.

———. *The Creation: An Appeal to Save Life on Earth.* New York: W. W. Norton, 2006.

Wood, John H., Gary R. Long, and David F. Morehouse. "Long-Term World Oil Supply Scenarios: The Future Is Neither as Bleak or Rosy as Some Assert." Energy Information Administration, U.S. Department of Energy, August 18 2004. www.eia.doe.gov/pub/oil_gas/petroleum/feature_articles/2004/worldoilsupply/oilsupply04.html.

Working Group III Technical Support Unit. "Workshop on New Emission Scenarios, 29 June–1 July 2005, Laxenburg, Austria." Intergovernmental Panel on Climate Change, Bilthoven, The Netherlands, August 2005.

World Commission on Environment and Development. *Our Common Future.* New York: Oxford University Press, 1987.

World Health Organization, World Meteorological Organization, and United Nations Environmental Program. *Climate Change and Human Health: Risks and Responses.* www.who.int/globalchange/climate/en/ccSCREEN.pdf.

World Resources Institute. *World Resources 1998–99: Environmental Change and Human Health?* New York: Oxford University Press, 1998.

———. *World Resources 2000–2001.* Washington, DC: World Resources Institute, 2000.

Worster, Donald. *Nature's Economy: The Roots of Ecology.* San Francisco: Sierra Club Books, 1977.

Wright, John H. *The Order of the Universe in the Theology of St. Thomas Aquinas.* Rome: Apud Aedes Universitatis Gregorianae, 1957.

Yarri, Donna. "Animals as Kin: The Religious Significance of Marc Bekoff's Work." *Zygon* 41.1 (2006):21–28.

Yergin, Daniel. "Long-Term World Oil Supply Scenarios." *Washington Post,* July 31, 2005.

Zemler-Cizewski, Wanda. "Reading the World as Scripture: Hugh of St Victor's *De tribus diebus.*" *Florilegium* 9 (1987): 65–88.

INDEX

Aalen, F. H. A., 183n78
Abba Amoun, 159
Abba Bes, 161
Abba Helle, 158, 183n92
Abban, 159
Abelard, Peter, 246n3
Abram, David, 111
Acton, Loren, 112
The Ages of Gaia (Lovelock), 108
Ailred of Rievaulx, 246n3
air, contemporary use and abuse of, 207–9, 225nn141–43
Alan of Lille, 76, 98n83
Albertus Magnus: appreciation for beauty of creation, 44, 47–48, 52, 59nn28–30; using creation with gratitude and restraint, 195–96, 197, 200–201
Allen, John L., 285n66
Alliance for the Great Lakes, 244
Ambrose of Milan, 246n3
American Association for the Advancement of Science, 203
Andersen, Signe Bech, 118n45
Anselm of Canterbury, 77
Anthony of Padua, 162, 164
anthropocentric biases in theological tradition, 8–9, 15n23, 52
Antony: battles with the devil, 178nn5–6; kinship and companionship with wild species and natural places, 153, 155–56, 158, 160, 181n42
Aquinas, Thomas: appreciation for the beauty of creation, 44, 47, 49, 54, 60n48, 60nn42n43; on the common good, 22–24, 27, 28, 31, 38n63, 38n69, 39n75, 39n77, 39nn88–89, 199; on the entire universe as revelatory of God, 78–79; and ethical framework for addressing environmental issues, 24, 39nn88–89; and God's grace/care for individual human beings, 23, 38n73,

272, 284n48; and God's love for creation, 257–58; and God's natural law, 22, 38n60; and God's valuation of the world, 25, 40nn97–98; and God's work through secondary causal agents, 140n36, 141n39, 269–70, 281n13; and the goodness of natural beings, 19–20, 34n17, 35n21, 35n23; and the hierarchy of beings, 20–21, 35n28, 36nn30–40, 37n43, 78–79, 99n101, 125–26, 141nn41–42, 194, 216n8, 216n10, 270, 282n16, 282nn18–19, 282n21; and human dominion over creatures, 26, 126, 141n45, 196; and human sin, 126; and human use of the Earth's sacramental goods, 85; and human valuation of the physical world, 26–27; and instrumental value of all creatures, 21, 22, 36nn36–37, 36n40, 38n62, 40nn97–98, 78–79, 194; and the intercooperation among natural entities, 23–24, 125, 140n30, 140n34, 141n38, 269–73; on intrinsic goodness/value of creation, 20, 26, 40n103, 42n125; and love for God's creation, 26, 259; and love of friendship, 258, 259, 260–61; on the moral virtues, 231–35, 239–45, 247n6; and the perfection of the physical universe, 22, 37nn55–56, 37n58; and poverty, 233, 247n28; sacramental/functional perspective on unity of creatures, 124–25; sacramental view of the world, 21, 37n43; and the unifying interactivity of diverse creatures, 124–26, 139nn28–29, 140n30, 140n36, 141nn38–45; and using creation/God's blessings, 194, 196, 198–99, 201, 218n48, 218n51, 218n57; virtuous cooperator model, 269–78, 281n13
Arian heresy, 67

Orthodox Christianity, 101n140
overconsumption and waste, 210–11,
    228nn171–73; average home sizes, 210,
    227n165; the world's poor, 211, 228n177
ozone holes, 109, 117n44, 118n45, 207–8

Pachome, 158–59
Palamas, Gregory, 79, 99n111
Palmer, Clare, 17
panentheism, 256
Parker, Tom, 42n120
Patrick, 152, 181n27
Paul the Hermit, 158, 160
Peacocke, Arthur, 100n121
Pearce, Fred, 117n44
Perisphysion (John Scotus Eriugena), 71,
    97n52, 216n15
Perrings, Charles, 147n132
Physica (Albertus Magnus), 200–201
Pickett, Steward, 42n120
Pieper, Josef, 19, 34n17
Poemen (holy hermit), 159
poor, world's: and living virtuously within
    the Earth community, 233, 247n28;
    McFague on "nature" as the "new
    poor," 147n129; and overconsumption
    and waste, 211, 228n177; and use of
    God's creation, 211, 228n177
population growth, 205–6, 222n109
Porter, Jean, 34–35n17
Possekel, Ute, 94–95n18
praise for God, creation's, 103–20; adding
    the human voice to the chorus of
    creation, 113; astronauts and the Earth
    viewed from space, 112, 119n65;
    Augustine's call for creation to praise
    God, 104–5; Basil and the languages of
    creatures/chorus of creation, 104,
    114nn1–2; behaviors, 111–13, 119n63;
    biospheric concept, 107–11; biospheric
    ethics/Gaian ethics, 109–11; consonance
    between patristic-medieval thinking and
    contemporary science, 106–11; Francis
    of Assisi and poetic calls to praise, 105;
    and Gaia, 107–11; John of the Cross and
    the symphony of creation, 105–6;
    patristic and medieval sources, 103–6;
    and Psalms, 104, 105, 114n1; respecting
    animate/inanimate ways of praising
    God, 112; respecting the biosphere's
    capacity to praise God, 112–13;
    respecting the interacting voices, 112
"The Praises To Be Said at All the Hours"
    (Francis of Assisi), 105
Pratum spirituale (John Moschus), 153,
    181n35

precautionary principle, 56, 62n72, 136,
    147n133, 276
process theologians, 86, 101n134
prokaryotes and eukaryotes, 166,
    186nn141–42
prudence, virtue of, 232, 240–41
Psalms: Augustine's commentaries on, 50,
    70, 104, 105; Basil's homilies on, 104,
    114n1
Pseudo-Dionysius, 71, 73, 77, 123–24, 256,
    257

Rahner, Karl, 102n143, 102n145, 262–63,
    274
Rasmussen, Larry L., 101n134
Rausch, Thomas P., SJ, 15n21
Raven, Peter H., 210
reason, human, 194–97, 212–13
Religions of the World and Ecology
    conferences (1996-1998) (Harvard
    University Center for the Study of
    World Religions), 61n57
Renewing the Earth (U.S. Conference of
    Catholic Bishops), 12n3, 86
Rio Declaration (1992) and the
    "precautionary principle," 62n72,
    147n133
Rio Earth Summit (1992), 89, 210, 276
rituals: for addressing the ecological crisis,
    89; Catholic sacraments of
    reconciliation and confirmation, 89–90;
    and confessing sins of ecological
    degradation, 89–90, 101n140; and
    exercise of moral virtues, 90; the
    meaning of, 89; and reverencing the
    sacramental universe, 89–91
Rolston, Holmes, III: and aesthetic
    appreciation as foundation for
    ecological ethics, 43, 48, 52, 57n4; and
    intrinsic value of the evolutionary
    process, 41n119; and value theory in
    environmental ethics, 17, 28, 33n4; and
    Wilson's reductionistic approach to
    biophilic ethics, 171–72
Romans, Paul's Letter to, 66, 67, 70, 72,
    73–74, 79, 80
Rufinus of Aquilea, 153, 156
Runyon, Theodore, 102n141
Russell, Jeffrey Burton, 178n6
Russell, Robert John, 4

Sabas, 158, 183n86
sacramental universe (reverence for),
    65–103; Alan of Lille, 76, 98n83;
    Aquinas, 21, 37n43, 78–79, 85, 99n101,
    100n127, 101n128; Athanasius, 67,